TABLE ◇ OF ◇ CONTENTS

Copyright

Copyright © Vault Editions Ltd 2025.

This book is a new work created by Vault Editions Ltd.

ISBN: 978-1-922966-73-5

ART SUPPLIES YOU'LL NEED

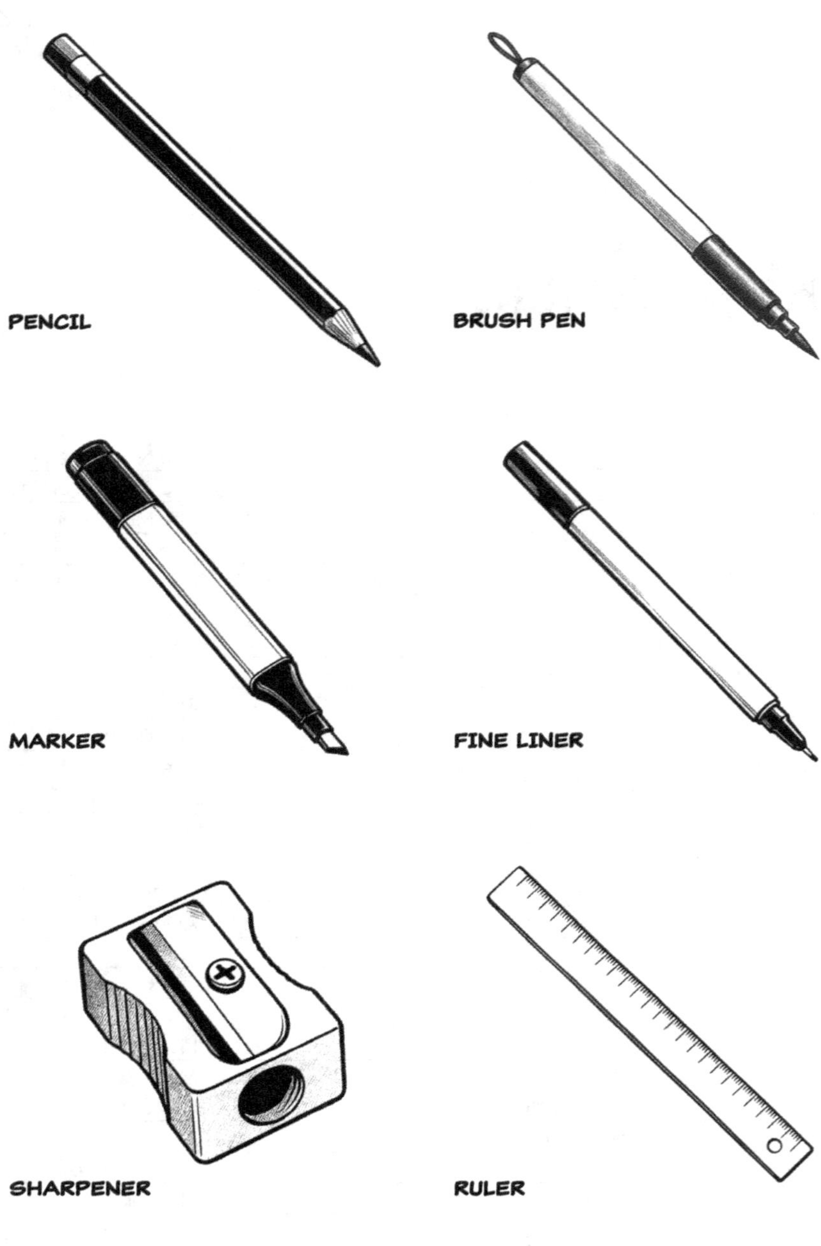

Pro Tip: These tools are all helpful to have, but not all of them are essential. You don't need a full kit to begin your manga journey: a simple pencil or pen and a piece of paper are enough. Fancy materials can make the process smoother, but they won't replace the value of practice. What matters most is that you start drawing, experiment freely and build confidence through repetition. Everything else can be added later as your skills grow.

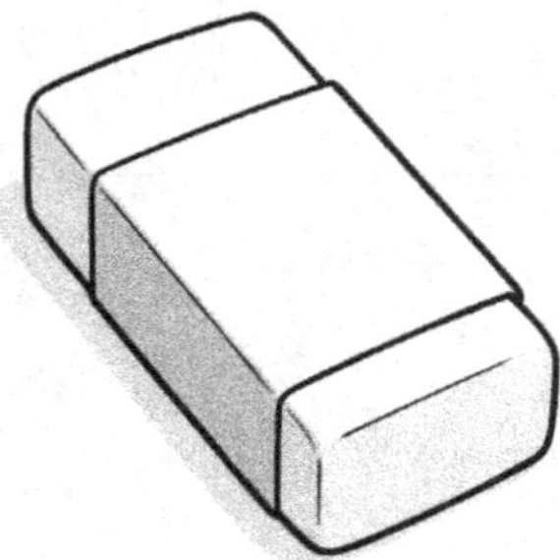

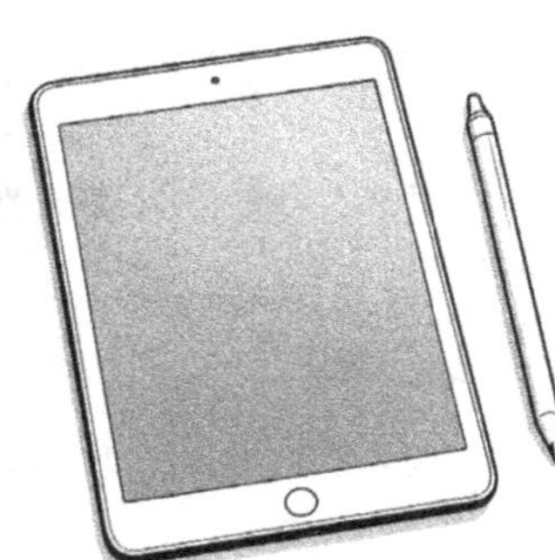

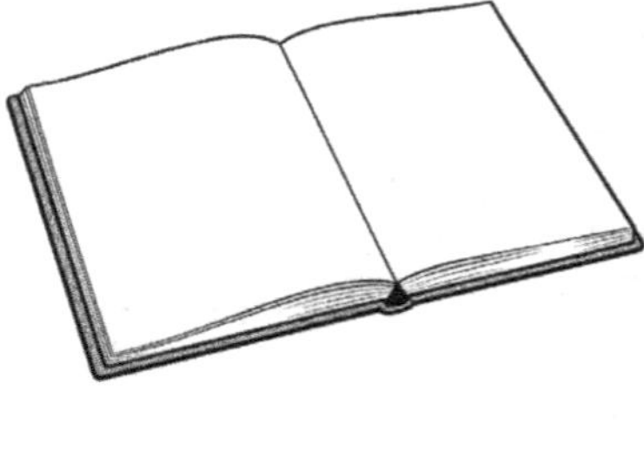

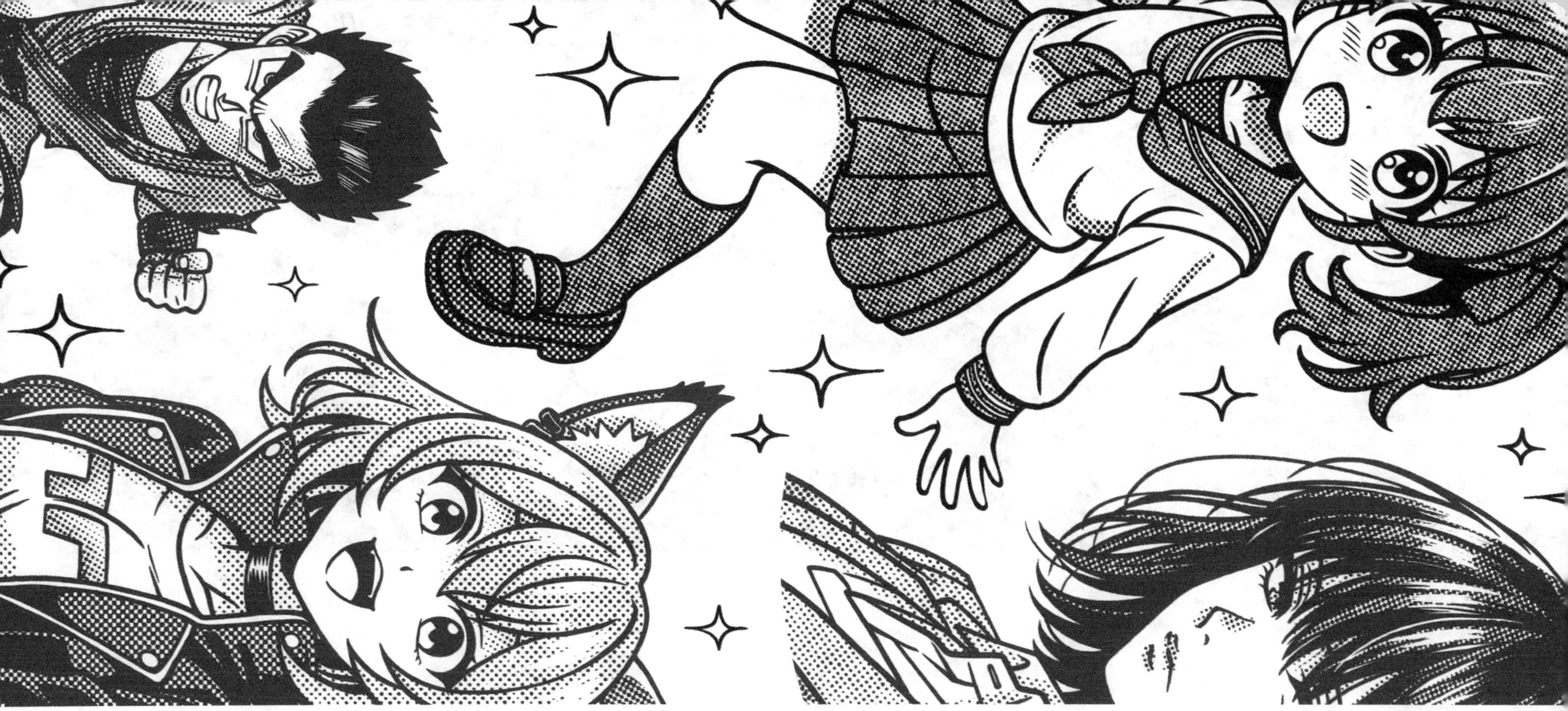

THE VAULT EDITIONS GUIDE TO
MASTERING
THE ART OF
DRAWING

HOW TO DRAW
MANGA AND ANIME

A HELPFUL MANUAL FOR
ARTISTS AND DESIGNERS

STEP BY STEP

HAND DRAWN
UNIQUE 40 DESIGNS
BEST QUALITY

EDITIONS
Vault

INTRODUCTION

Manga and anime have become some of the most recognisable visual styles in contemporary illustration, defined by expressive faces, stylised anatomy, and dynamic storytelling. Behind these striking characters are clear drawing principles: proportion, gesture, expression, and a visual language that artists have carefully developed over decades.

How to Draw Manga and Anime for Beginners introduces these foundations through the Vault Editions 12-step drawing method. Each subject is broken into simple, guided stages that show you how to construct characters from basic shapes to finished drawings. This approach removes the guesswork and builds confidence as your skills develop.

Inside, you'll find essential lessons on faces, body types, hairstyles, clothing, chibi proportions, expressions, and dynamic poses, along with popular archetypes and impactful comic effects. Every design has been chosen for its relevance to the manga style and its value to beginner artists.

Clear, intentional artwork makes each step easy to follow, helping you understand not just what to draw, but why it works. Whether you're new to drawing or exploring manga for the first time, this book provides a structured, accessible way to learn the fundamentals and begin creating your own characters and stories.

Download Your Files:

This book includes downloadable files to support your drawing practice. You'll find instructions on how to access them on the final pages of this book.

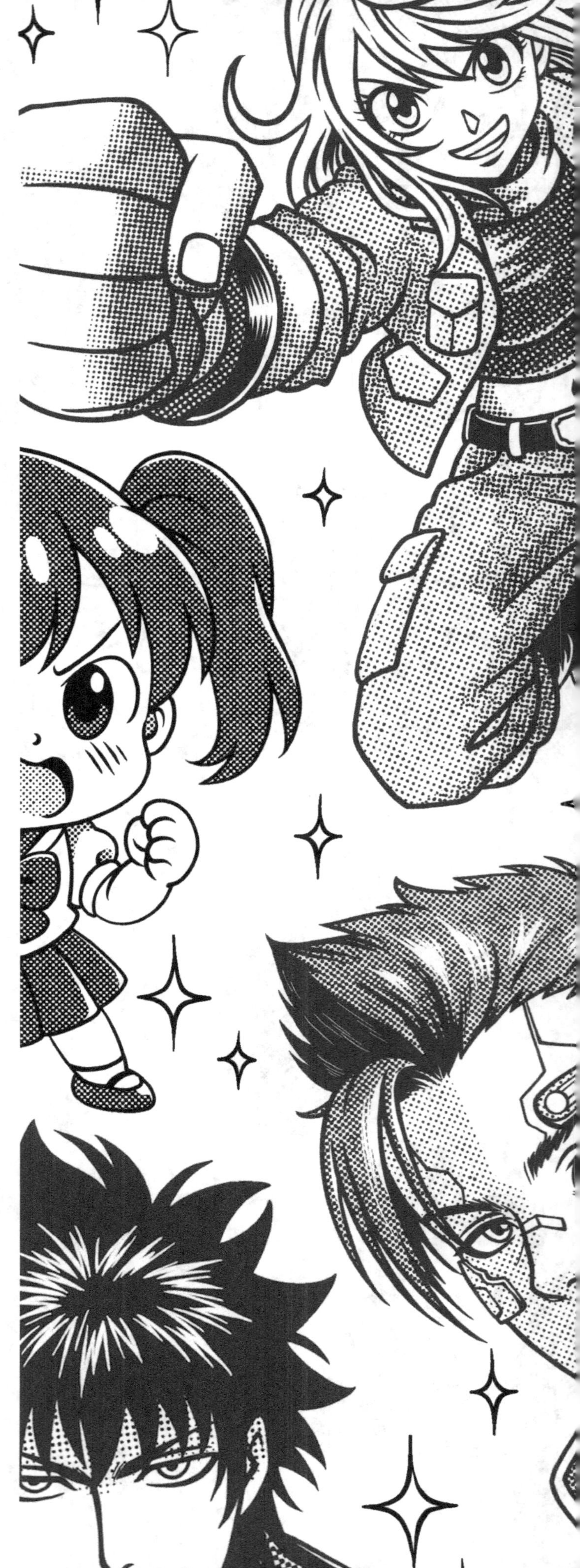

A MINDSET FOR SUCCESS

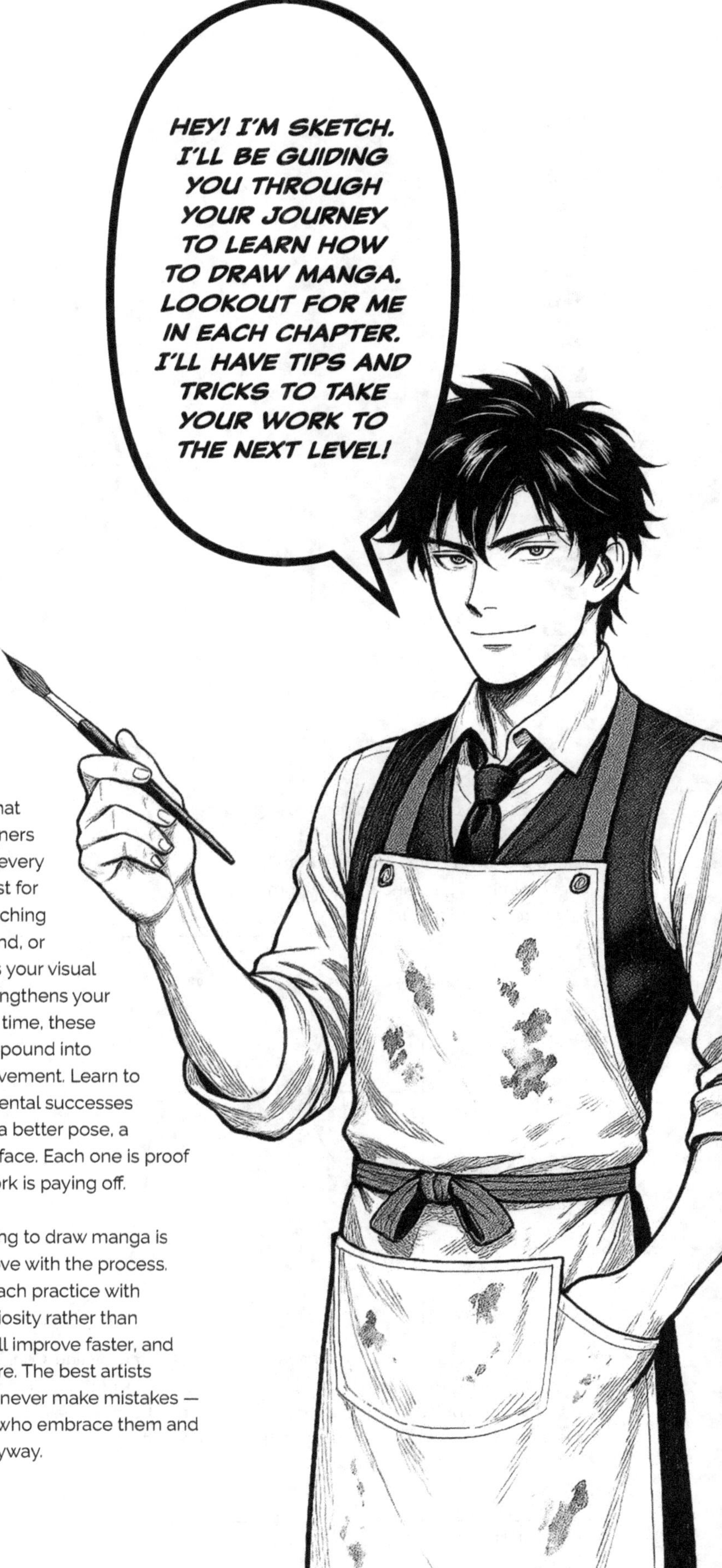

Pro Tip: Learning to draw manga is as much about mindset as it is about technique. When you start, it's easy to get caught up comparing your work to the artists you admire, but every one of them began exactly where you are — with clumsy lines and uncertain strokes. The key is to accept that progress in drawing isn't about perfection, it's about persistence. Your goal isn't to make a masterpiece every time you pick up a pencil; it's to build the habit of drawing, to show up each day and make something.

One of the most important skills you'll develop early on is resilience. You'll have days when your proportions feel wrong, when your characters look stiff, or when you can't capture the emotion you imagined — that's normal. Instead of judging those drawings harshly, use them as markers of growth. Every page you fill brings you closer to control, confidence, and understanding. Finishing a sketch, even one you don't love, is far more valuable than abandoning it in frustration.

Consistency is what transforms beginners into artists. Draw every day, even if it's just for ten minutes. Sketching a single head, hand, or expression builds your visual memory and strengthens your line control. Over time, these small efforts compound into noticeable improvement. Learn to celebrate incremental successes — a cleaner line, a better pose, a more expressive face. Each one is proof that your hard work is paying off.

Ultimately, learning to draw manga is about falling in love with the process. When you approach practice with patience and curiosity rather than expectation, you'll improve faster, and you'll enjoy it more. The best artists aren't those who never make mistakes — they're the ones who embrace them and keep drawing anyway.

DRAWING THE MALE FACE

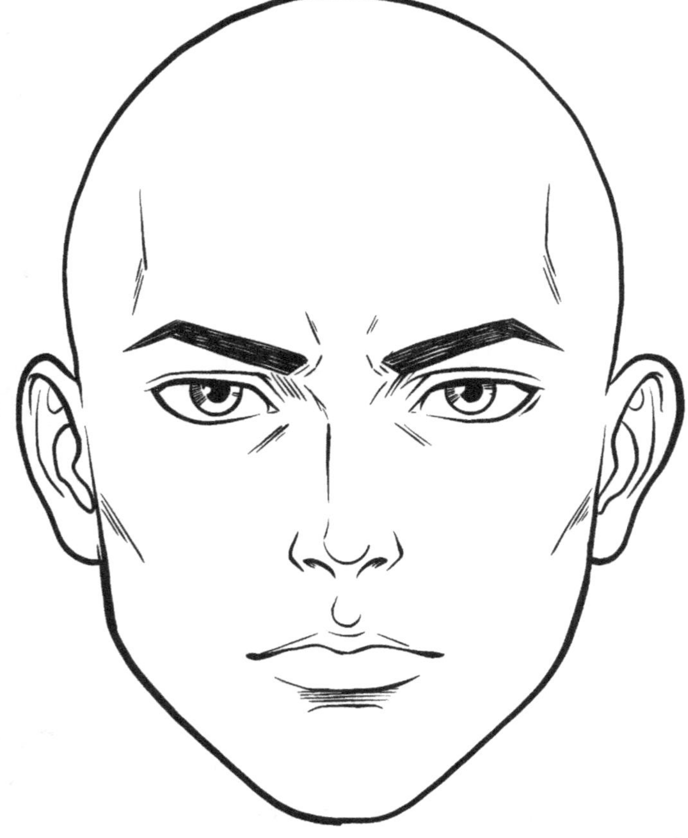

Pro Tip: Keep your construction lines light and consistent—these guides are the backbone of your drawing. Use them to check symmetry, balance, and alignment as you refine the features.

01

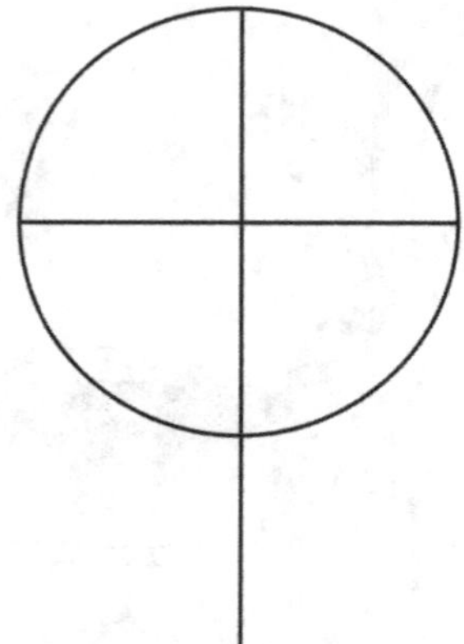

Start by drawing a circle. Divide it evenly into quarters, then extend a vertical line down from the bottom half of the circle. This will form the centre line of the face.

02

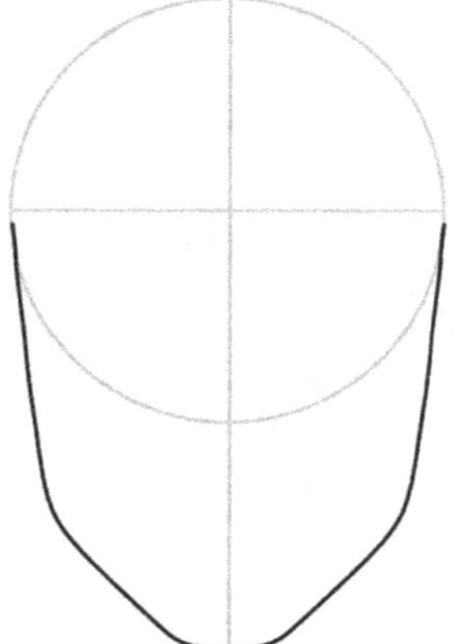

Sketch the jawline. Connect the left and right sides of the circle to the end of the vertical centre line to create the shape of the chin.

03

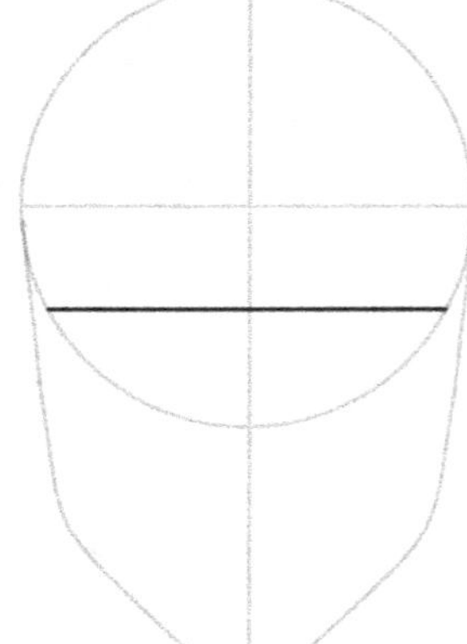

Draw a horizontal guideline halfway down the circle. This marks the position of the eyes and the bridge of the nose.

04

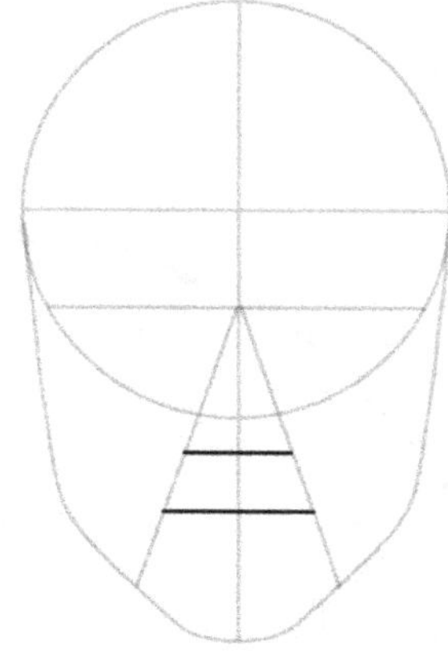

From the bridge of the nose, draw an equilateral triangle pointing downward. This defines the overall width of the nose and mouth.

05

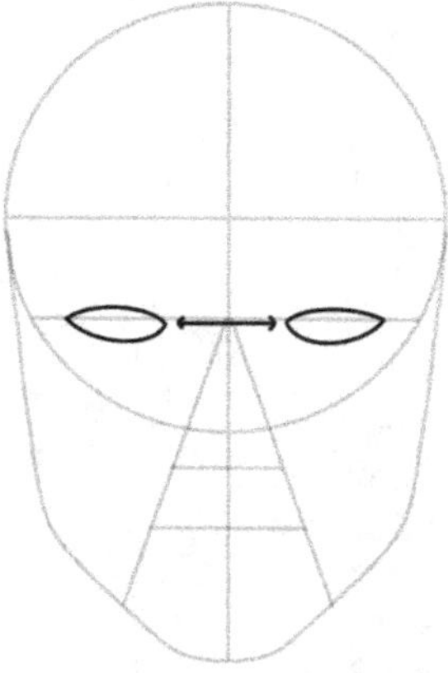

The first line down from the top of the triangle will dictate the position of the base of the nose. The second line will be the centre of the mouth.

06

To determine the width of the eye, know that the head will be 4 eyes wide. The space between the eyes will measure one eye width.

07

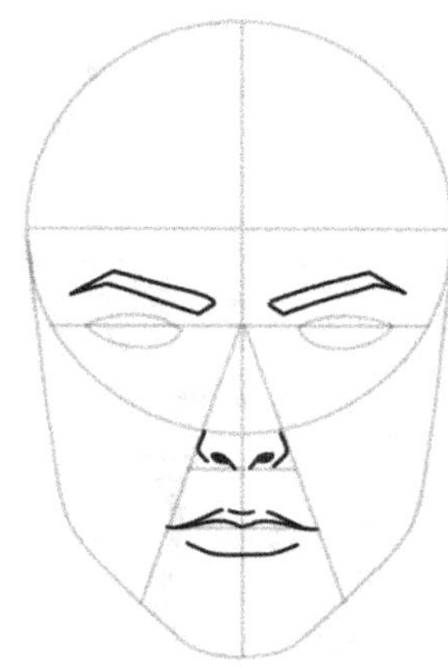

Draw in the basic shape of the nose and mouth using the gudielines you drew earlier for placement.

08

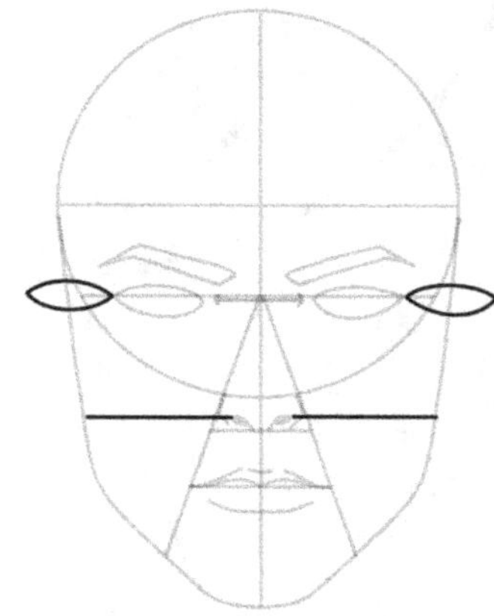

To help you in drawing natural looking ears. Draw one eye width out from the left and right eye. Also draw a line extending out from the nostrils.

09

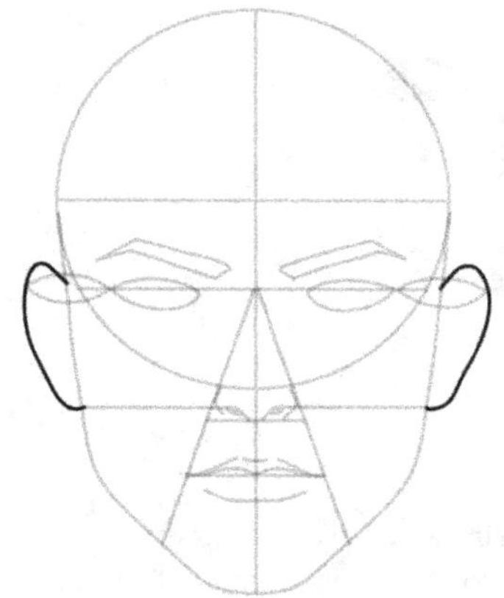

Draw in the ears. They extend up slightly from the eyeline and taper in slightly to the line you have drawn extending out from the nostrils.

10

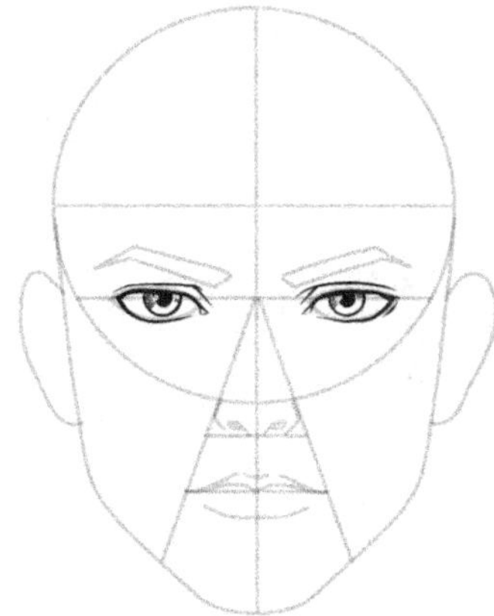

Using an inking pen, start adding in the details of the eyes.

11

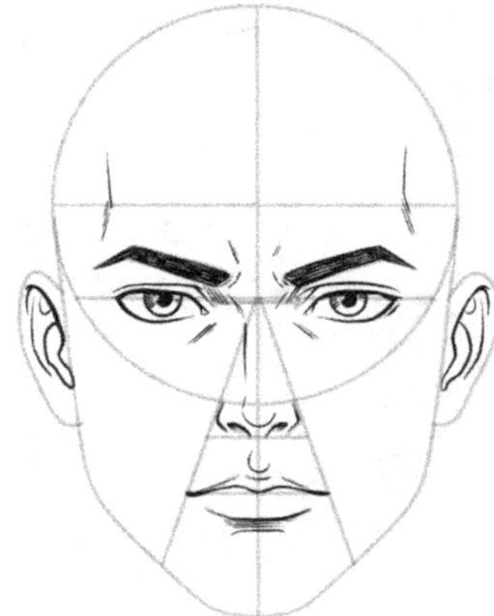

Continue adding details to the nose, mouth and ears. Be sure to add in some additional skin fold lines around the eyes to help define the features and give the face a natural look.

12

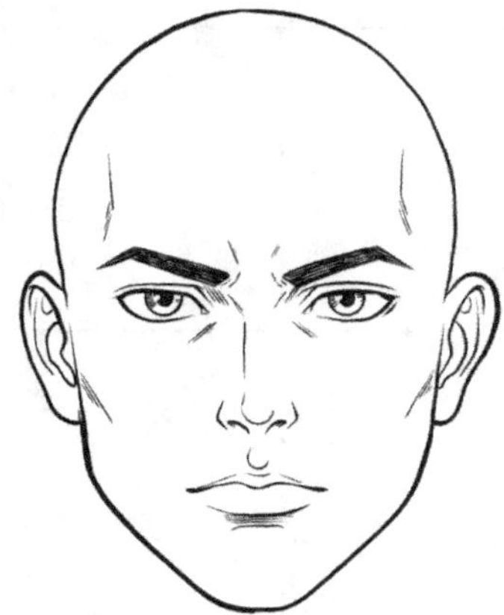

Draw in the outline of the face and erase any exisiting guidelines.

HOW TO DRAW ANIME

DRAWING THE MALE FACE IN PROFILE VIEW

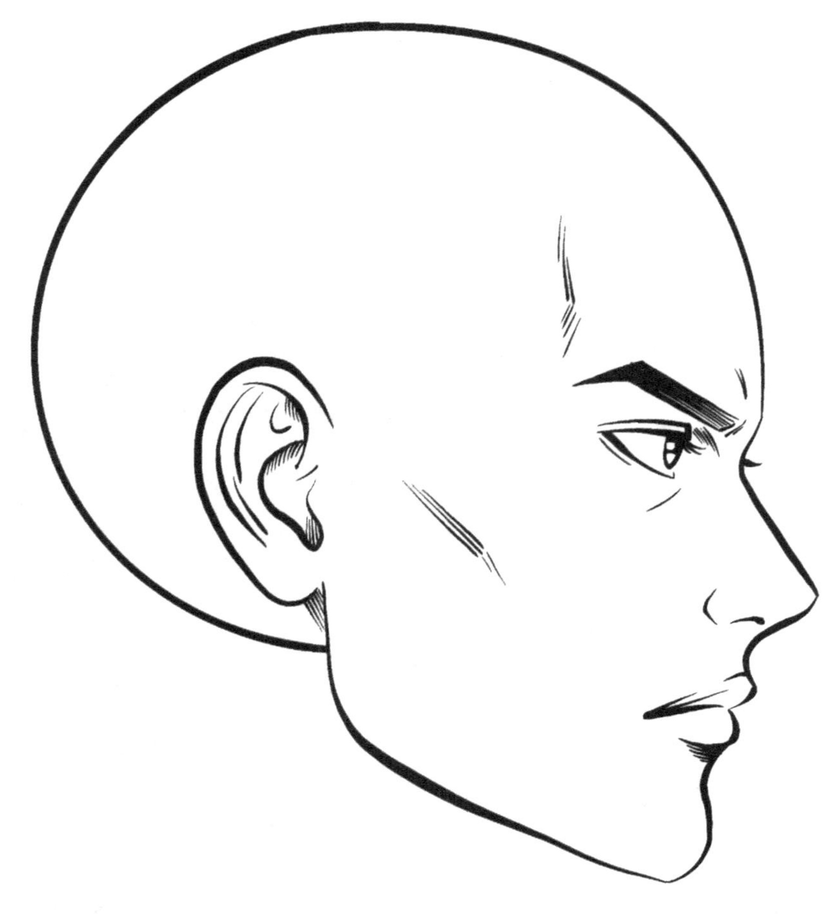

Pro Tip: When sketching in profile, focus on how each feature aligns along the vertical centre and horizontal lines. Visualising these relationships early helps maintain correct proportions.

01

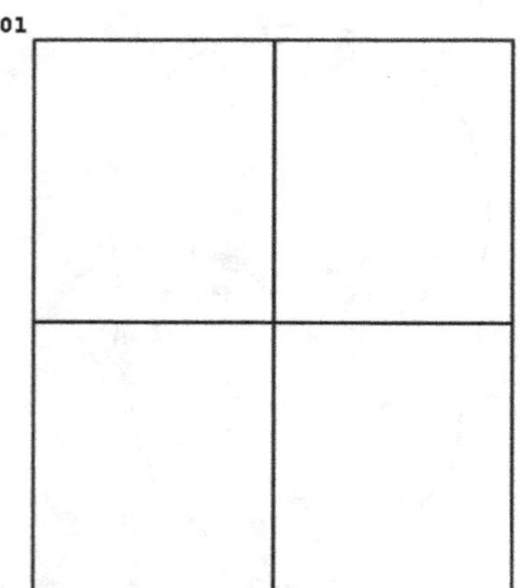

Start by drawing a rectangle. Imagine a square lightly stretched upwards. Now divide it into 4 quarters.

02

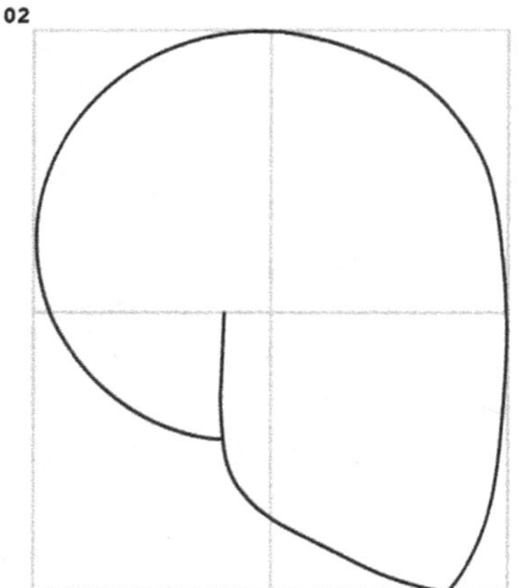

Sketch in a rough head shape. Use the grid you have created as a reference for where to position the various features.

03

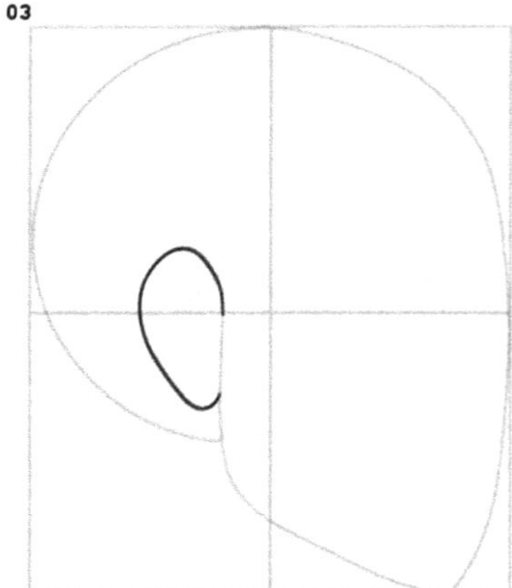

Sketch it in the ear. Notice that it extends directly up from the jawline and extends downward to approximately 1/3 of the lower left quarter along the jawline.

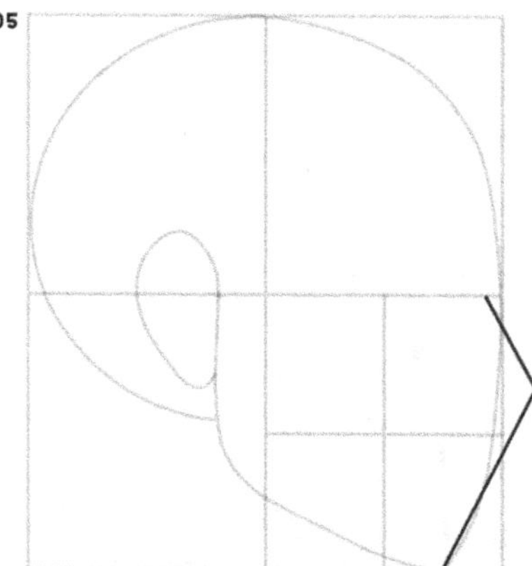

04

Divide the bottom right panel into 4 even quarters to assist you in positioning the facial features.

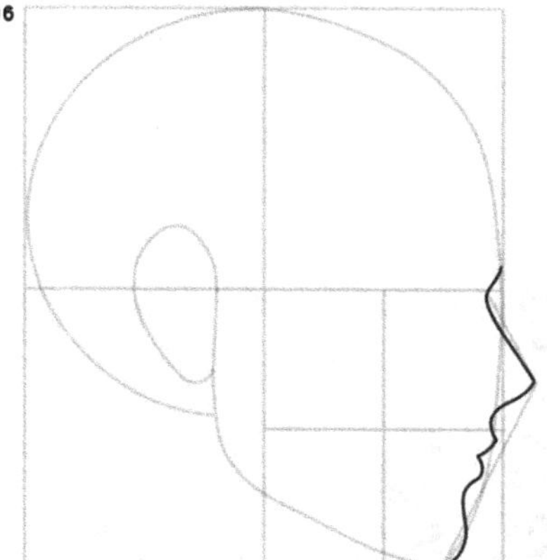

05

A horizontal line should extend outwards 1/3 of the top quarter, and down 2/3 of the top quarter. Draw a connecting line down to the bottom.

06

Use your guideline to sketch in the nose mouth and chin. Pay close attention to where they are positioned in relation to the reference above.

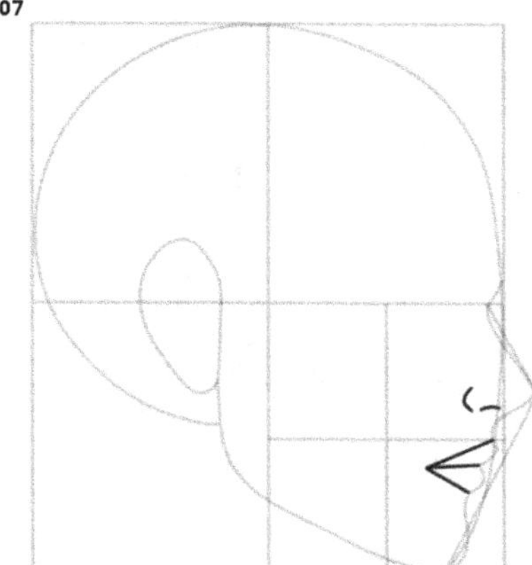

07

Draw simple lines to define the position of the lips. Note they extend back 3/4 horizontally of the lower-right quarter. Sketch in the nose also.

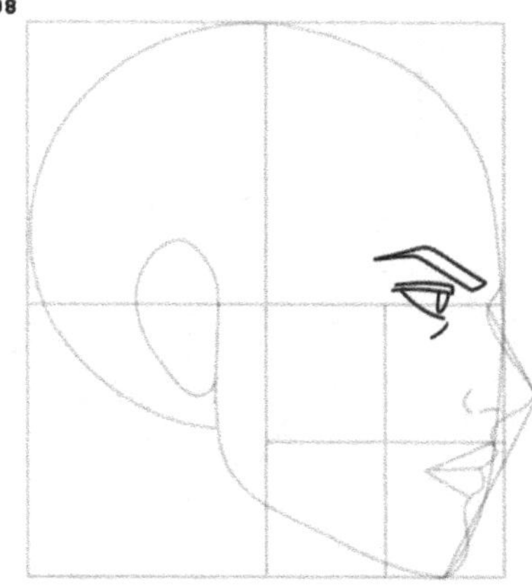

08

The eyeline is the horizontal line that bisects the rectangle. Note that the outside of the eye aligns perfectly with the vertical line beneath it.

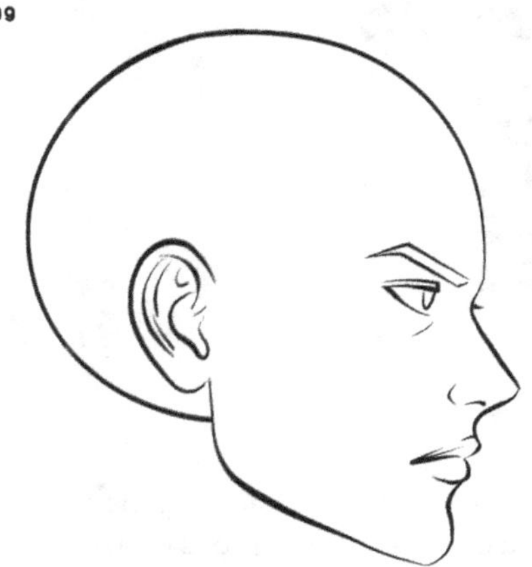

09

Draw in the outline of the head and erase any exisiting guidelines.

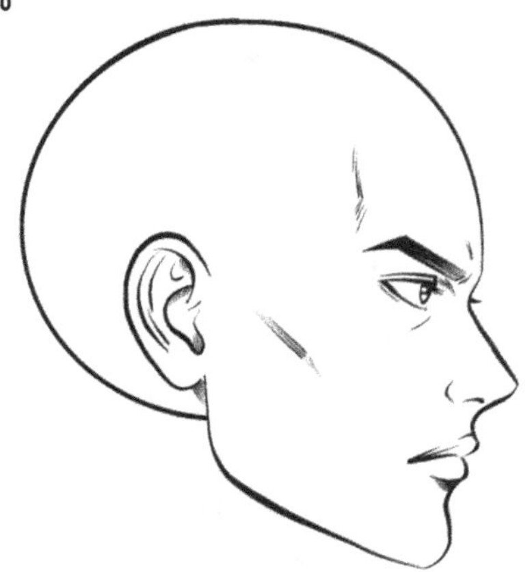

10

Be sure to add in some additional skin fold lines around the eyes and shadow under the lip to define the features and give the face depth and a natural look.

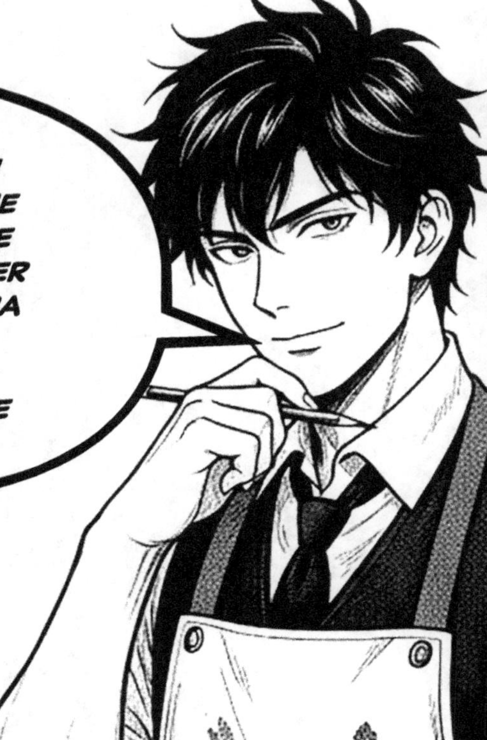

DRAWING THE MALE FACE IN ³/₄ VIEW

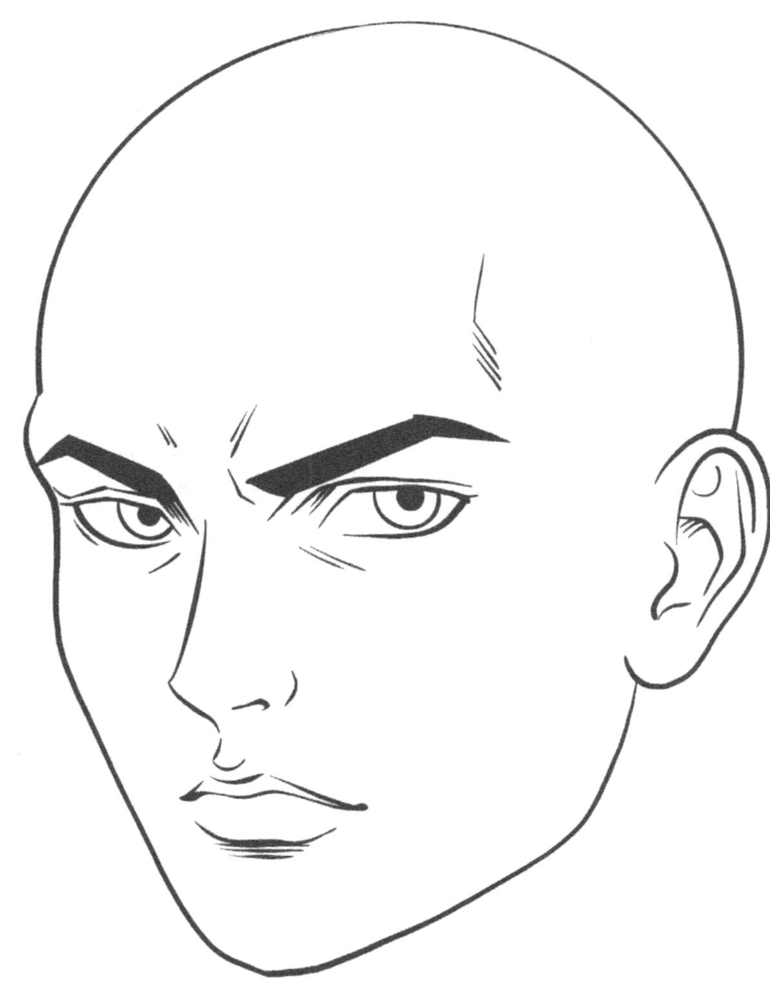

Pro Tip: Anchor all features to the centre and eye lines. These guides keep the tilt consistent and the face balanced in perspective.

01

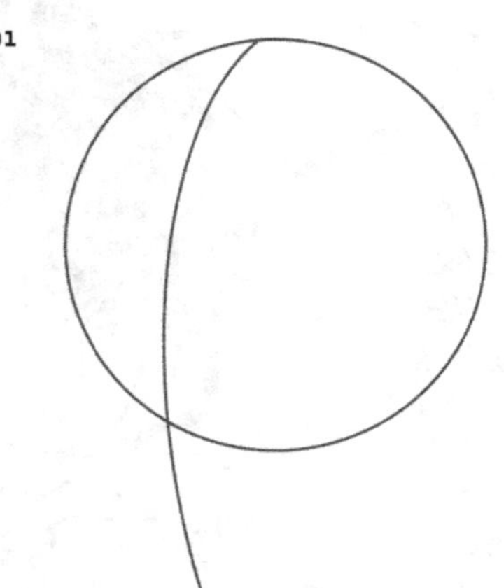
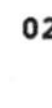

Draw an arced line downward from the top the circle. The line should extend past the base approximately 50% of the height of the circle.

02

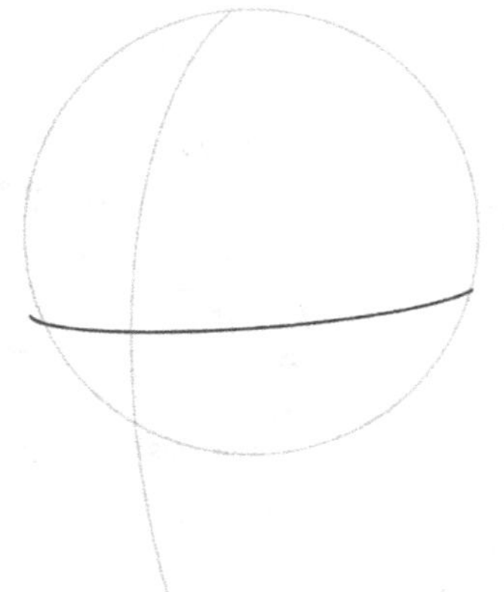

Now draw a horizontal arced line on a slight leftward leaning slant approximately 1/3 of the height of the circle from the base. This will be the eyeline.

03

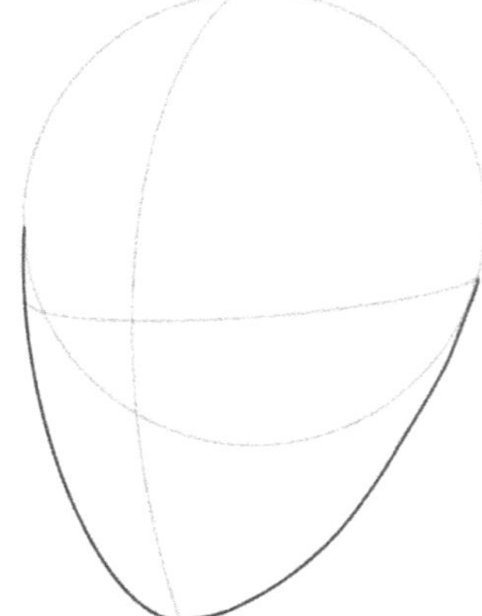

Sketch in the chin shape by connecting an arced line from each point of the eyeline. Note that on the left, it extends just above the eyeline. Be sure to include this detail.

04

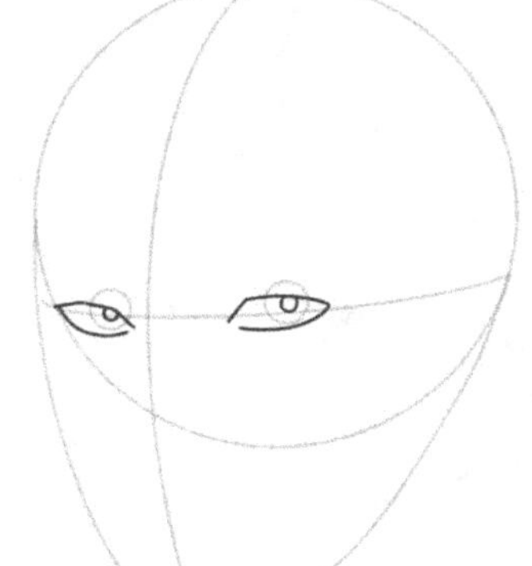

Place the eyes on the eyeline just like the reference above.

05

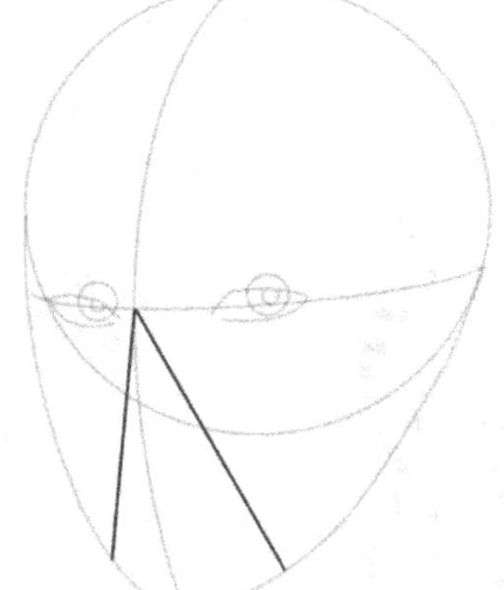

Sketch the in the eyelids to start giving the eyes some structure.

06

Draw a triangle shape from the centre point of the intersecting lines. This will help you determine the width and position of the nose and mouth.

07

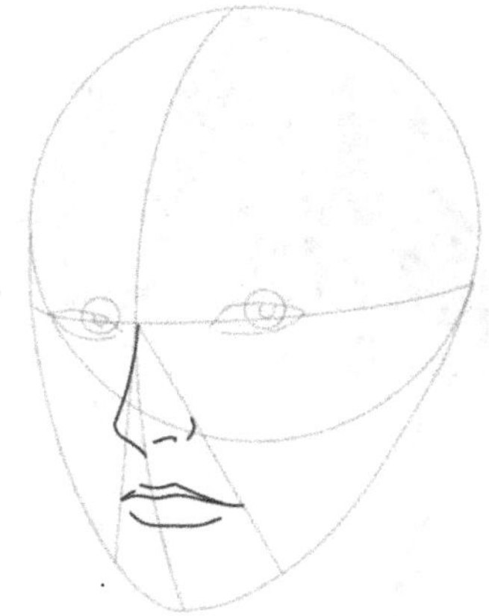

The mouth sits approximately halfway down the triangle. Note that the nose extends outside the triangle due to the angle of the face.

08

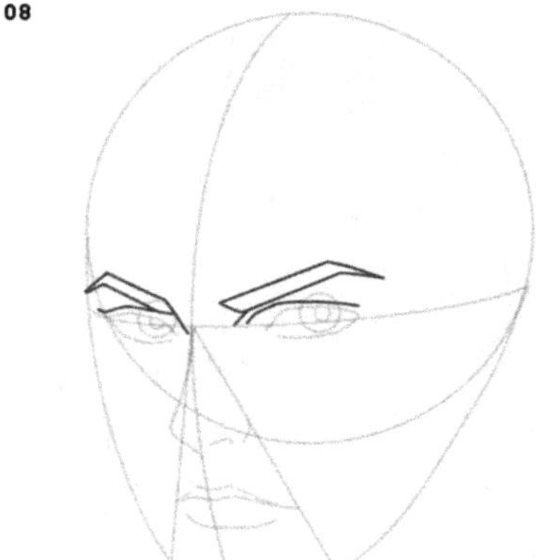

Sketch in the eyebrows. Add an additional fold line above the eyeline for a more natural look.

09

It's important that you draw the ears set in from the edge of the circle. If you do not, it will look as though the ear is placed behind the skull.

10

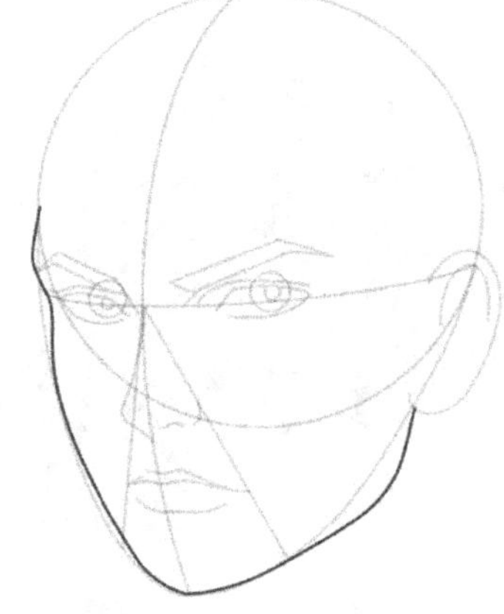

It's time to add a more natural-looking structure to the face. On the left, at the eyeline, notice that the contour of the line goes in and then back out again. This captures the definition of the cheekbones and brow.

11

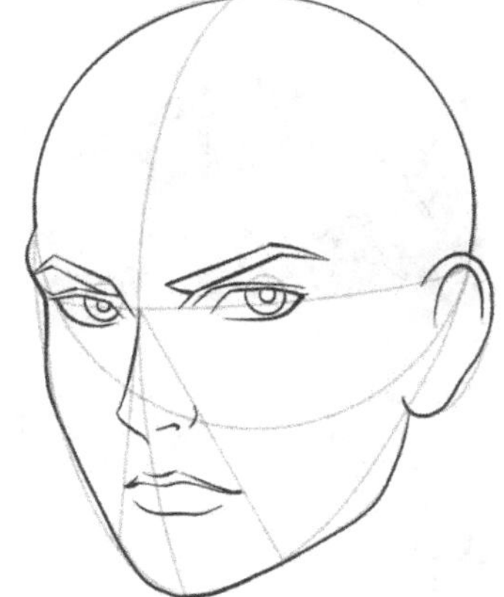

Using an inking brush, outline the skull and facial features.

12

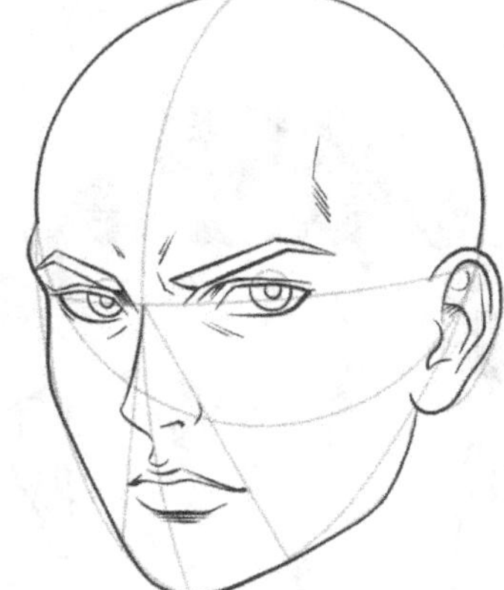

Now add some additional skin fold lines around the eyes and shadow under the lip to define the features and give the face a natural look.

DRAWING MALE HAIR, FACIAL HAIR, AND ACCESSORIES

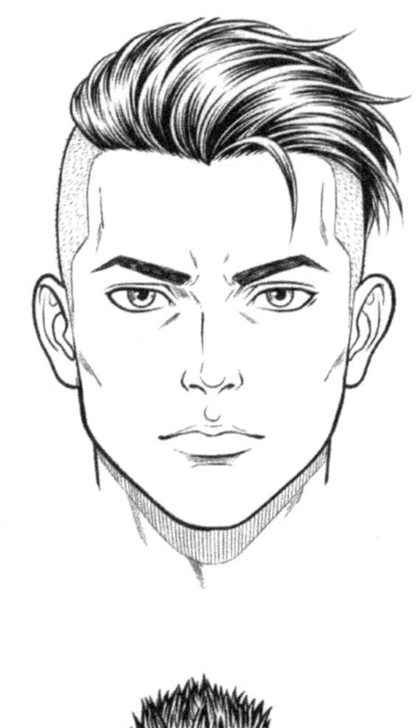

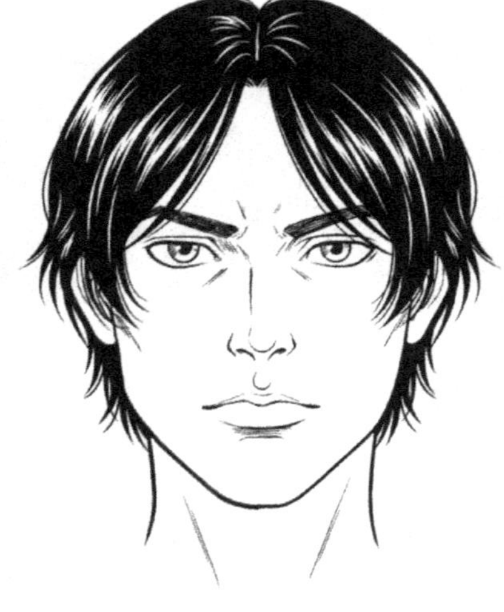

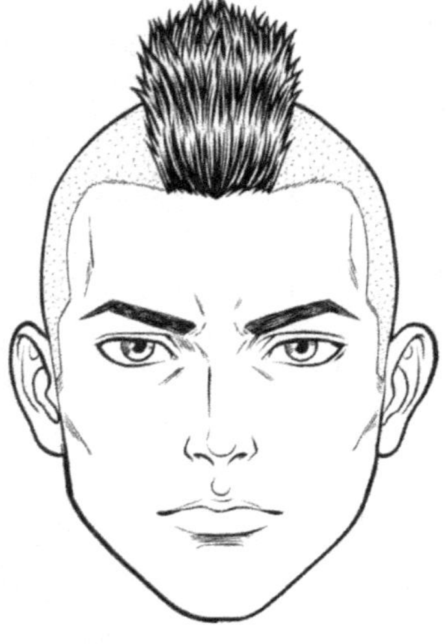

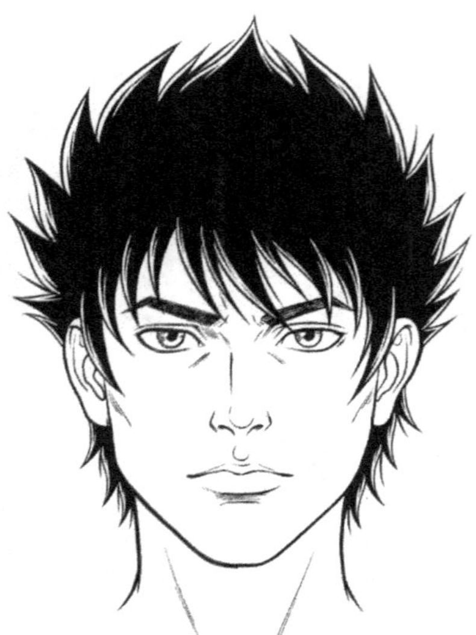

Pro Tip: Hairstyles, facial hair, and accessories express personality. Experiment with different looks to show age, attitude, and individuality while keeping proportions consistent.

01   02   03

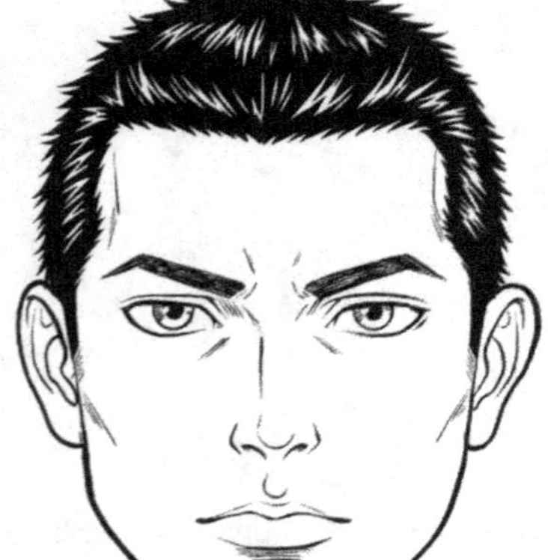

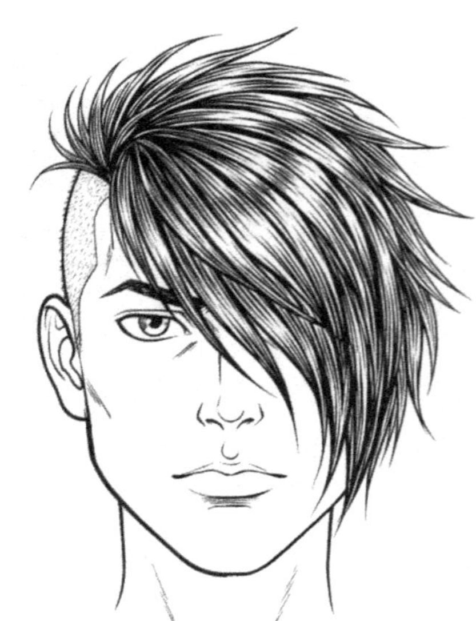

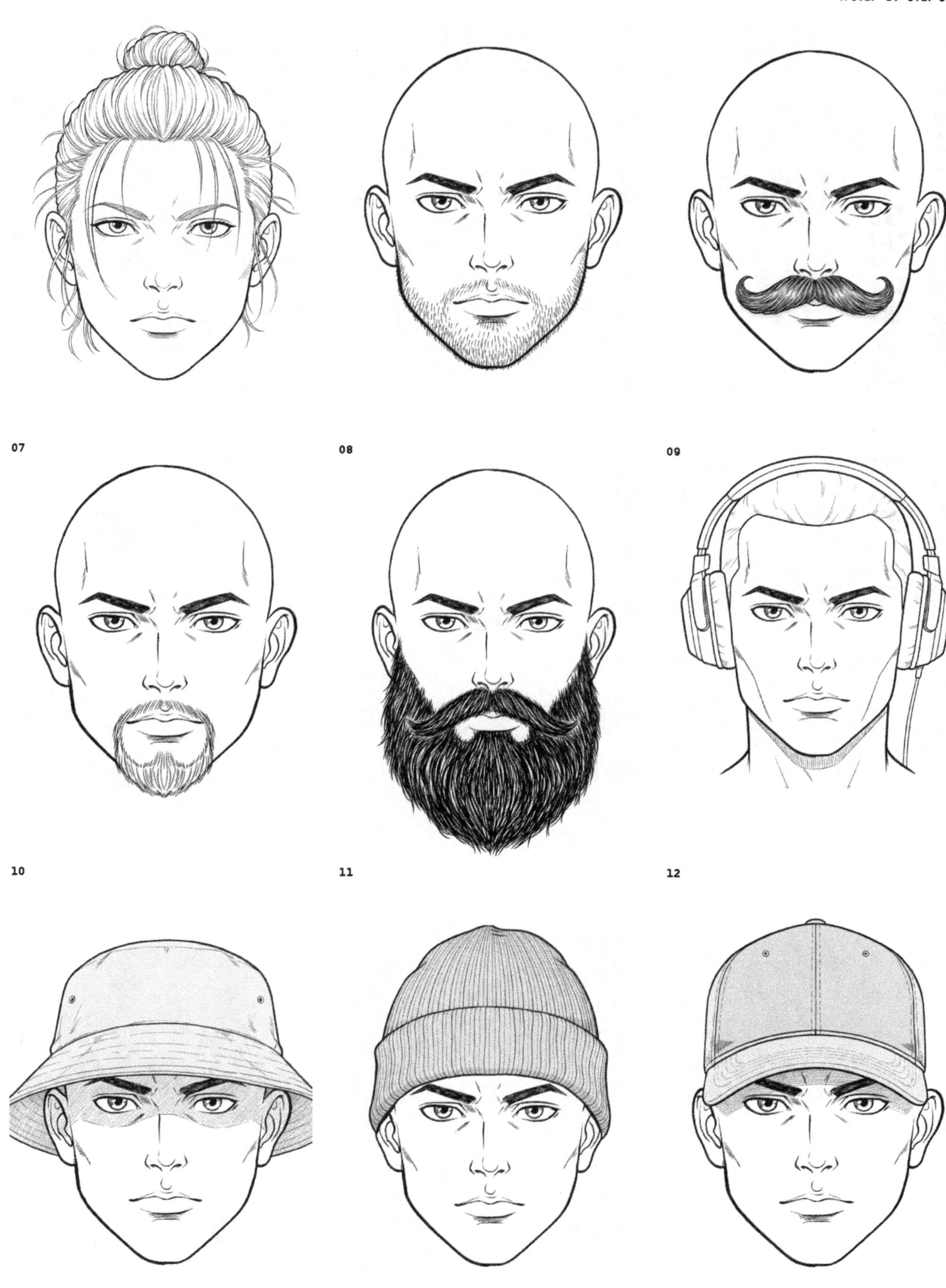

07
08
09
10
11
12
HOW TO DRAW ANIME

DRAWING THE MALE FACE FROM VARIOUS ANGLES

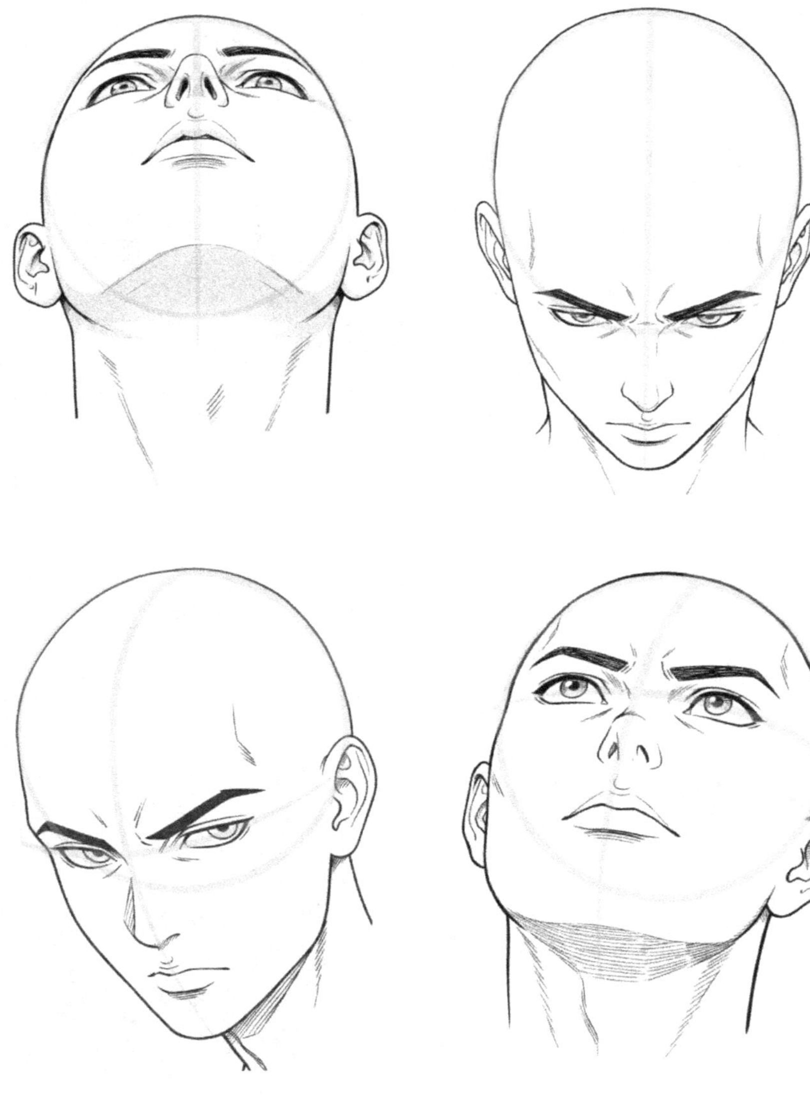

Pro Tip: When drawing the head from extreme angles, use perspective lines to guide proportion. Keep features aligned to maintain structure and avoid distortion.

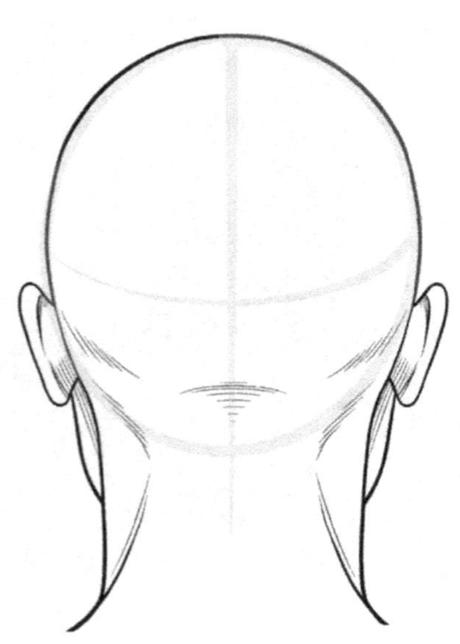

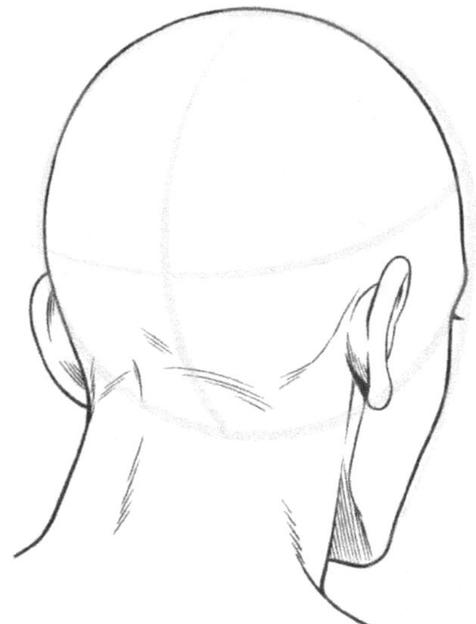

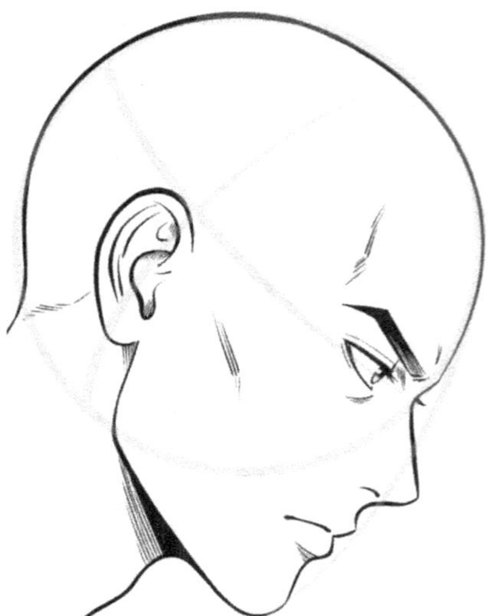

DRAWING MALE FACIAL EXPRESSIONS

Pro Tip: Facial expressions give your characters energy. Adjust the eyes and brows for intensity, and use subtle mouth shapes to show surprise, anger, happiness, or determination.

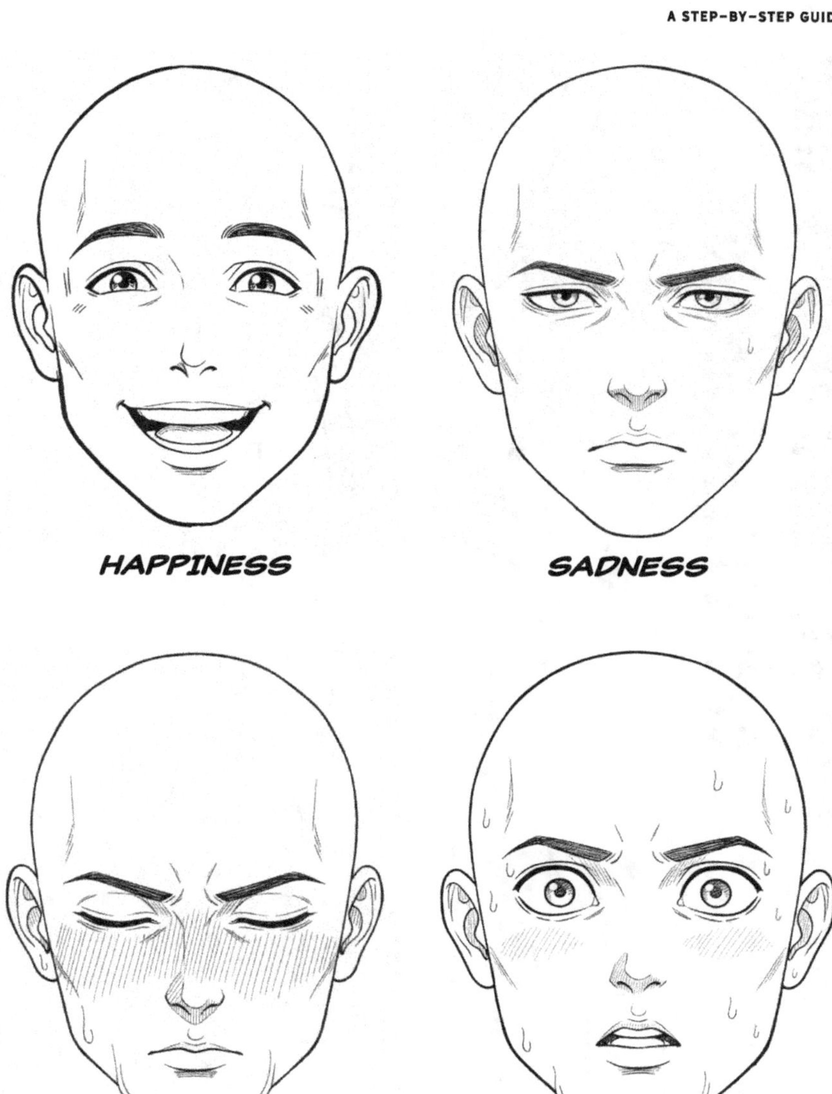

HAPPINESS

SADNESS

EMBARRASSED

FEAR

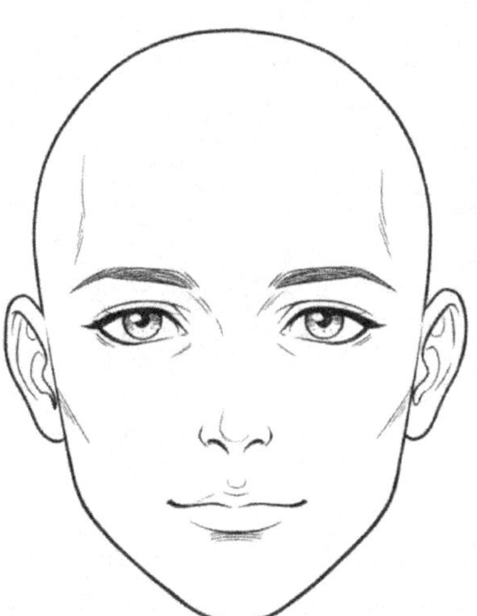

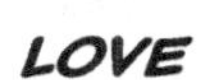

LOVE

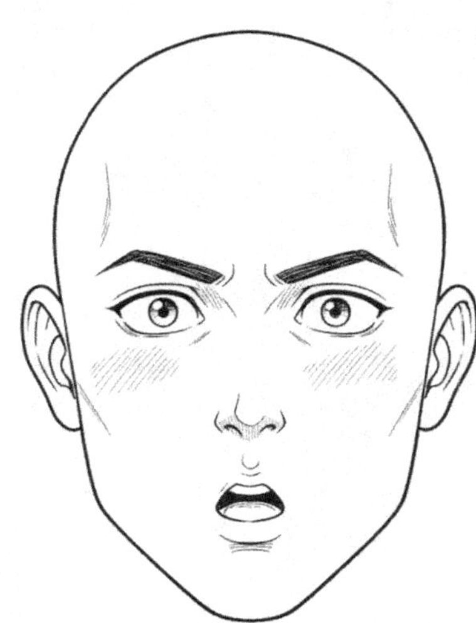

SURPRISED

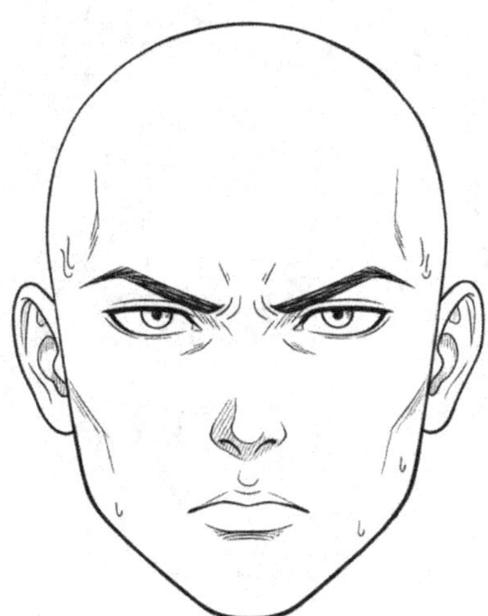

ANGER

UNDERSTANDING PROPORTIONS OF THE MAILE ANATOMY

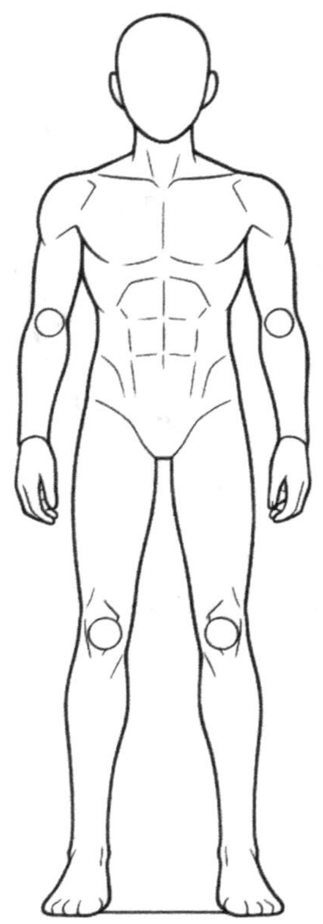
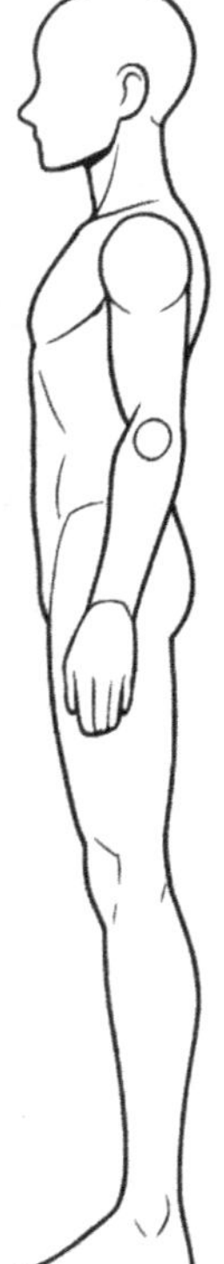
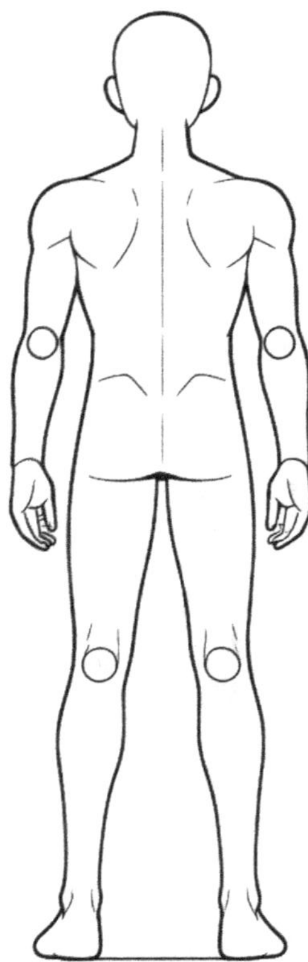

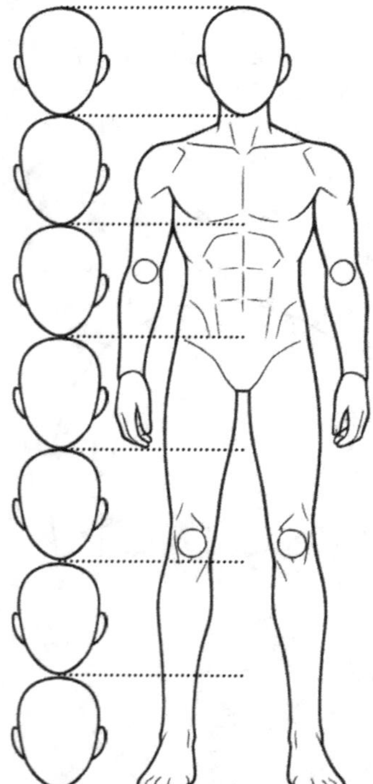

1. The average male body measures roughly seven heads tall. Use the head as a unit to keep proportions consistent.

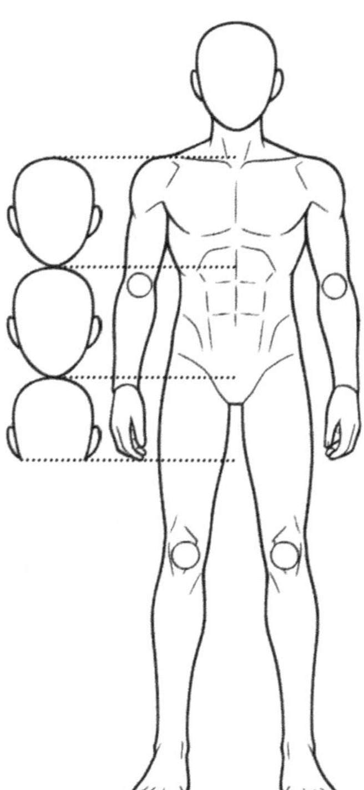

The arm, from the shoulder to the tips of the fingers, measures approximately 2½ heads.

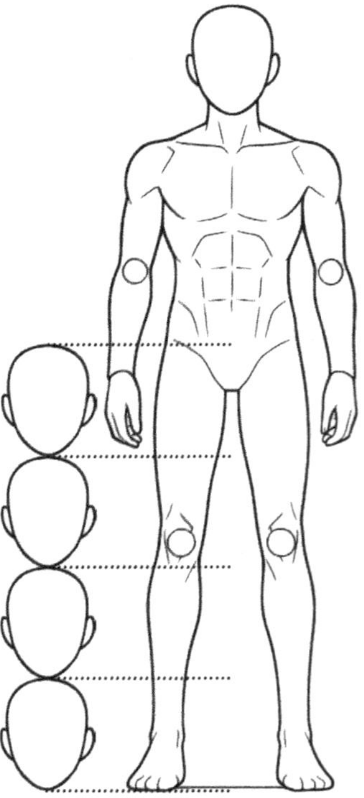

From the hips to the feet, the lower body measures around four heads.

Pro Tip: When drawing the human figure, start by establishing the head first. Once you've drawn it, you've created a unit of measurement that can be used to map out the rest of the body with accuracy and consistency.

Using head lengths as your universal measuring tool keeps the proportions of the figure balanced. For example, an average adult figure is roughly seven and to eight heads tall. This method helps you locate key landmarks, such as the position of the shoulders, chest, waist, hips, knees, and feet—relative to the size of the head. By stacking and comparing these head lengths as you work, you can build the entire figure confidently, maintaining harmony and realism throughout your drawing.

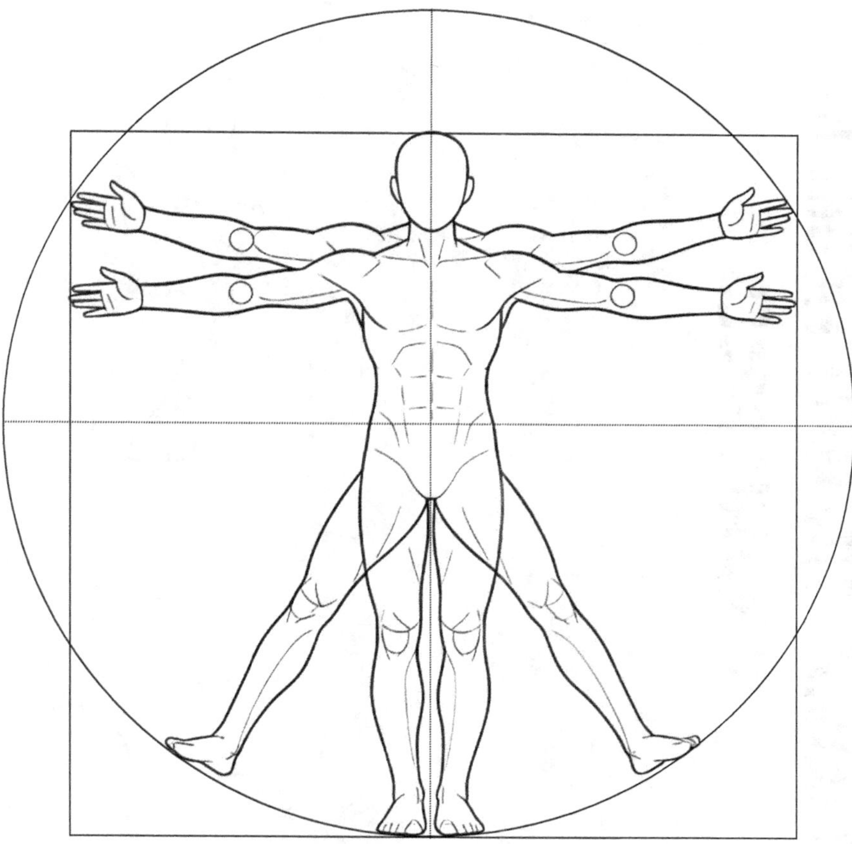

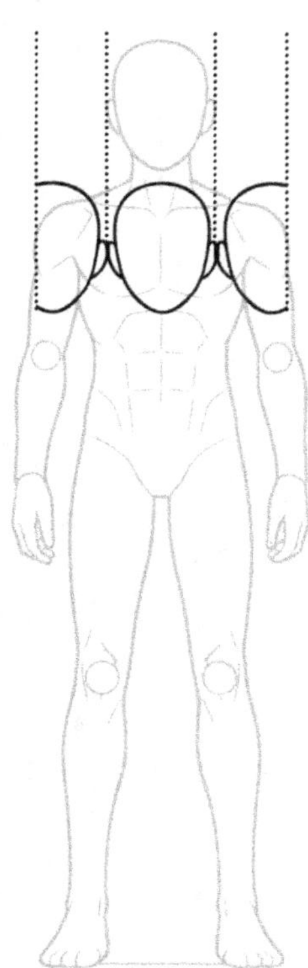

The shoulders sit approximately two head widths apart.

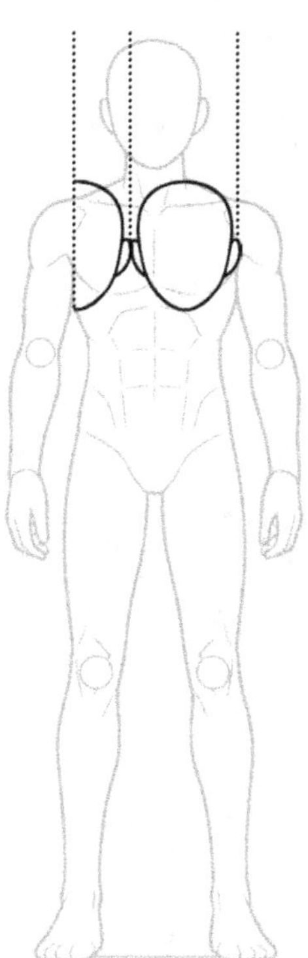

The chest spans approximately 1½ head widths.

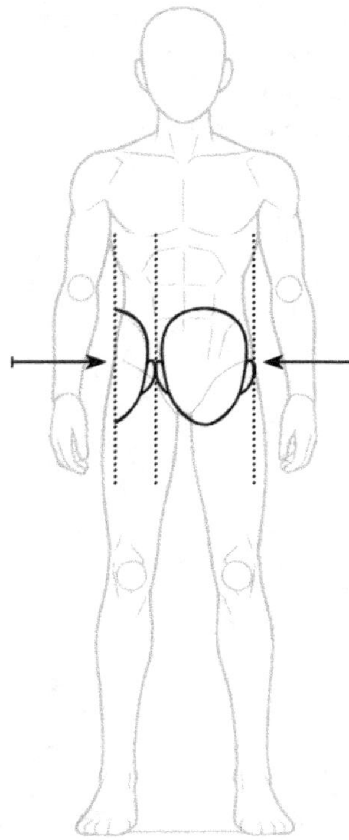

The waist measures about 1⅓ head widths at the top of the pelvis.

DRAWING THE MALE FIGURE IN DYNAMIC POSES

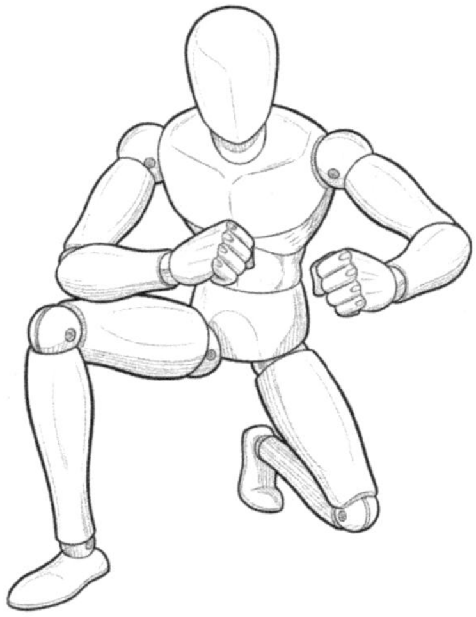

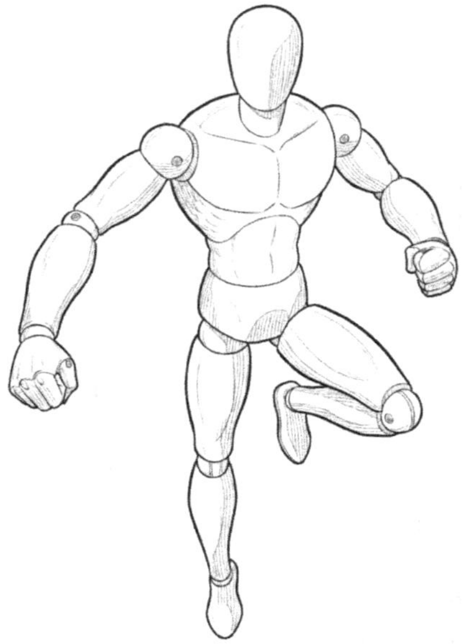

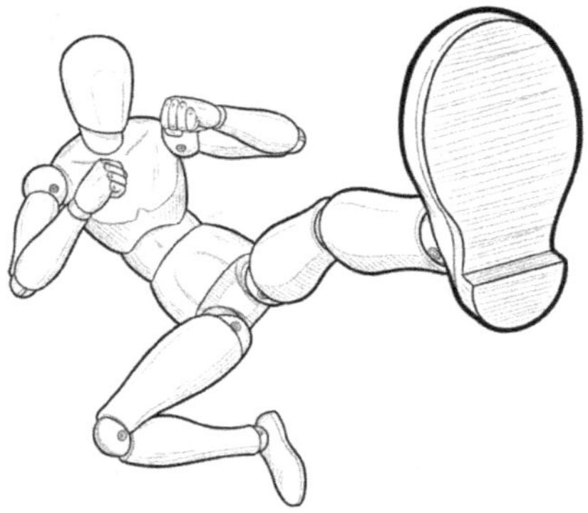

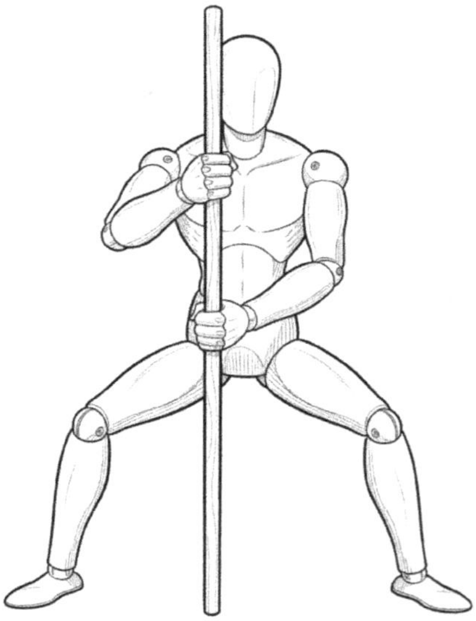

Pro Tip: Start with loose, sweeping lines to capture the movement before tightening the form. Keep the centre of gravity in mind to anchor your figure.

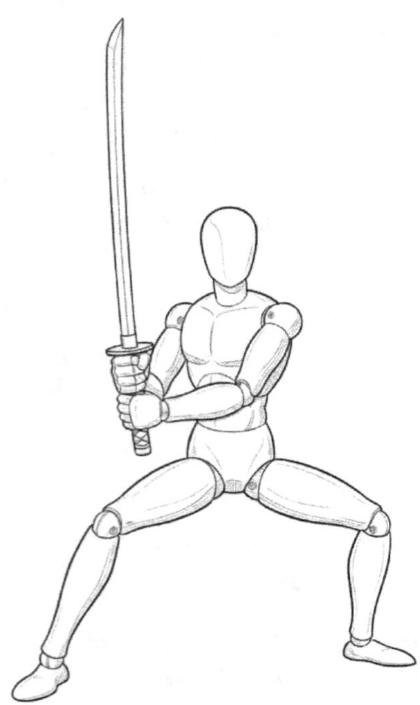

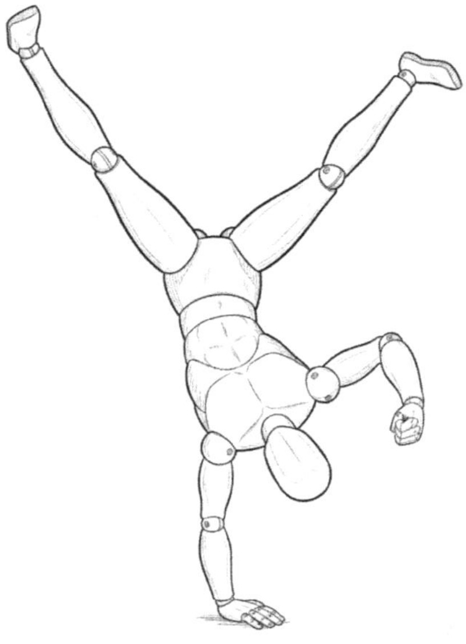

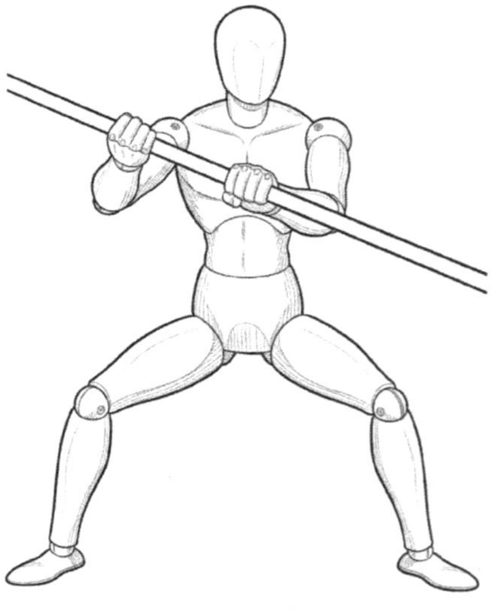

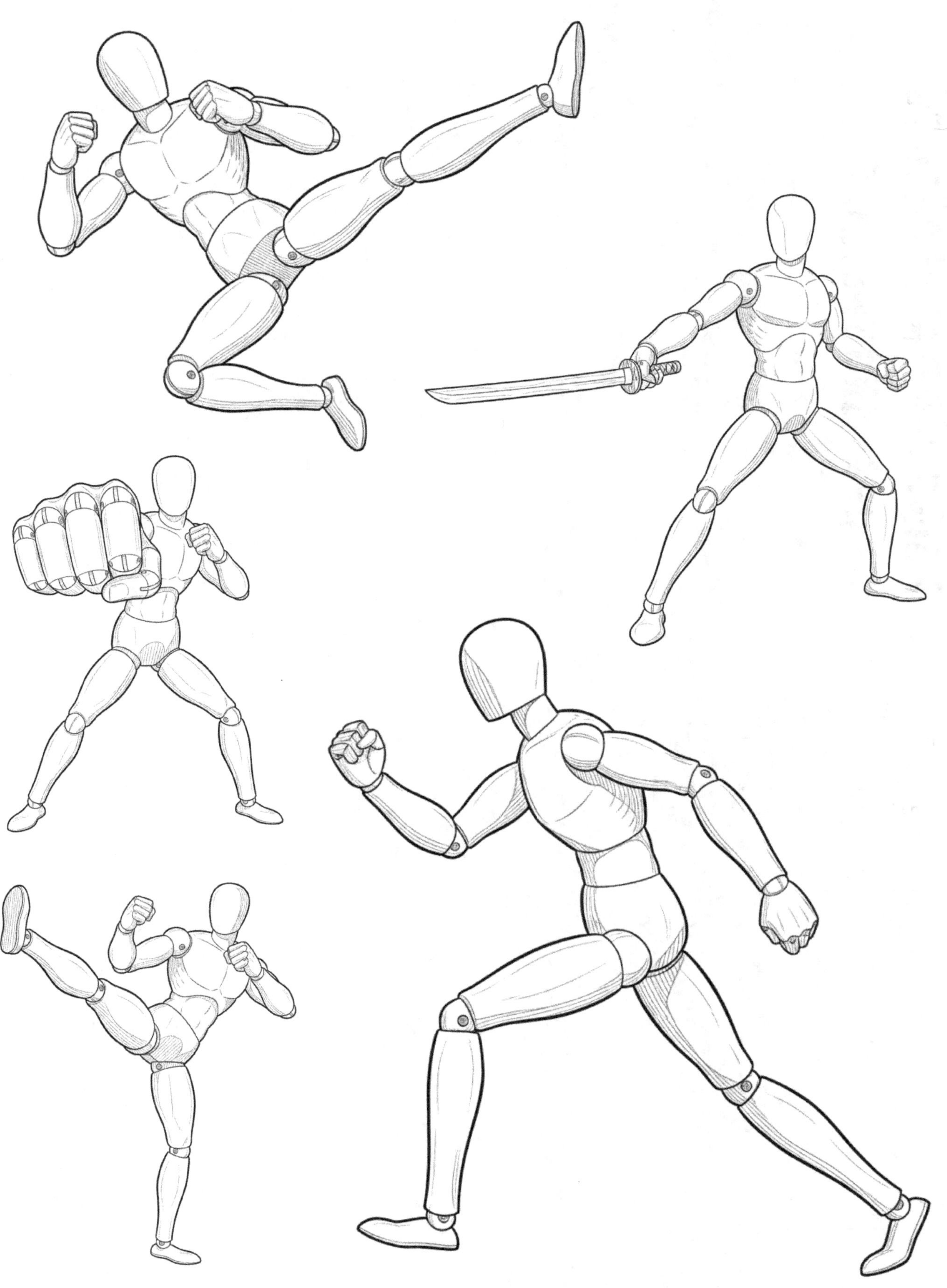
HOW TO DRAW ANIME

A SIMPLIFIED APPROACH TO DRAWING THE HAND

Drawing the hand is one of the most challenging yet rewarding studies for any artist. It combines structure, movement and expression. By breaking it into simple shapes and understanding its proportions, you can capture its form and expressive character.

01

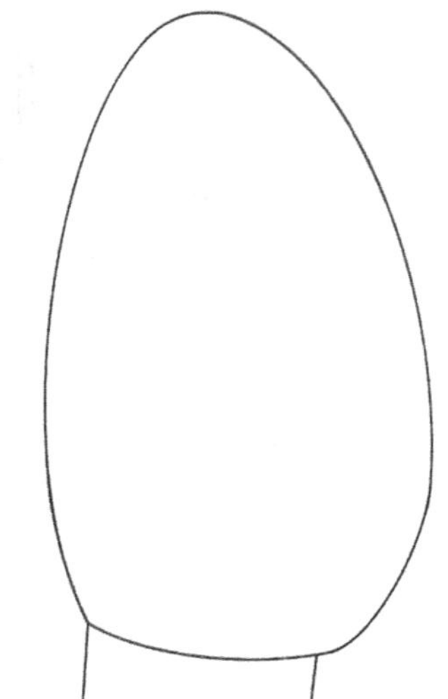

02

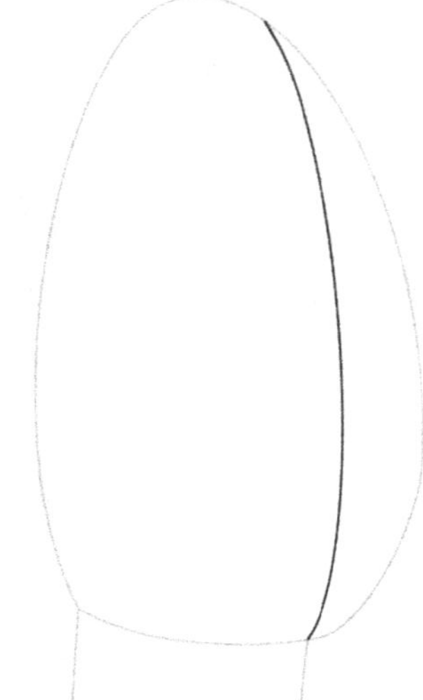

03

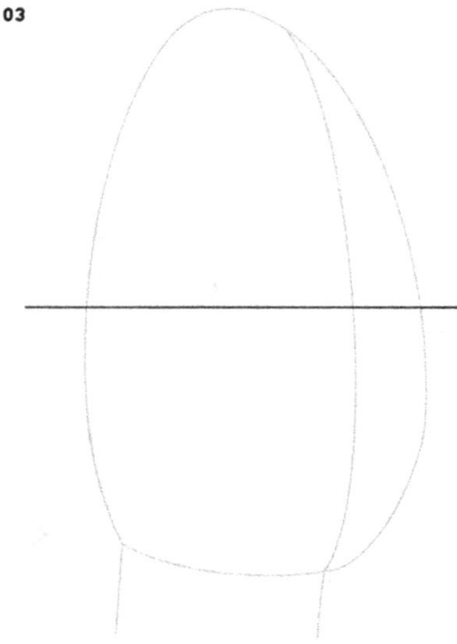

04

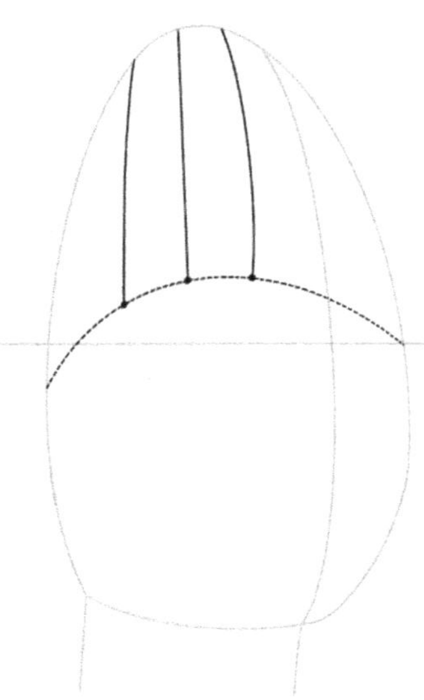

05

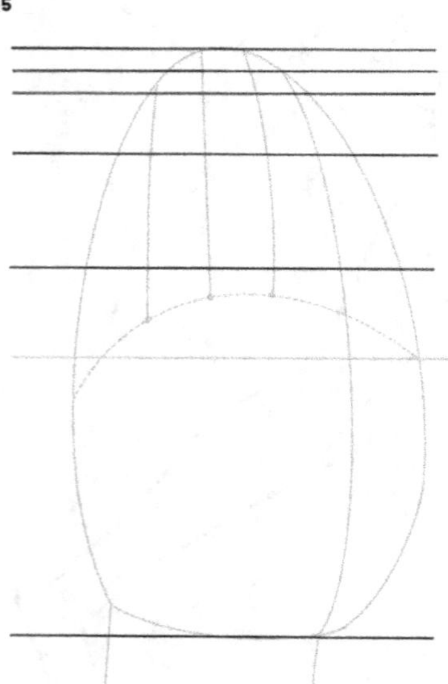

06

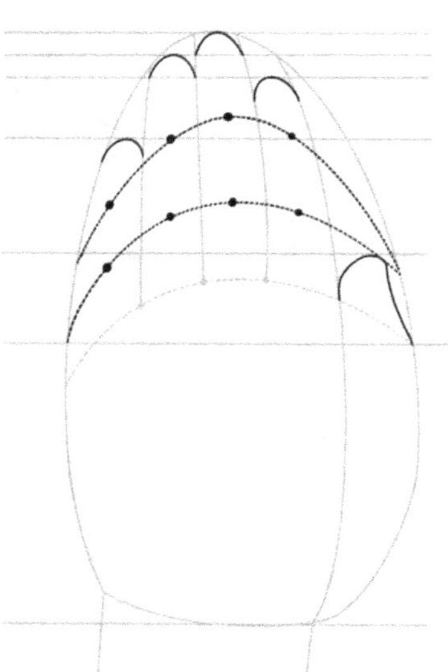

07

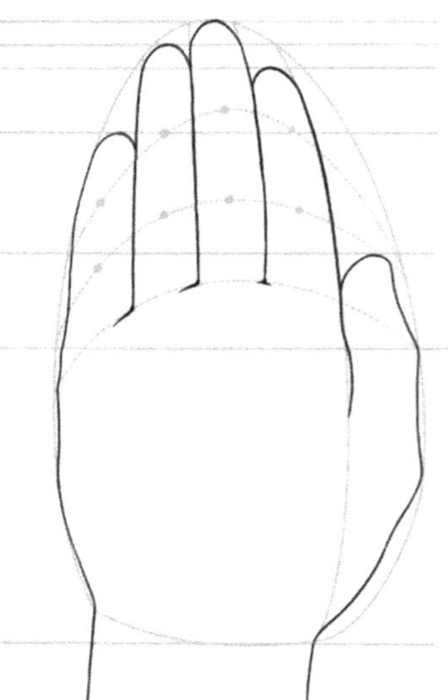

Step.1

Start by sketching an oval shape for the palm. Think of it as a smooth pebble—solid and slightly flattened. This shape represents the main mass of the hand and gives you a base to build on.

Step.2

Extend a short line from the bottom centre of the oval to suggest the wrist. The thumb attaches at an angle from the side, and curves naturally towards the character's fingers.

Step.3

Draw a horizontal line halfway between the top and bottom of the oval. This will help you place the base of the fingers in proportion to the rest of the hand.

Step.4

Above this halfway line, draw a curved guide to mark where the fingers begin. The curve should dip slightly below the line at the little finger's base and rise at the index finger's base.

Step.5

Use this curve to measure the finger lengths. The middle finger is usually the longest, the index and ring fingers are roughly equal, and the little finger is shorter. The thumb starts slightly higher than the base curve of the fingers.

Step.6

Round off the fingertips, keeping each finger slightly tapered. Imagine three arcs running across the hand: one arc for the knuckles, one arc for the middle joints, and one arc for the fingertips. The thumb connects along these same curves, completing the natural rhythm of the character's hand.

Step.7

At the base of the fingers, notice a short, curved fold of skin that runs across the palm. This crease follows the natural arc where the fingers bend and helps define the base of the palm.

Step.8

When the hand is flat and the thumb is curved inward, you'll see a deep crease running from the thumb's base toward its top joint. This forms an inverted "T" shape with the main fold of the palm and defines the thumb's movement.

Step.9

Add the two main crease lines across the palm as indicated. The small pits between the finger bases can be slightly darkened, and you might include a subtle fold line running across the wrist for added realism.

Step.10

Some hands show double lines at the finger joints, depending on size and flexibility. A single line will usually do, but adding a faint secondary crease can suggest more realism.

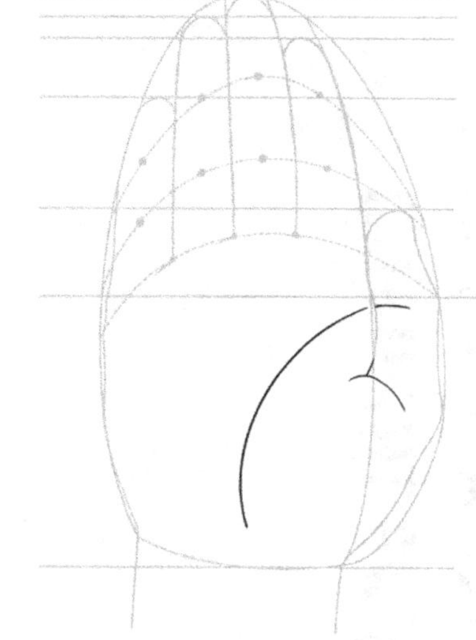

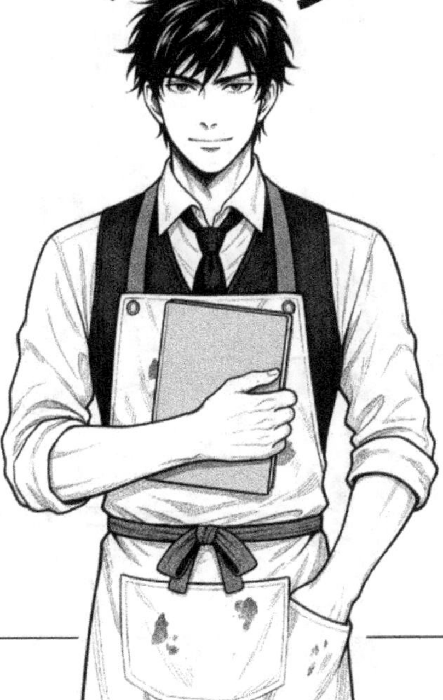

08

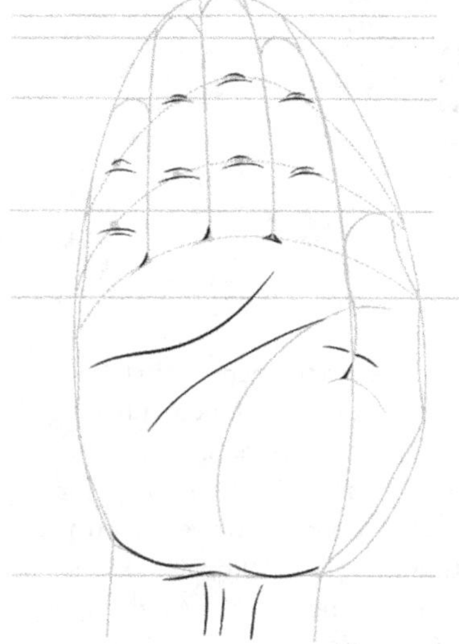

09

10

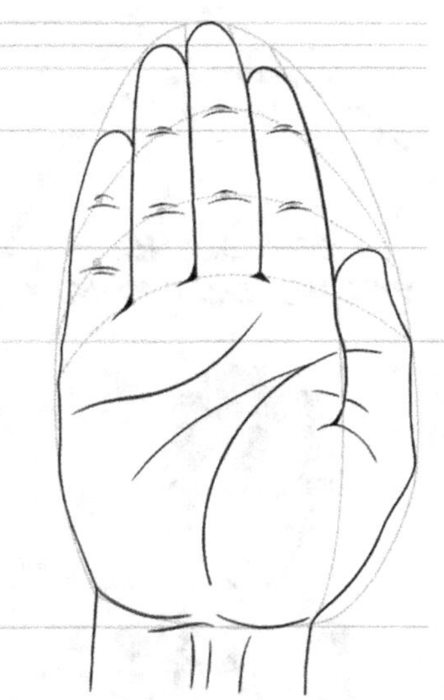

HOW TO DRAW ANIME

A SIMPLIFIED APPROACH TO DRAWING THE HAND

Understanding the hand from the side view is essential for capturing its structure and movement. From this angle, the hand reveals its subtle planes, step-downs, and the powerful form of the thumb base. By simplifying it into basic geometric shapes, you can grasp its proportions more easily while building a solid foundation for drawing hands in any position.

01

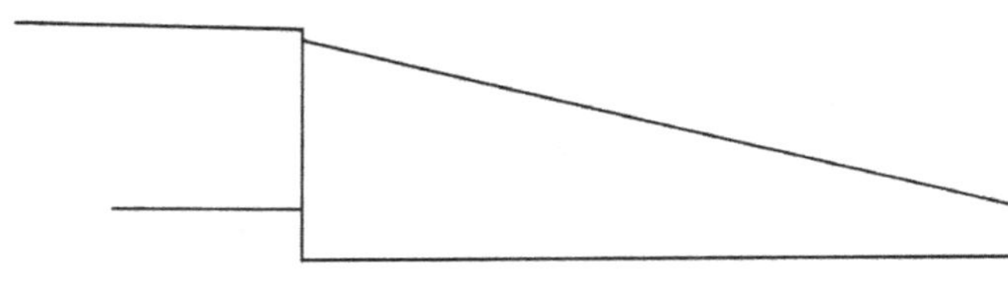

02

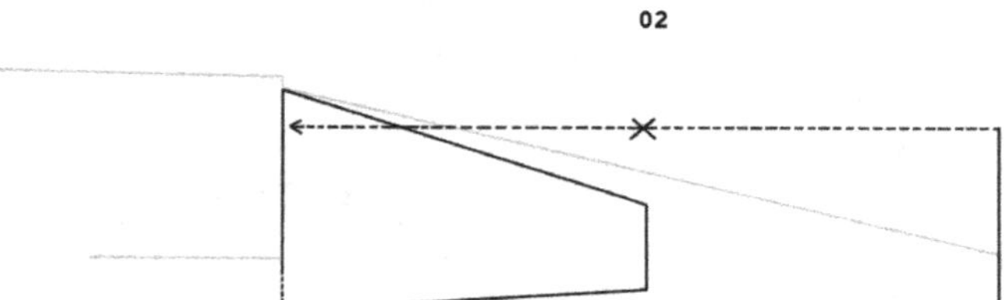

03

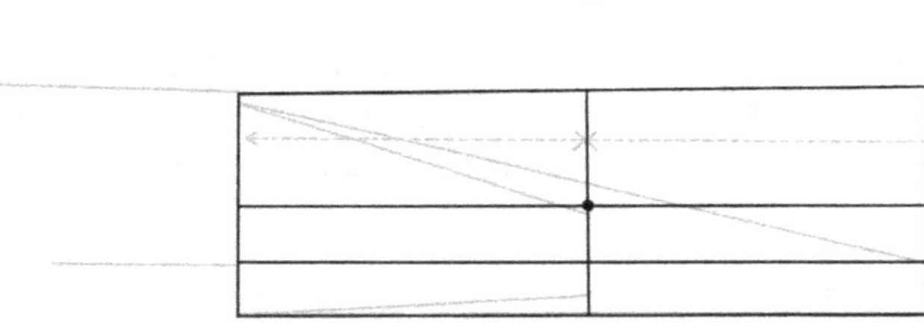

04

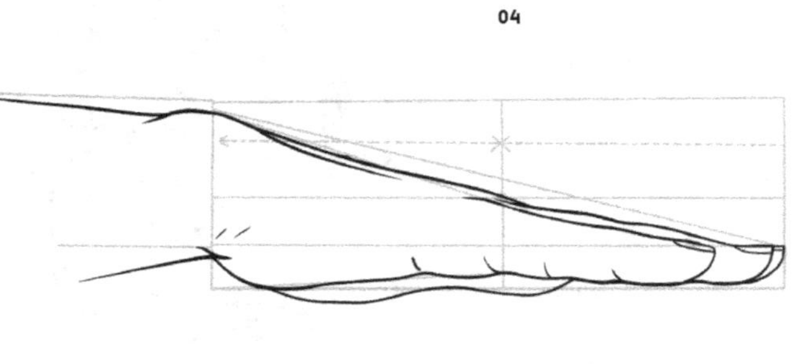

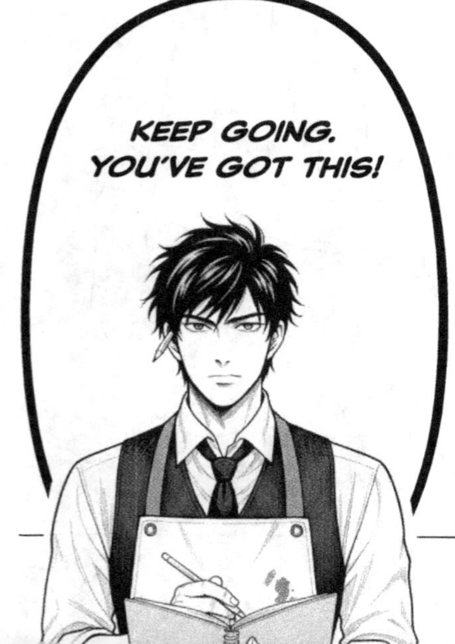

Step.1

From the side, the hand can be simplified into a tapered trapezoid. The base on the little finger side is thicker than on the thumb side. Notice the clear step down where the wrist meets the hand—there's always a change in direction at this point.

Step.2

A smaller trapezoid runs from the wrist to the base of the little finger, about half the overall length of the hand.

Step.3

You can establish proportions by drawing a rectangle around the hand. The midpoint marks the hand's thickness, while the lower quarter indicates where the wrist connects. This also helps define the width of the fingers.

Step.4

The completed side view should look sleek and dynamic, with a smooth, aerodynamic contour.

Step.5

On the thumb side, the wrist and palm meet with a more pronounced drop, forming a subtle curve on the underside of the hand.

Step.6

The thumb's knuckles align with the nail joint, showing a strong step down between the wrist and thumb. Remember, the ball of the thumb is a prominent feature and gives the hand much of its power and shape.

Step.7

Because the thumb base drops lower, the hand appears slightly wider when viewed from this angle. The halfway point across the thumb aligns roughly with its top knuckle.

Step.8

When the thumb rests against the hand, its base contracts slightly, creating an elliptical shape that makes the muscle fold inward.

05

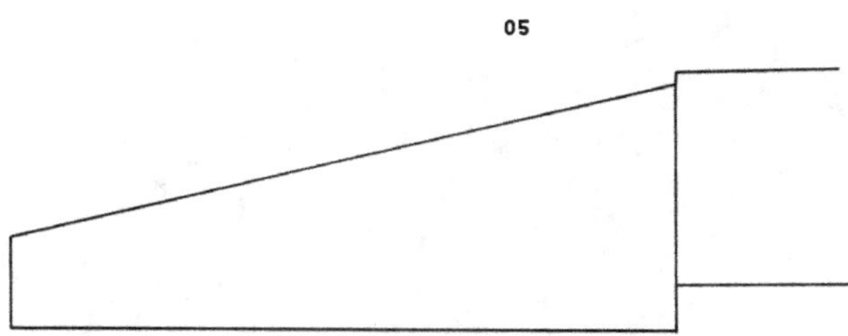

06

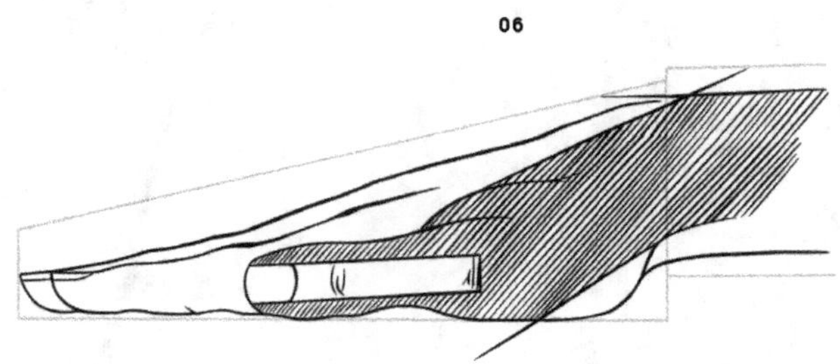

07

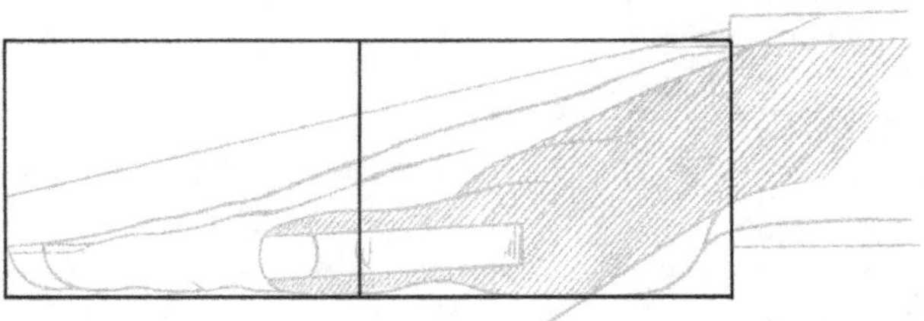

08

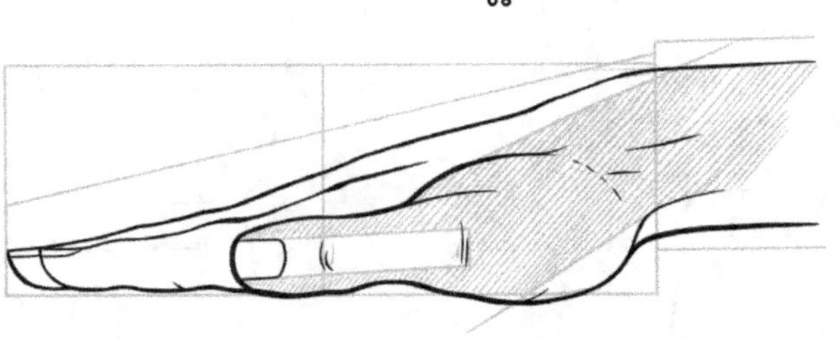

DRAWING THE HAND AND HAND GESTURES

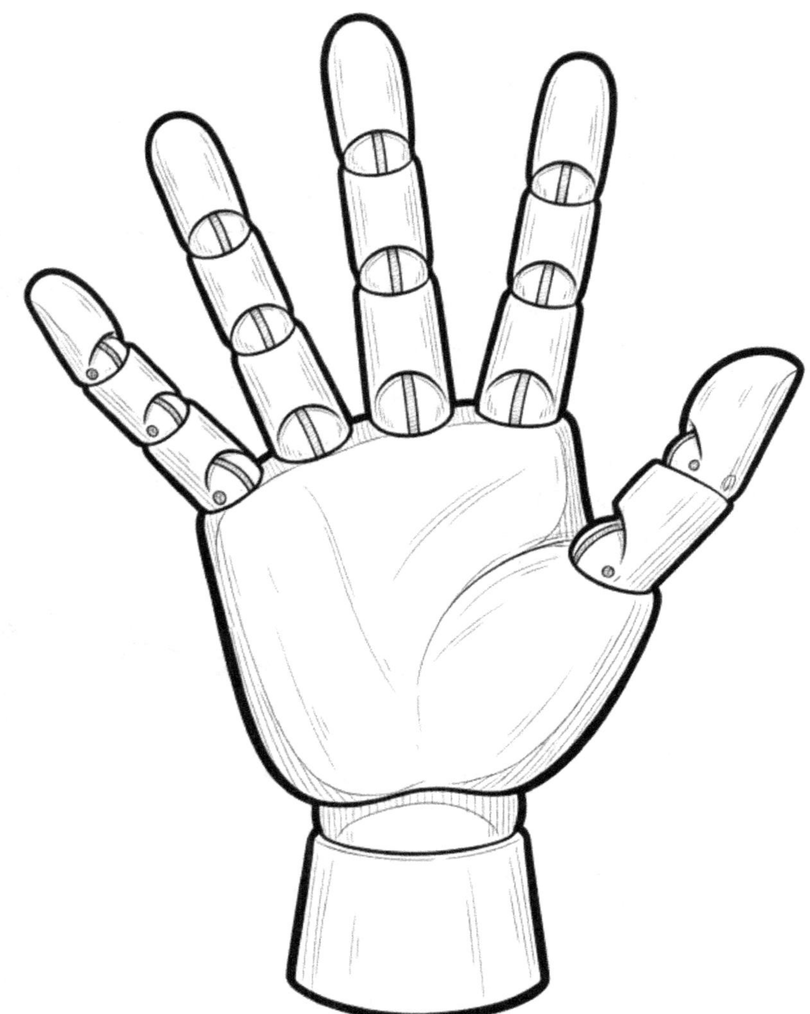

Pro Tip: When drawing hands, think of them as a series of boxes and cylinders. Start simple to capture proportion and angle, then refine the details like knuckles and creases.

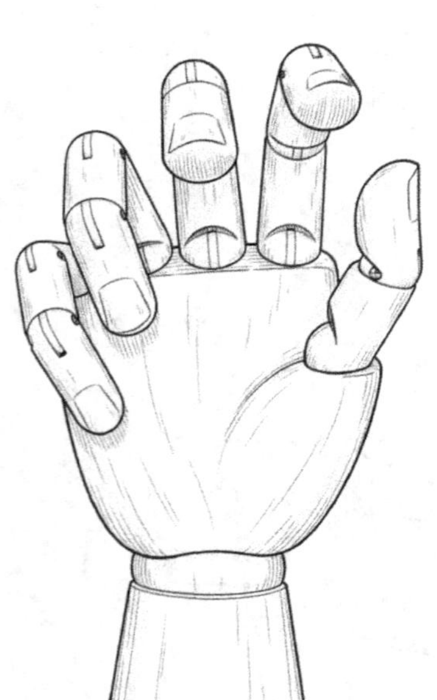

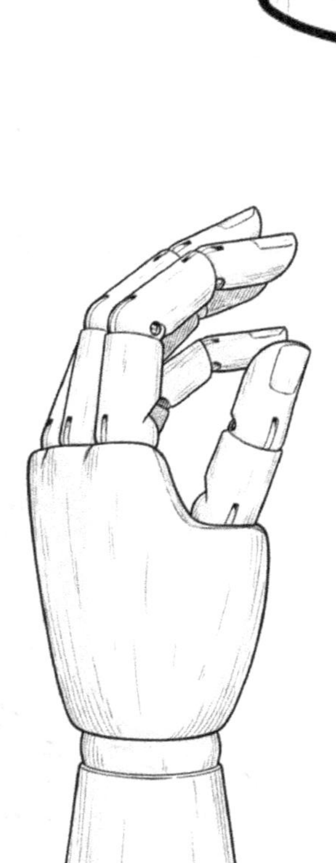

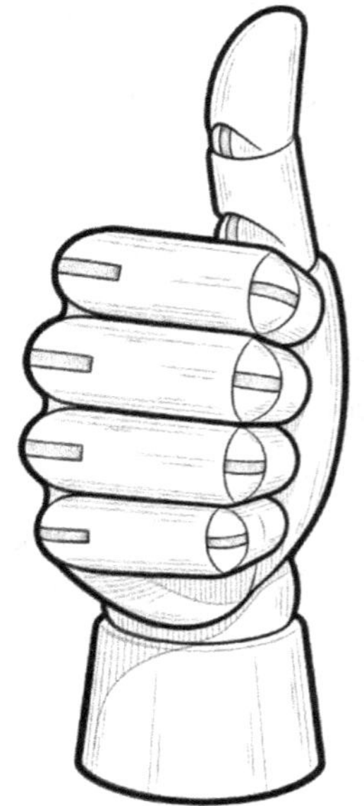

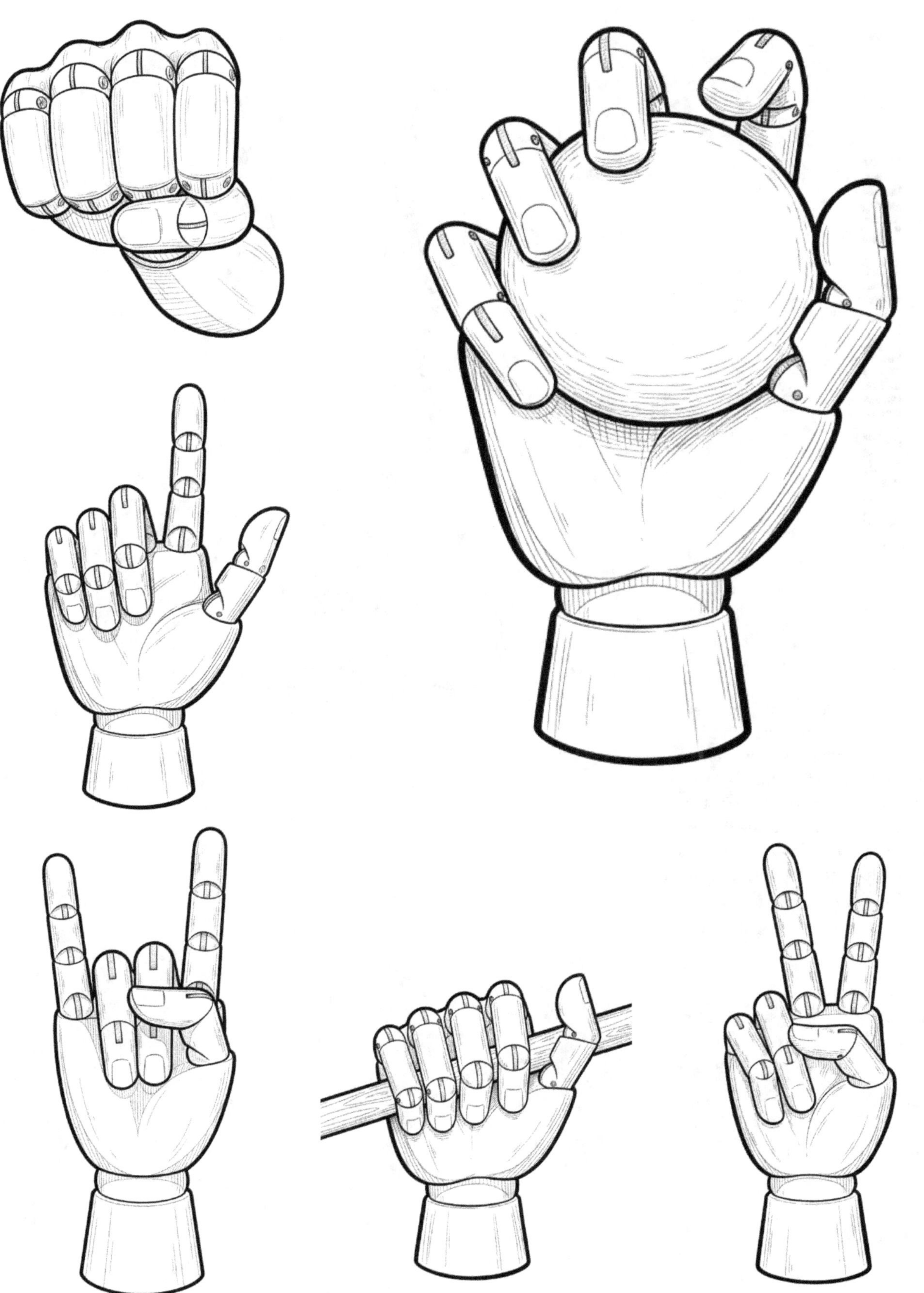

A SIMPLIFIED APPROACH TO DRAWING THE FOOT

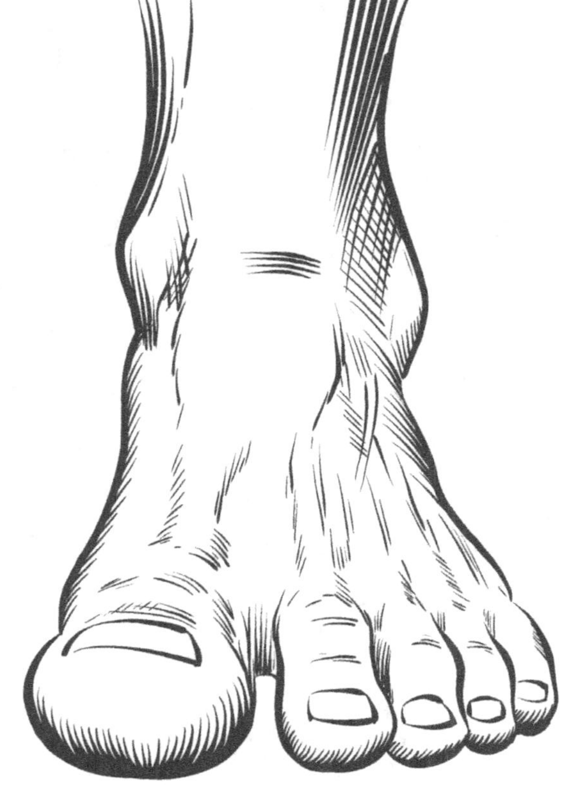

Pro Tip: The ankle isn't level—its inner side sits higher than the outer. This happens because the tibia (inner ankle bone) extends lower than the fibula (outer ankle bone). When drawing the foot, use an angled line across the ankle to show this tilt. It instantly makes your figure feel more grounded and anatomically correct.

01

02

03

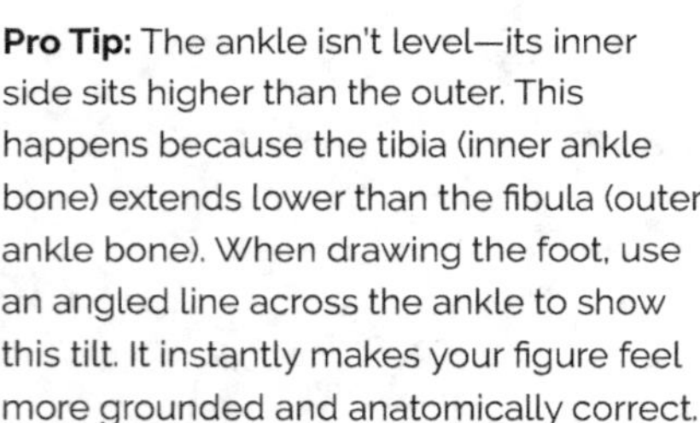

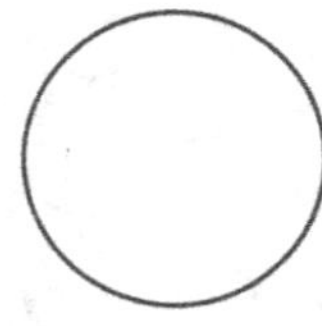

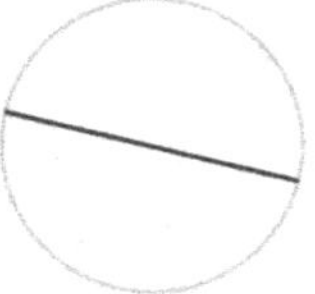

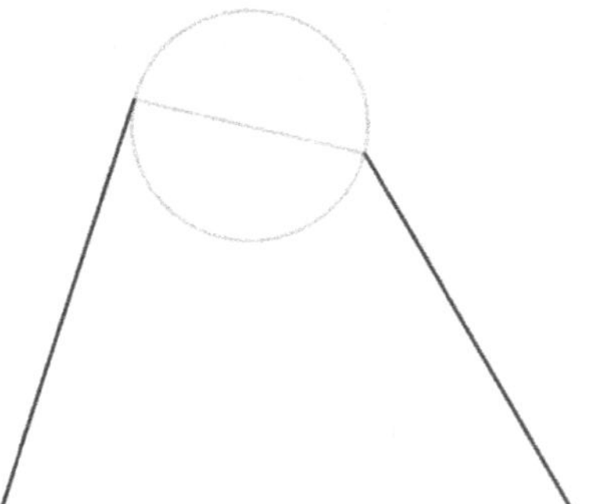

04

05

06

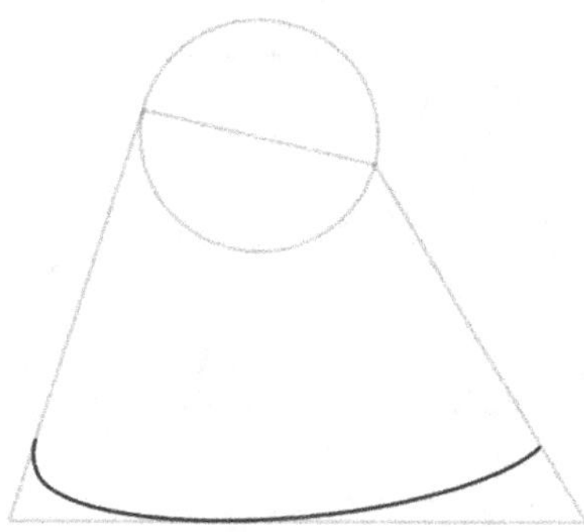

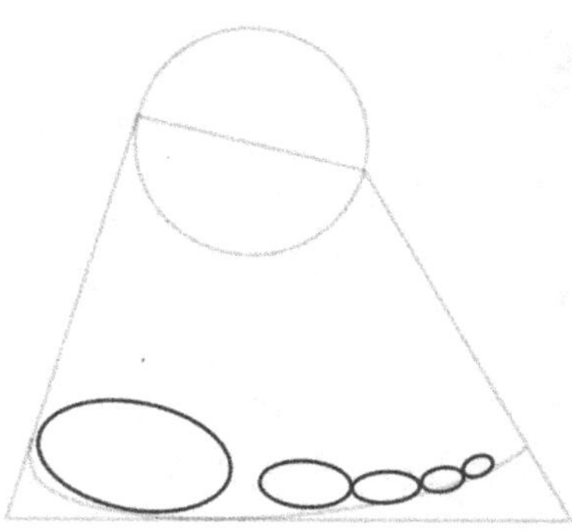

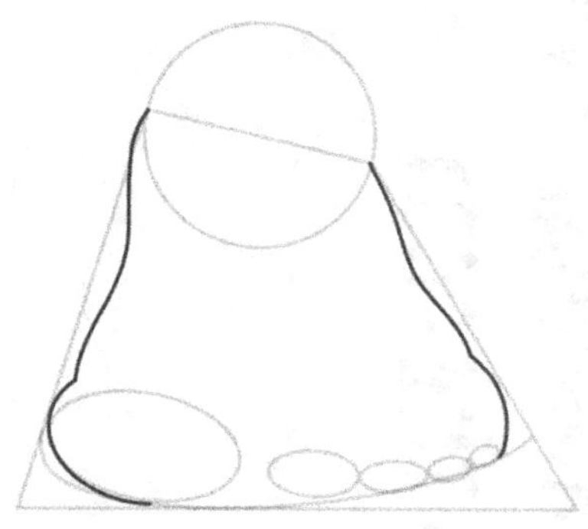

07

08

09

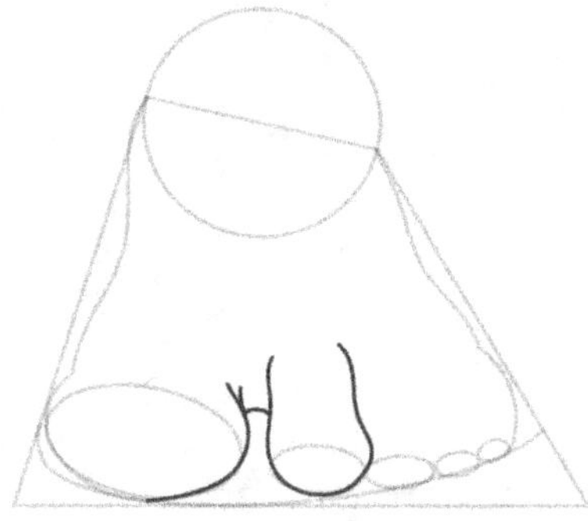

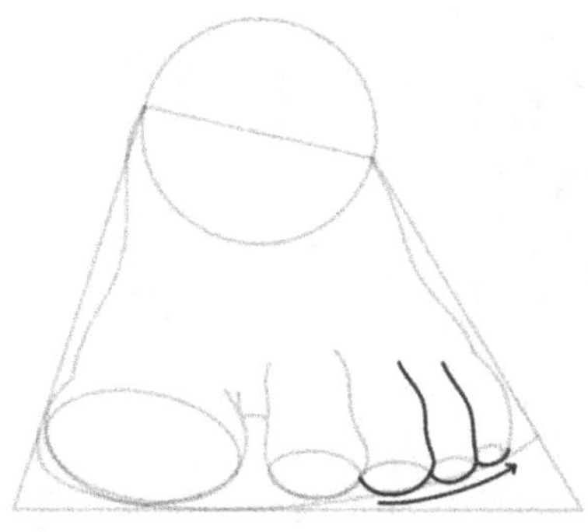

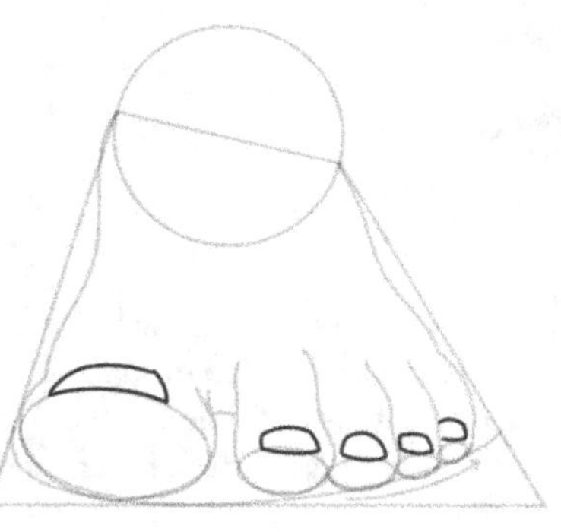

10

11

12

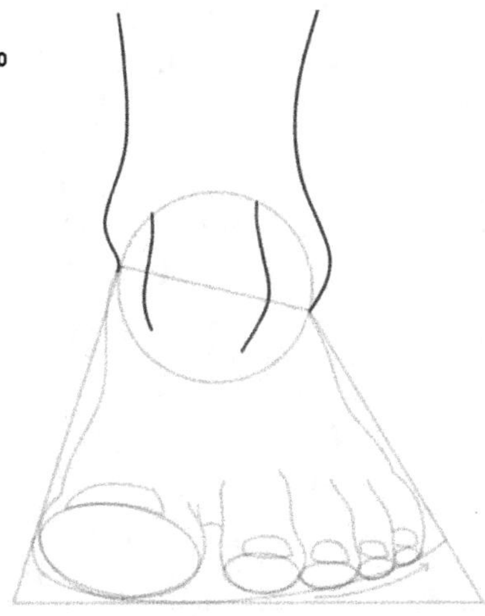

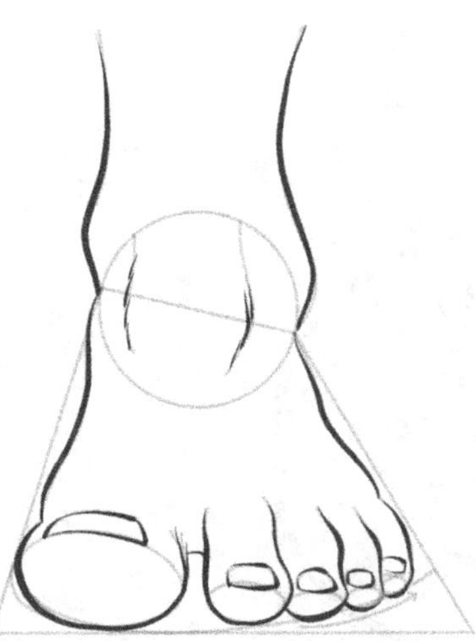

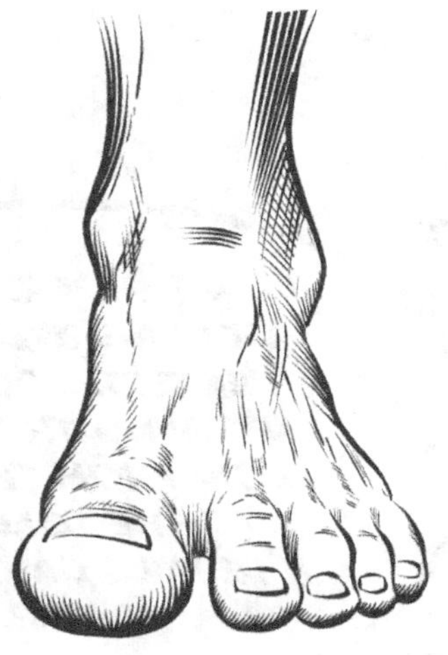

A SIMPLIFIED APPROACH TO DRAWING THE FOOT

Pro Tip: The foot supports the entire body, yet its form is often misunderstood. By reducing it to simple geometric shapes, you can grasp its structure and proportions before adding detail. This exercise will help you build the foot from the ground up, focusing on balance, rhythm and the relationship between the heel, arch and toes.

01

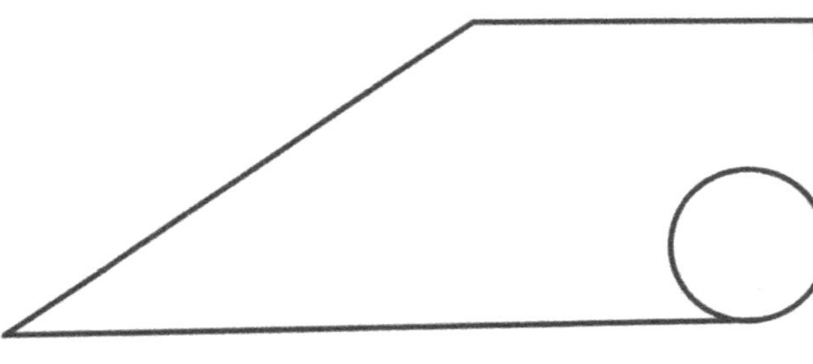

02

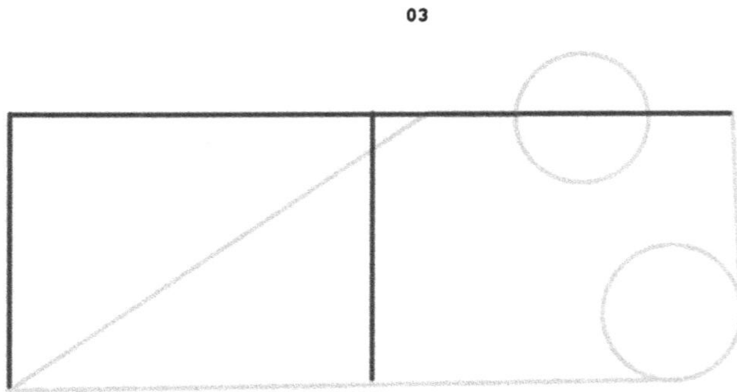

03

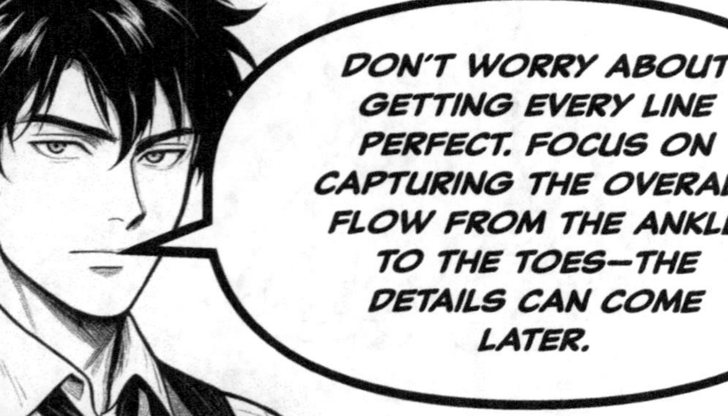

04

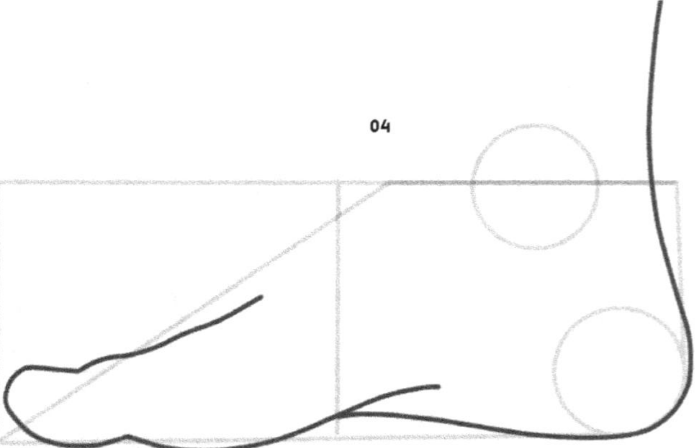

Step.1
Begin with a simple wedge shape to represent the foot's overall form. The top edge tilts slightly downward, showing the slope from the ankle to the toes. Add a circle at the back to mark the heel.

Step.2
Add another smaller circle slightly higher and forward from the heel to indicate the ankle joint. This second circle helps you understand how the ankle connects to the foot and sets the angle for the leg.

Step.3
Enclose the shape in a rectangle to define the proportions. The front half represents the forefoot (toes and ball), and the back half represents the arch and heel. The diagonal line across the box helps visualise the downward slope from the ankle to the toes.

Step.4
Begin sketching the foot's contour over the guide shapes. Use the lower line for the sole and the upper slope for the top plane of the foot. Keep the arch slightly raised and the toes angled downward.

Step.5
Add the front plane of the leg and refine the joint connection. The top circle marks where the ankle meets the leg, while the lower circle still defines the heel mass. Keep the lines light and structural.

Step.6
Outline the ankle bones and refine the curves around the top of the foot. Remember, the inner ankle sits higher and more forward than the outer one— this subtle tilt gives the foot its natural, grounded appearance.

Step.7
Refine the drawing with more confident contour lines. Emphasise the weight-bearing structure of the foot: the heel, arch, and ball. Notice how the line from the ankle to the toes flows in one continuous rhythm.

Step.8
Finish with surface details such as tendons with subtle shading.

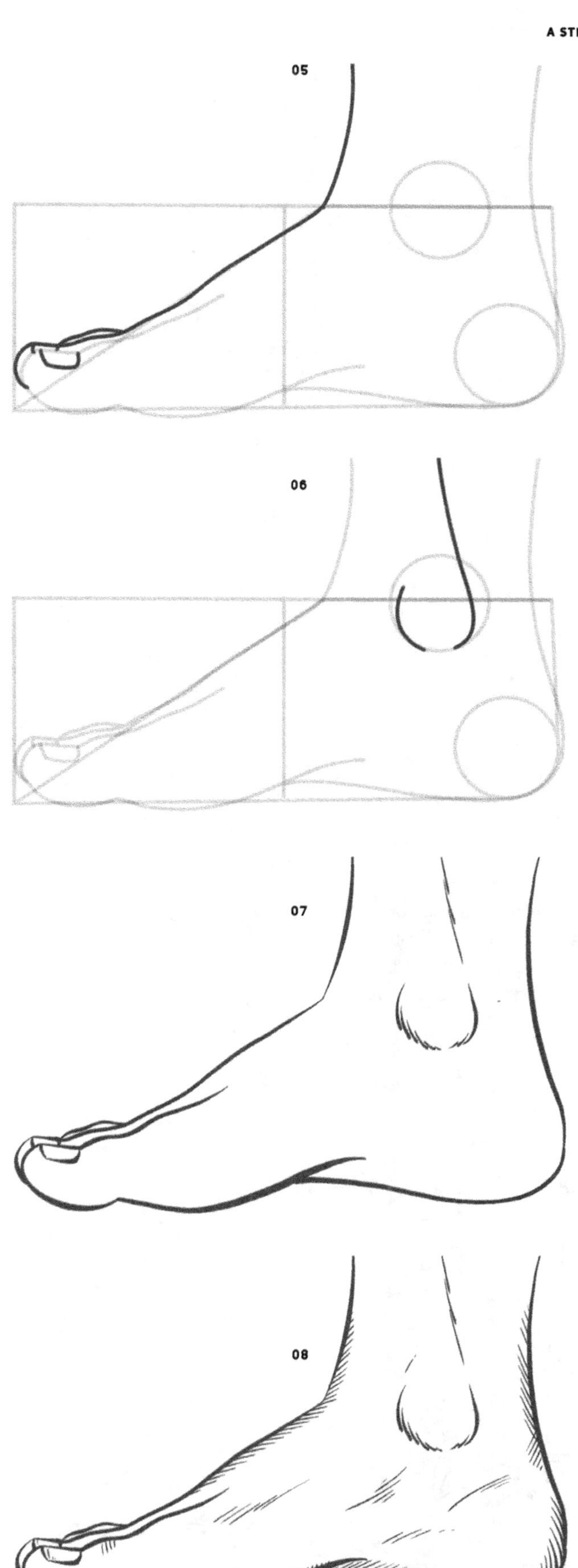

HOW TO DRAW ANIME

DRAWING FEET FROM VARIOUS ANGLES

Pro Tip: When drawing feet, think of them as wedges or blocks. Start with basic shapes to establish angle and weight before refining the toes and/or shoe details.

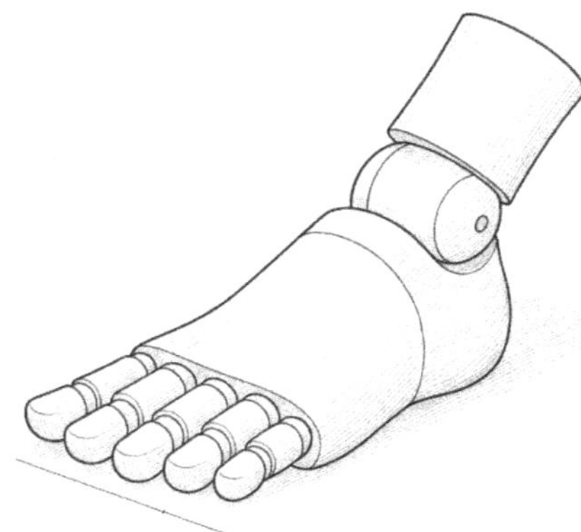

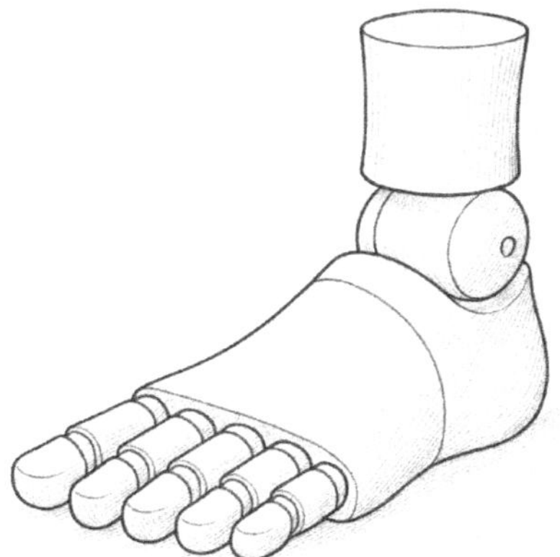

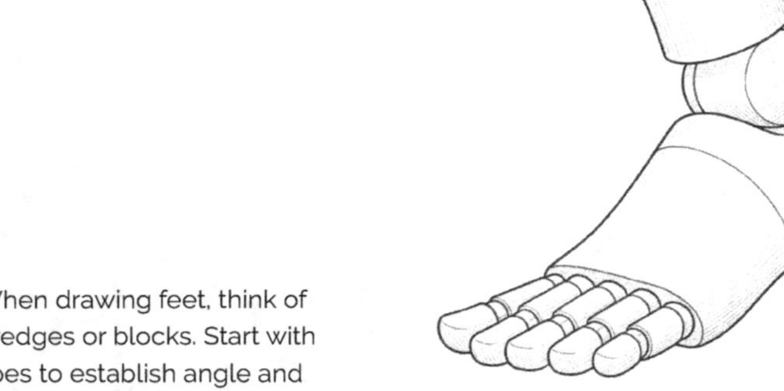

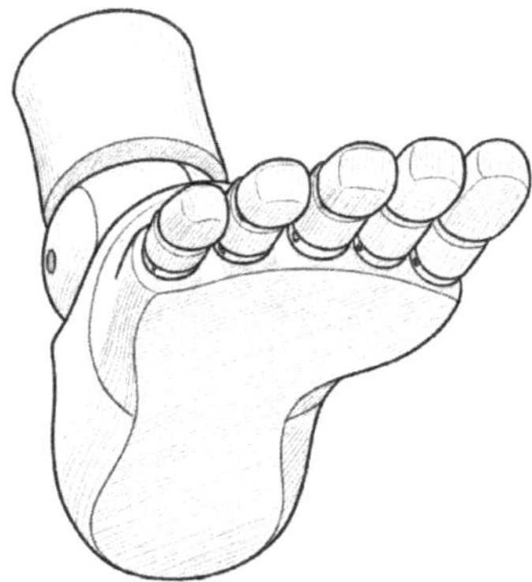

01

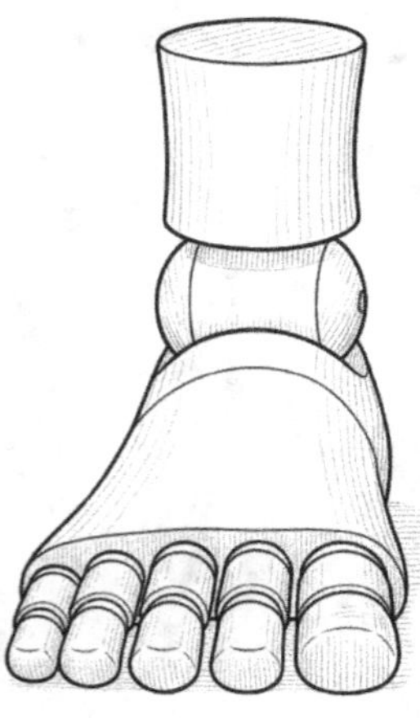

02

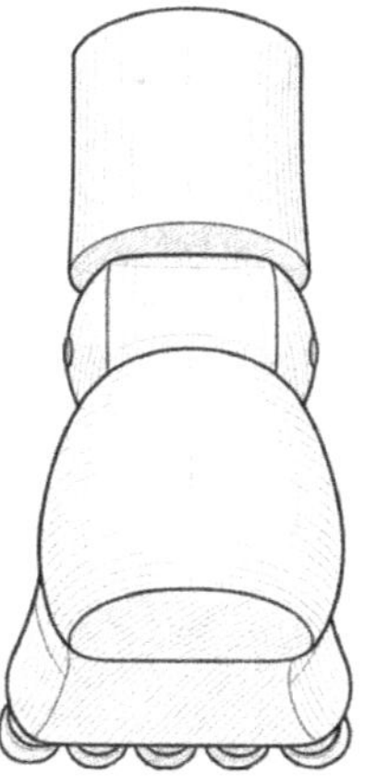

03

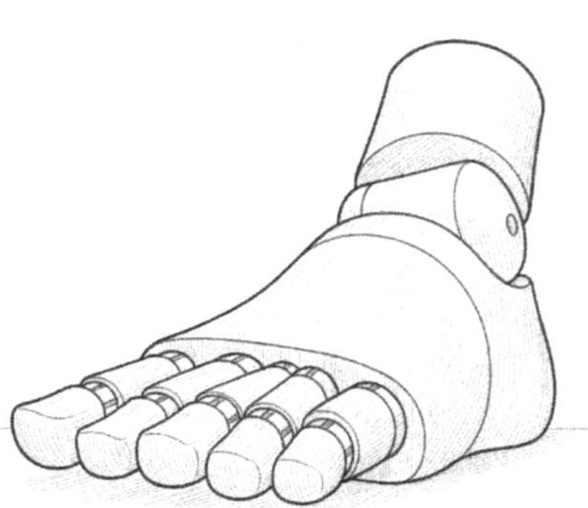

DRAWING FOOTWEAR

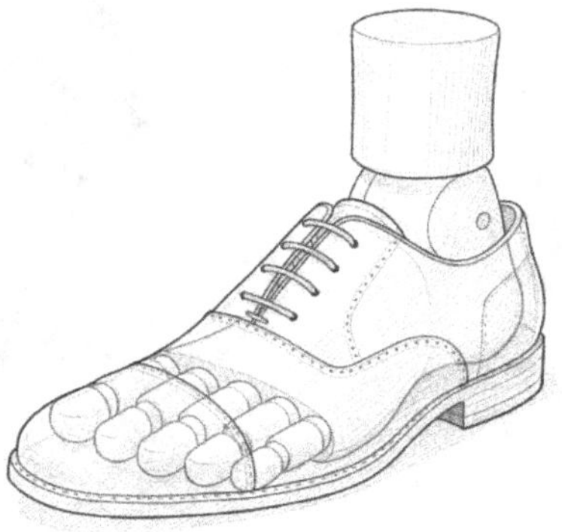

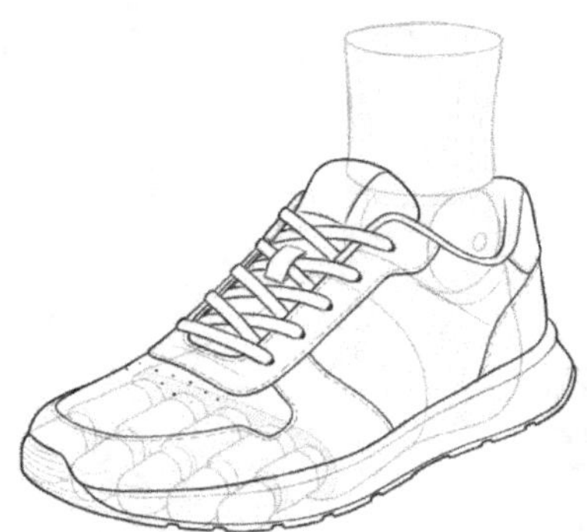

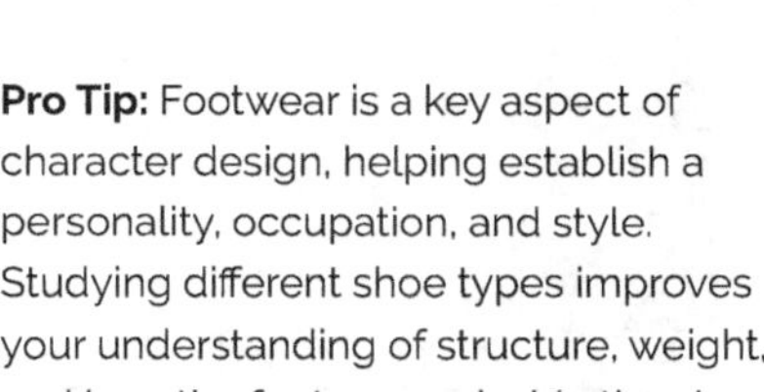

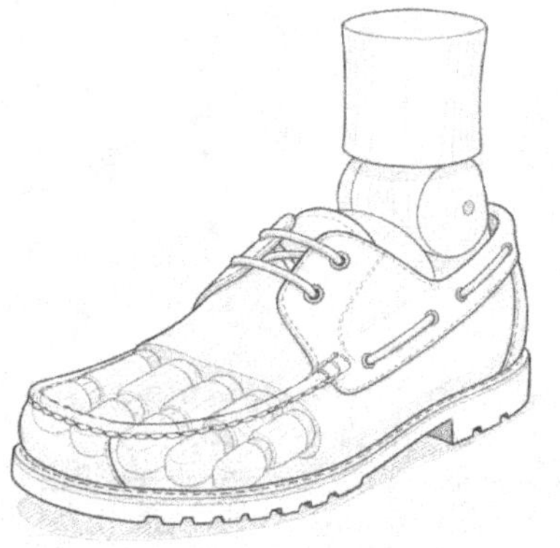

Pro Tip: Footwear is a key aspect of character design, helping establish a personality, occupation, and style. Studying different shoe types improves your understanding of structure, weight, and how the foot moves inside the shoe.

01

02

03

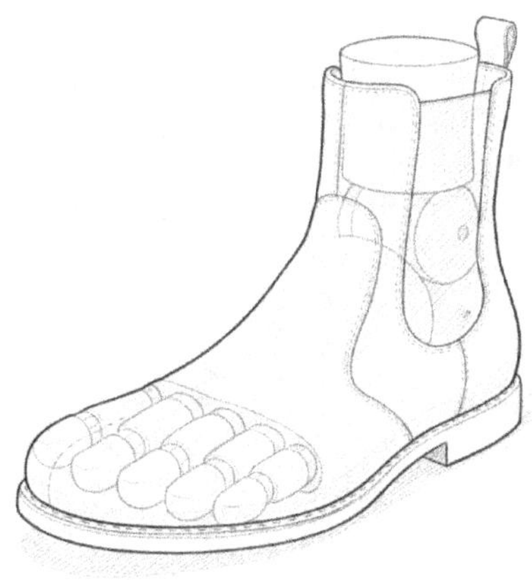

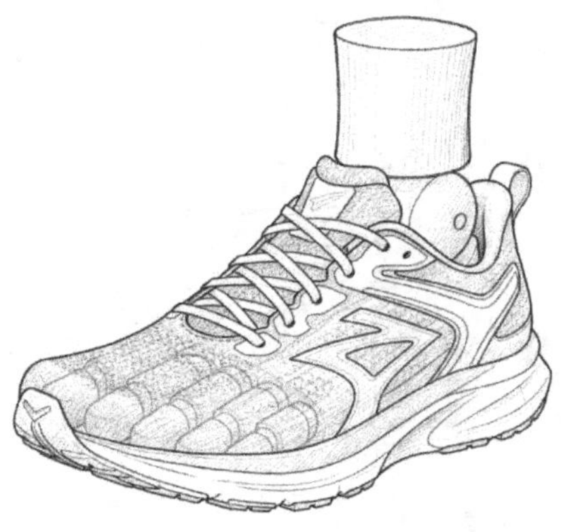

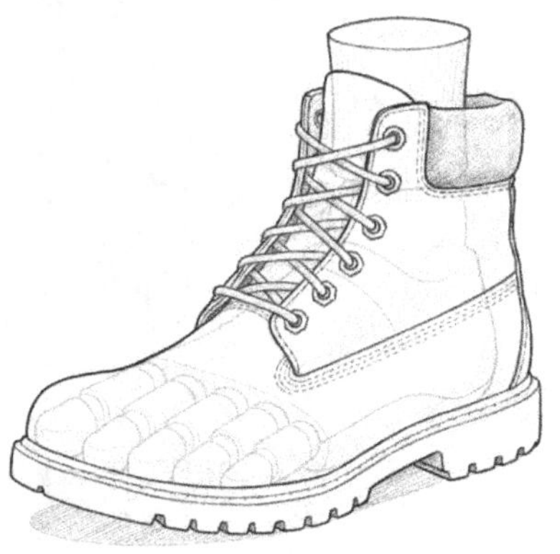

YOUNG MALE

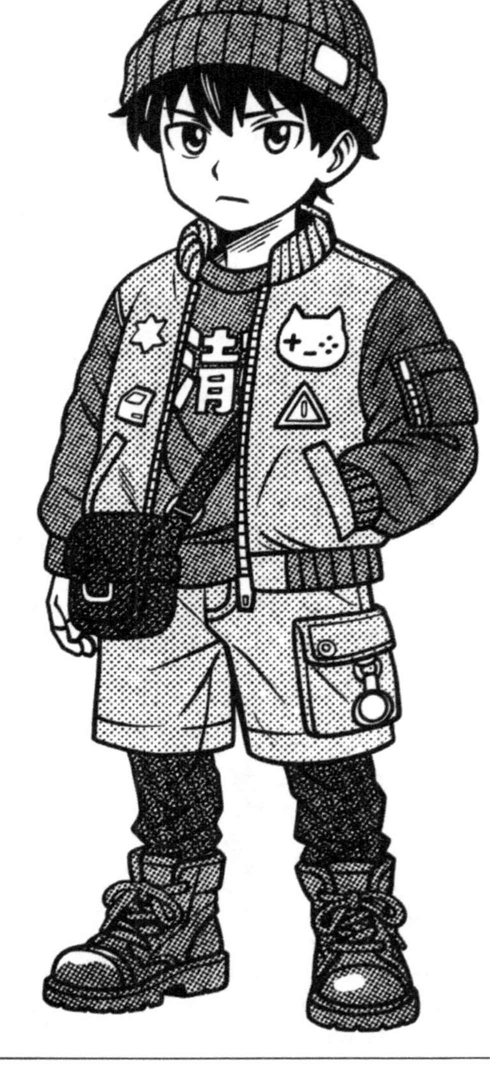

Pro Tip: For a young male manga character, aim for a height of around five heads tall. Keep the torso short and the limbs slightly elongated but slender to suggest youth and agility.

01

02

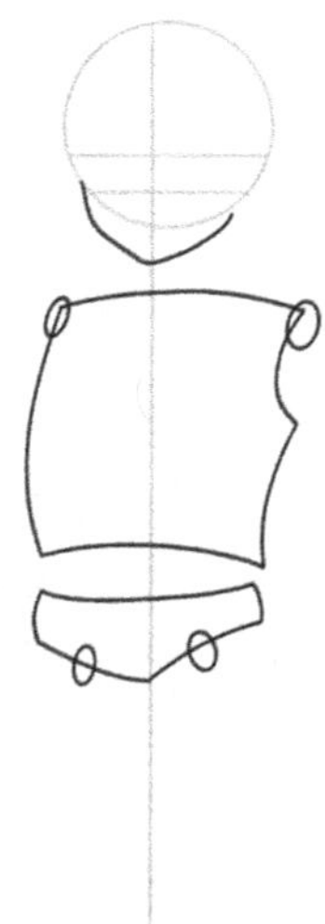

03

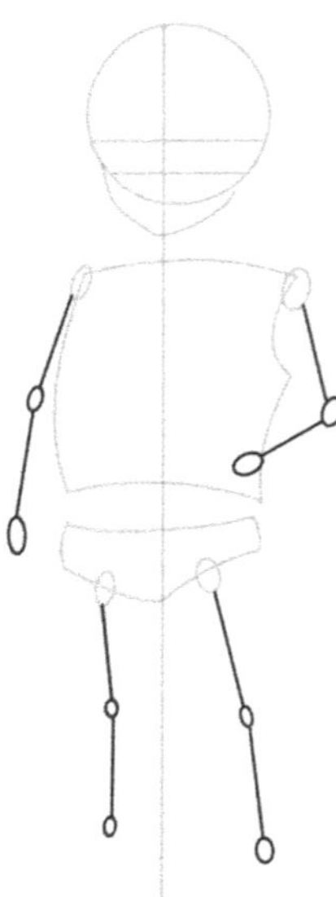

04

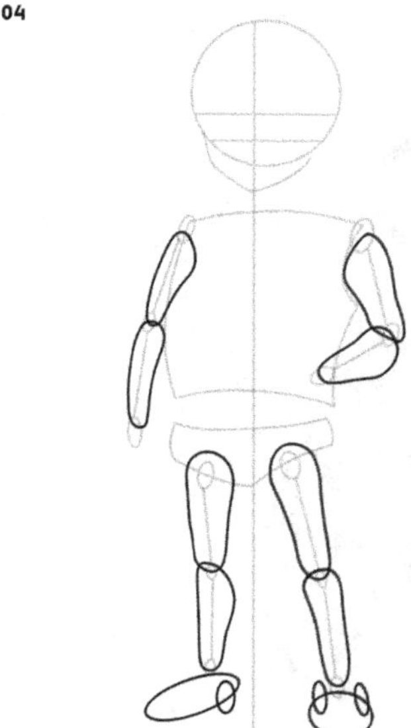

05

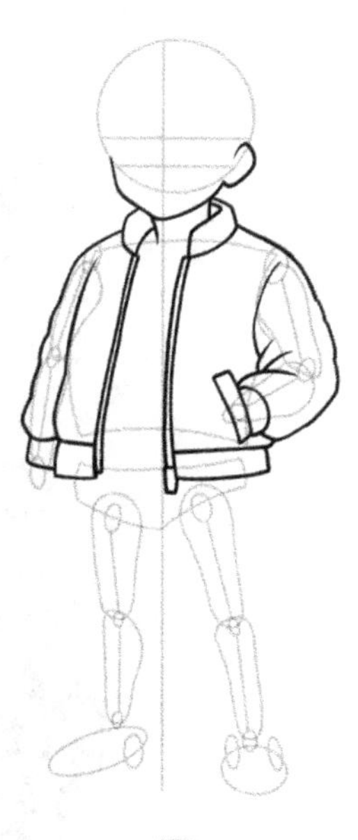

06

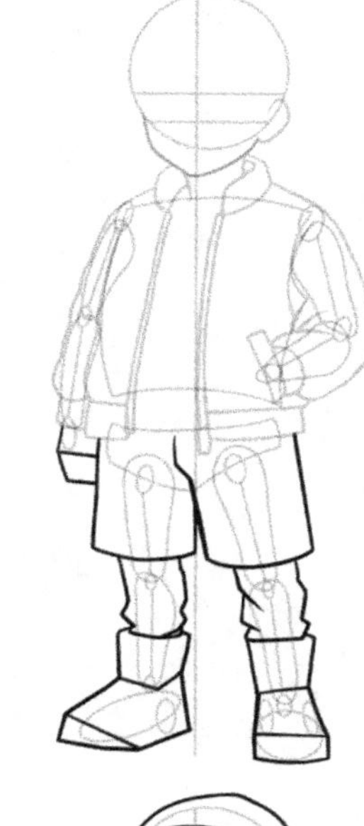

07

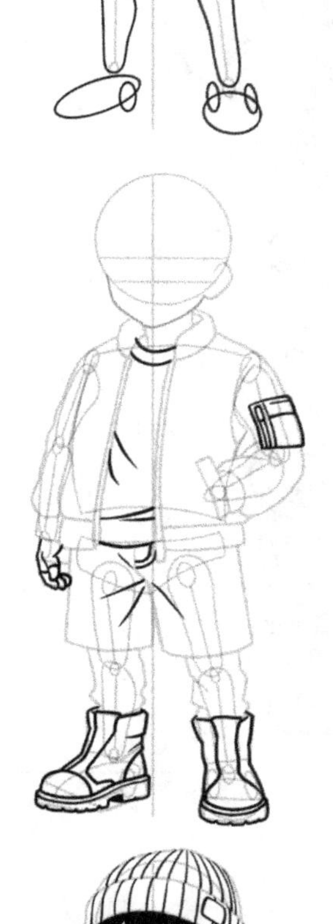

08

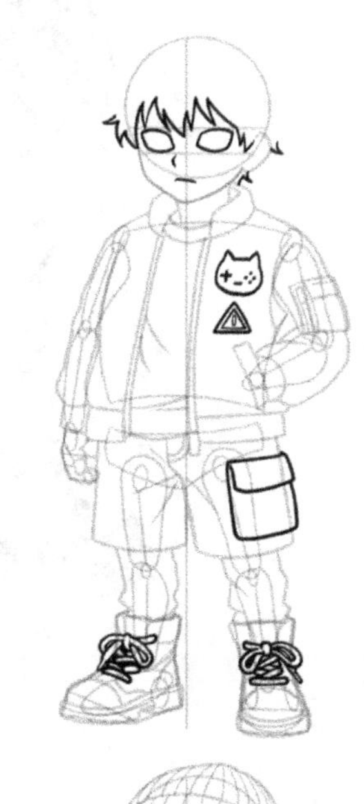

09

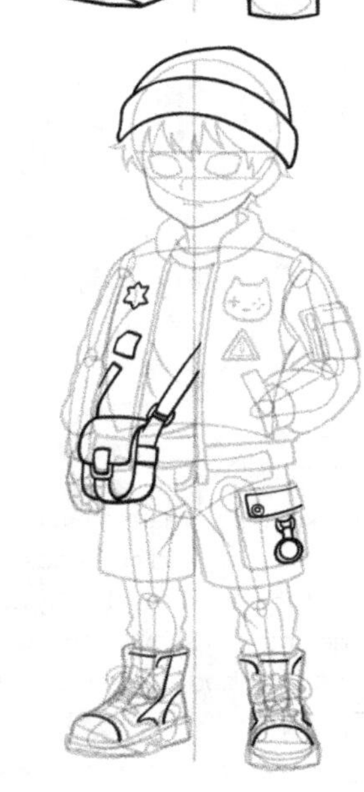

10

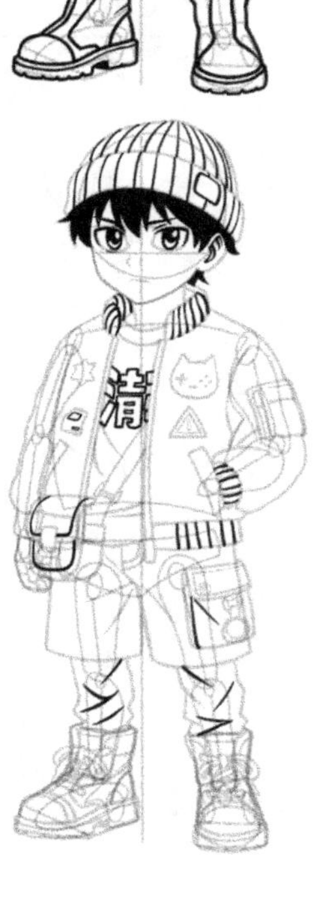

11

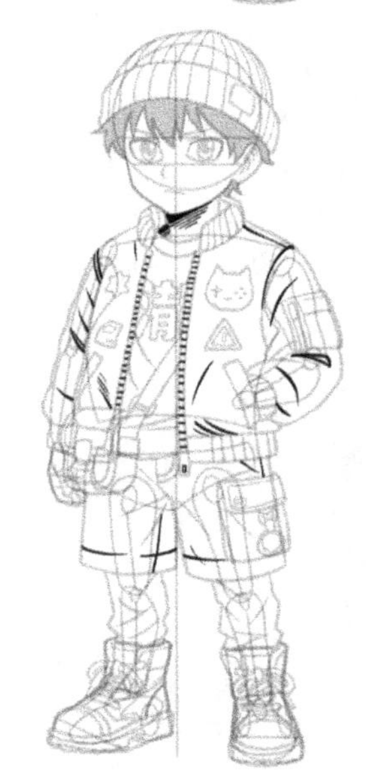

12

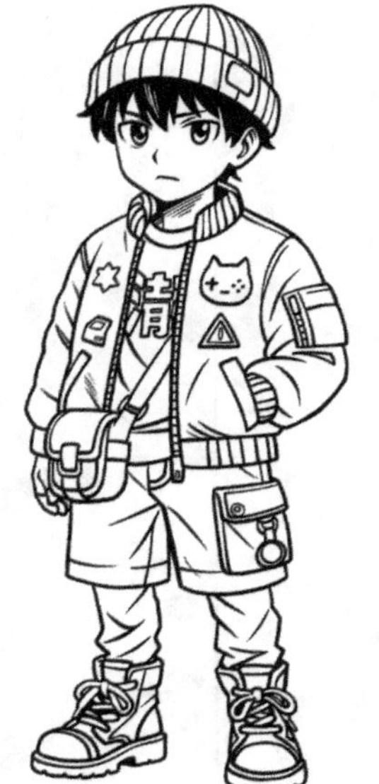

MALE TEENAGER

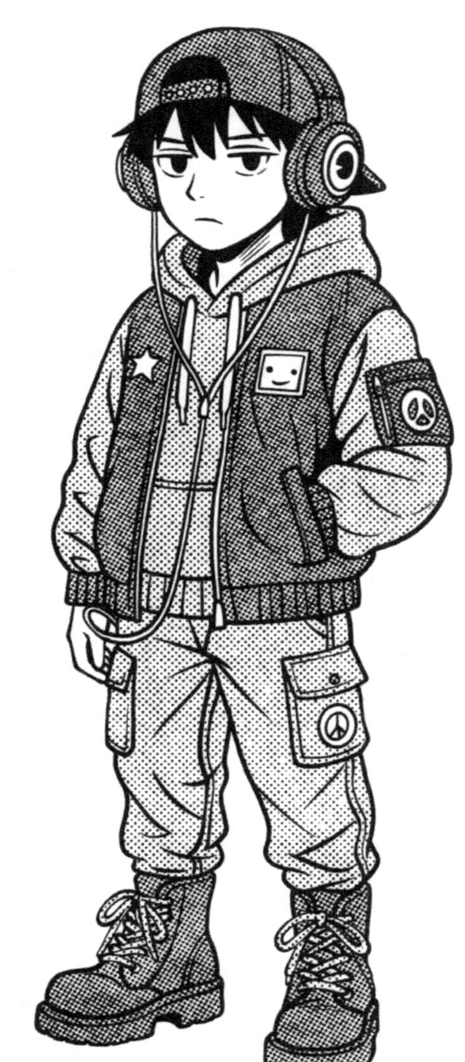

Pro Tip: For a teenage male character, aim for a height of around six heads tall. Broaden the shoulders slightly and lengthen the limbs to show growing maturity. Keep the body lean and angular.

01

02

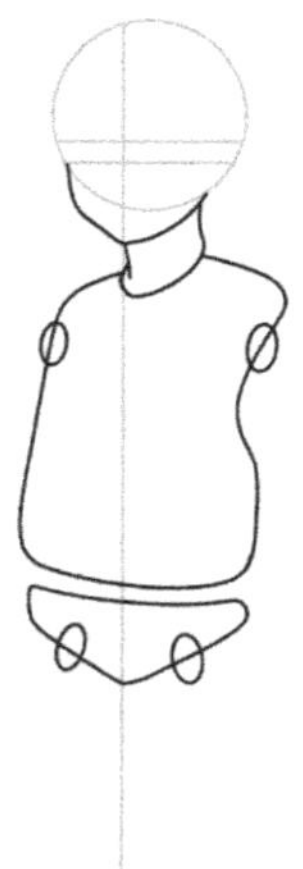

03

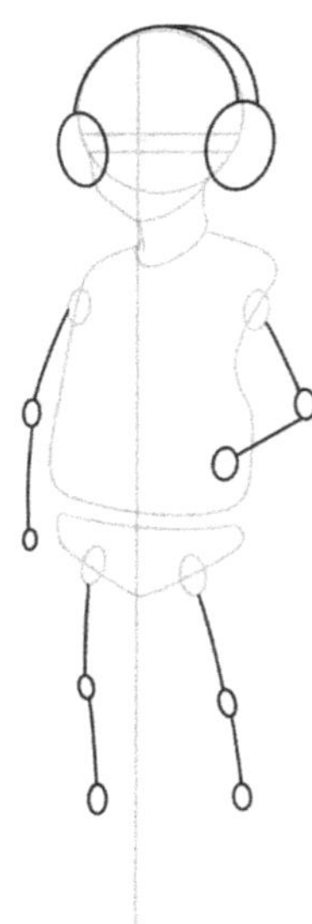

04

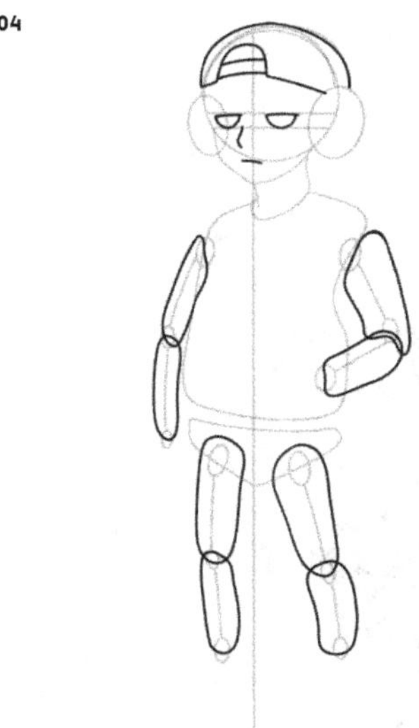
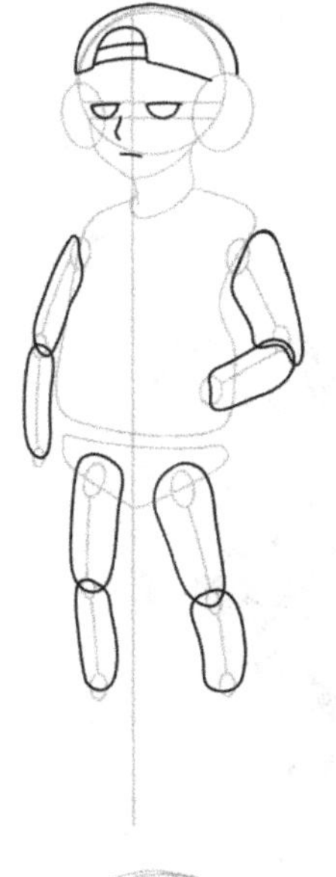

05

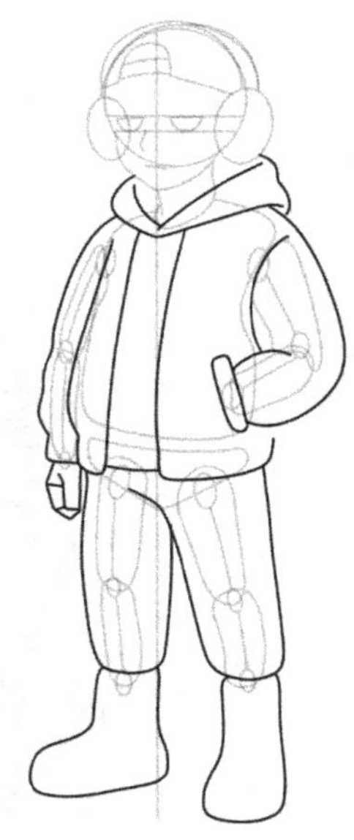

06

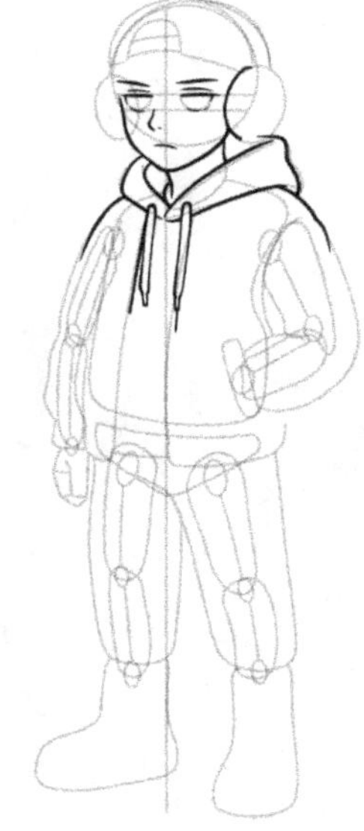

07

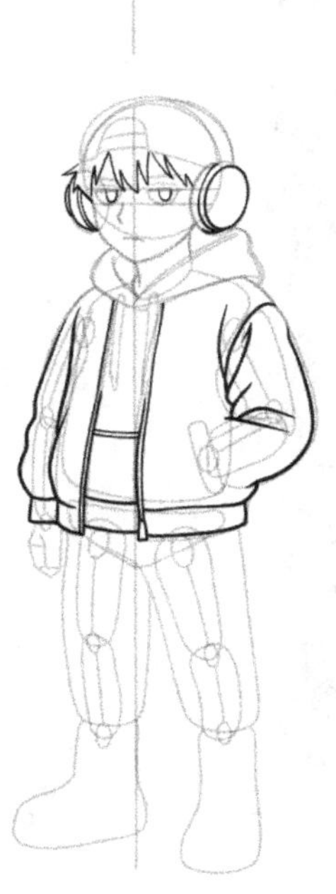

08

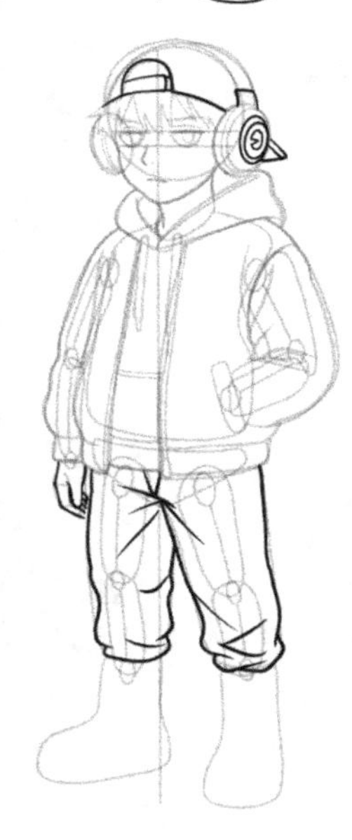

09

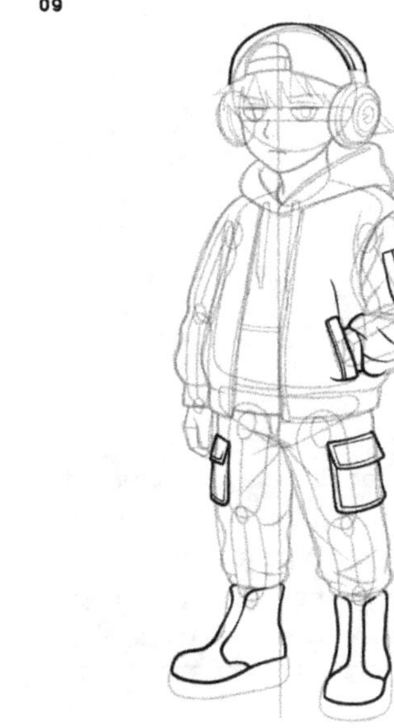

10

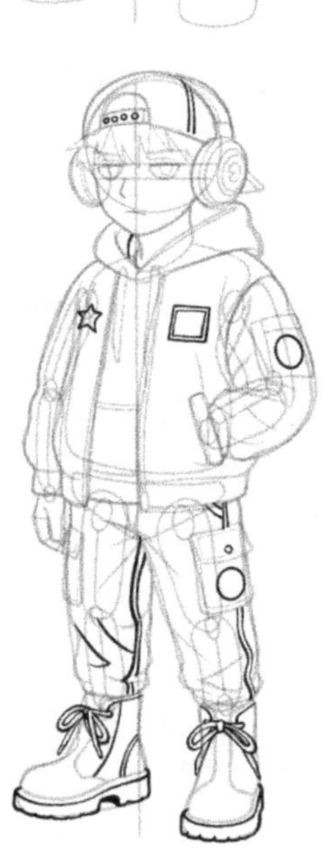

11

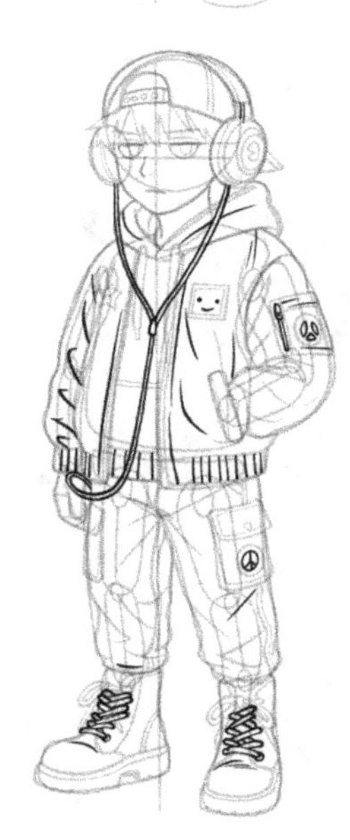

12

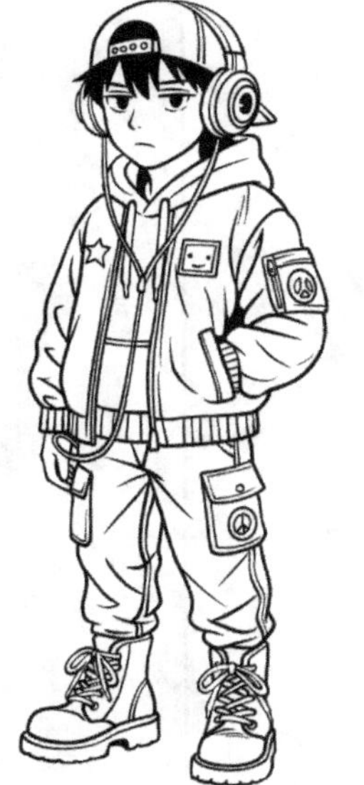

ADULT MALE

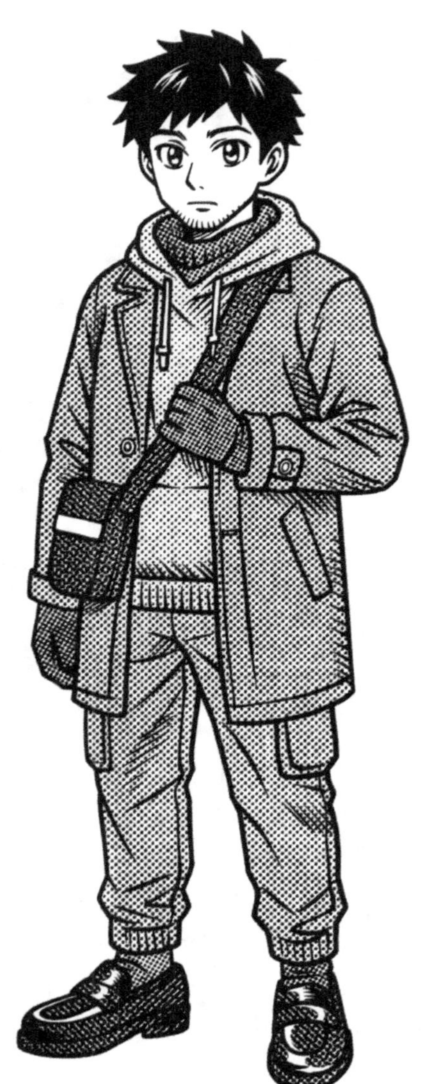

Pro Tip: For an adult male character, aim for a height of about seven and a half heads tall. Broaden the shoulders, narrow the hips and keep the legs slightly longer to create a balanced, mature build.

01

02

03

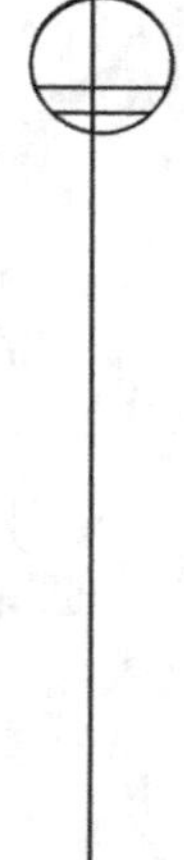

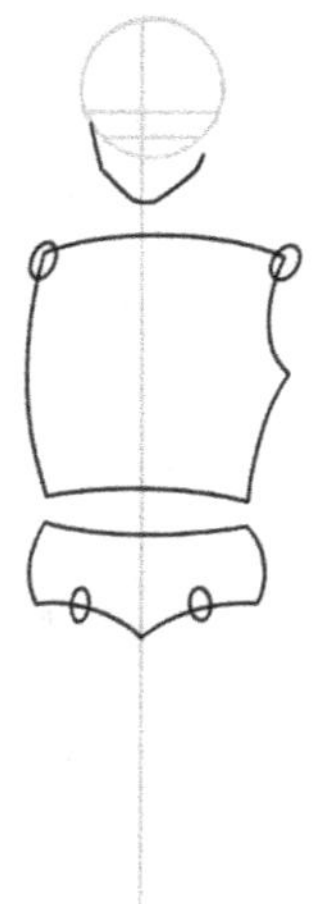

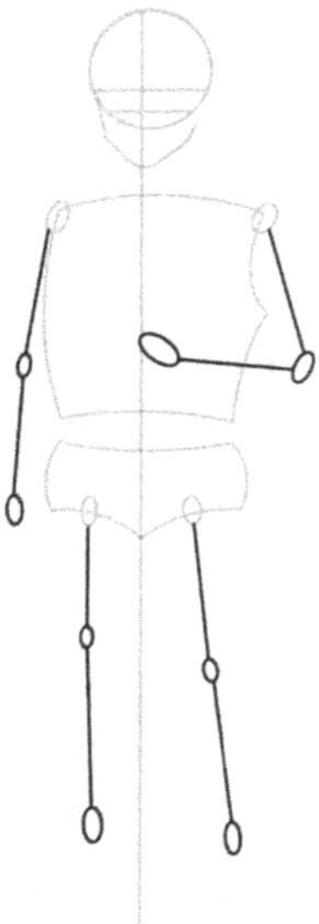

04

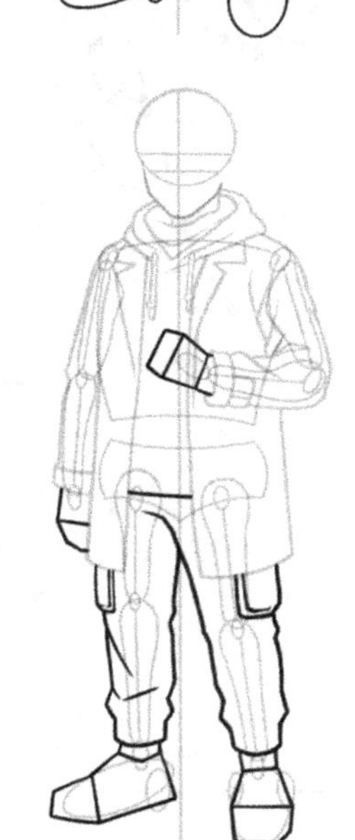

05

06

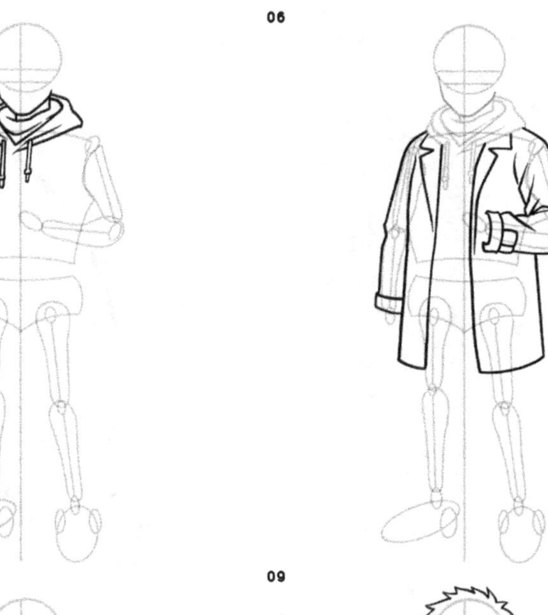

07

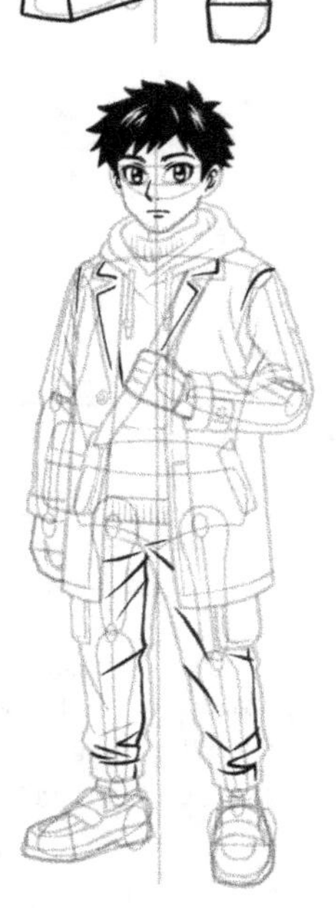

08

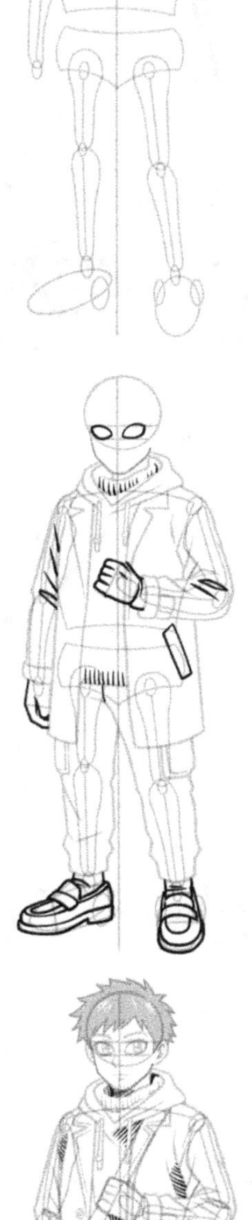

09

10

11

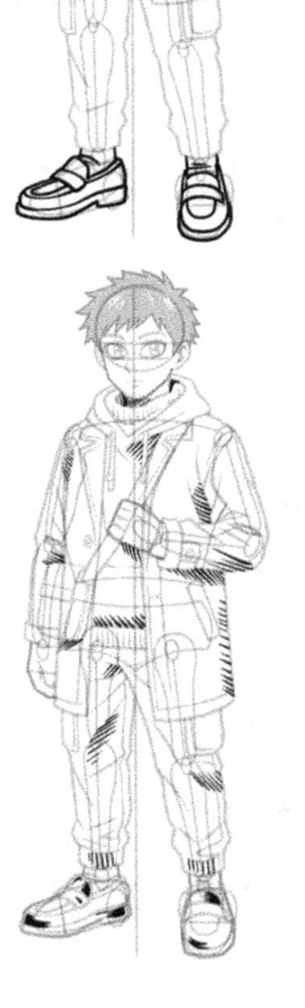

12

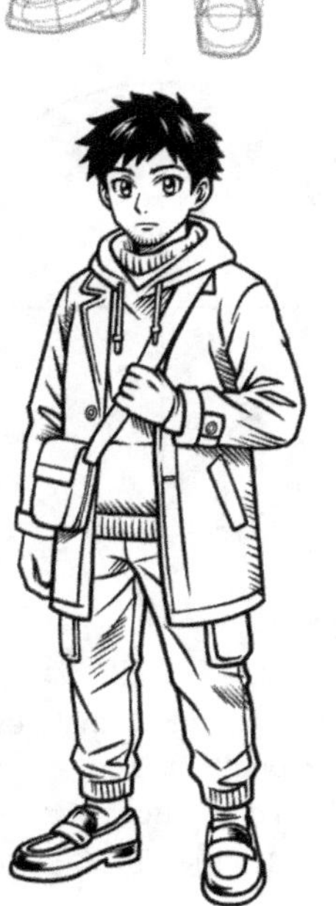

DRAWING THE FEMALE FACE

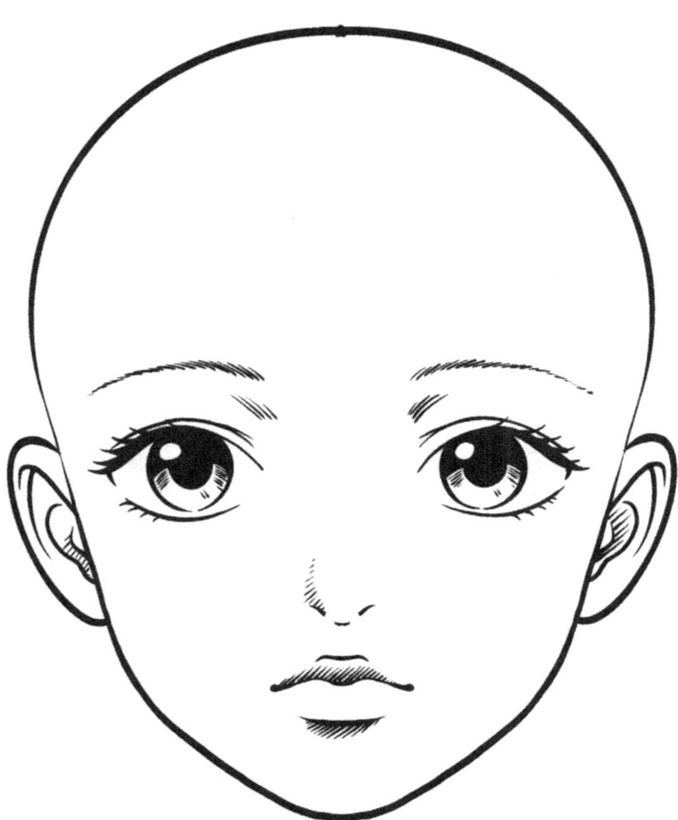

Pro Tip: The triangle acts as a precise guide for placing the nose and mouth. Its upper point defines the bridge of the nose, while the lower edges mark the width of the mouth.

01

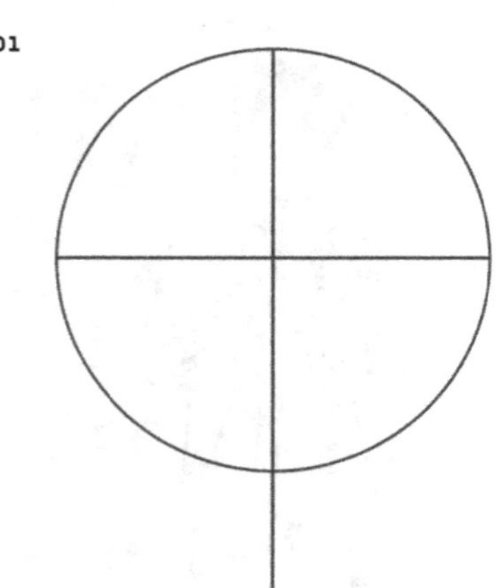

Start by drawing a circle that's evenly divided into quarters. Draw a line that extends from the bottom of the circle that measures 1/3 of the circle's height.

02

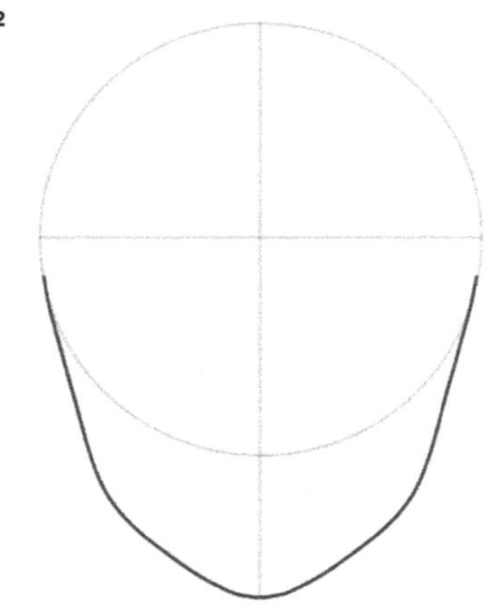

Now, draw in a chin shape that connects the left and right points of the circle with the line that extends from the bottom of the circle.

03

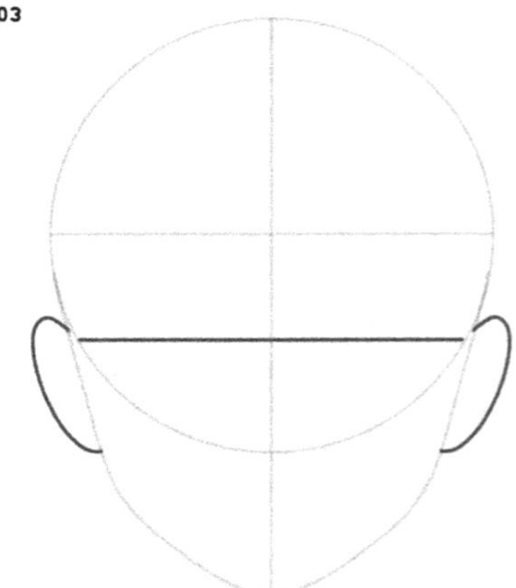

Draw a horizontal line at the halfway point in the lower half of the circle. This will give you the exact position to place the eyes and the bridge of the nose. Also sketch in the ears.

04

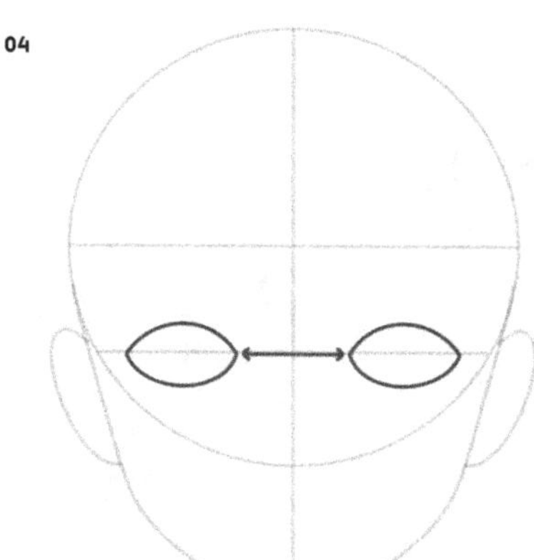

To determine the width of the eye, remember that the head will be 3.5 eyes wide. The space between the eyes will be one eye width.

05

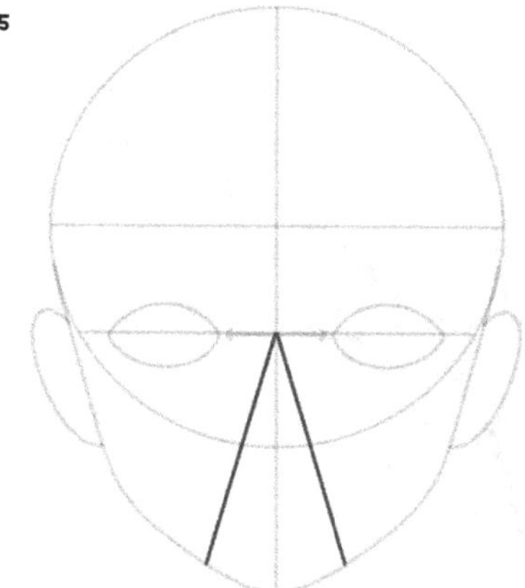

Draw an equilateral triangle out from the bridge of the nose, similar to the example above. This will define the width of the nose and mouth.

06

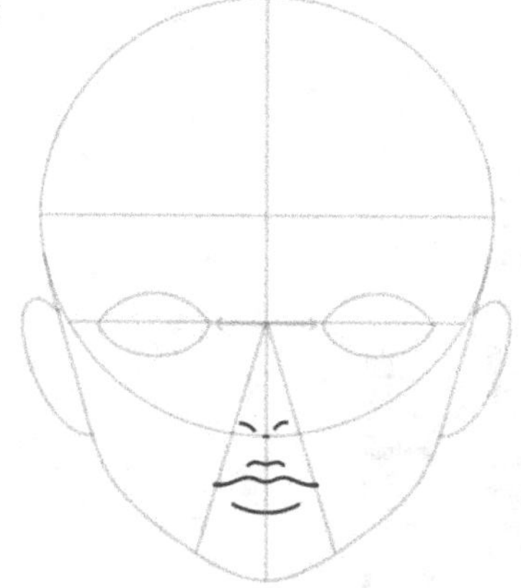

The mouth sits approximately halfway down the triangle. Note that the base of the nose is at the bottom of the circle.

07

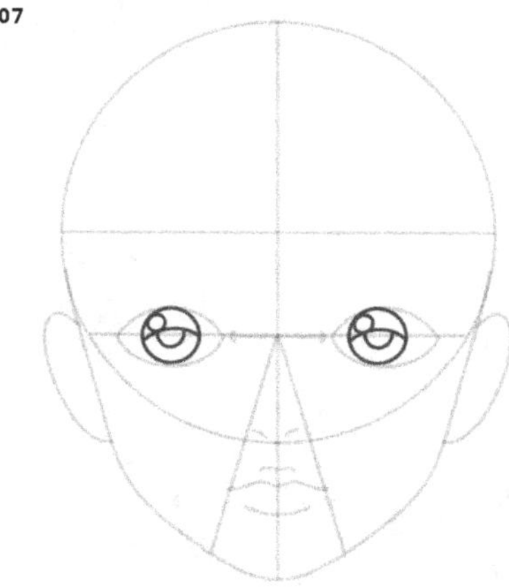

Start adding details to the eyes. They should be bright and wide with space allocated for reflections.

08

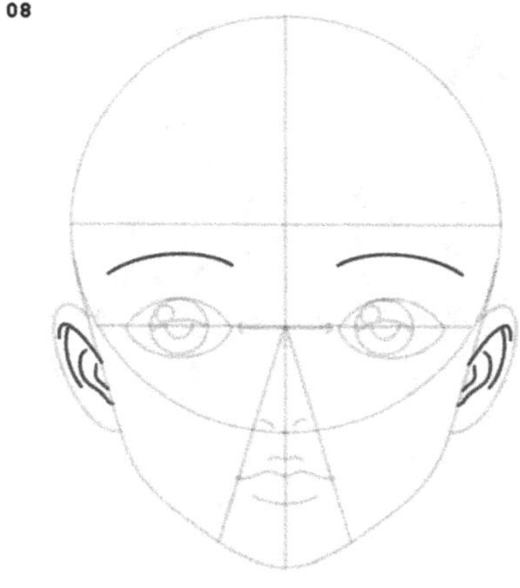

Draw is the eyebrows just below the horizontal line bisecting the circle. Also add in details to the ears.

09

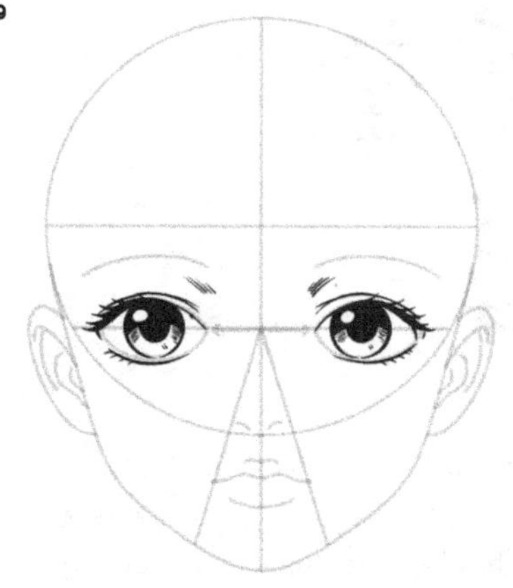

With an inking brush, start detailing the eyes. Avoid adding too many eyelashes; it looks amateur. Instead, try just drawing a few thick lines.

10

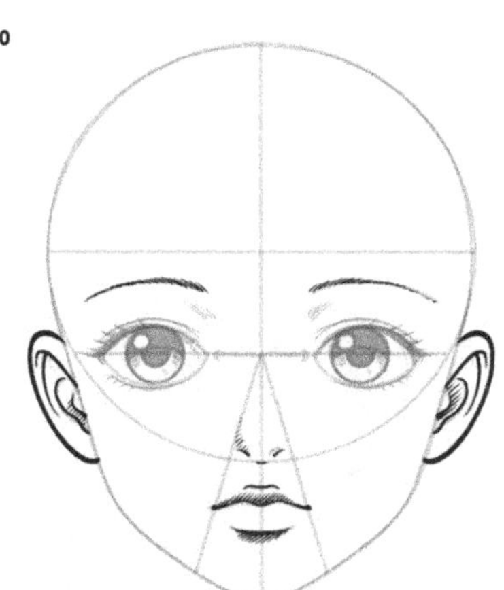

Ink the eyebrows, ears, nose and mouth. Add some light shading with thin lines for the nose and mouth to add depth to your character's face.

11

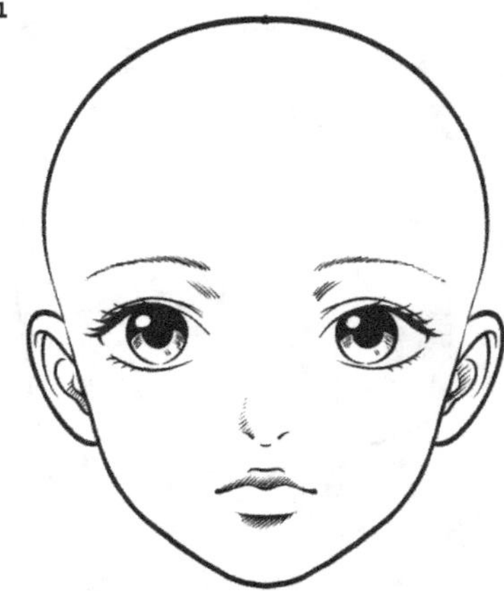

Now outline the skull and erase any existing guidelines. You're done!

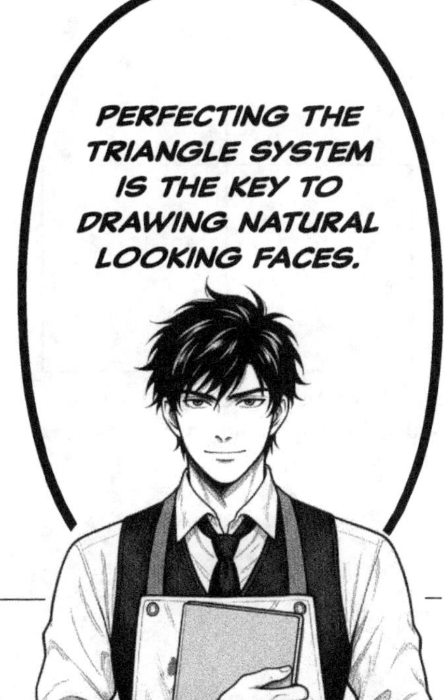

HOW TO DRAW ANIME

DRAWING THE FEMALE FACE IN PROFILE VIEW

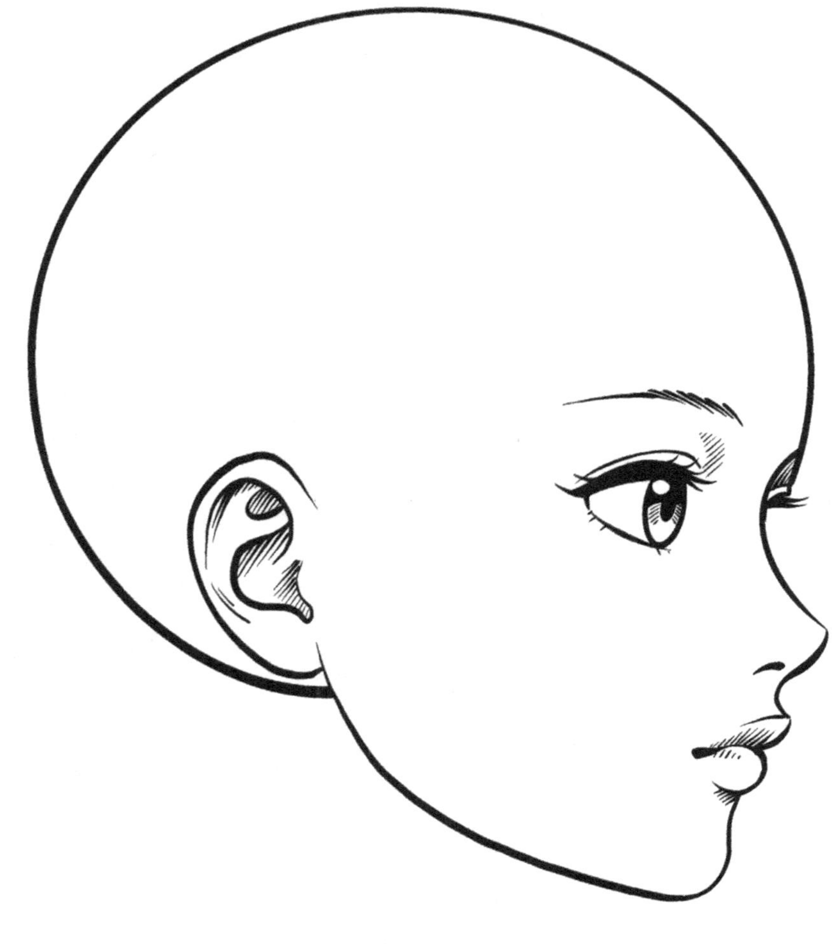

Pro Tip: When sketching in profile, focus on how each feature aligns along the vertical centre and horizontal lines. Visualising these relationships early helps maintain correct proportions.

01

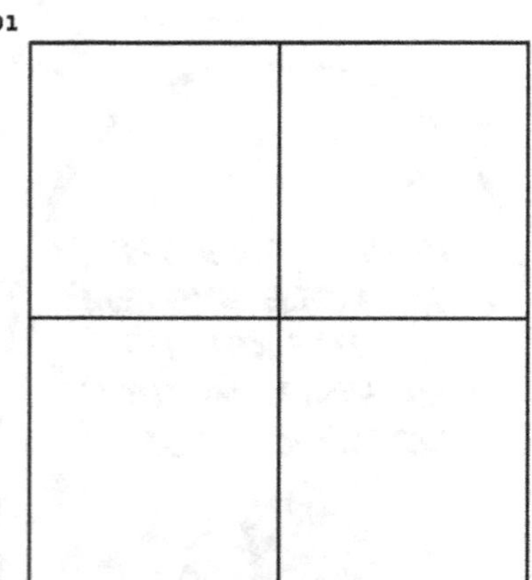

Start by drawing a rectangle. Imagine a square, slightly stretched upwards. Now divide it into 4 quarters.

02

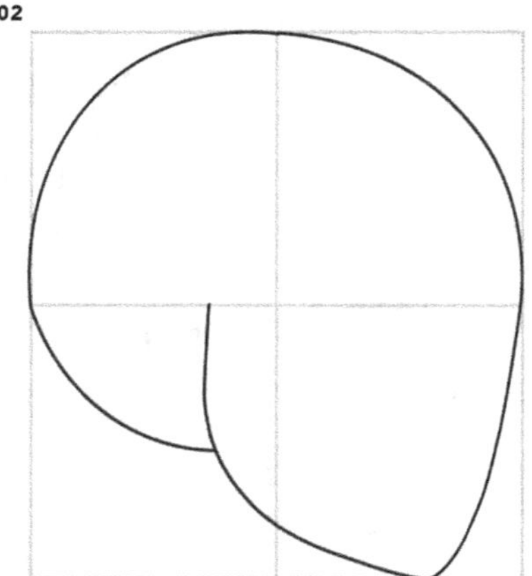

Sketch in a rough head shape. Use the grid you have created as a reference for where to position the various features. Note that the jawline finishes exactly at the horizontal line.

03

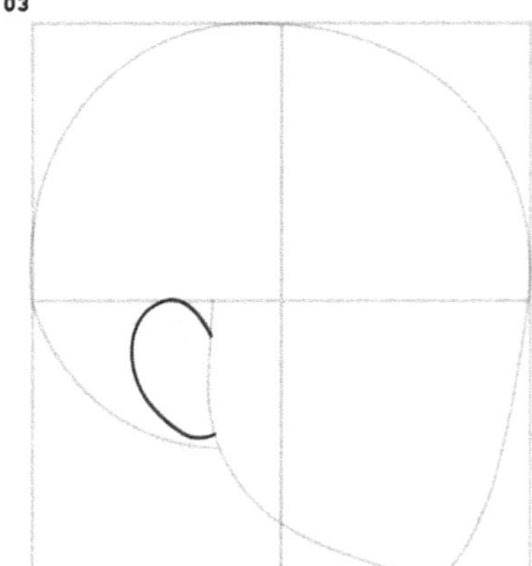

Now, sketch in the ear. Notice that it extends directly out from the jawline but does not go above it.

04

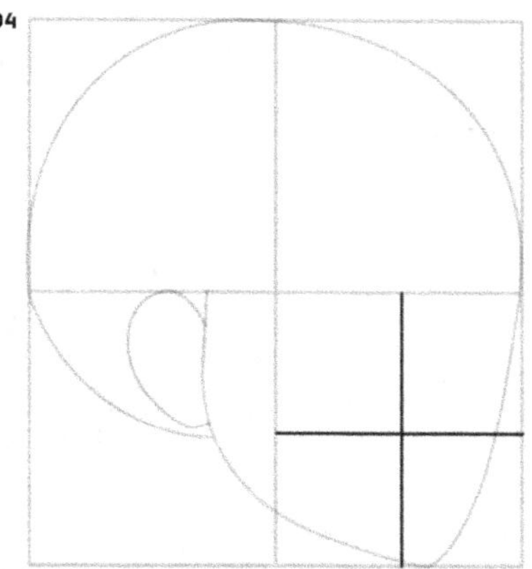

Divide the bottom right panel into 4 even quarters to assist you in positioning the facial features.

05

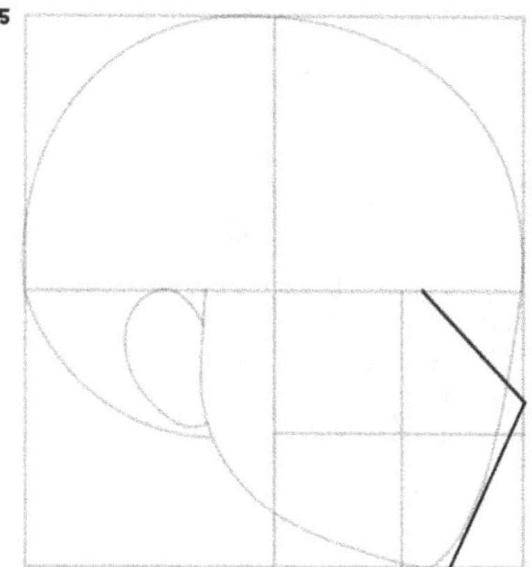

A horizontal line should extend outwards ⅓ of the top quarter and down ⅔ of the top quarter. Draw a connecting line down to the chin.

06

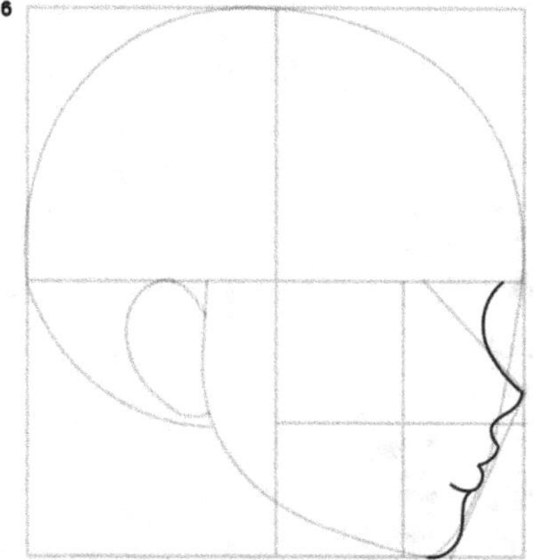

Use your guideline to sketch in the nose, mouth and chin. Pay close attention to where they are positioned in relation to the reference.

07

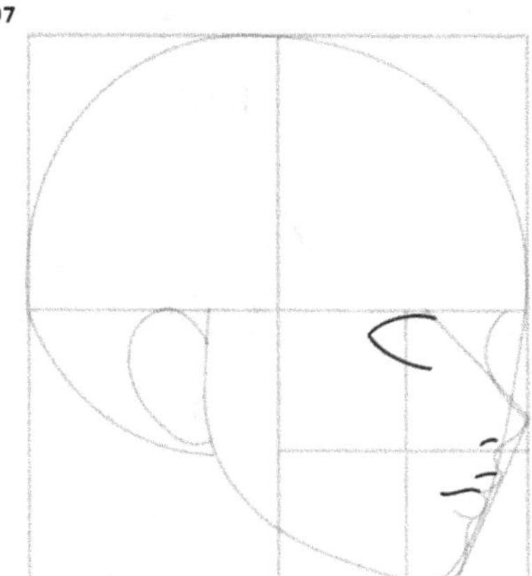

Draw simple lines to define the position of the lips and nose.

08

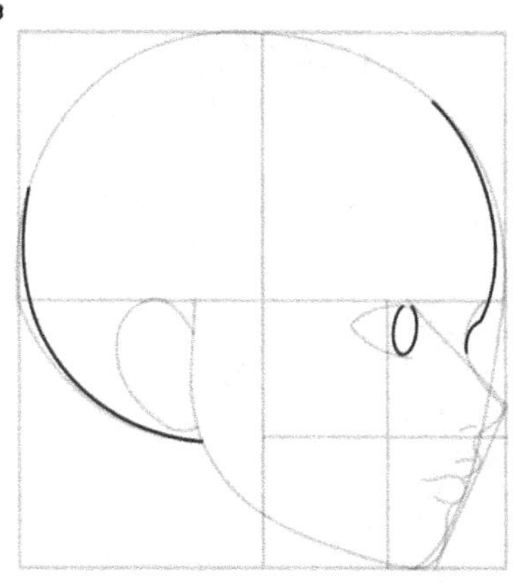

Refine the shape of the skull and brow to give the character a natural look.

09

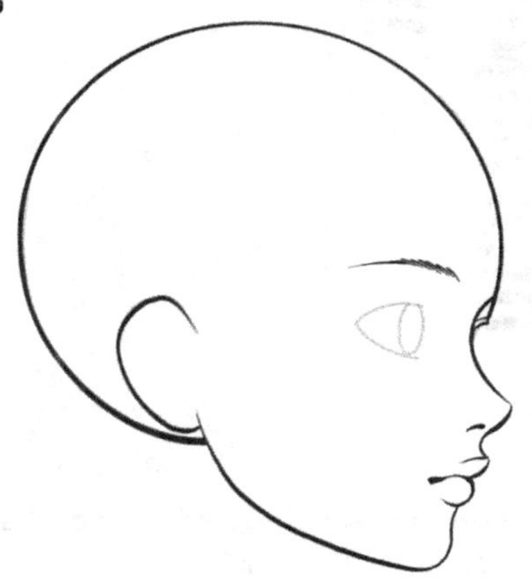

With an inking brush, draw the outline of the head and erase any guidelines.

10

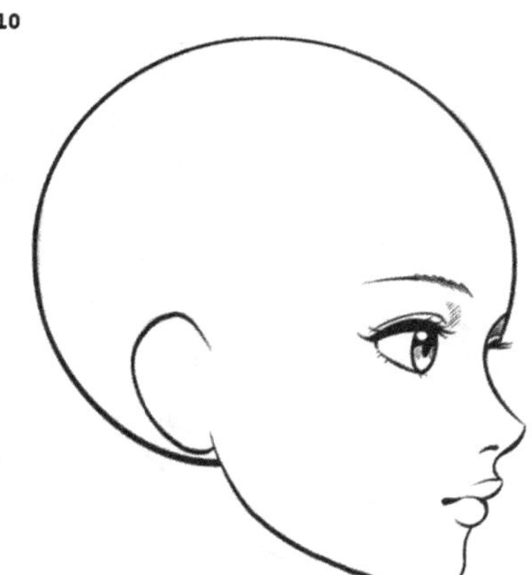

Start detailing the eyes. Avoid adding too many eyelashes; it looks amateur. Instead, try just a few thick lines.

11

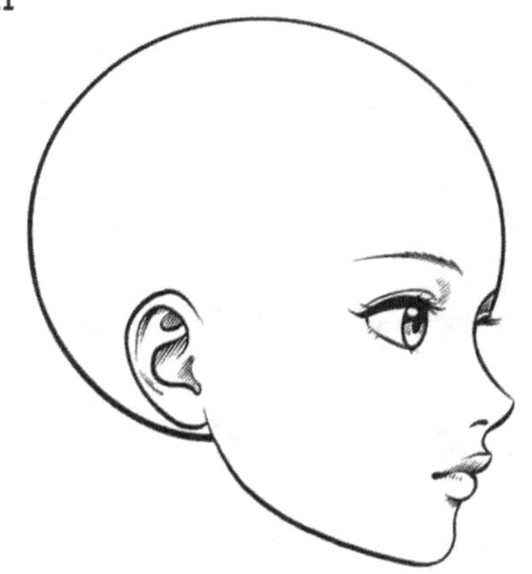

Add some shadow on and under the lip and ear to define the features and give them depth.

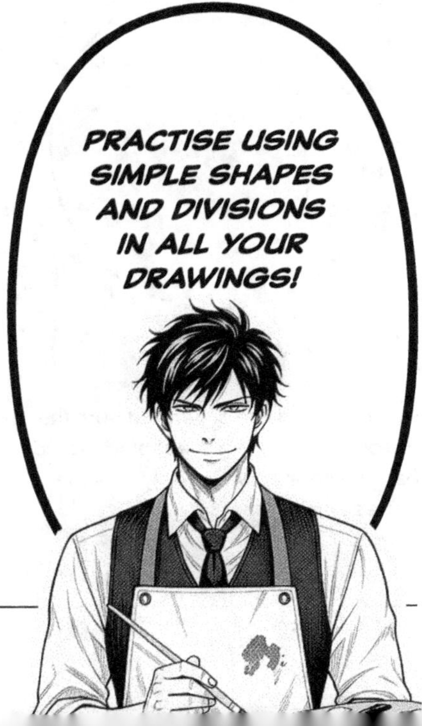

DRAWING THE FEMALE FACE IN ³/₄ VIEW

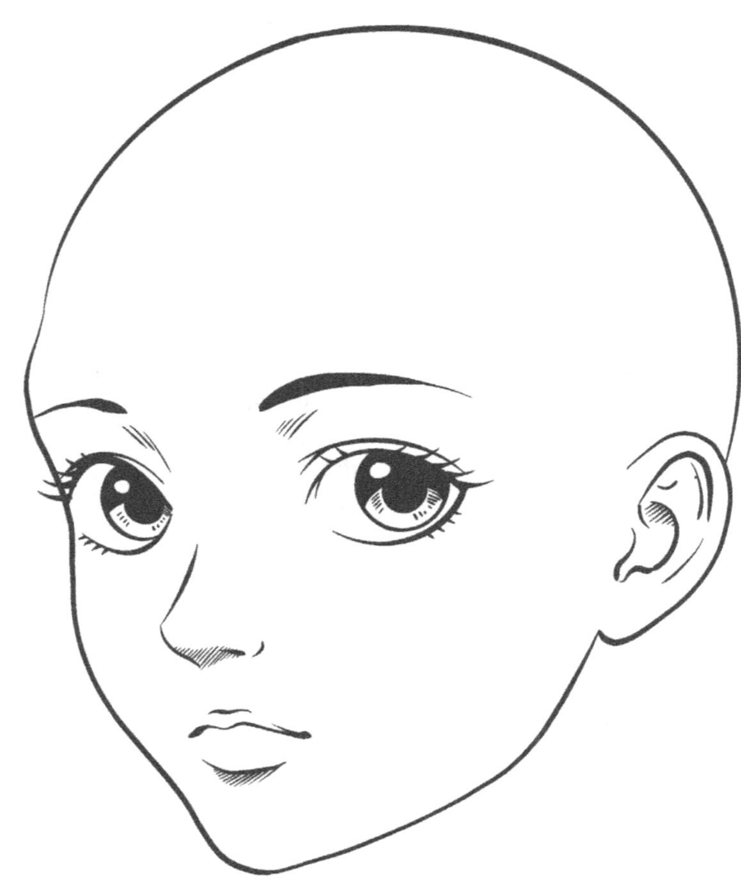

Pro Tip: Anchor all features to the centre and eye lines. These guides keep the tilt consistent and the face balanced in perspective, creating a natural look.

01

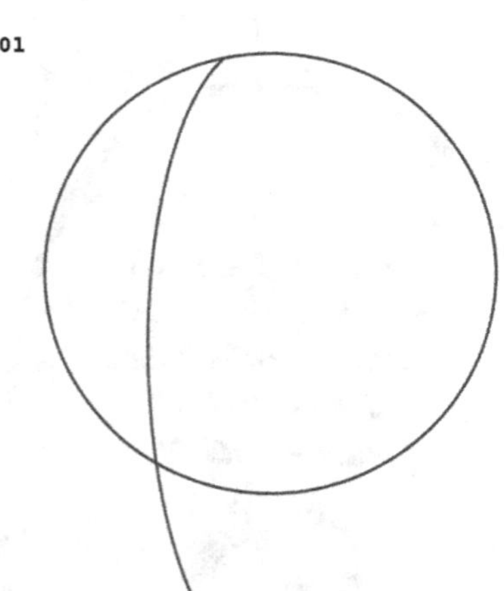

Draw an arced line downward from the top of the circle. The line should extend past the base approximately ⅓ of the circle's height.

02

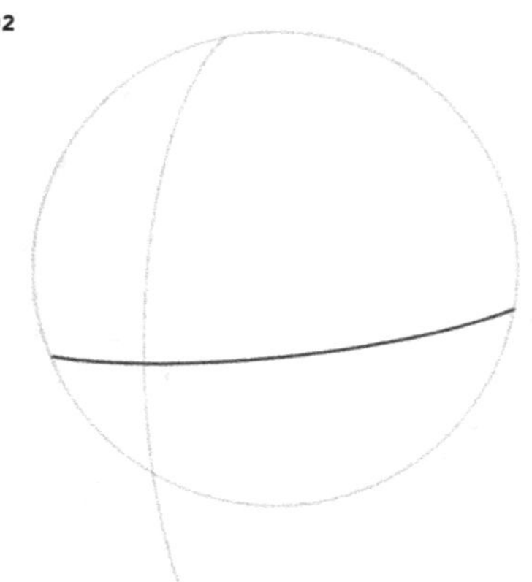

Now, draw a horizontal arced line on a slight leftward leaning slant, roughly ⅓ of the height of the circle from the base. This will be the eyeline.

03

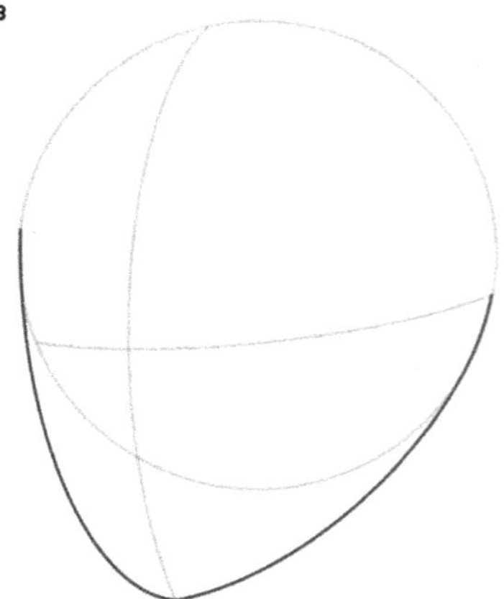

Sketch in the chin shape by connecting an arced line from each point of the eyeline. Note that on the left, it extends just above the eyeline. Be sure to include this detail.

04

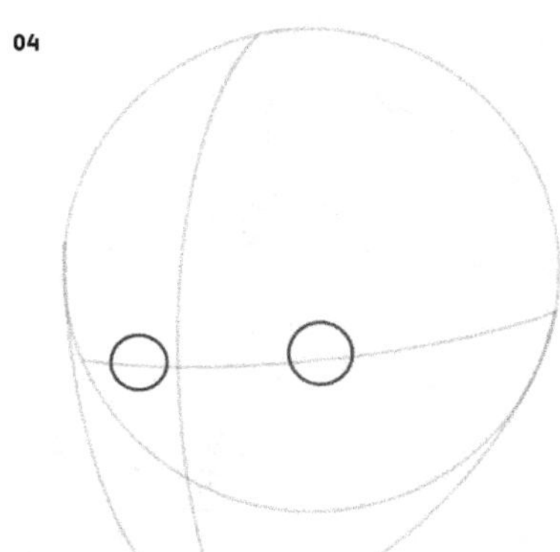

Place the eyes on the eyeline, as shown in the reference above.

05

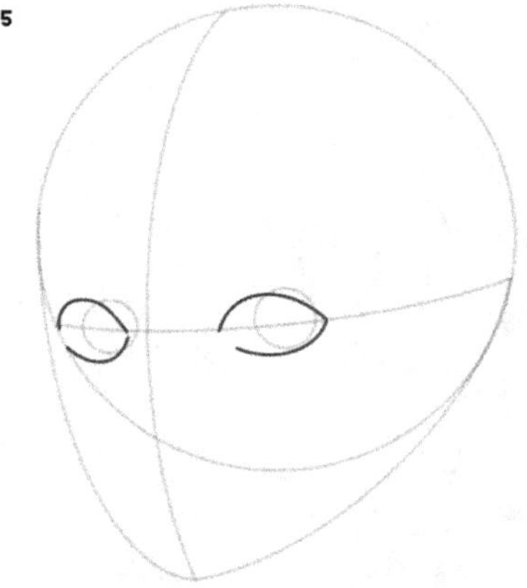

Sketch in the eyelids to start giving the eyes some structure.

06

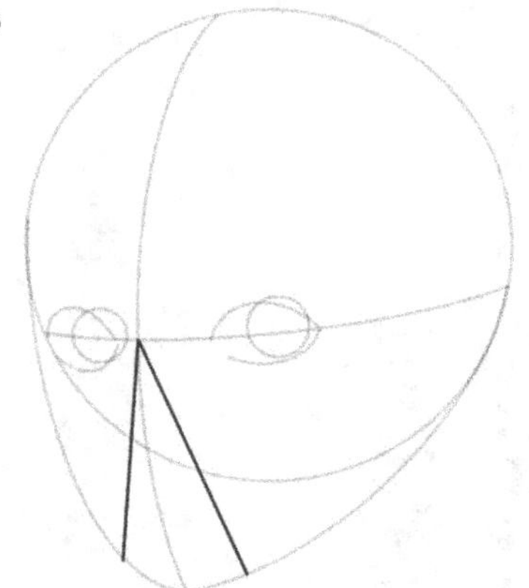

Draw a triangle shape down from the centre point of the intersecting lines. This will help you determine the width and position of the nose and mouth.

07

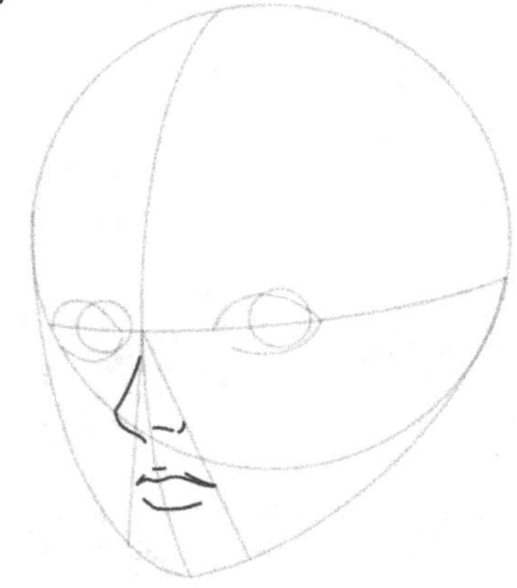

The mouth sits approximately halfway down the triangle. Note that the nose extends outside the triangle due to the angle of the face.

08

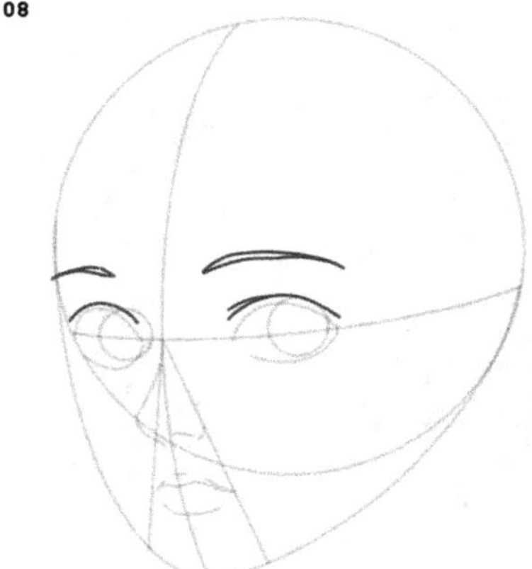

Sketch in the eyebrows. Add an additional fold line above the eyeline for a more natural look.

09

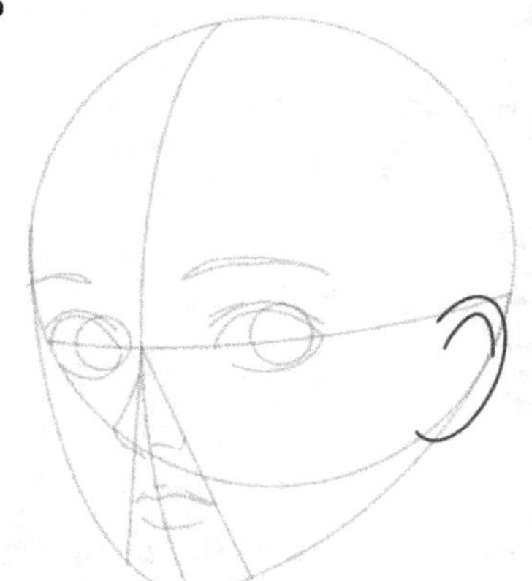

It's important that you draw the ear set in from the edge of the circle. If you do not, it will look as though the ear is placed behind the skull.

10

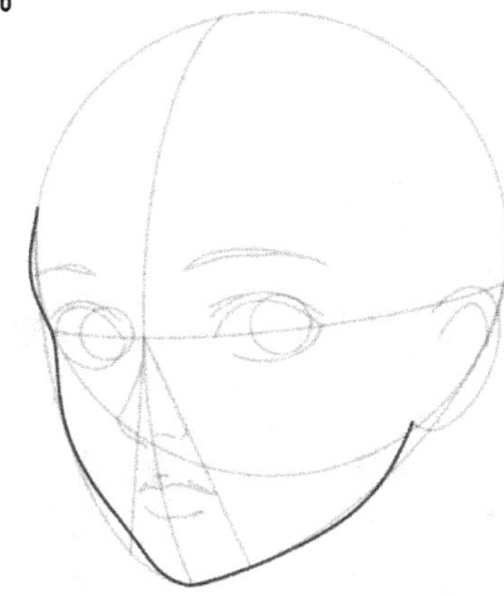

It's time to add a more natural-looking structure to the face. On the left, at the eyeline, notice that the contour of the line goes in and then back out again. This captures the definition of the cheekbones and brow.

11

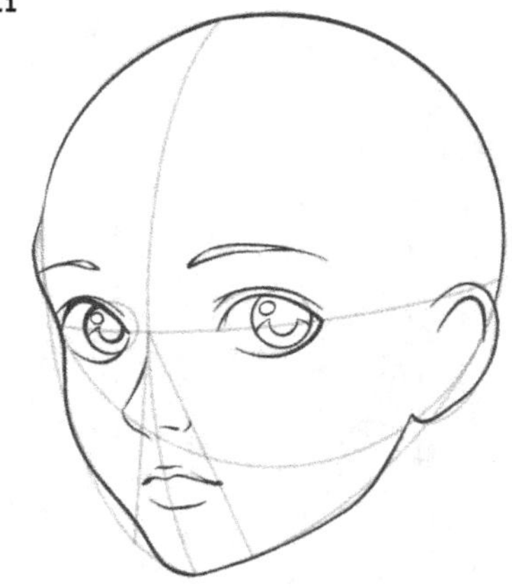

With an inking brush, outline the skull and facial features that you have drawn.

12

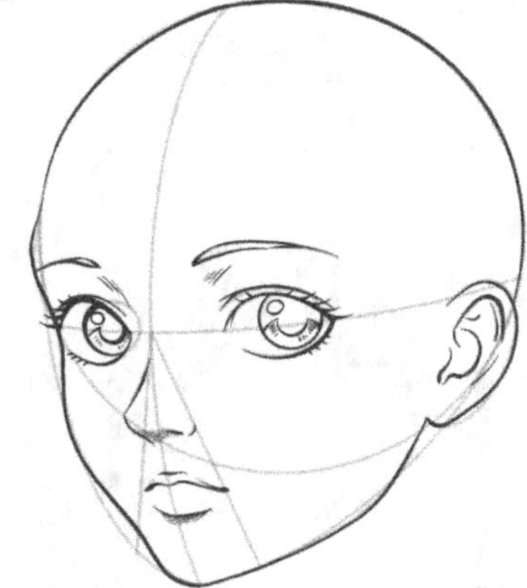

Now add some additional skin fold lines around the eyes and ear. Add a shadow under the lip and nose to define the facial features and give them depth.

DRAWING FEMALE HAIRSTYLES AND ACCESSORIES

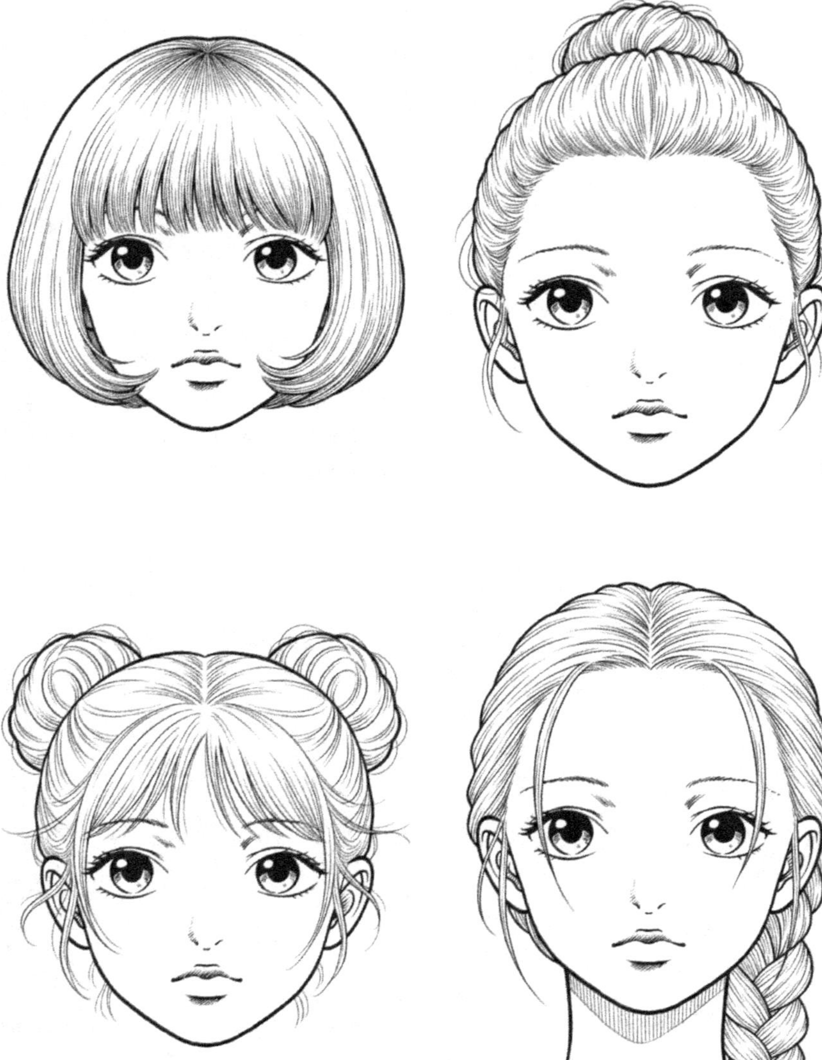

Pro Tip: Hair helps define the personality of your character. Sketch broad, flowing outlines first to capture volume and direction before adding individual strands or accessories.

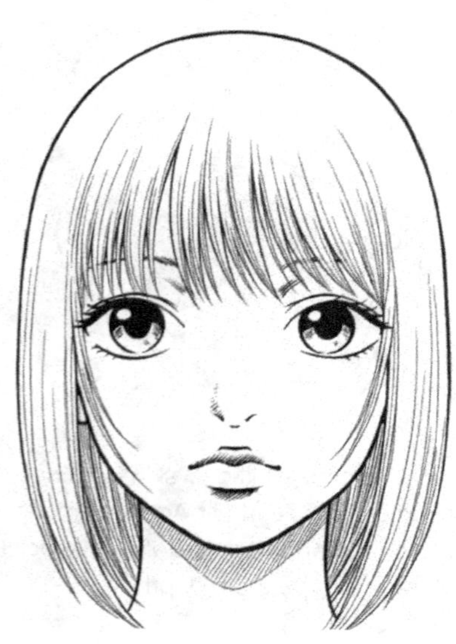

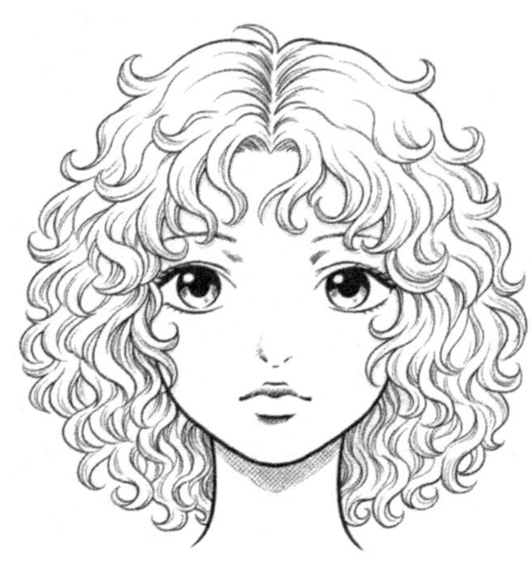

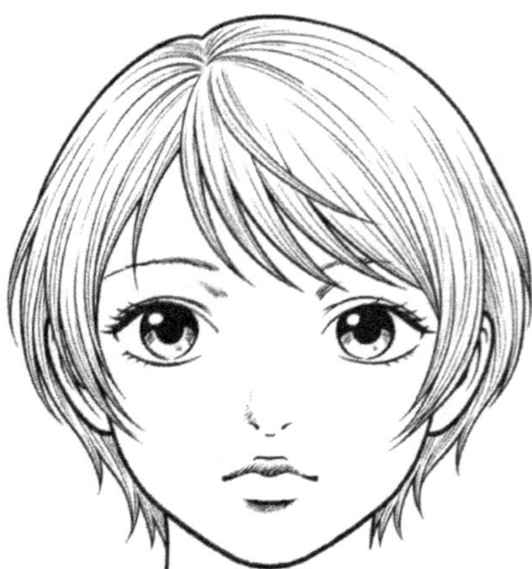

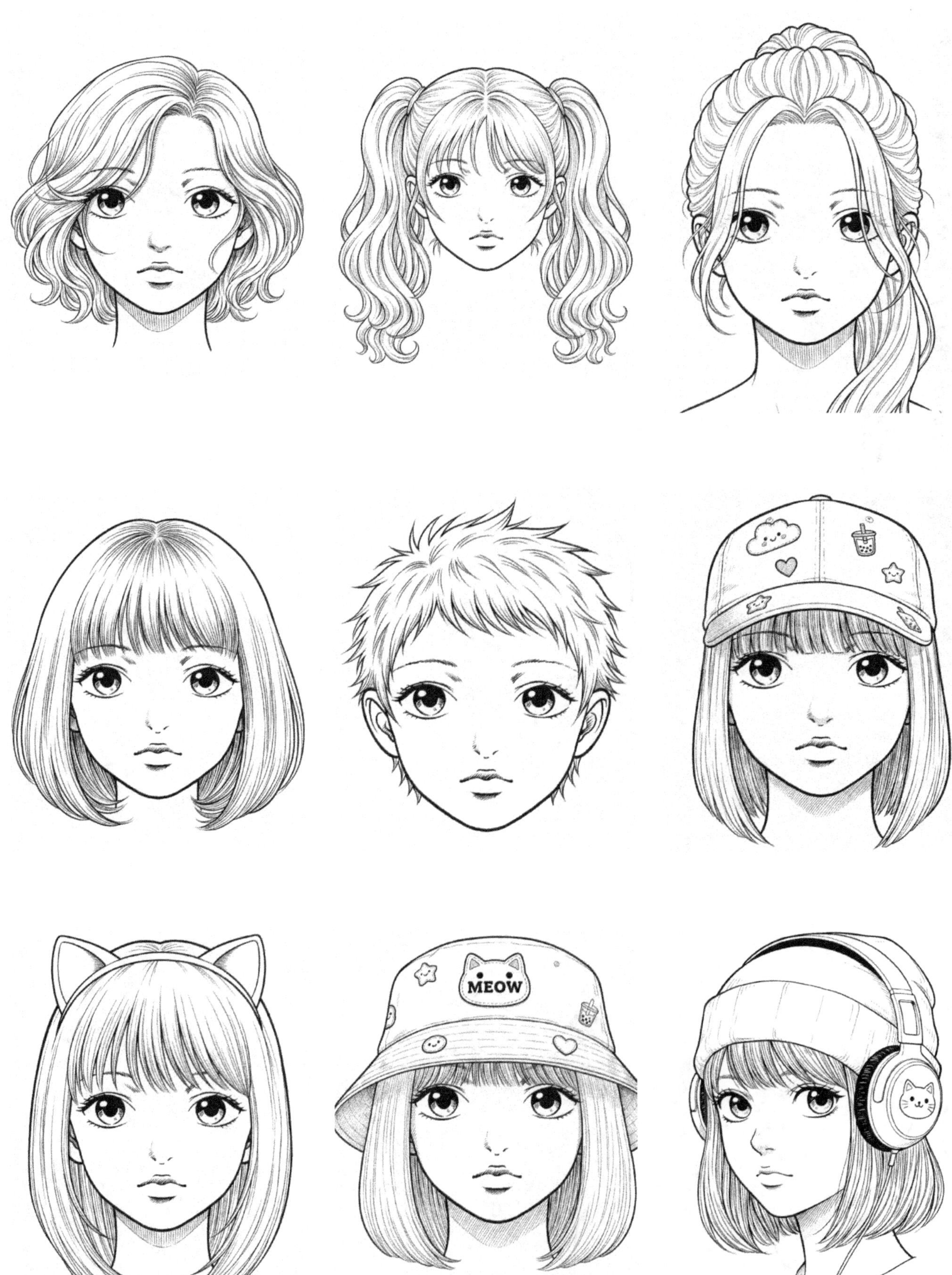

DRAWING THE FEMALE FACE FROM VARIOUS ANGLES

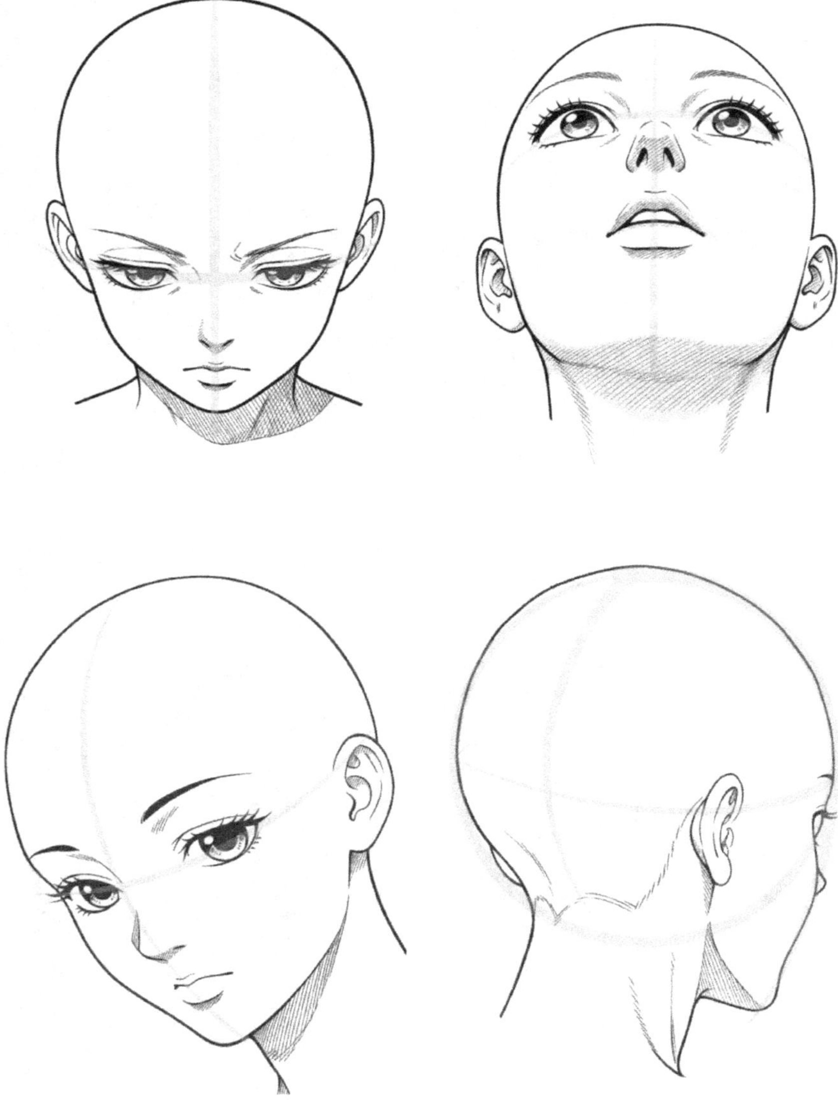

Pro Tip: Keep facial features aligned to the head's perspective lines. Softer curves and subtler shading help maintain a gentle, balanced appearance from every angle.

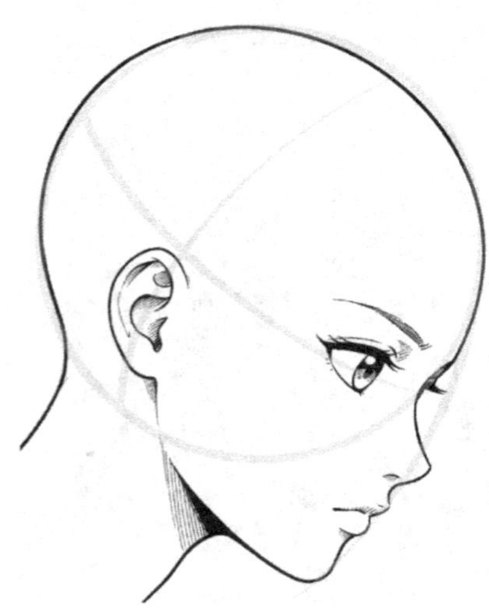

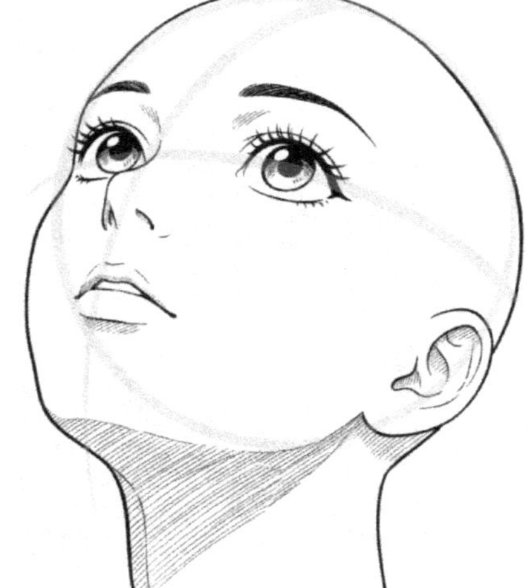

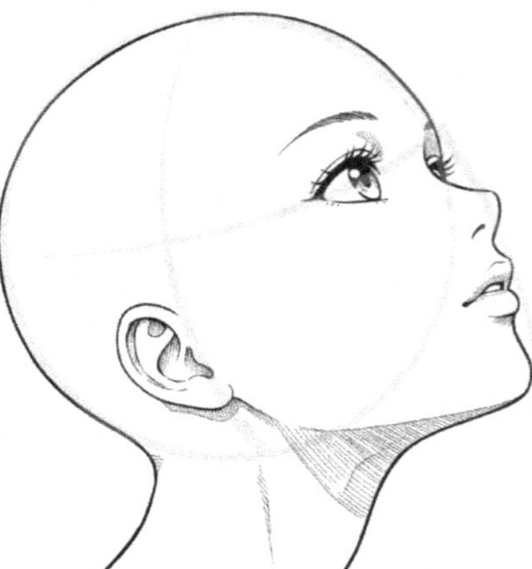

DRAWING FEMALE FACIAL EXPRESSIONS

Pro Tip: In manga, eyes are key to expressing emotion. Combine expressive eyes with subtle changes in the eyebrows and mouth to show everything from joy to heartbreak.

HOW TO DRAW ANIME

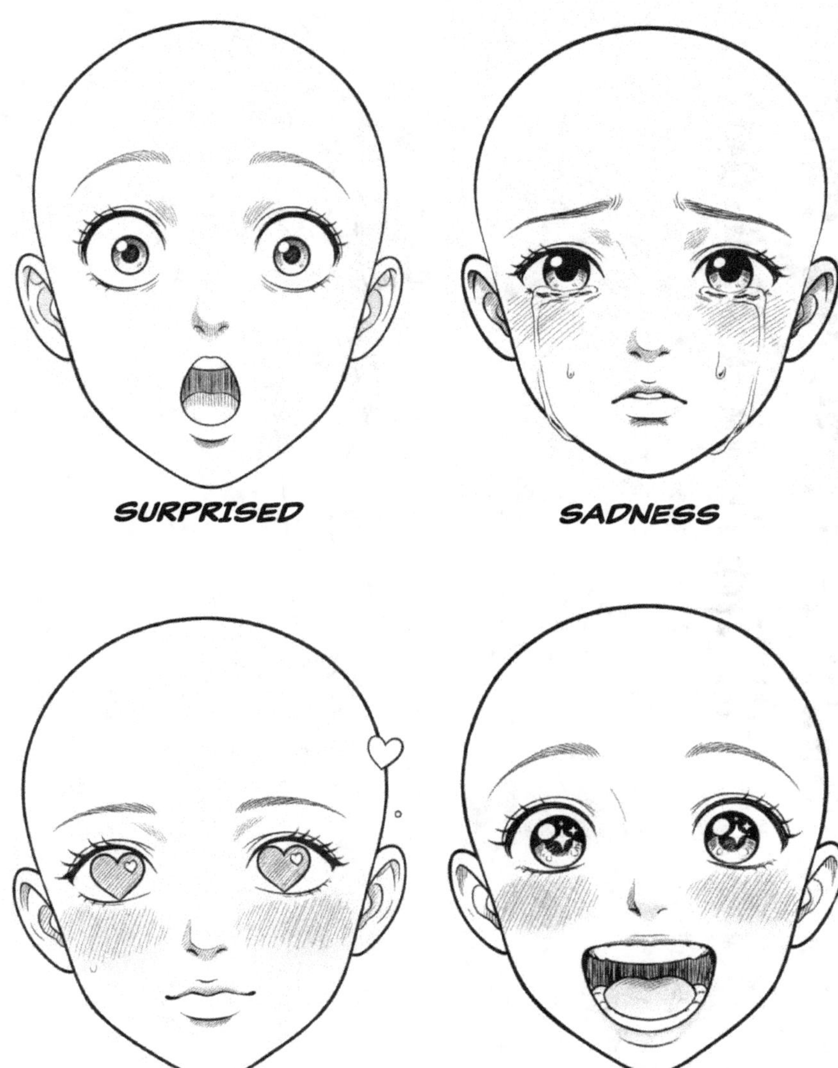

SURPRISED

SADNESS

LOVE

EXCITEMENT

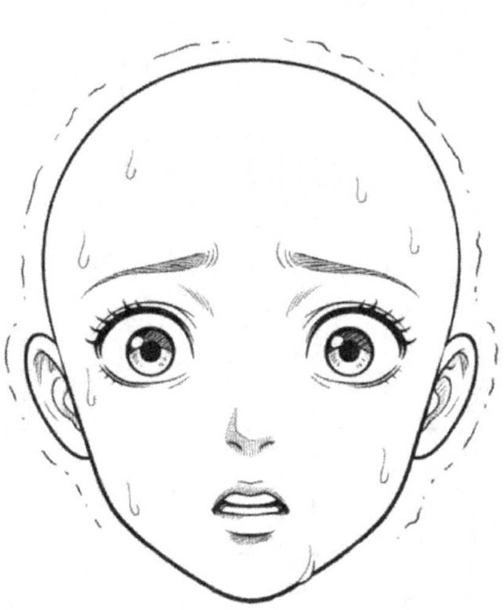

FEAR

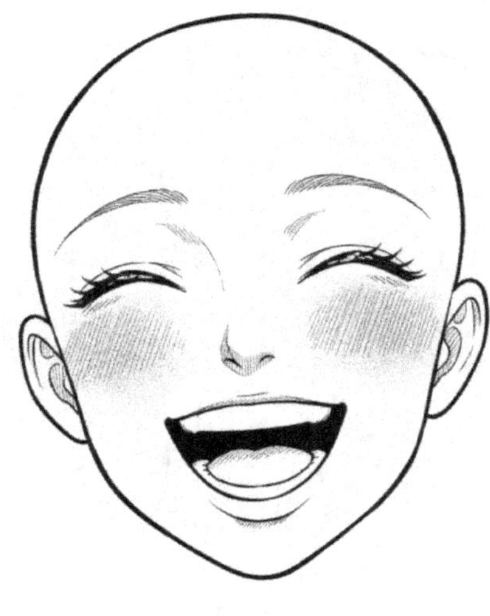

JOY

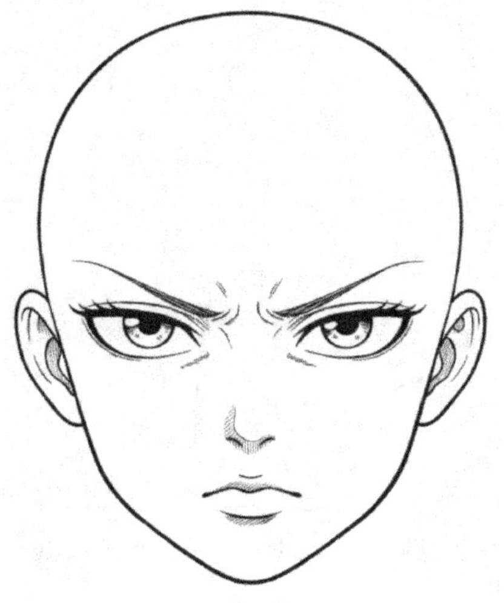

ANGER

UNDERSTANDING PROPORTIONS OF THE FEMALE ANATOMY

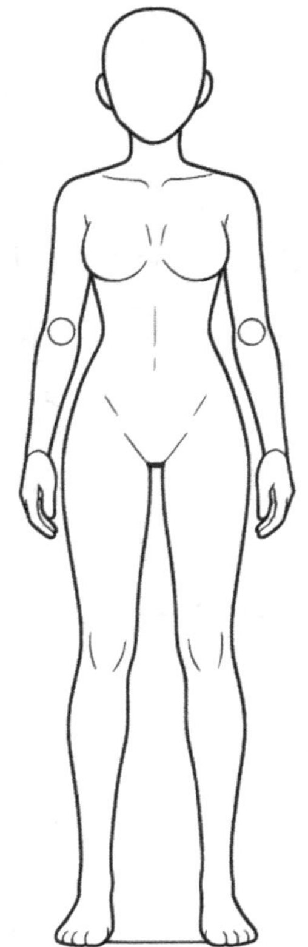
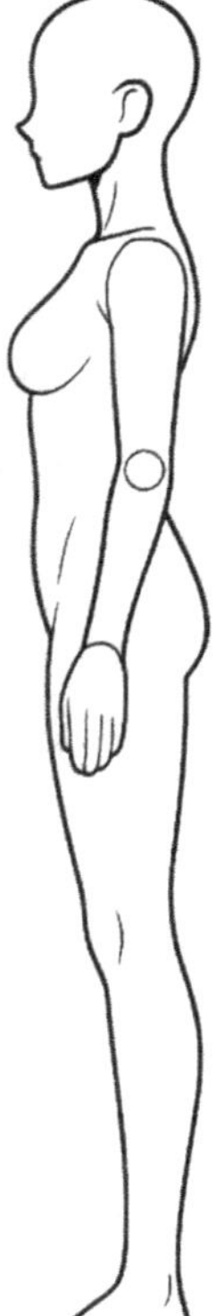
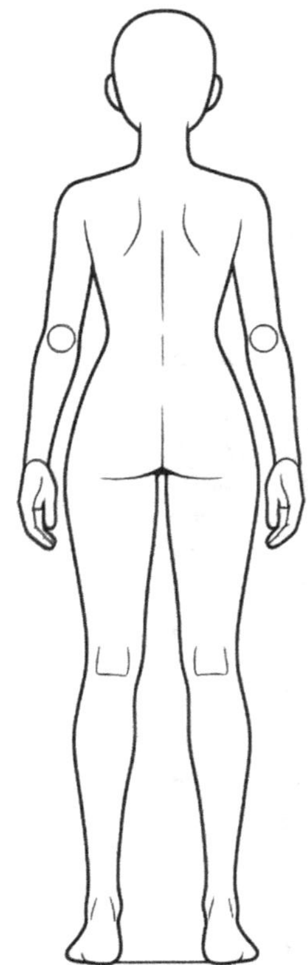

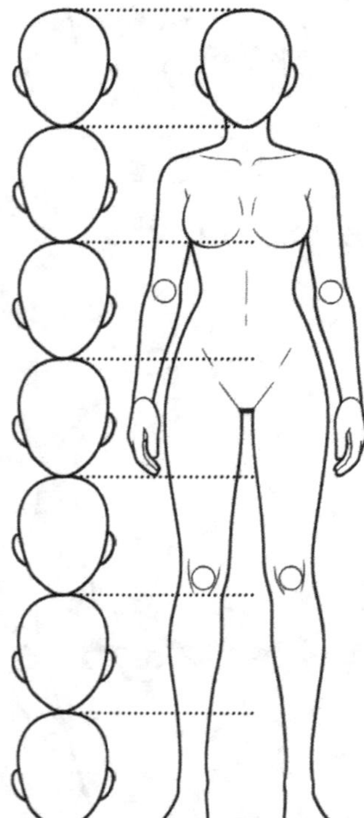

The average female figure stands seven heads tall.

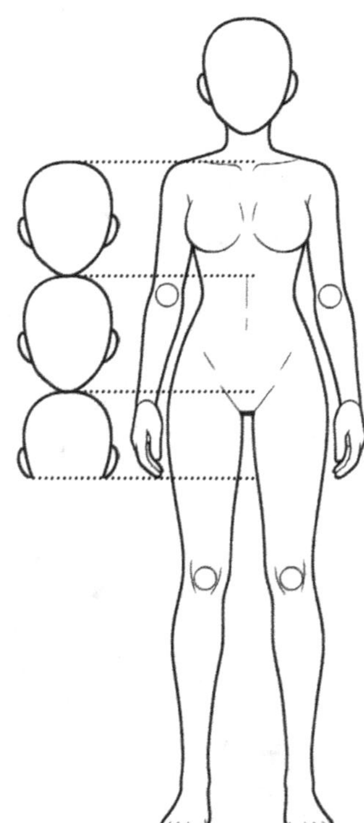

The arm, from the shoulder to the top of the fingers, measures roughly 2½ heads.

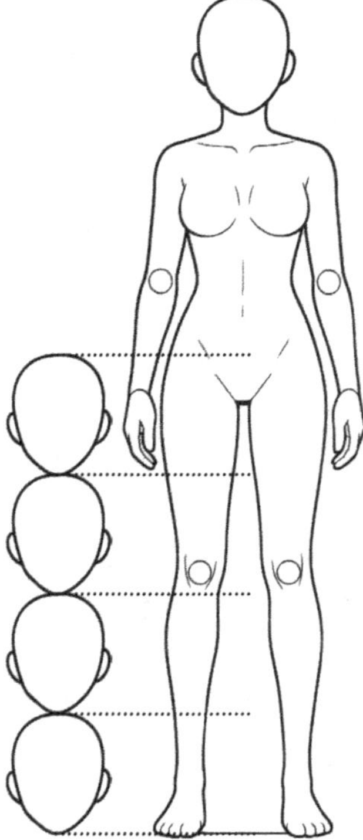

From the hips to the feet, the lower body measures around four heads.

Pro Tip: When drawing the female figure, begin by sketching the head first. This gives you a reliable unit of measurement for building the rest of the body in proportion.

Using head lengths as your guide ensures the figure remains balanced and graceful. The average female figure is about seven and a half heads tall. This approach helps you place key features—like the shoulders, bust, waist, hips, knees, and feet—in the correct relationship to one another. By stacking these head lengths as you draw, you can construct a well-proportioned figure with natural rhythm and flow.

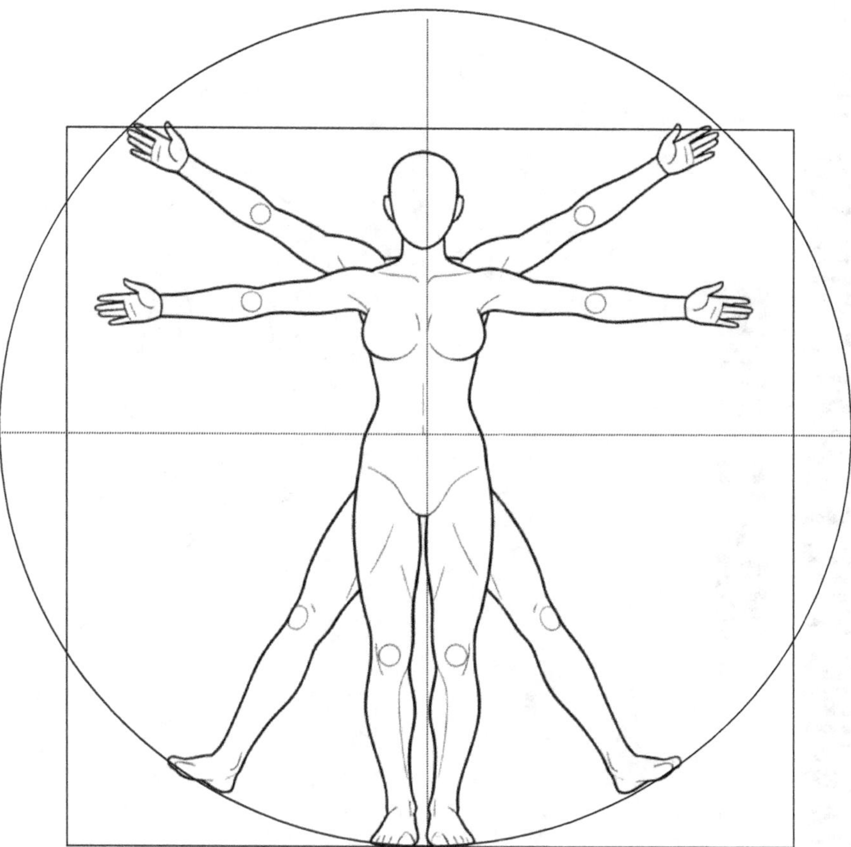

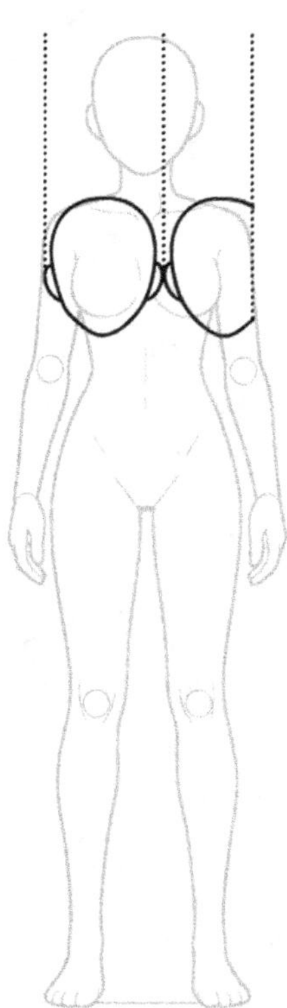

The shoulders sit approximately two head widths apart.

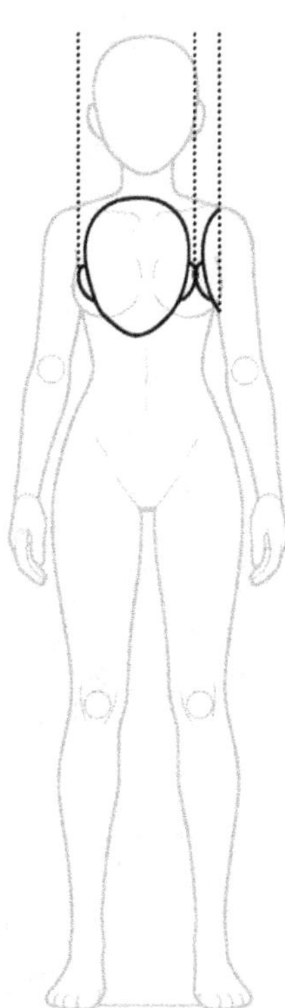

The chest measures the width of roughly 1¾ heads.

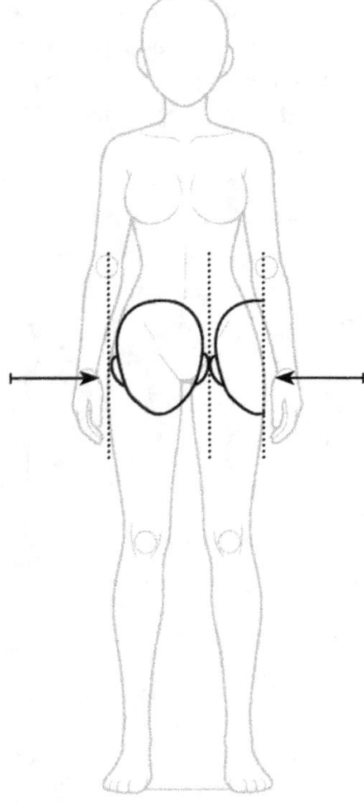

The waist measures about 1½ head widths at the top of the pelvis.

DRAWING THE FEMALE FIGURE IN DYNAMIC POSES

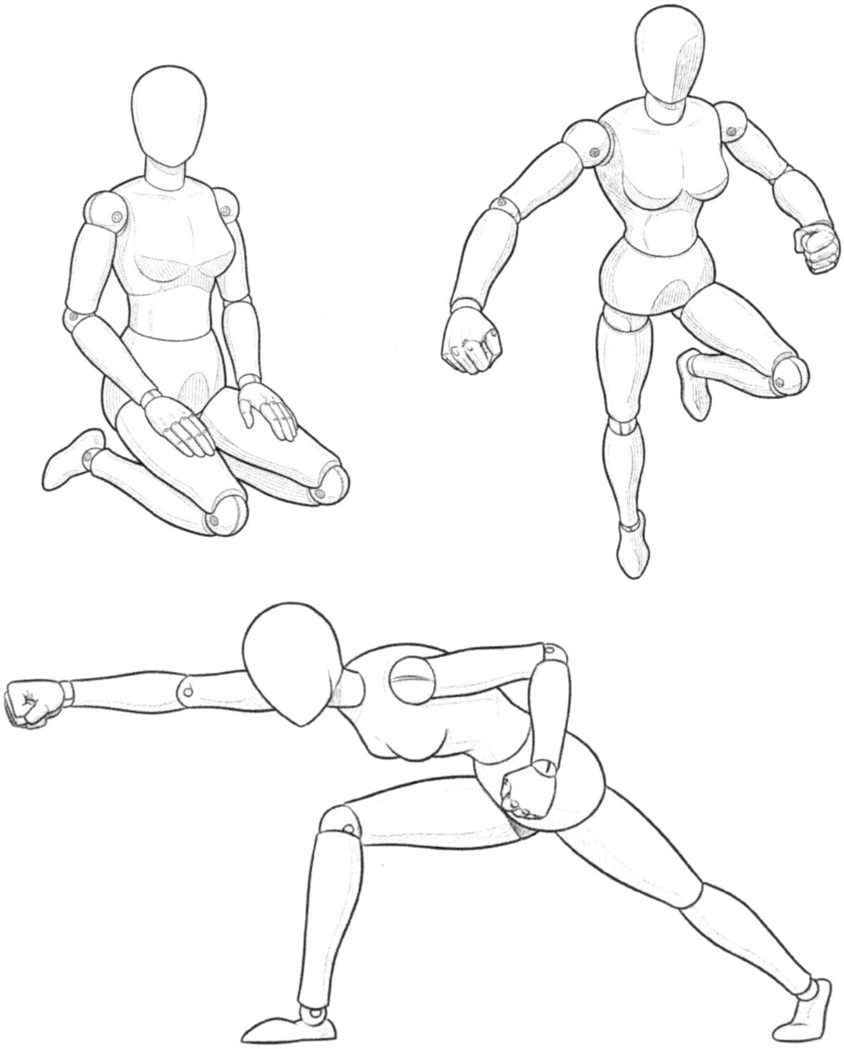

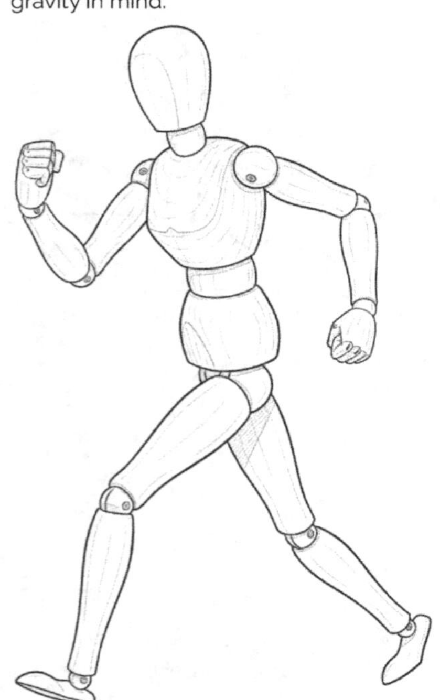

Pro Tip: Begin with loose, flowing lines to capture the gesture and rhythm of the pose before refining the form. Focus on balance and flow—keeping the centre of gravity in mind.

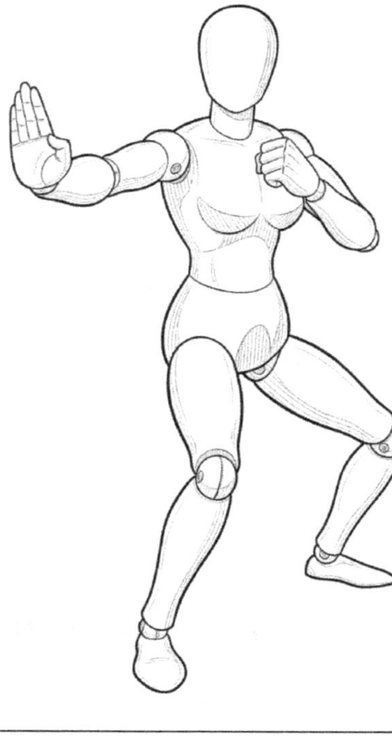

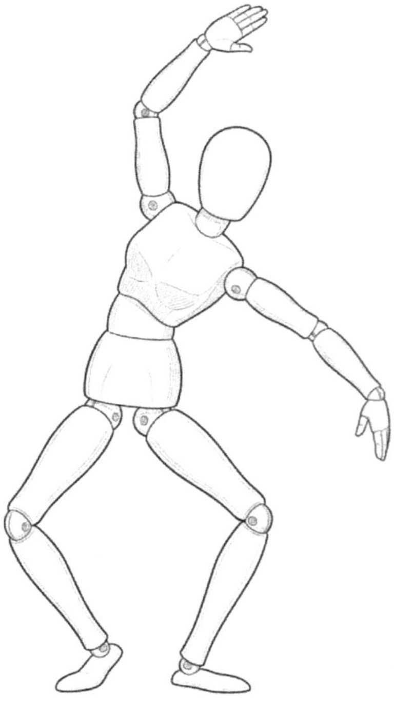

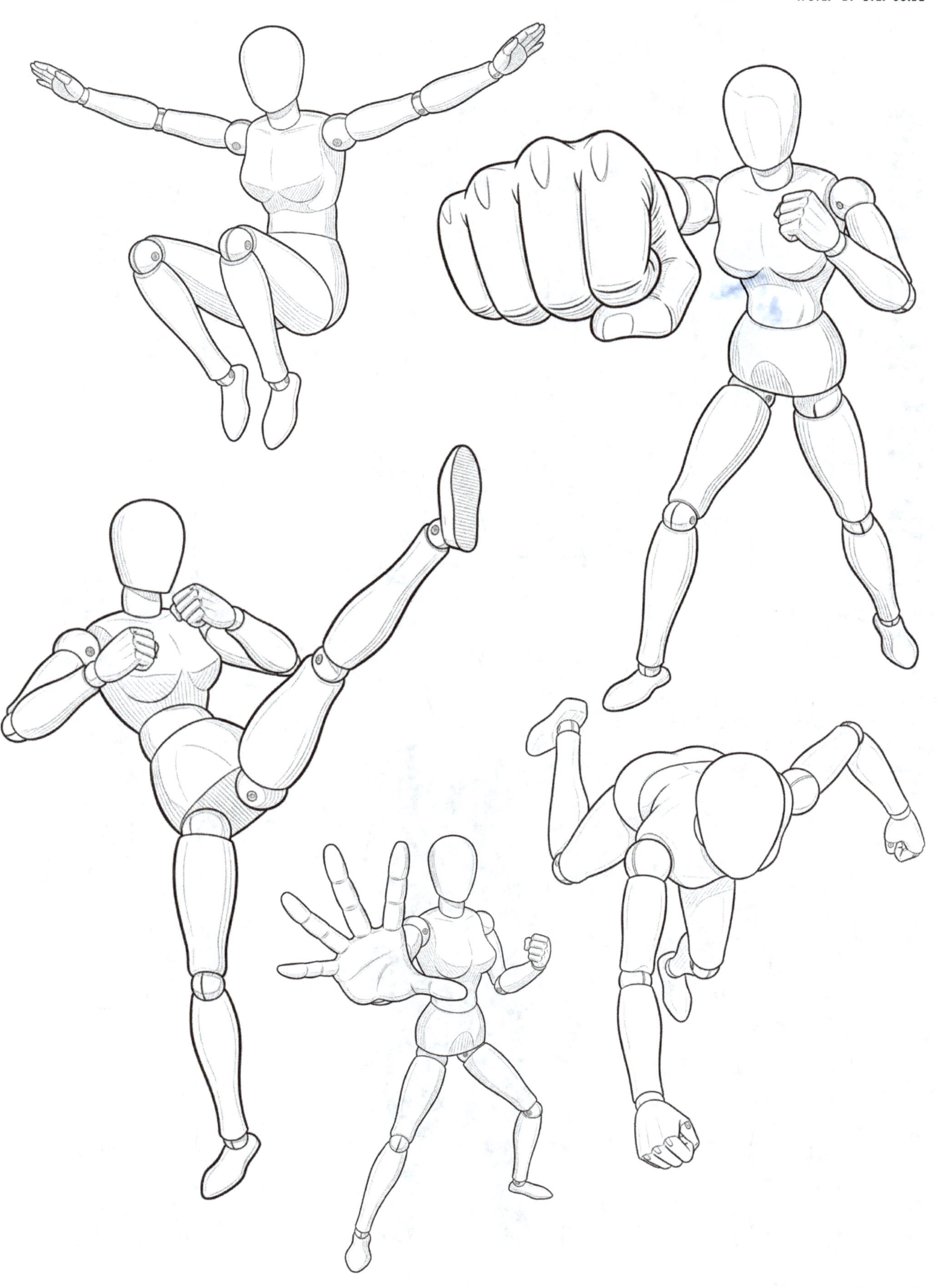

DRAWING FEMALE FASHION

Pro Tip: Start with the body's silhouette before adding garments. Observe how fabric drapes and folds over the form to convey weight, texture, and movement.

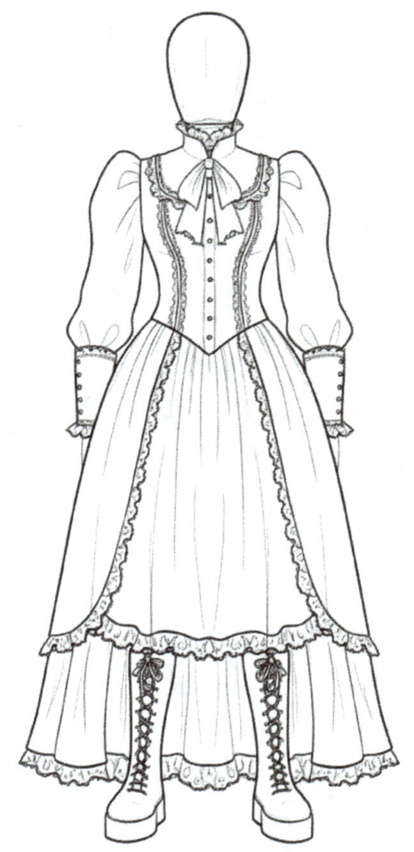

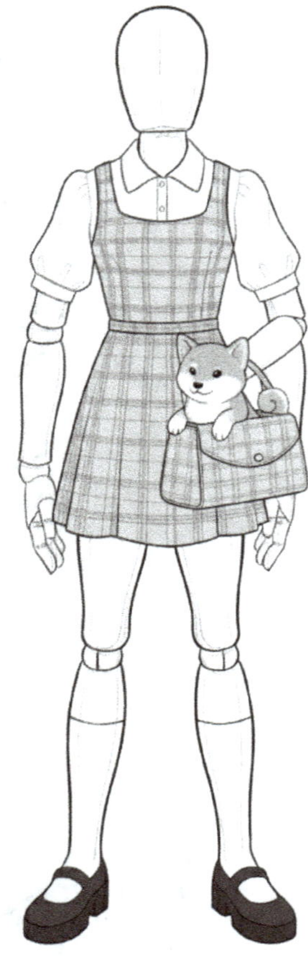

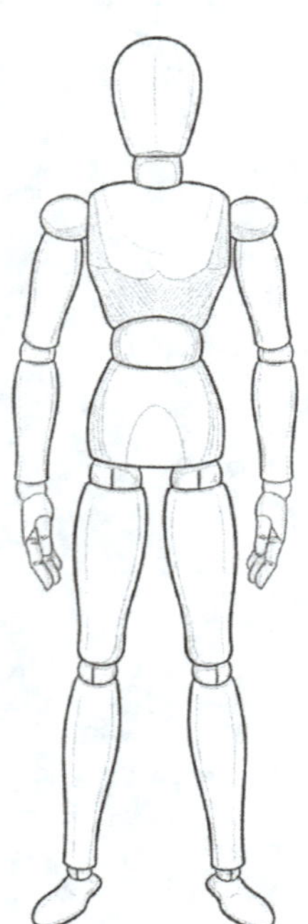

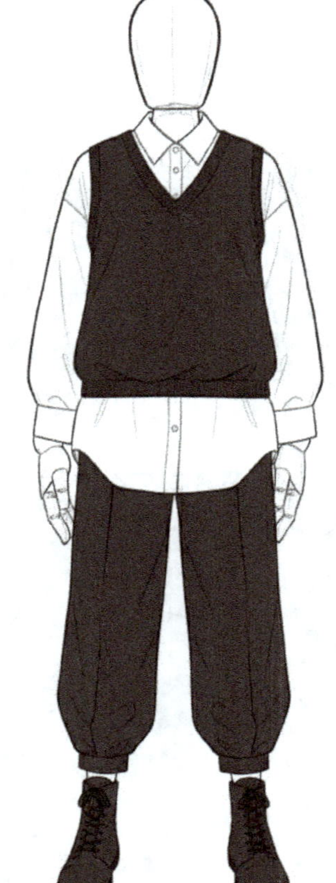

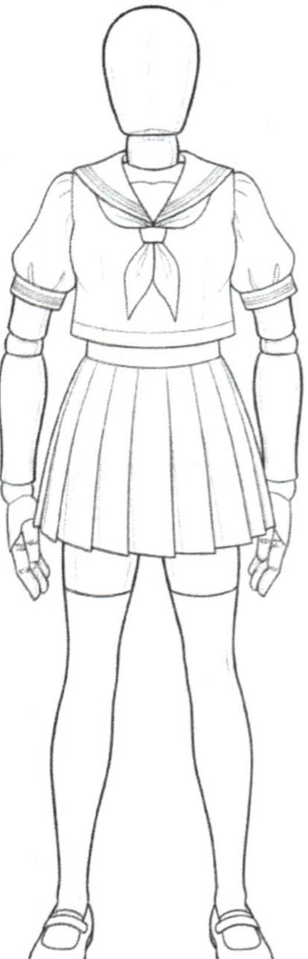

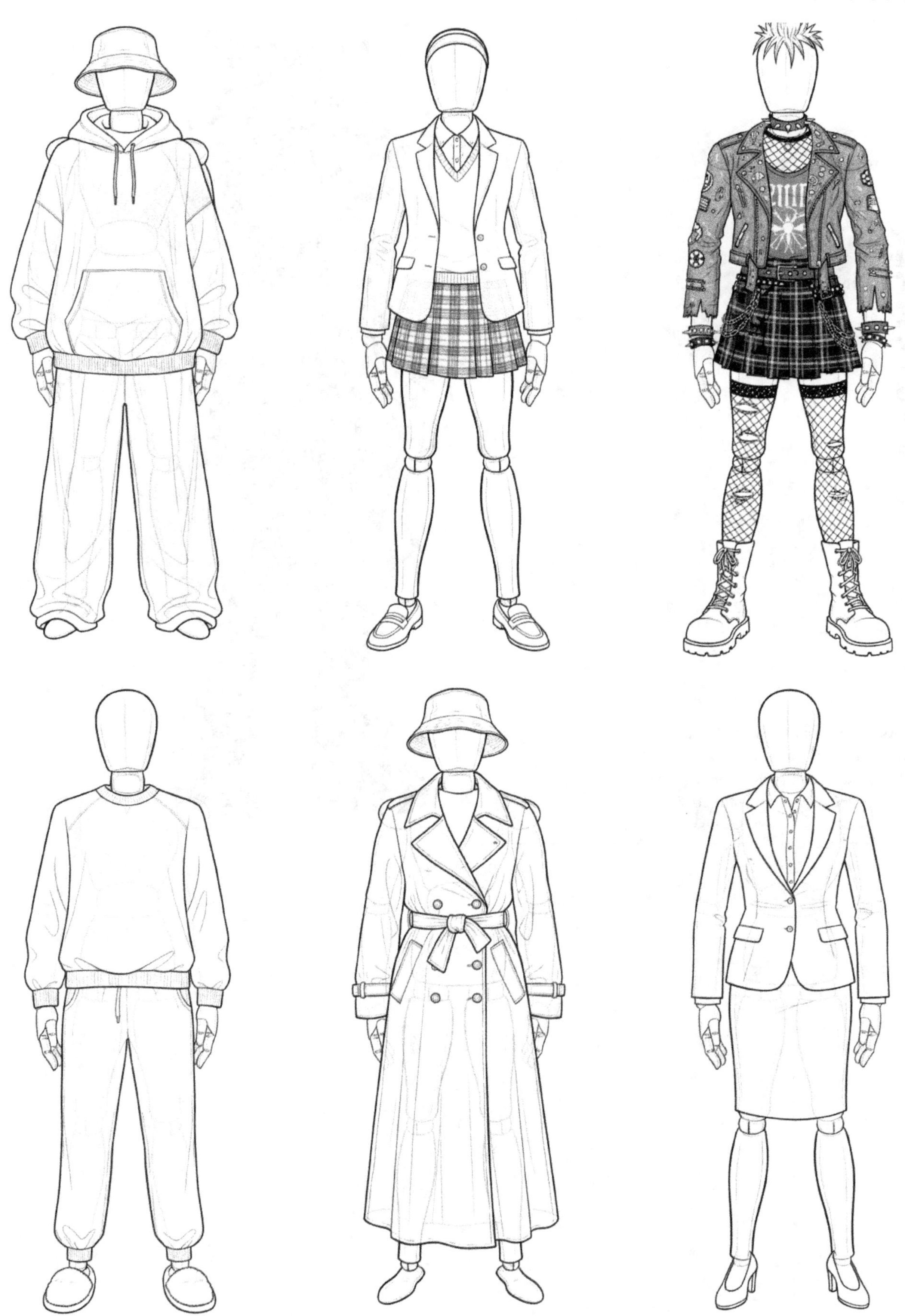

YOUNG FEMALE

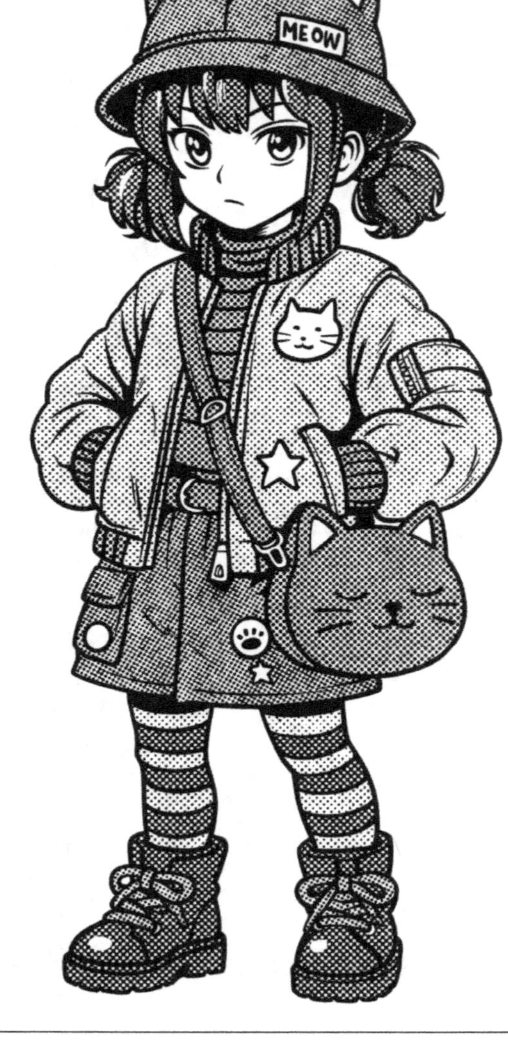

Pro Tip: For a young female character, aim for a height of around five and a half heads tall. Keep the torso short, the limbs soft and rounded, and the stance slightly narrower to suggest youthfulness.

01

02

03

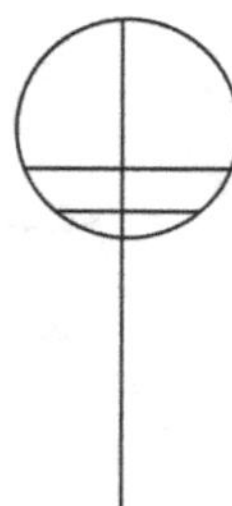

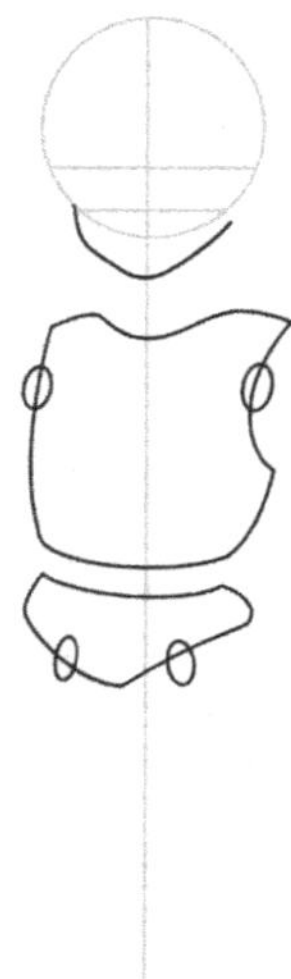

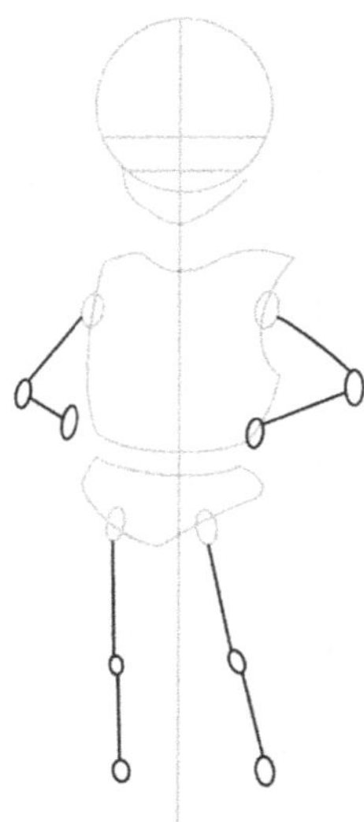

04

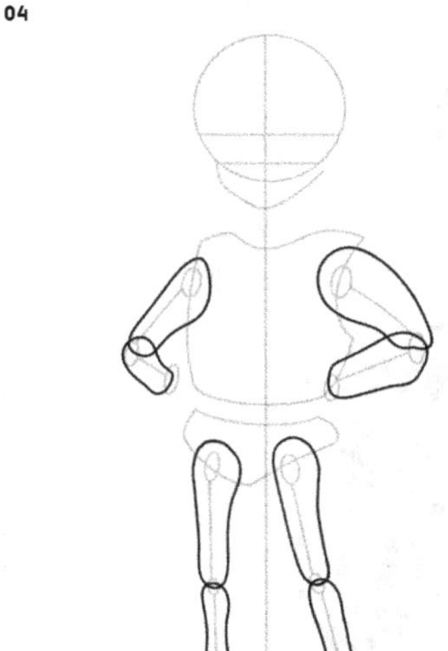

05

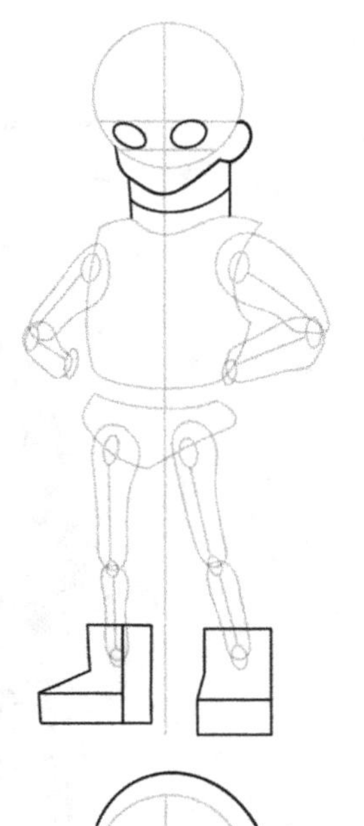

06

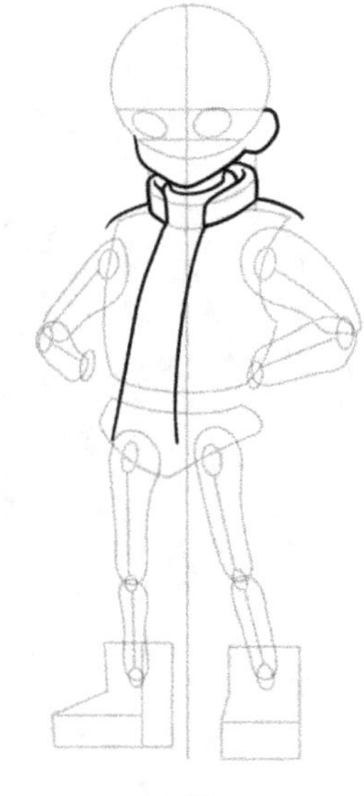

07

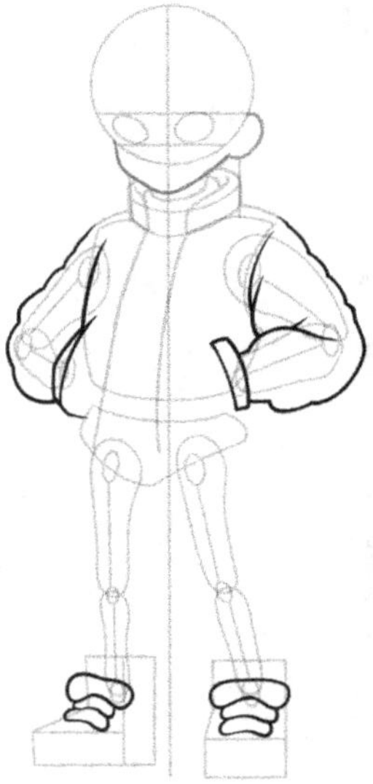

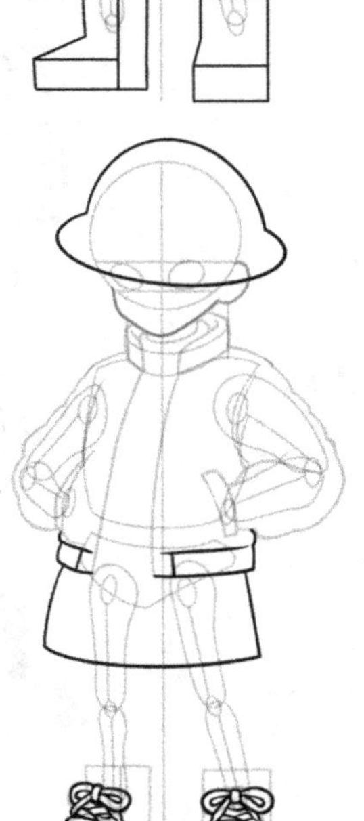

08

09

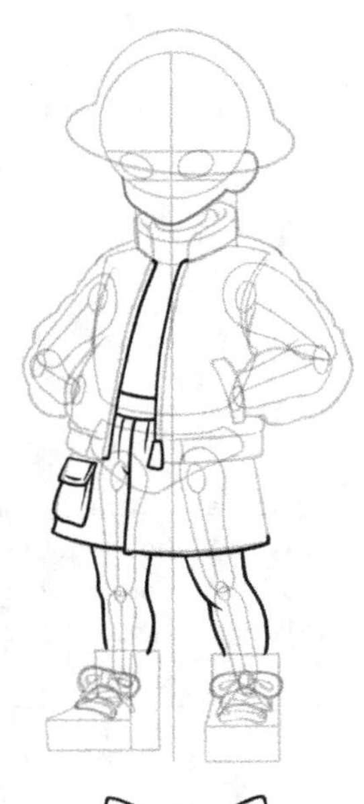

10

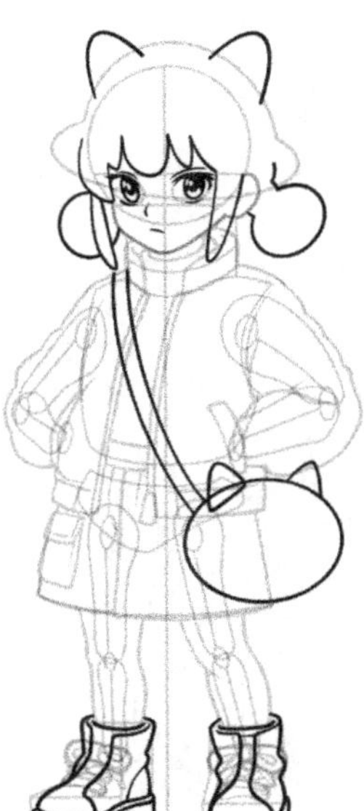

11

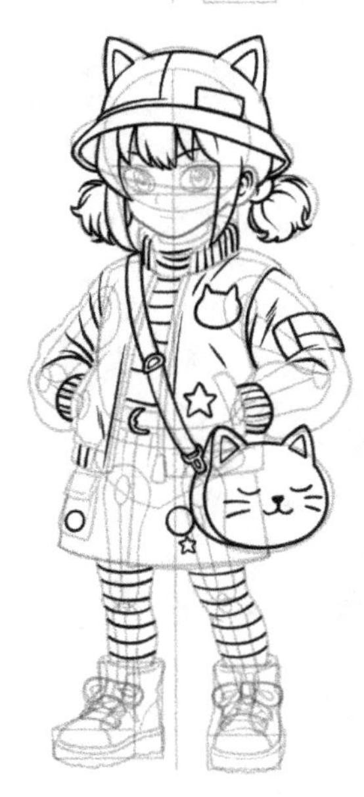

12

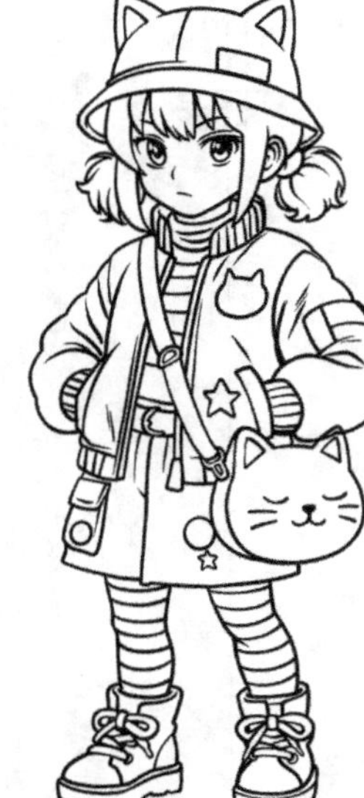

FEMALE TEENAGER

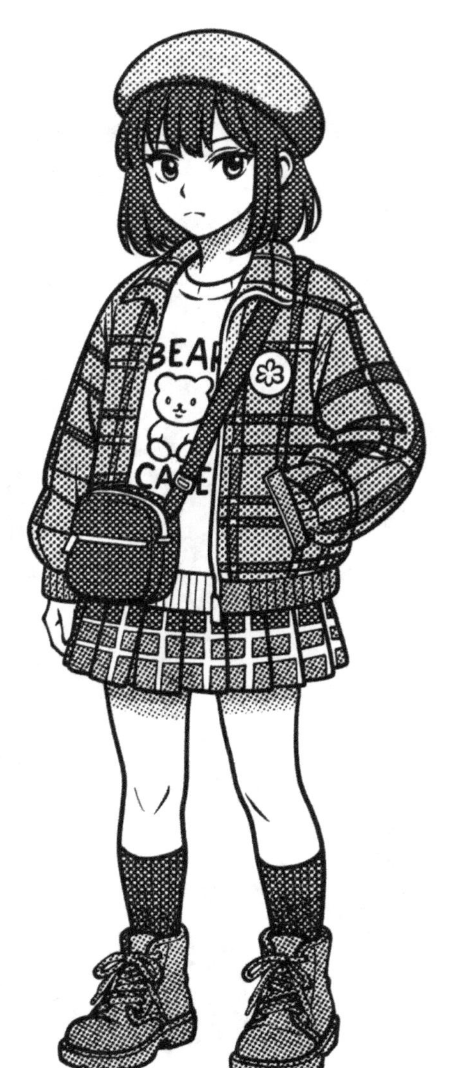

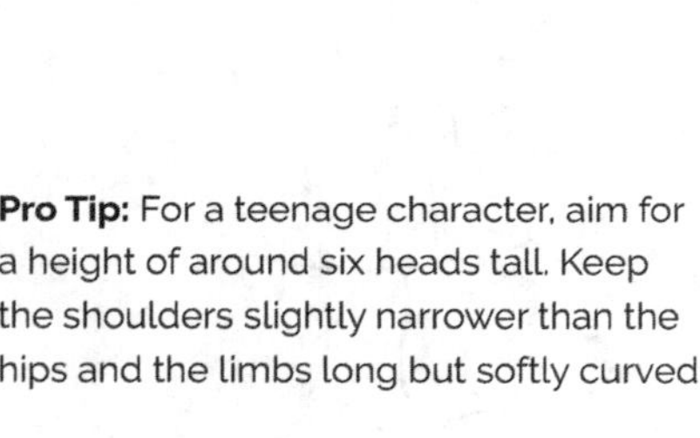

Pro Tip: For a teenage character, aim for a height of around six heads tall. Keep the shoulders slightly narrower than the hips and the limbs long but softly curved.

01

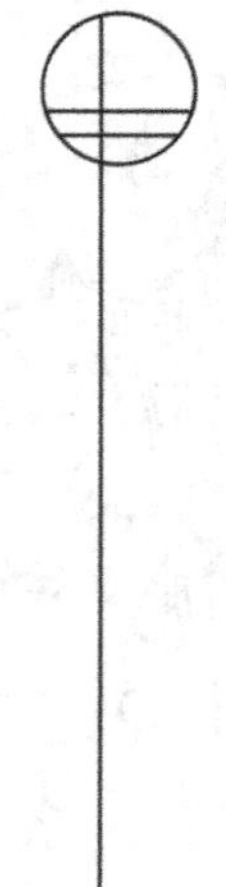

02

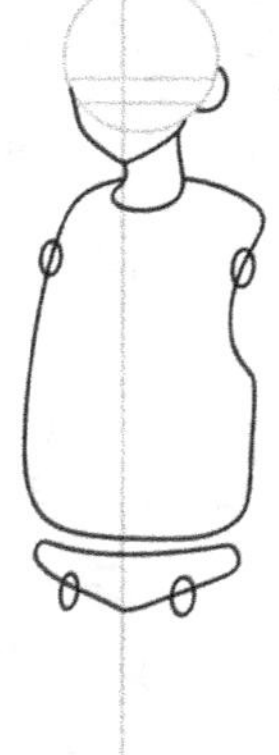

03

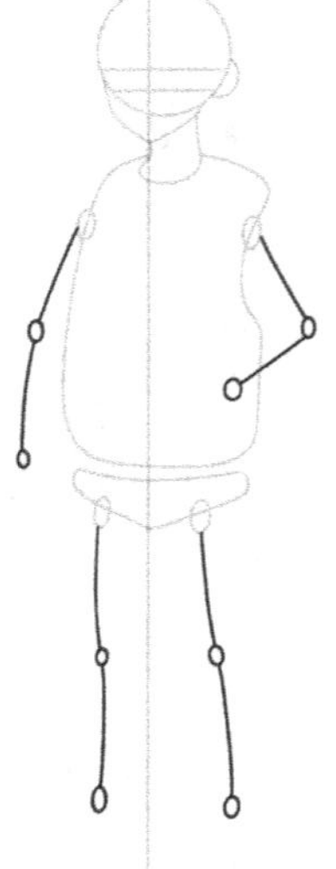

04

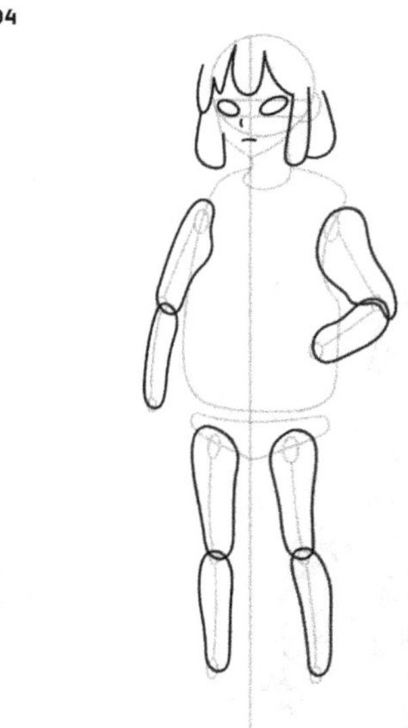

05

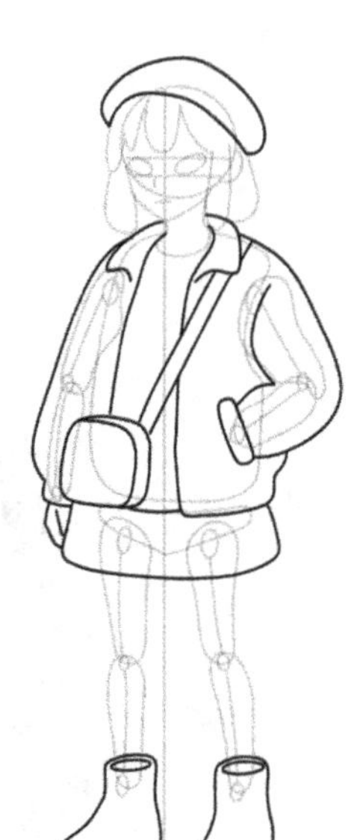

06

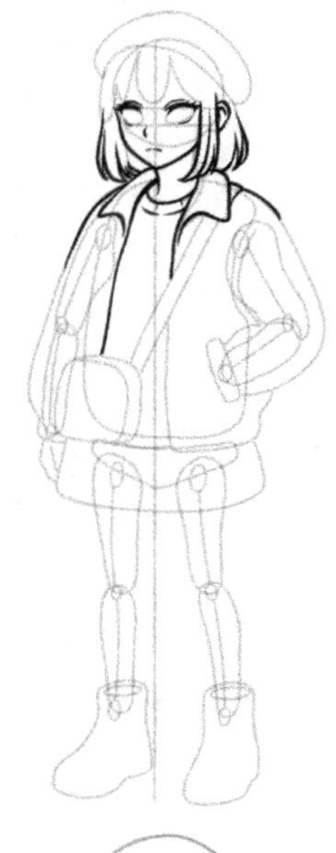

07

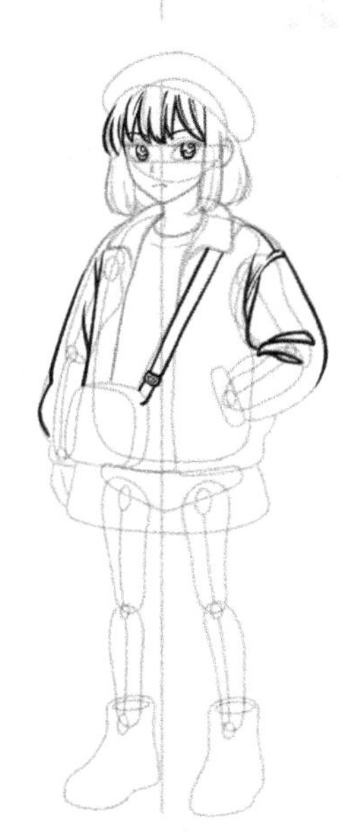

08

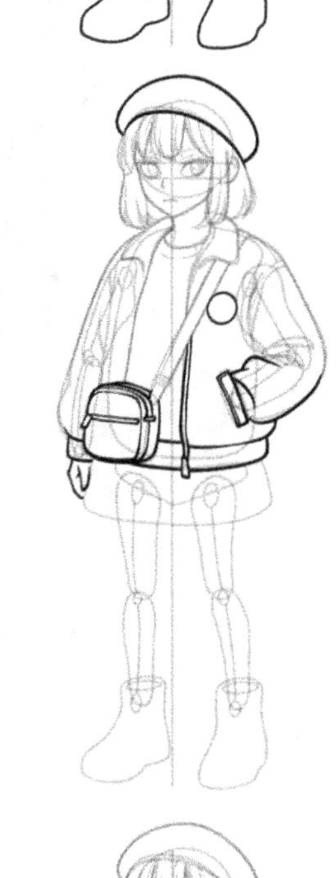

09

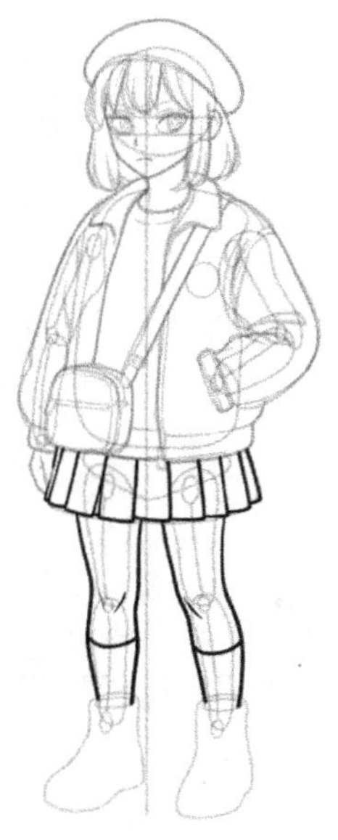

10

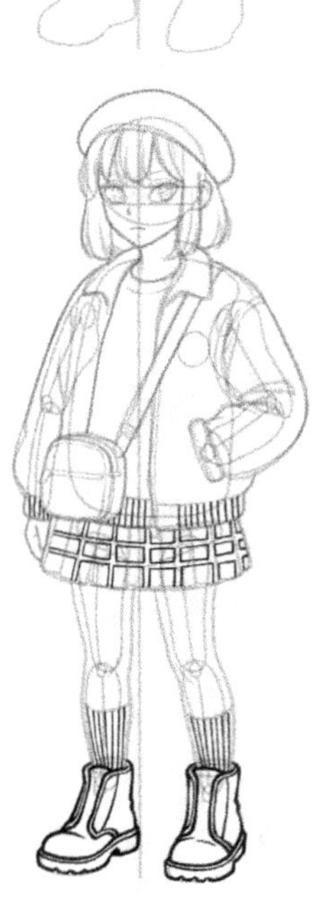

11

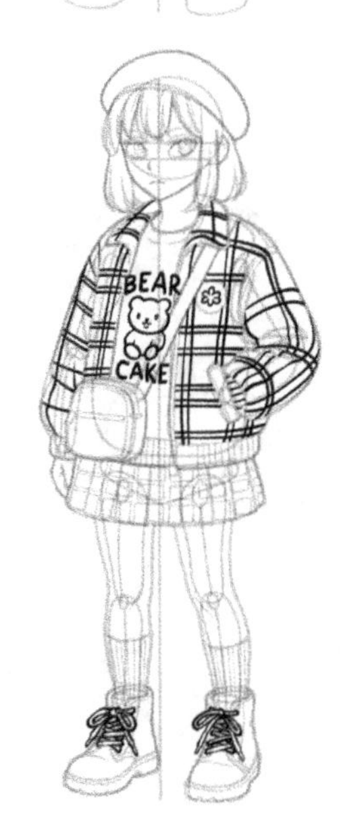

12

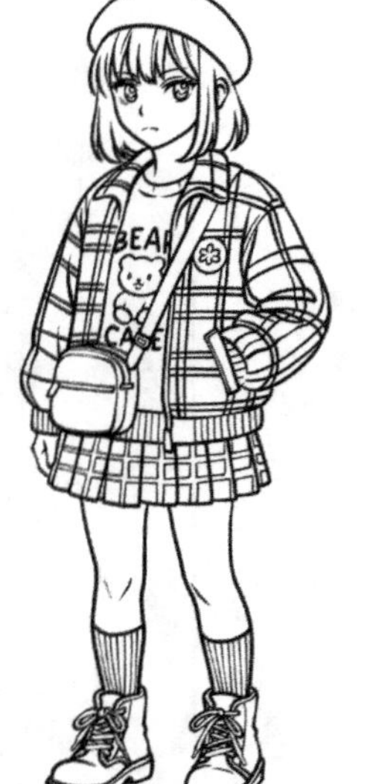

ADULT FEMALE

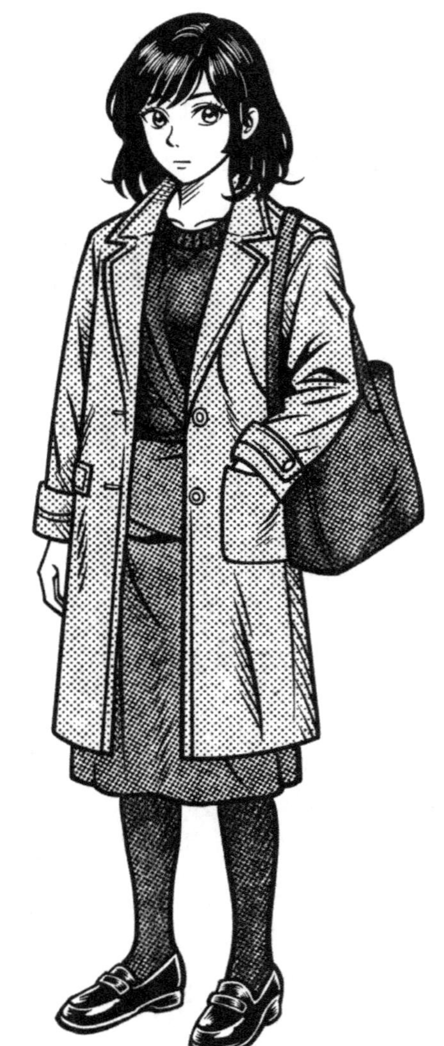

Pro Tip: For an adult female character, aim for a height of about seven heads tall. Keep the shoulders soft, the hips wider, and use smooth lines for a natural, balanced look.

01

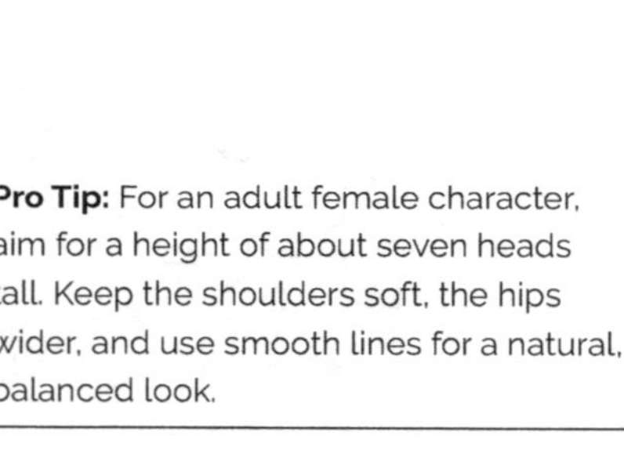

02

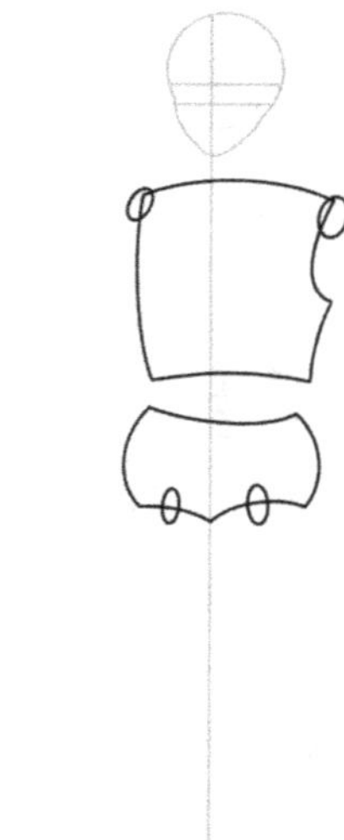

03

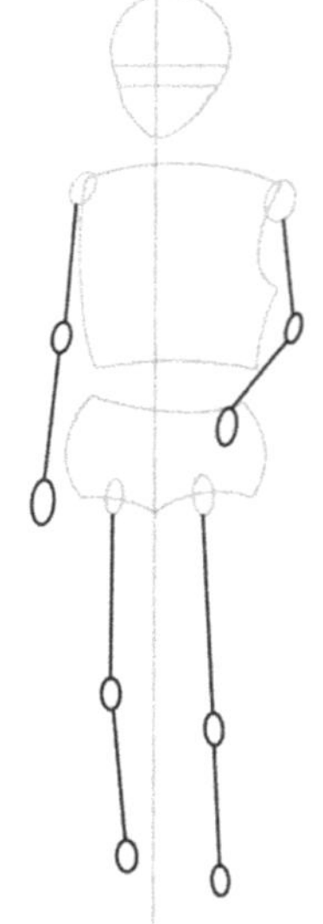

04

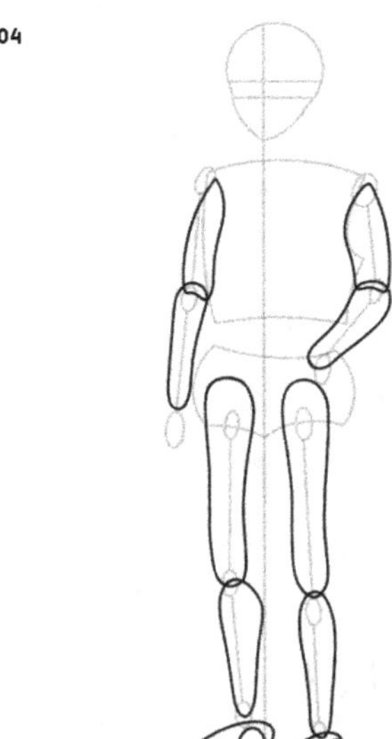

05

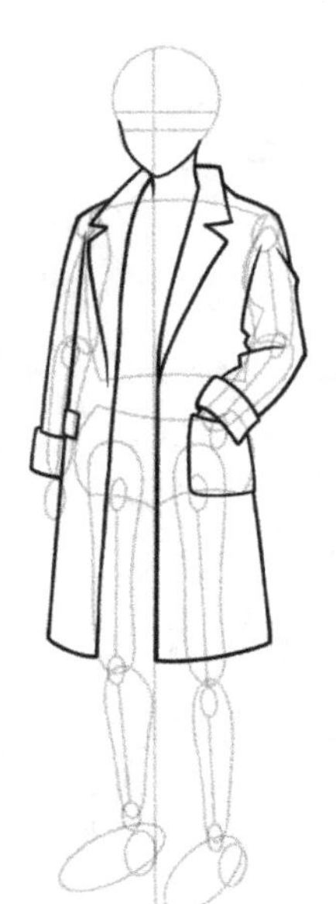

06

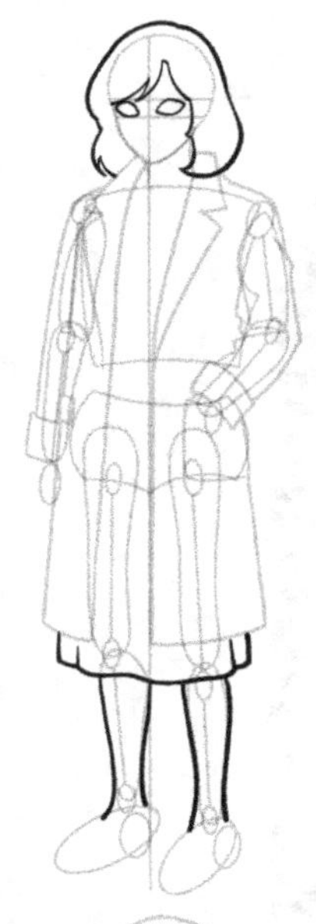

07

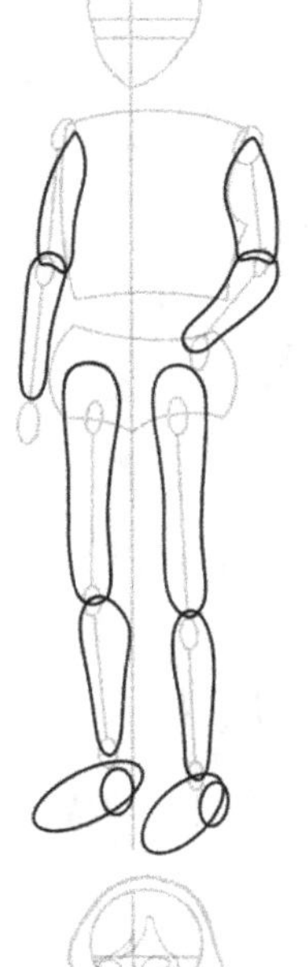

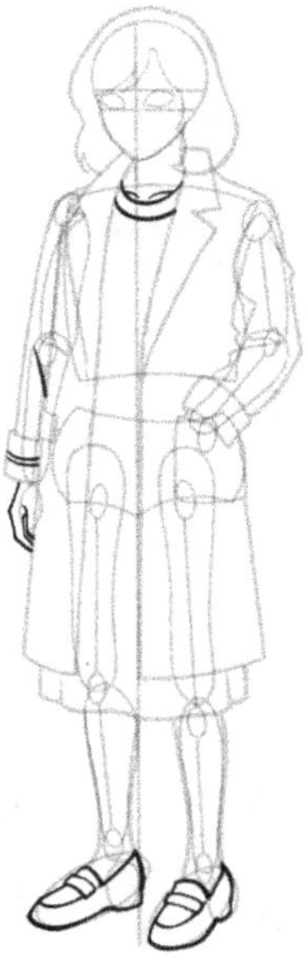

08

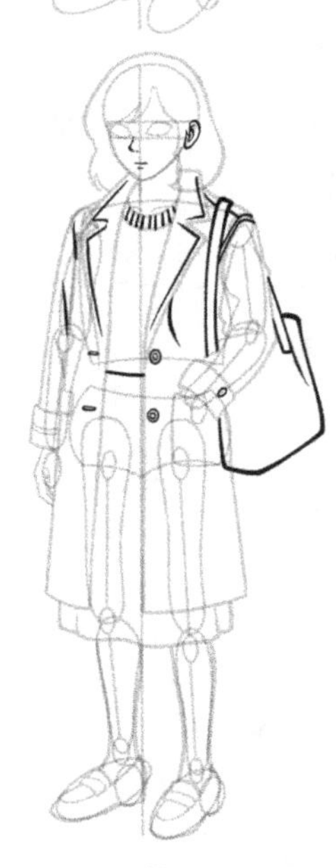

09

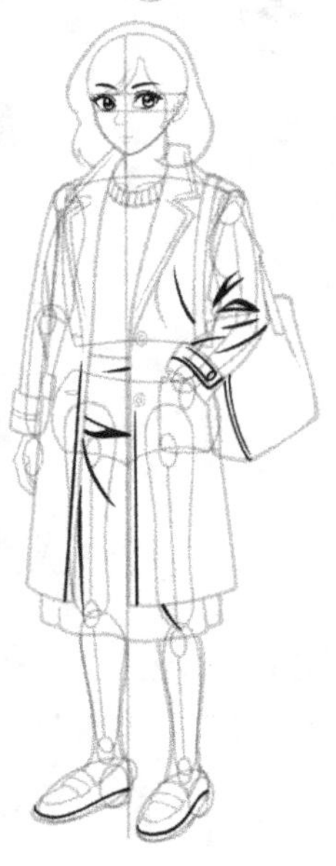

10

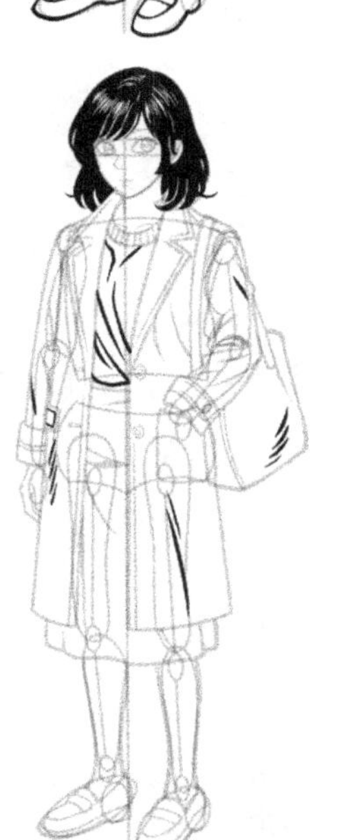

11

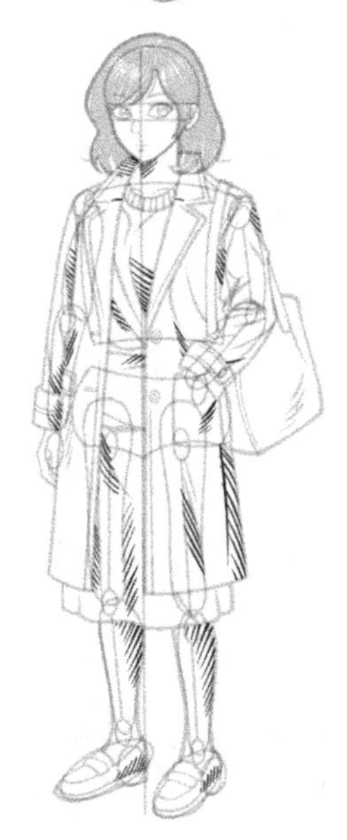

12

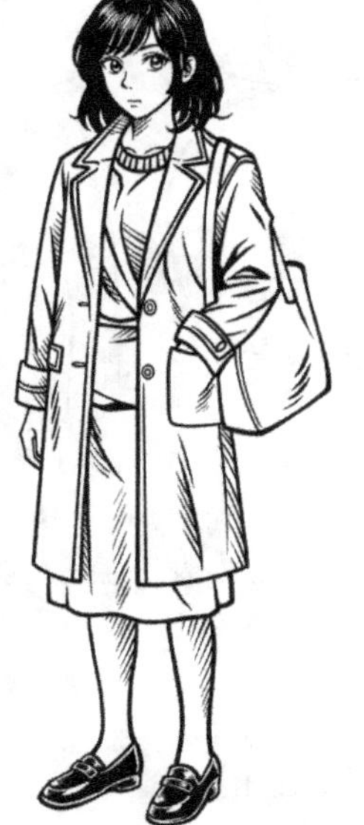

UNDERSTANDING PROPORTIONS OF THE CHIBI ANATOMY

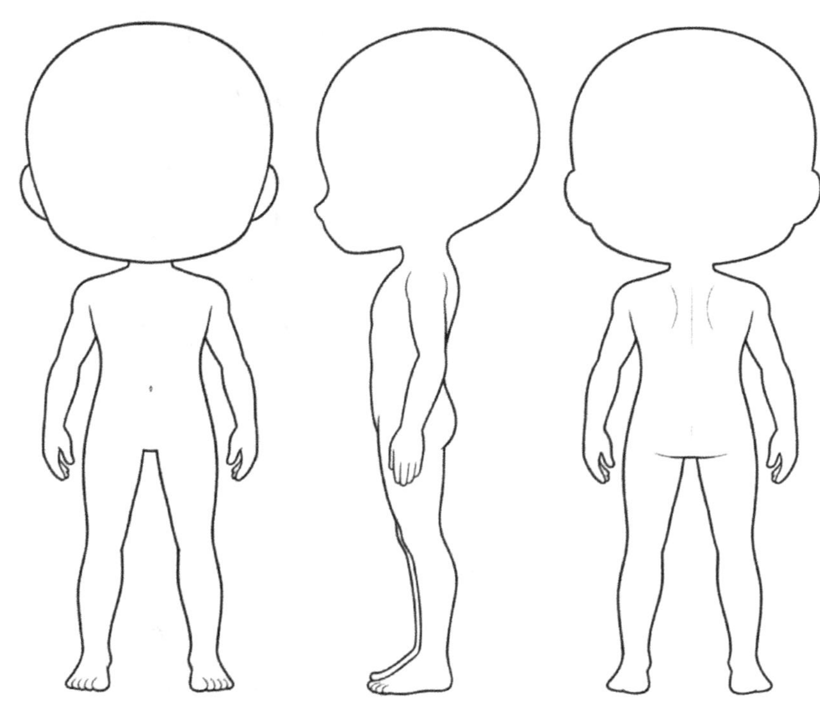

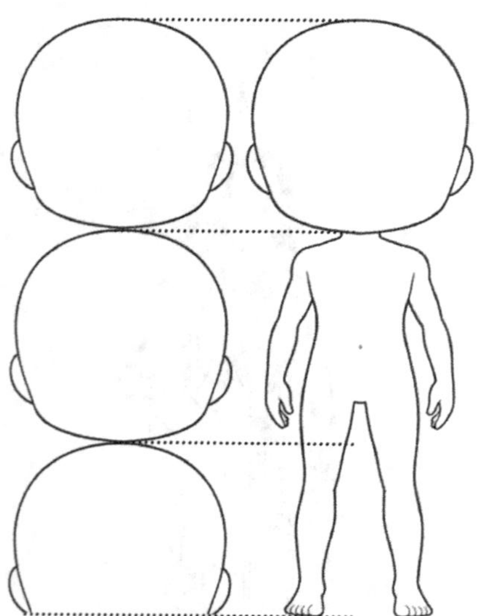

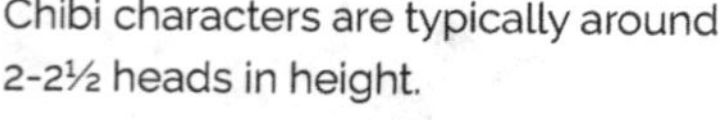

Chibi characters are typically around 2-2½ heads in height.

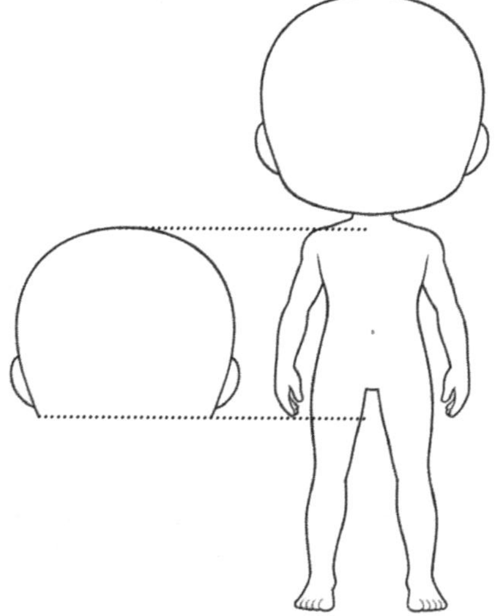

The chibi arm measures about ¾ of a head in height.

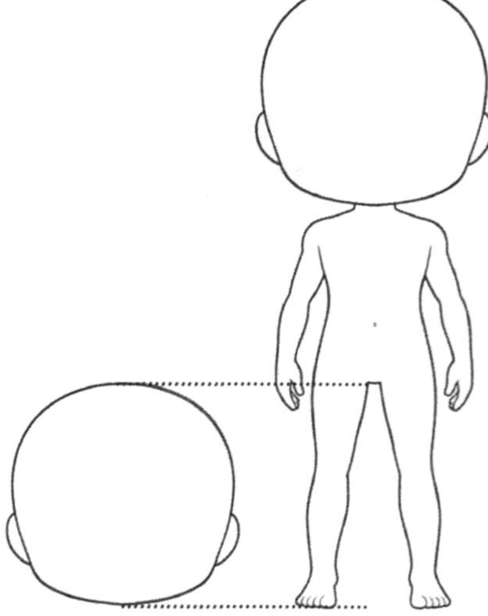

The leg, from the groin down, is roughly 1 head in height.

Pro Tip: When drawing chibi characters, start with the head—it's your main unit of measurement for the whole body.

Chibi proportions are much shorter and cuter, usually around two to three heads tall. Using head lengths as your guide helps you place the torso, arms, and legs in the right balance while keeping the overall look compact and appealing. This approach keeps your character's proportions consistent and enhances that signature chibi charm.

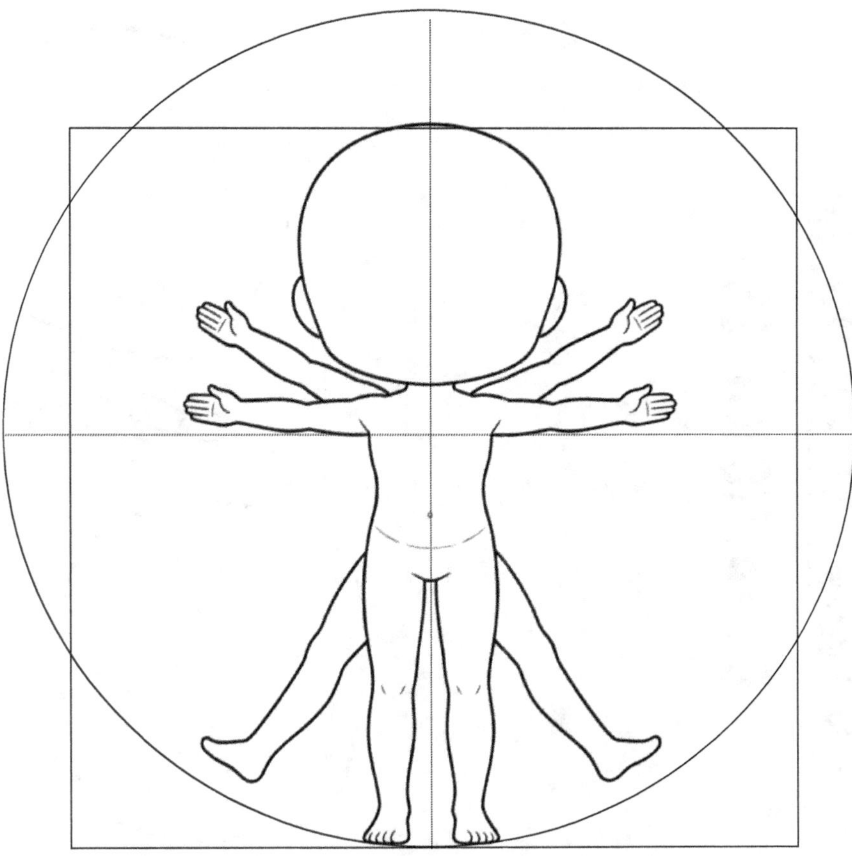

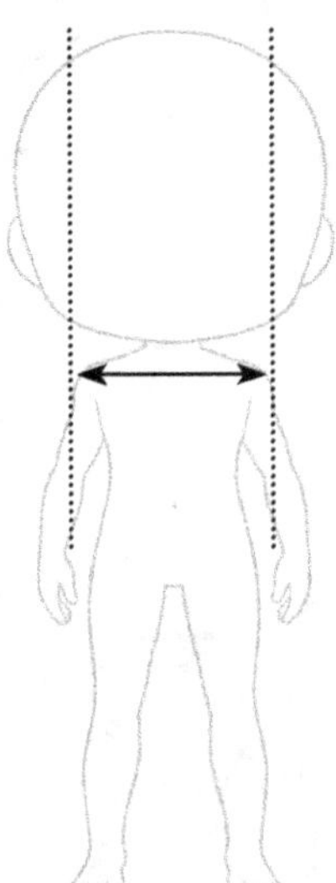

Chibi shoulders measure approximately ¾ of a head wide.

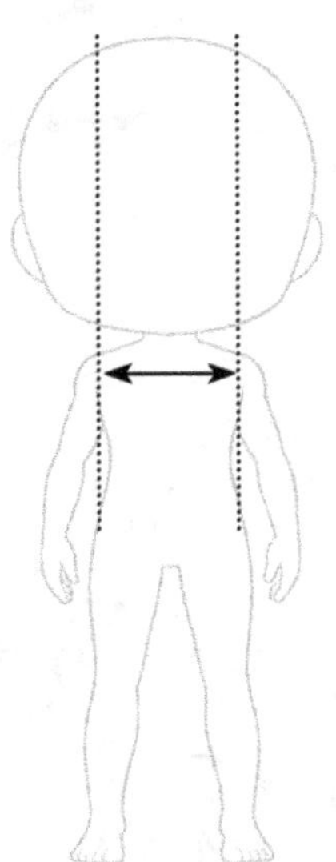

Chibi's torsos measure roughly ⅓ of a head wide.

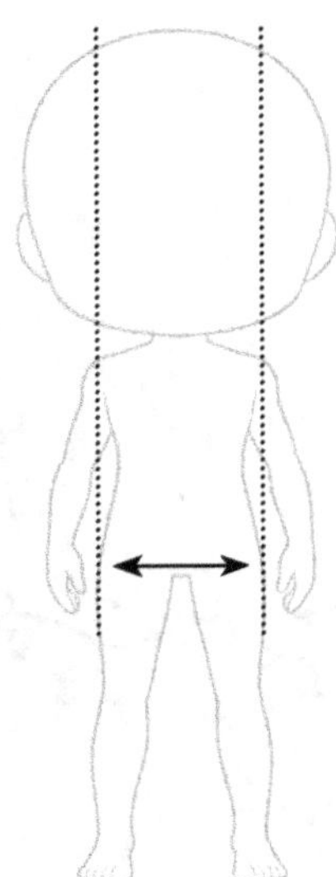

The hips of a chibi are approximately ½ of a head in width.

DRAWING THE CHIBI IN DYNAMIC POSES

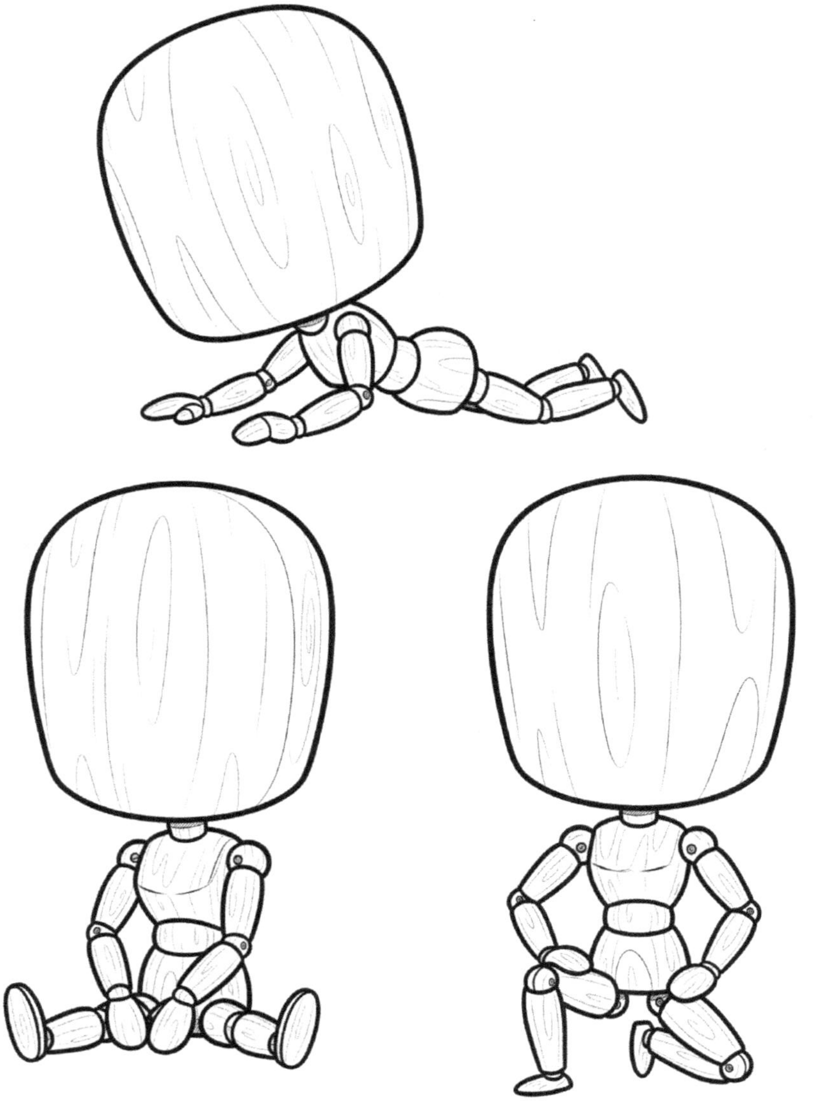

Pro tip: Chibi bodies comprise of simple, readable shapes, so focus on a clear silhouette over anatomy.

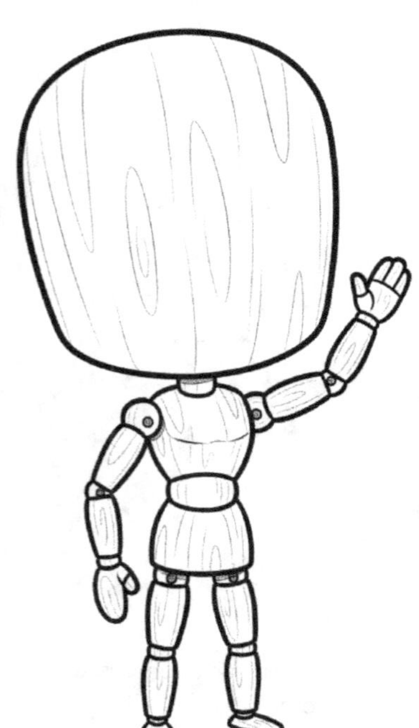

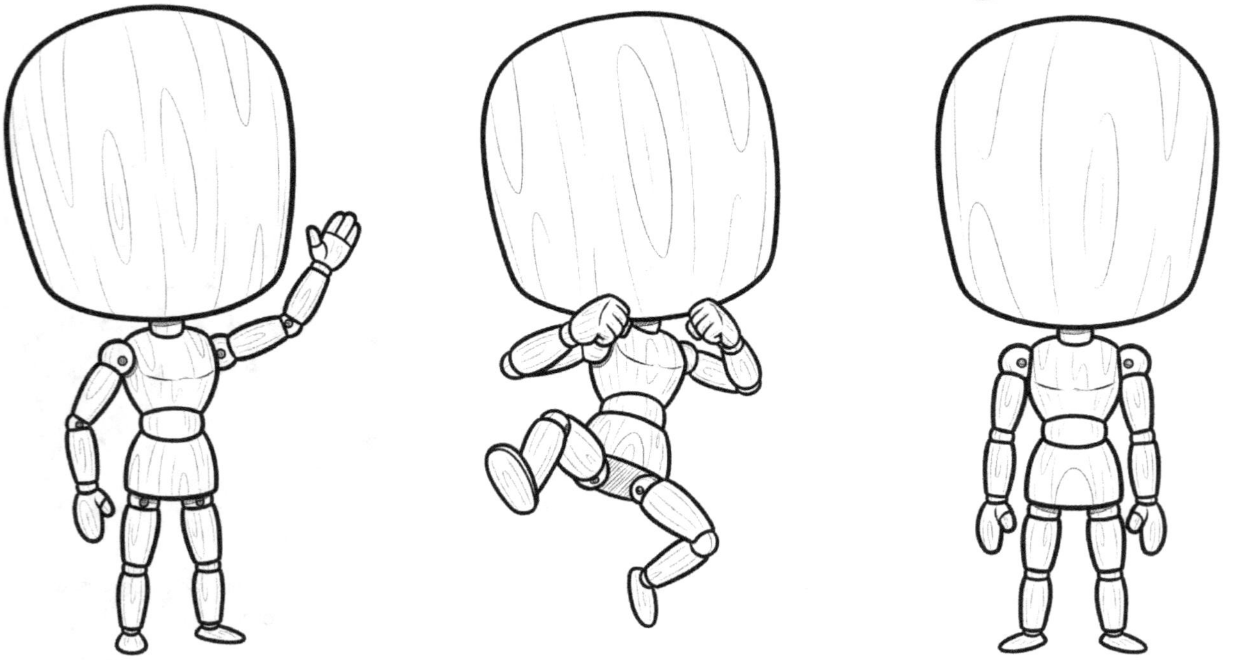

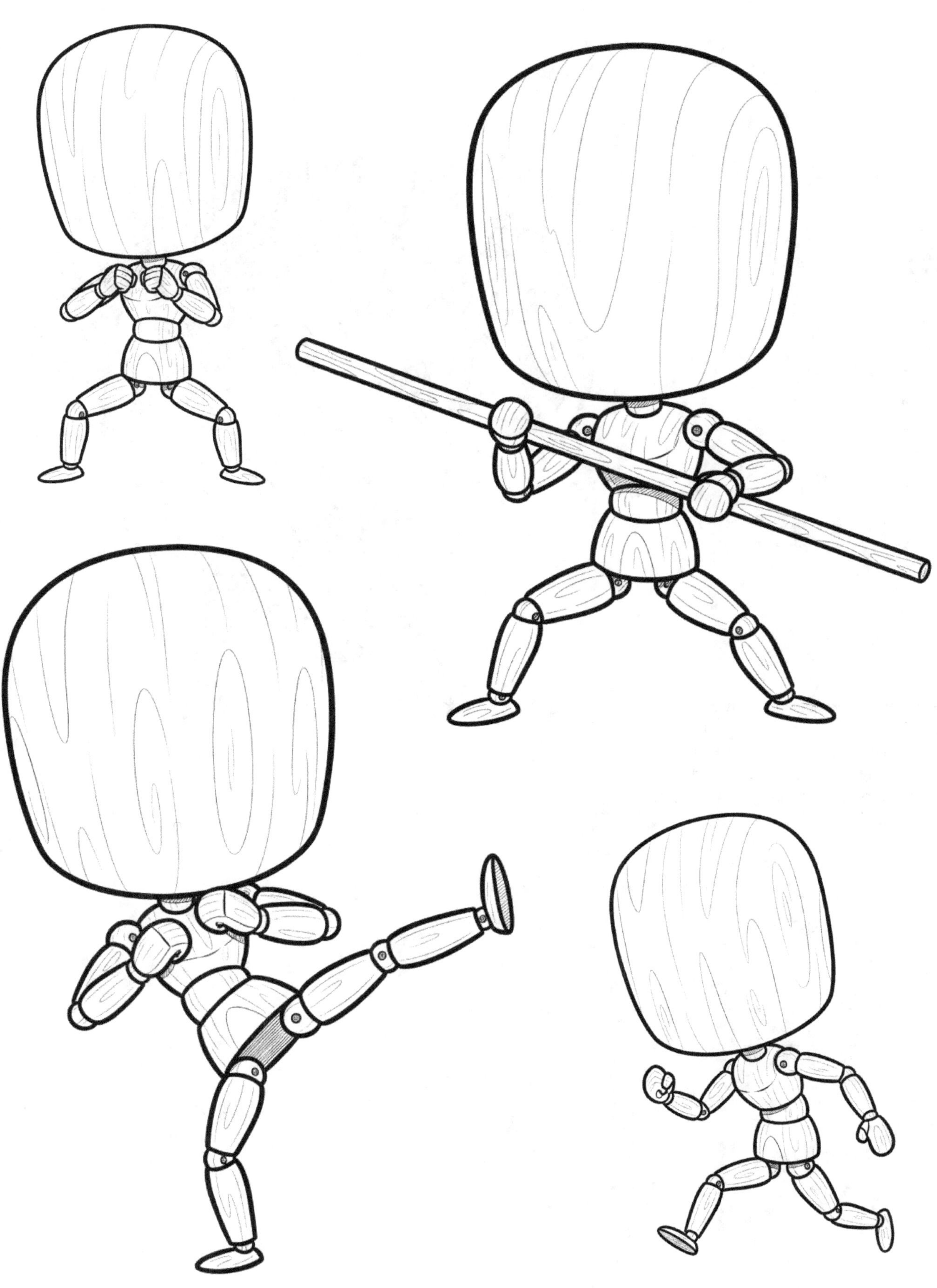

FEMALE CHIBI

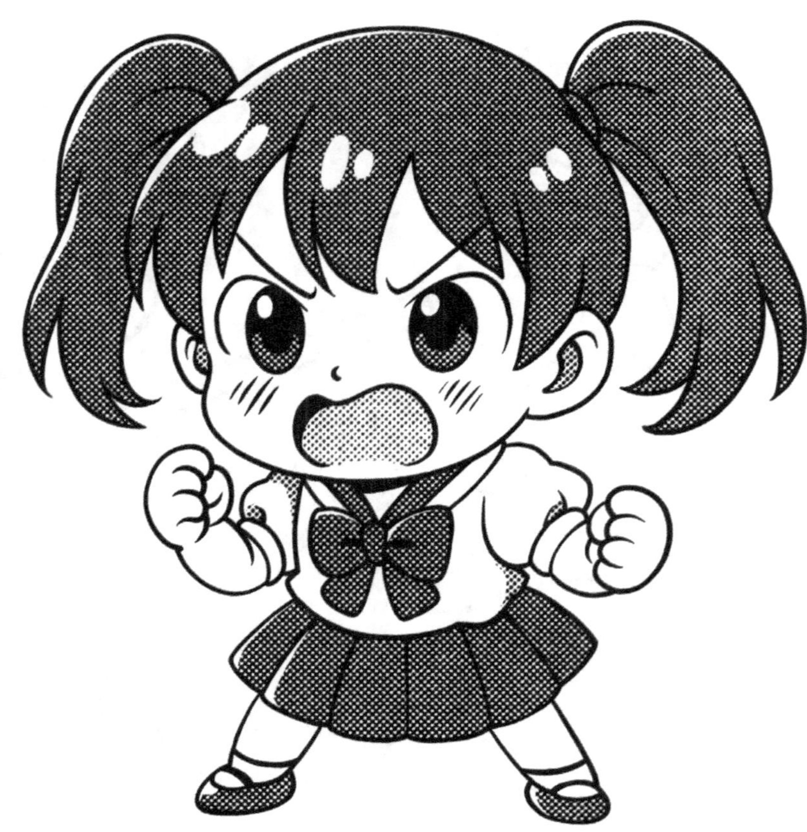

Pro Tip: For a female chibi character, aim for a height of about two and a half heads tall. Keep the limbs short and rounded, and exaggerate the head size to emphasise cuteness and youthful appeal.

01

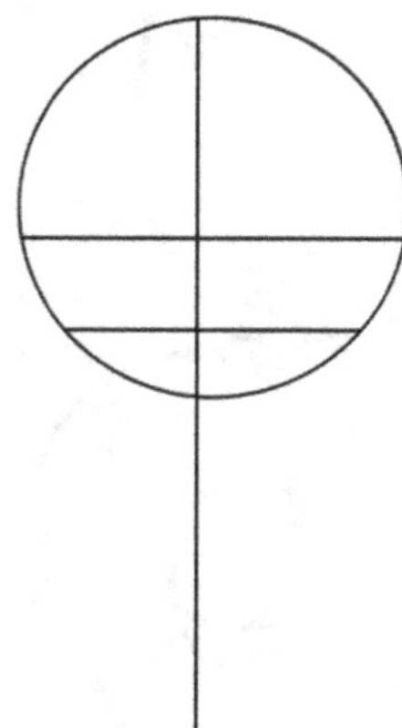

02

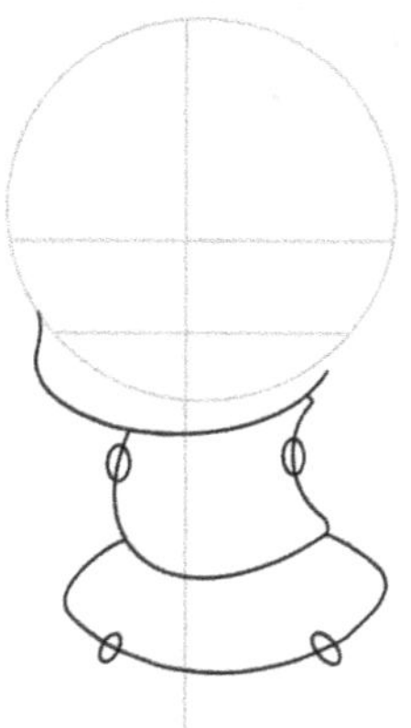

03

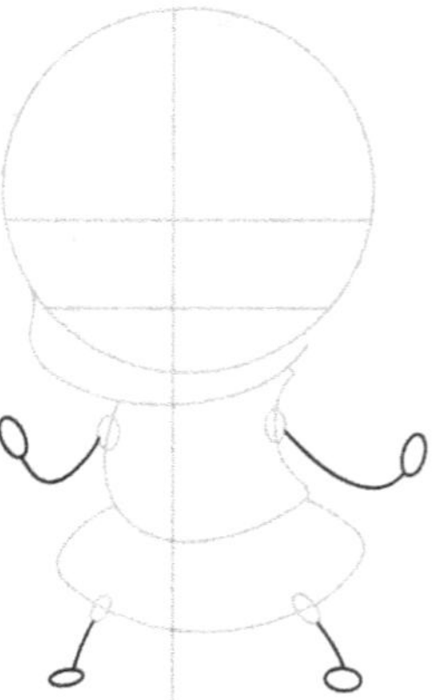

04

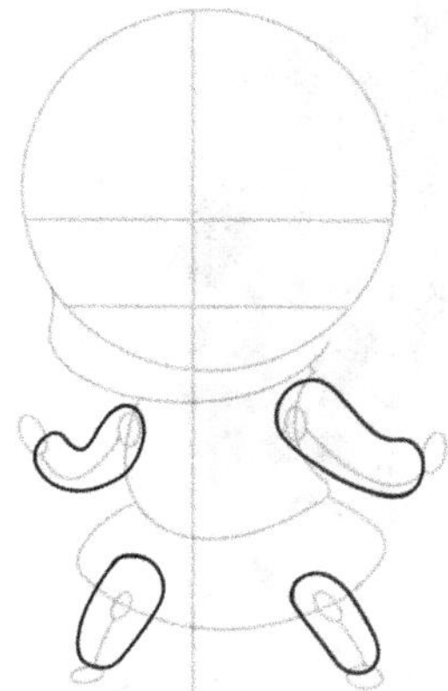

05

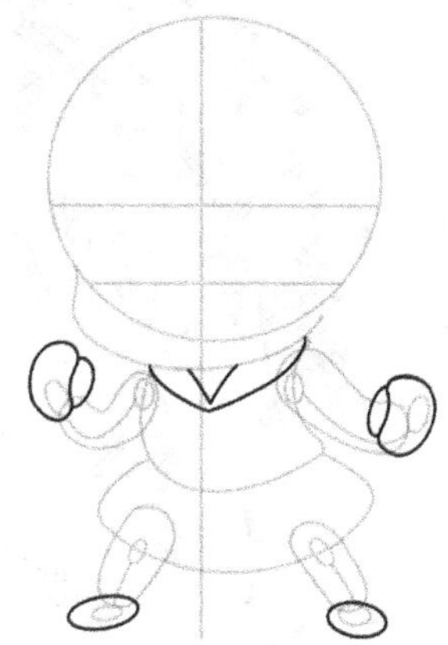

06

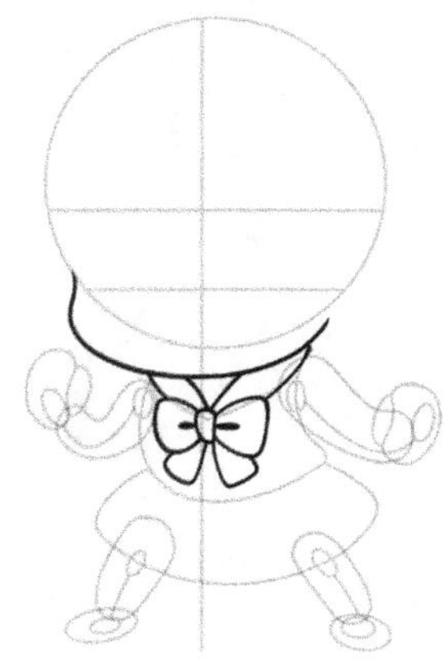

07

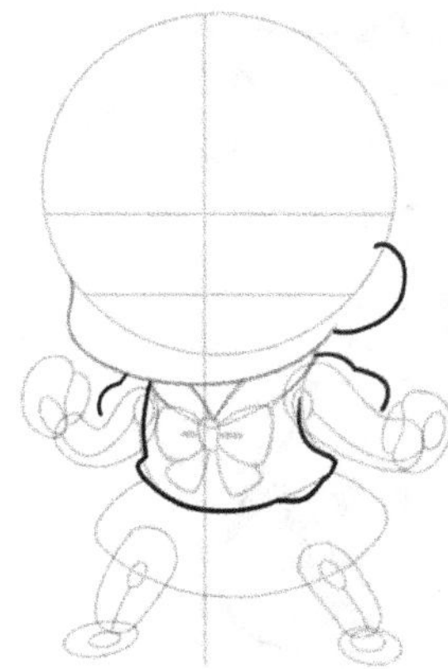

08

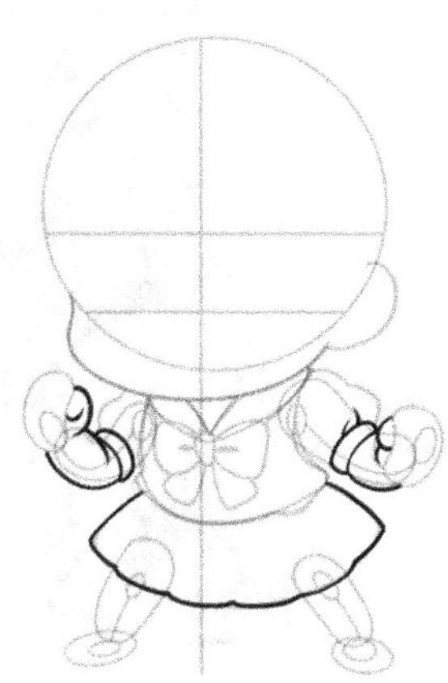

09

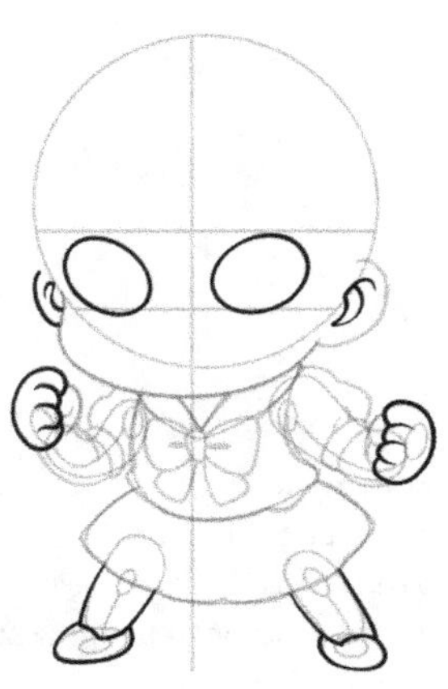

10

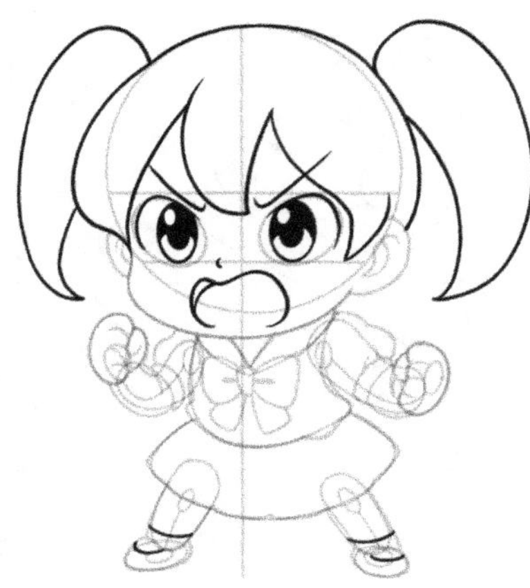

11

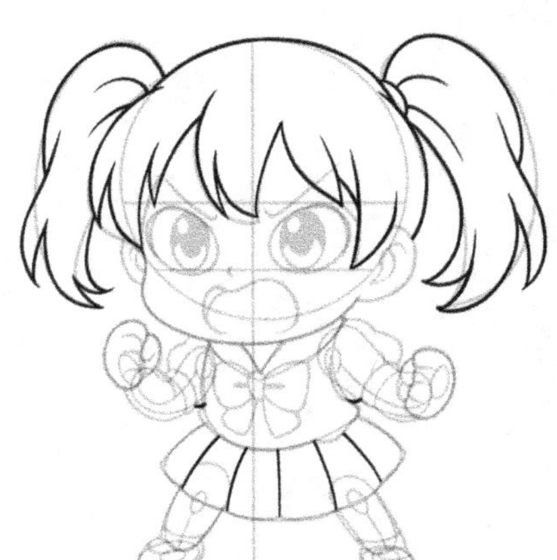

12

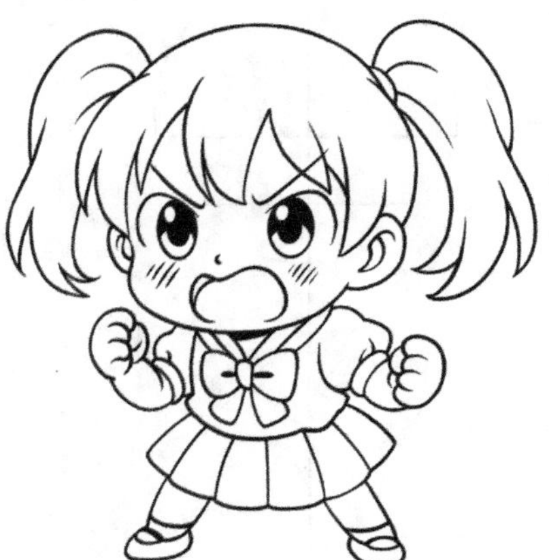

MALE CHIBI

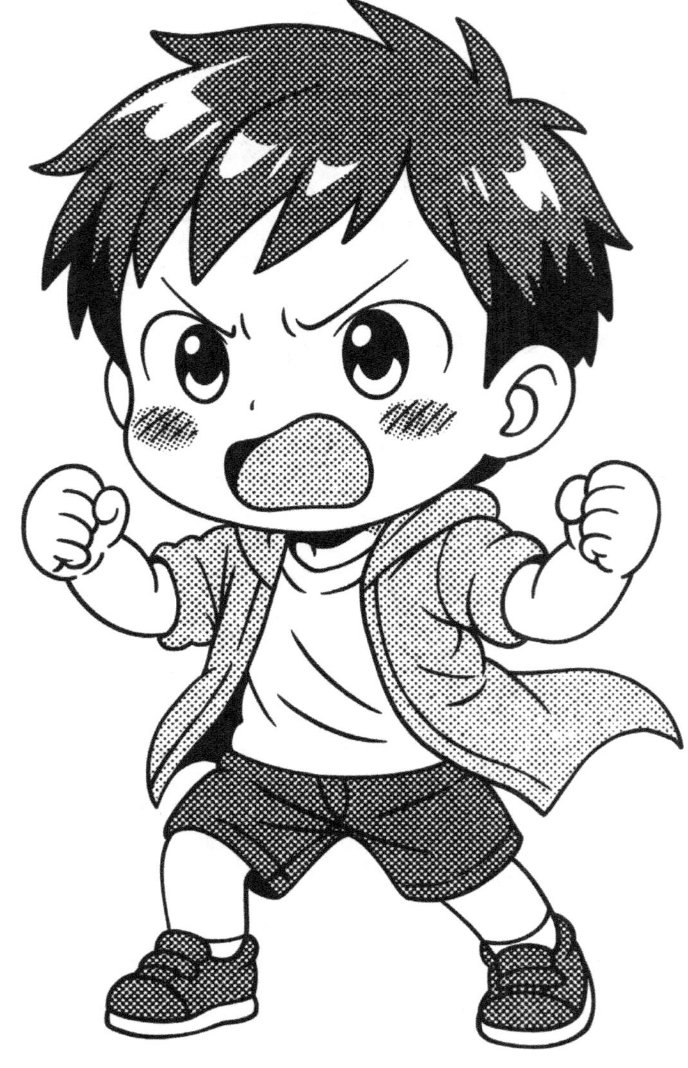

Pro Tip: For a male chibi character, aim for a height of about two and a half heads tall. Keep the limbs thick and expressive, and exaggerate the pose to show strong emotion and energy.

01

02

03

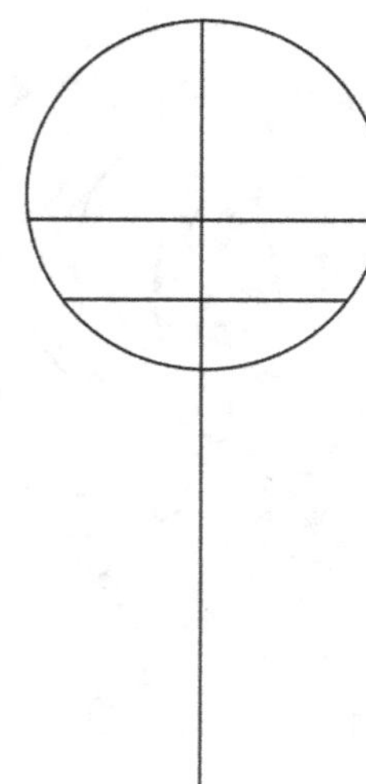

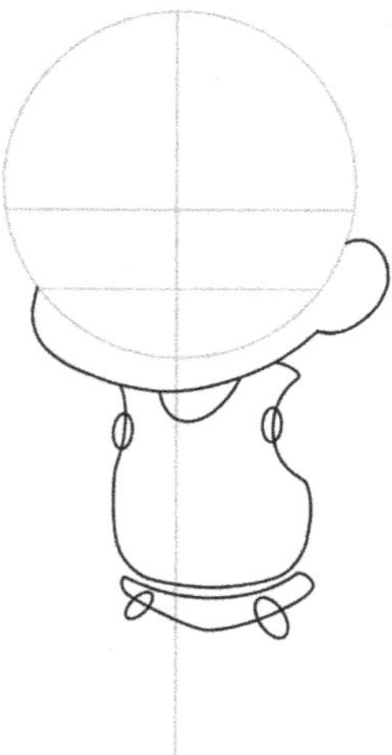

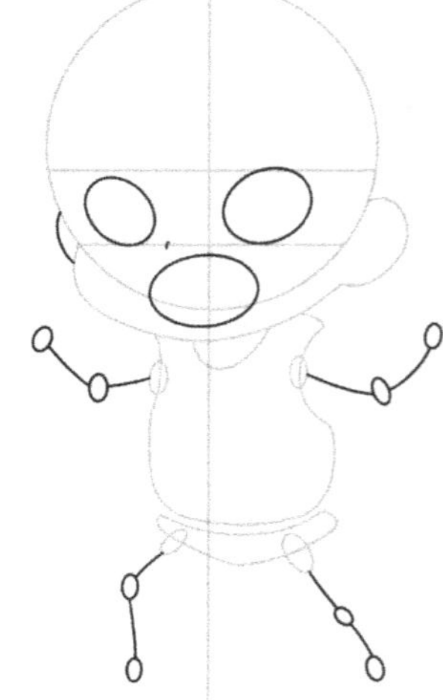

04

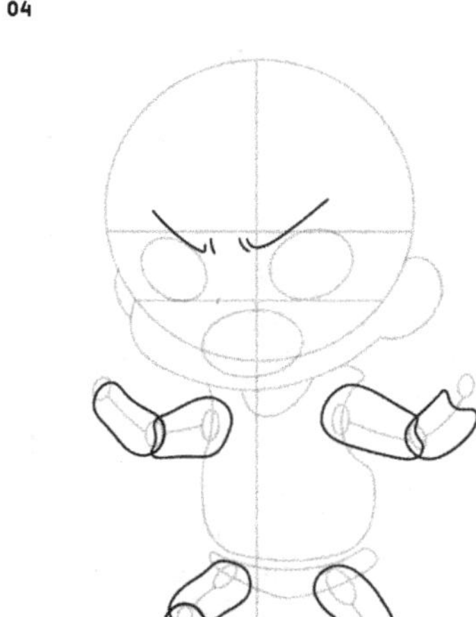

05

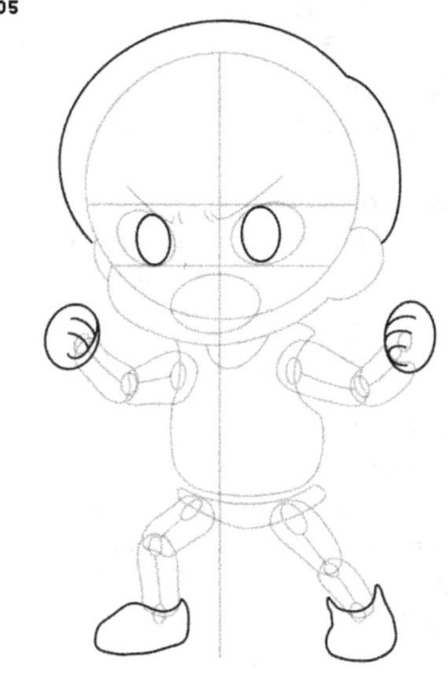

06

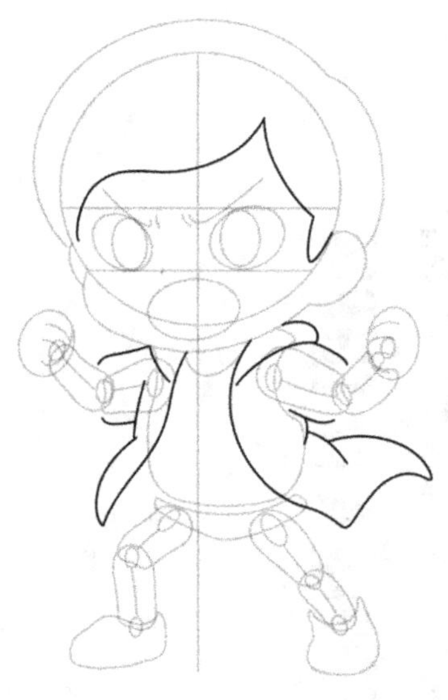

07

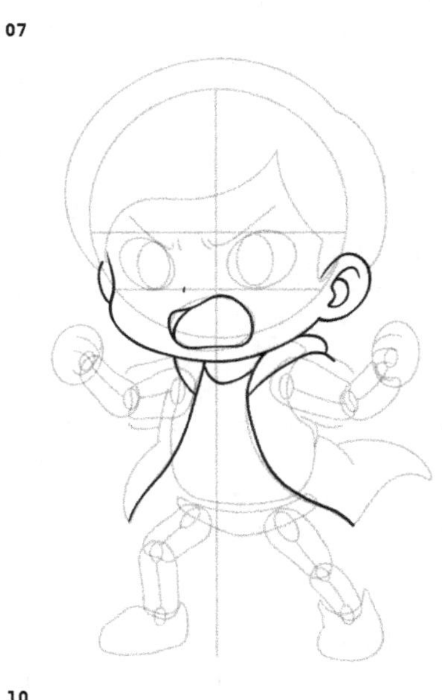

08

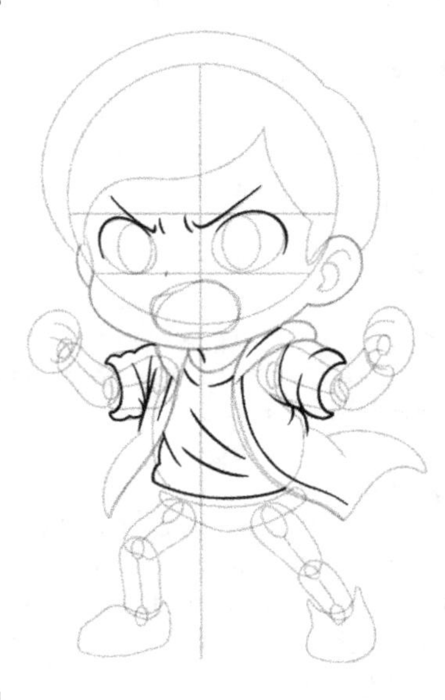

09

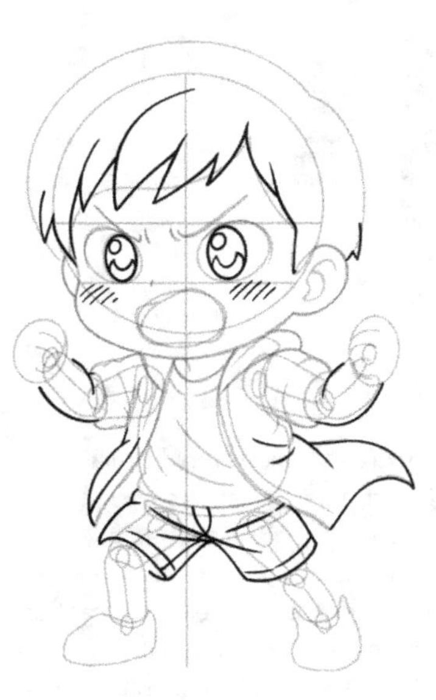

10

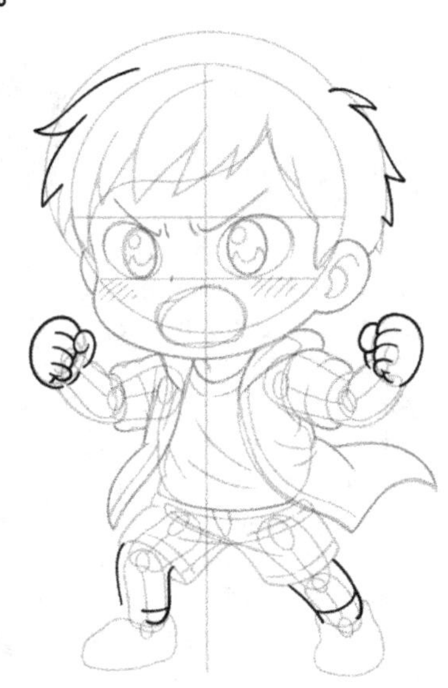

11

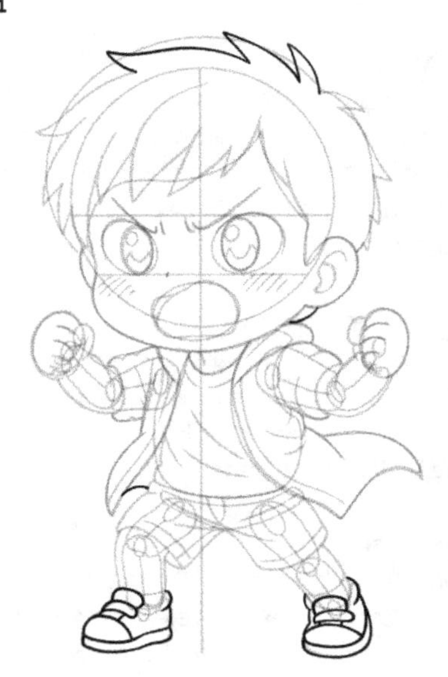

12

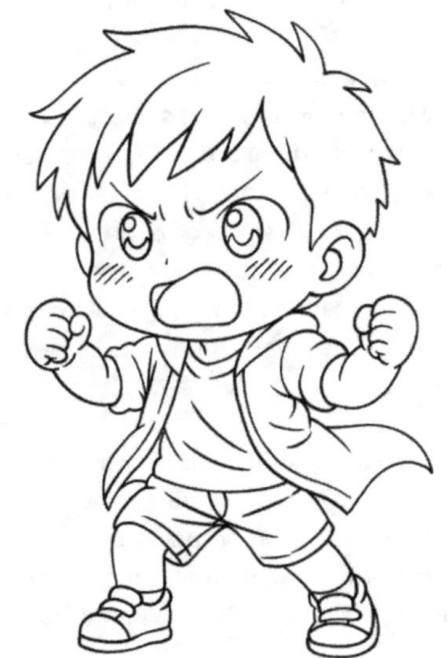

HOW TO DRAW ANIME

MANGA ARCHETYPES AND HOW TO DRAW THEM

Every great manga story is built on unforgettable characters, and those characters are often shaped by enduring archetypes. Understanding these archetypes—their personalities, emotions, and defining traits—gives you the foundation to design characters that feel authentic and visually compelling.

By studying common personality types, you'll learn how to express character through proportion, pose, and expression. A confident hero stands tall and open; a shy dandere averts her gaze and draws inward. Every design choice, from the angle of a stance to the shape of an eye, communicates who a character is before they even speak.

In this chapter, we'll explore some of the most recognisable manga archetypes. Use these as a starting point to experiment, combine traits, and create characters that not only look right but feel alive.

Young Male Hero

The rookie fighter. Impulsive, passionate and full of energy, he's driven by a desire to prove himself against impossible odds.

Young Female Hero

The spirited warrior. Bold, expressive and daring, she combines enthusiasm with compassion, often leading through emotion and instinct.

Adult Male Hero

The classic protagonist. Strong, honourable and courageous, he stands as the moral centre, ready to protect or fight for his ideals. Often a leader or mentor figure, he embodies resilience and conviction, inspiring others through action and unwavering purpose.

Adult Female Hero

The fearless leader. Agile, focused and brave, she represents independence and the power of will over circumstance.

Samurai

The disciplined warrior. Guided by honour, restraint and precision, this archetype embodies focus, purpose and mastery through self-control.

The Action Hero

Defined by explosive energy and physical power, this archetype channels raw emotion into action. Their strength often reflects their determination, making every blow a symbol of resolve.

The Ninja

Stealthy, disciplined and elusive, this archetype thrives on strategy and silence. Precision and agility define every movement, blending mystery with a lethal grace.

The Action Heroine

A fierce fighter who balances speed and strength. Her movements are deliberate and sharp, embodying skill, confidence and tactical intelligence.

The Muscle Man

Pure strength incarnate. Defined by size, confidence and explosive emotion, he's both protector and unstoppable force.

The Sensei

He is wise, calm and formidable. A master of discipline who teaches through his experience and example rather than his words.

The Martial Arts Expert

Centred, powerful and precise. Every movement reflects years of mastery and inner balance.

The Loner

Detached but observant, this character moves to his own rhythm. Reserved and mysterious, he often hides depth beneath indifference.

The Mysterious Figure

A figure of intrigue and restraint. Rarely expressive, their presence evokes tension, secrecy and quiet power.

The Villain

Confident, calculated and charismatic. Whether charming or ruthless, this archetype personifies ambition unbound by morality.

The Rival

Prideful and driven, the rival mirrors the hero's potential, pushing both characters toward their limits and revealing their true strength through intense competition and contrast.

The Delinquent

Rebellious and confident, this archetype thrives on defiance. Beneath the swagger, there's often vulnerability and loyalty.

The Reluctant Hero

Burdened by doubt or regret, this character doesn't seek glory but finds strength in necessity and their personal moral awakening.

The Cyberpunk

Cool, detached and tech-enhanced, this archetype merges humanity with machinery, representing rebellion and the cost of progress. Often cynical yet idealistic, they question control and humanity.

The Mecha Pilot
Disciplined and tactical, the pilot's resolve is tested by technology and teamwork. They are a symbol of courage and control.

The Butler
Refined, articulate and controlled. This archetype serves with grace, concealing intelligence and strength beneath reserved formality.

The Comic Relief
Exaggerated, clumsy and lovable. This character breaks tension through over-the-top emotion and physical comedy.

The Animal Sidekick
Loyal, funny and expressive. Often a guide or companion, providing comic relief and emotional connection.

The Witch
Mysterious and alluring, she bridges the mystical and the human. Often wise, mischievous or morally ambiguous.

The Goddess
Graceful and commanding, embodying beauty, wisdom and authority. She inspires awe and reverence through presence alone.

Moe-Style Cute Girl
Bright, innocent and irresistibly expressive. Large eyes and open gestures convey warmth, curiosity and personal charm.

Idol Singer
Charismatic and radiant, this character shines with confidence and emotional energy, embodying joy and performance.

The Magical Girl
The embodiment of hope and transformation. She channels courage and love into power, balancing vulnerability with strength.

Kemonomimi Girl
Playful and instinctive. Animal features blend with human traits to create charm, agility and unpredictable energy. Their expressive ears and tails often mirror emotions and feelings.

The Dandere
Quiet, shy and introspective. She communicates through subtle gestures and silences, revealing depth through their stillness.

The Kuudere
Cool and controlled, showing emotion only in rare moments. Her restraint makes every glance or smile meaningful.

The Yandere
Obsessive love personified. Sweet on the surface but dangerously intense beneath, driven by devotion that borders on madness.

The Tsundere
Tough exterior, soft heart. Combines pride and vulnerability, often hiding affection behind irritation or denial.

Understanding archetypes is the first step toward designing characters that connect with readers. Each of these profiles captures a familiar personality, emotion or motivation that helps you communicate identity through form and gesture. As you practise drawing them, pay attention to how posture, proportion and expression reveal who a character is. Once you're comfortable, start blending traits, subverting expectations and inventing your own combinations. Every great manga artist learns the rules of archetypes not to follow them rigidly, but to transform them into something uniquely their own.

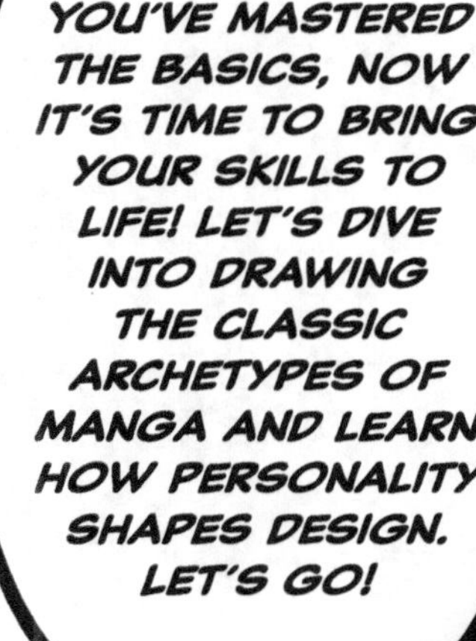

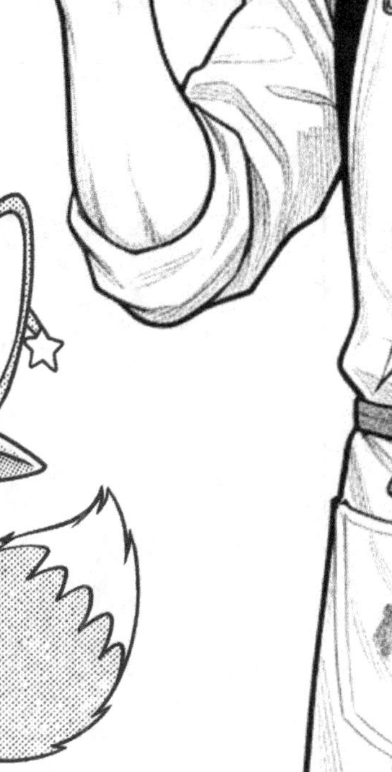

YOUNG MALE HERO

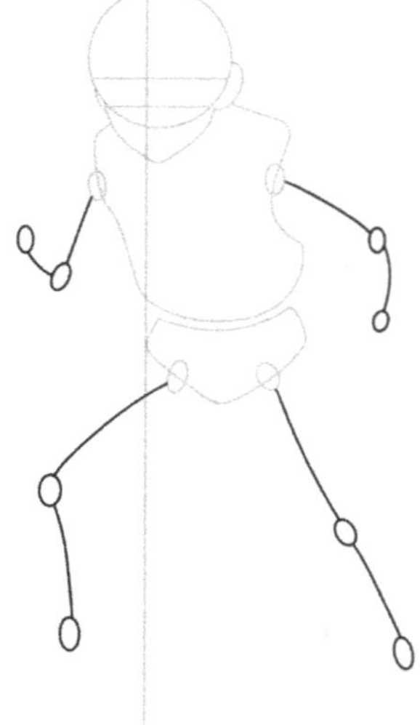

Pro Tip: Lower the stance and bend the knees to show tension and readiness. Keep the fists raised near the chest to add s sense of determination and power to the pose.

01

02

03

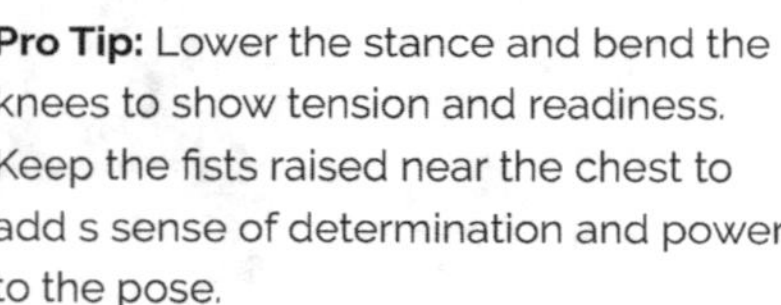

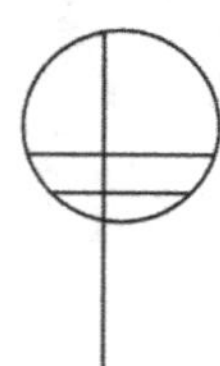

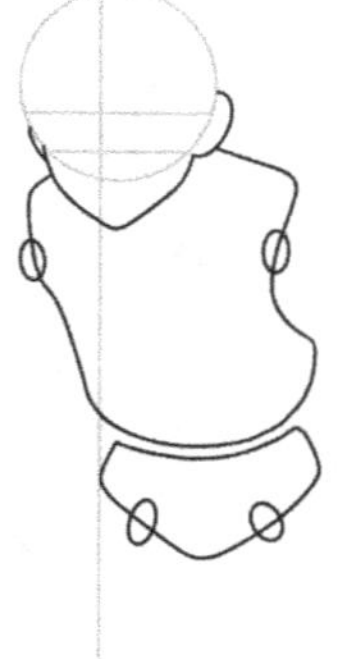

04

05

06

07

08

09

10

11

12

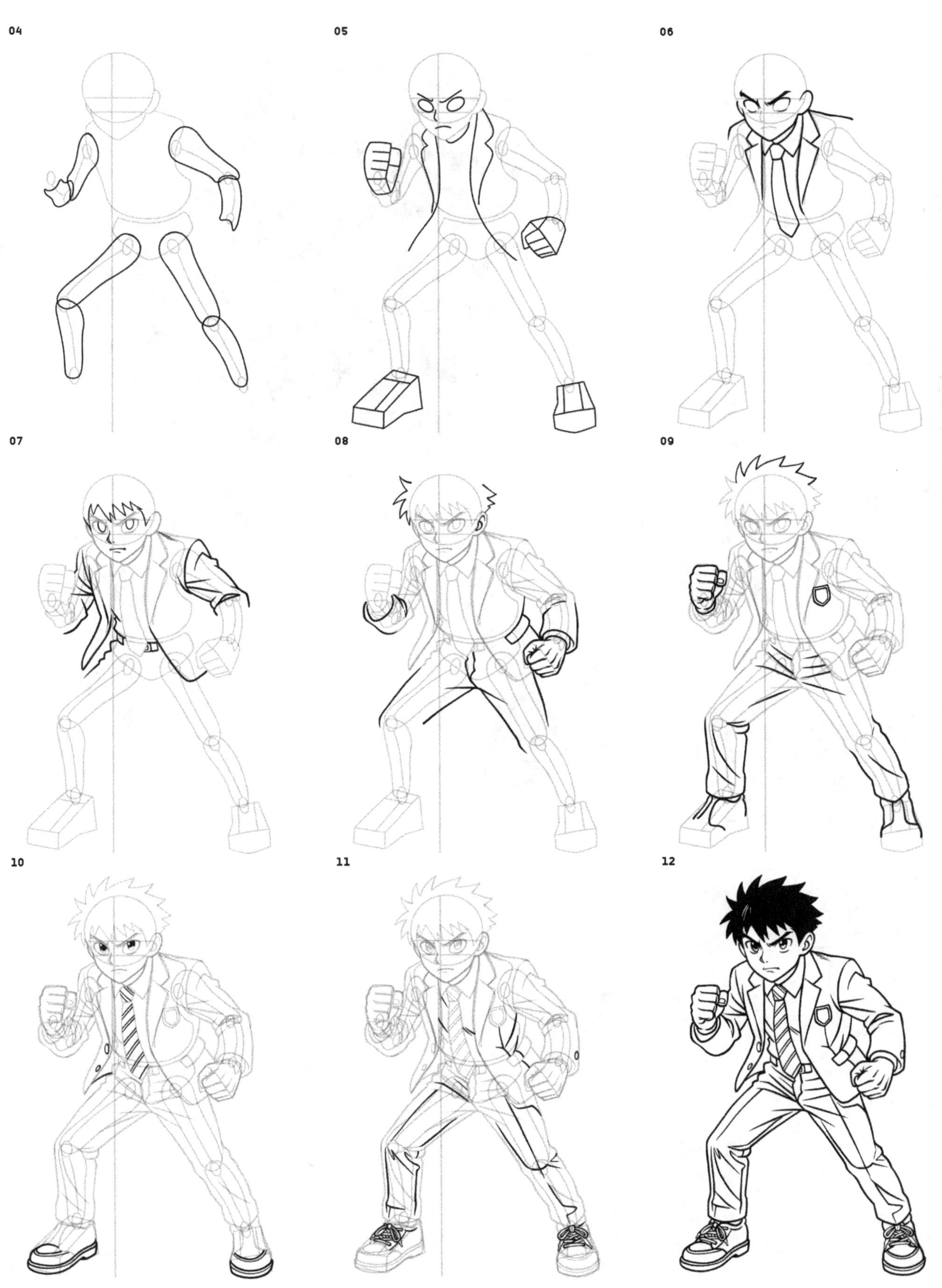

YOUNG FEMALE HERO

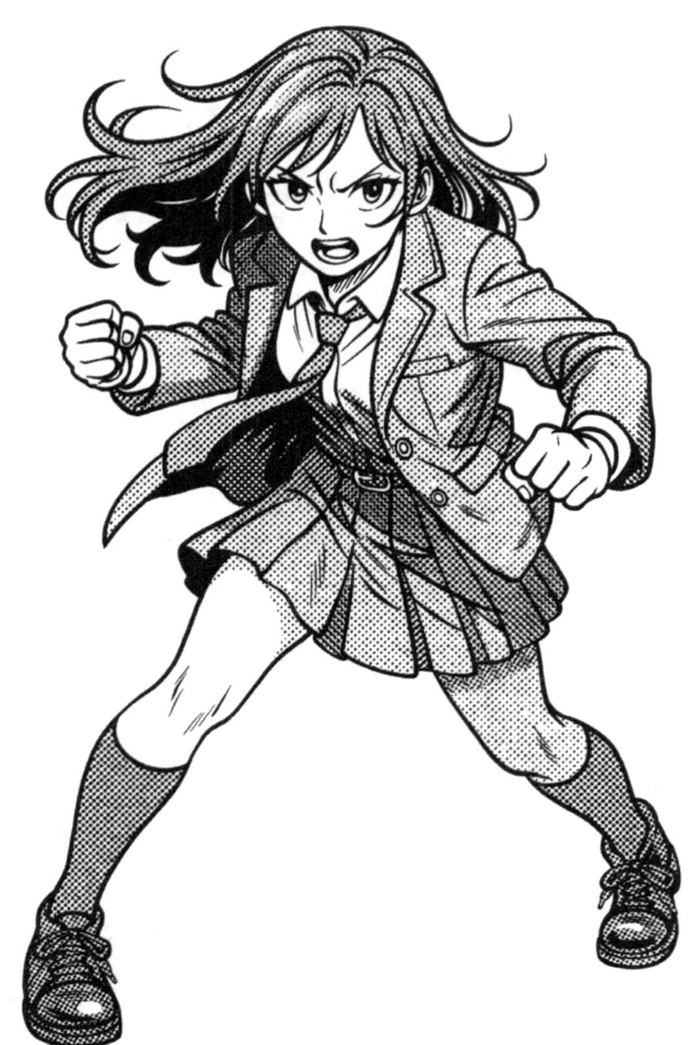

Pro Tip: Keep the stance wide and balanced, with one shoulder slightly forward. Use flowing hair or clothing lines to enhance movement and add a sense of energy in the pose.

01

02

03

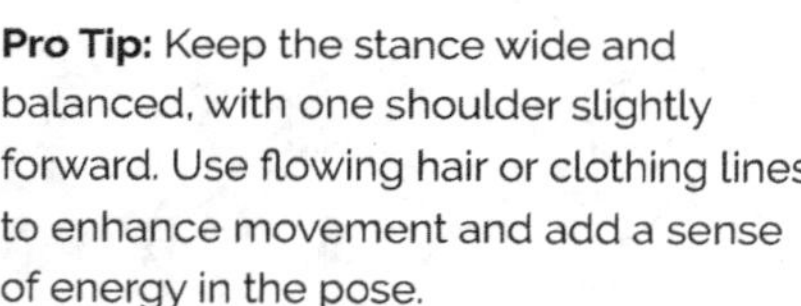

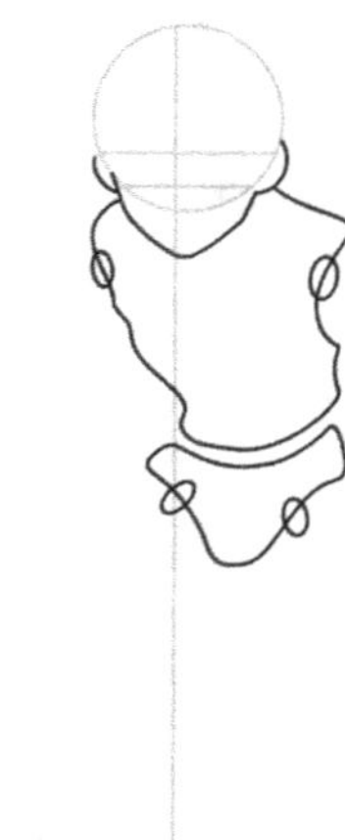

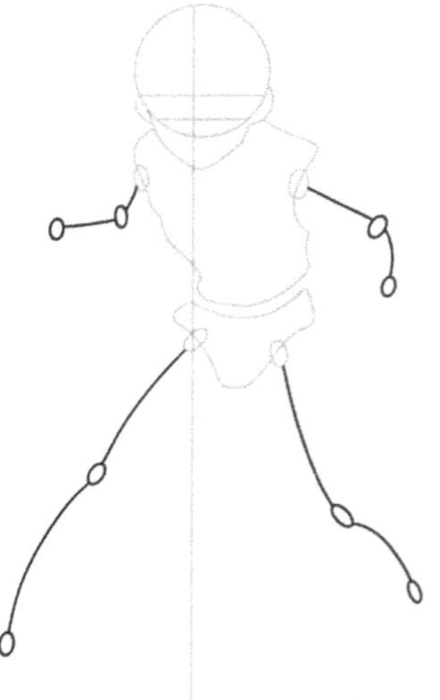

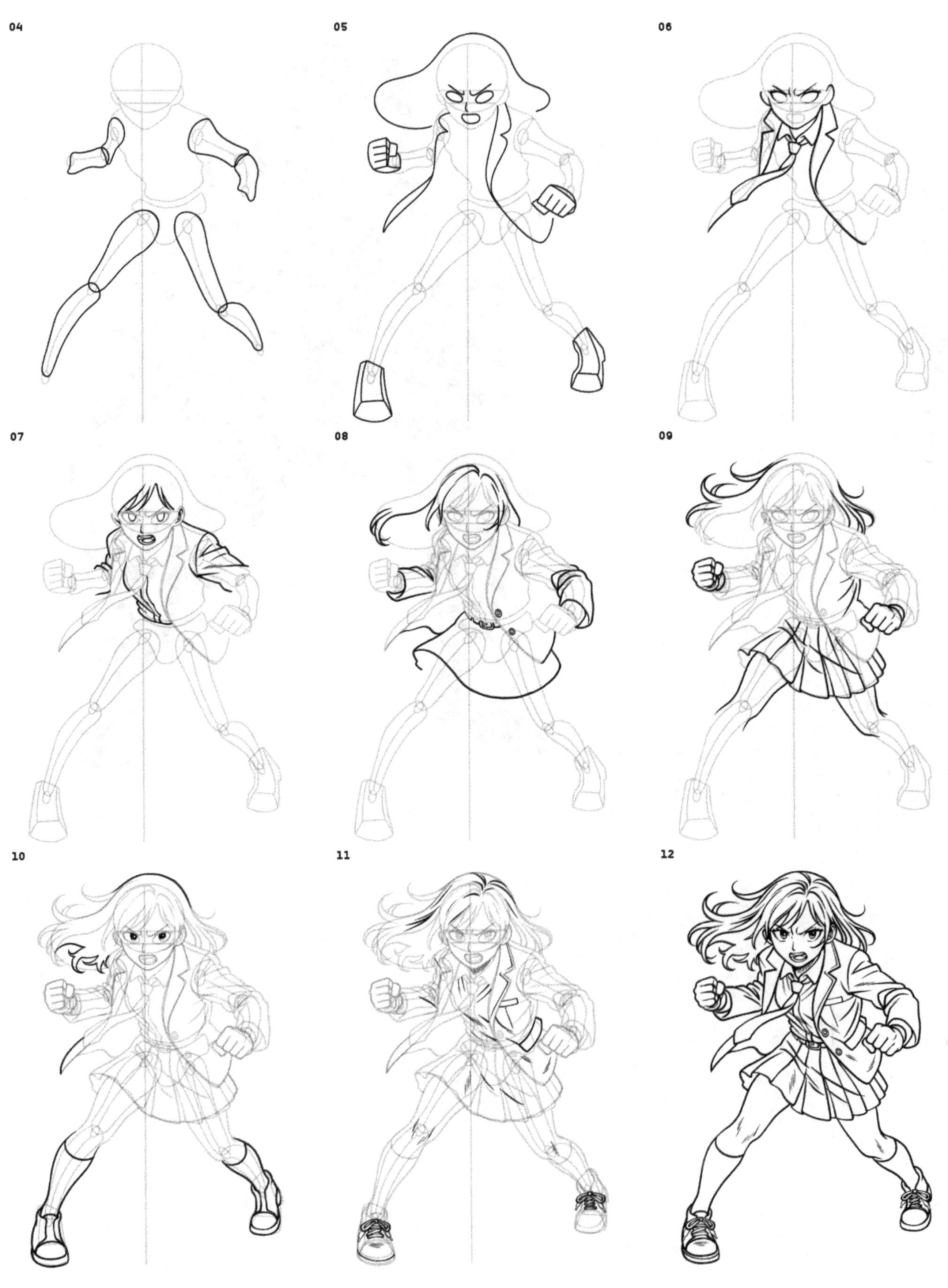

04
05
06
07
08
09
10
11
12
HOW TO DRAW ANIME

ADULT MALE HERO

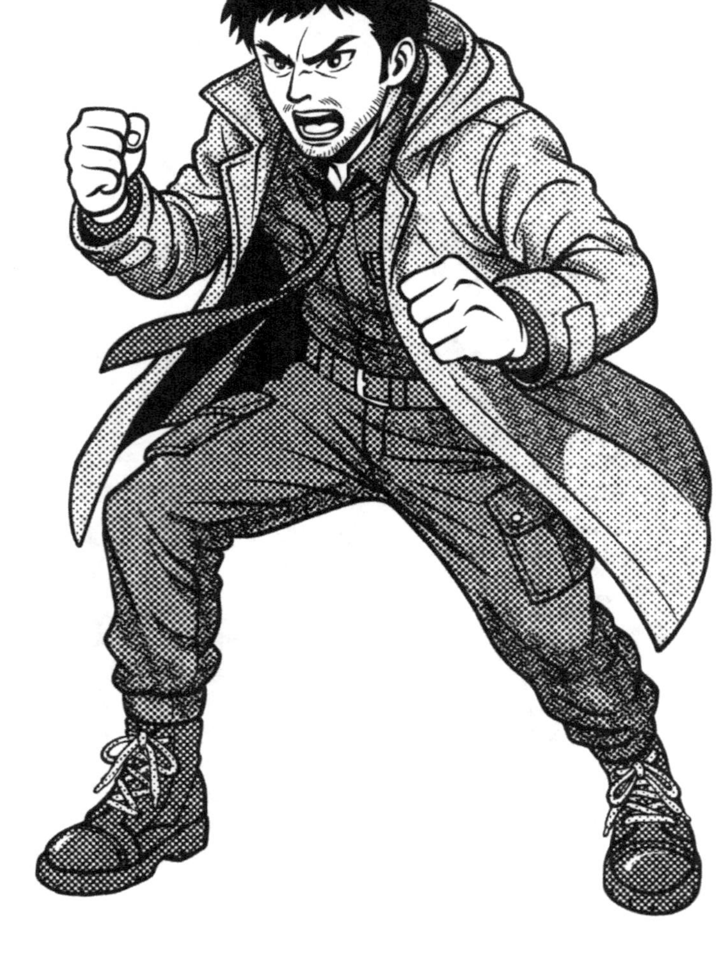

Pro Tip: Hero pose - widen the stance and lower the centre of gravity to show strength and stability. Keep the fists level with the chest and angle the shoulders forward to add power and intensity.

01

02

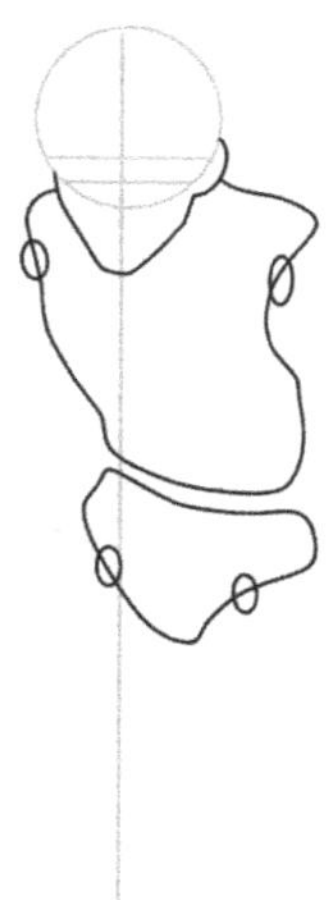

03

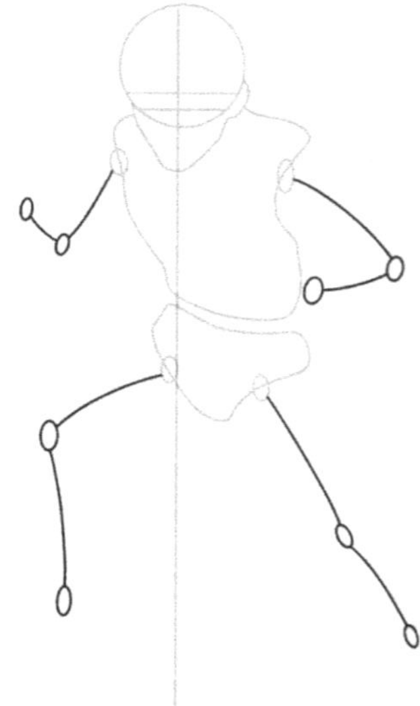

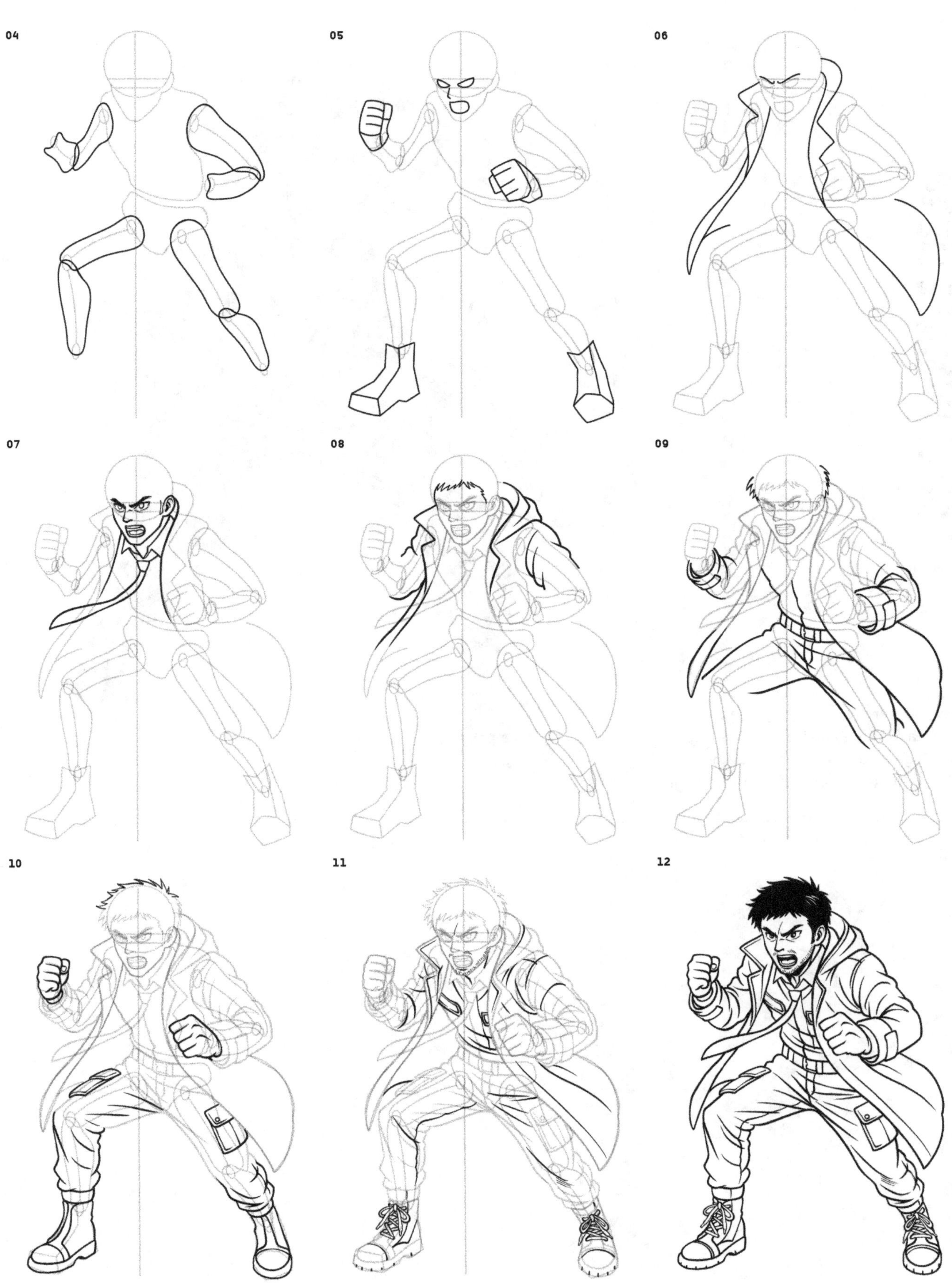

04

05

06

07

08

09

10

11

12

HOW TO DRAW ANIME

ADULT FEMALE HERO

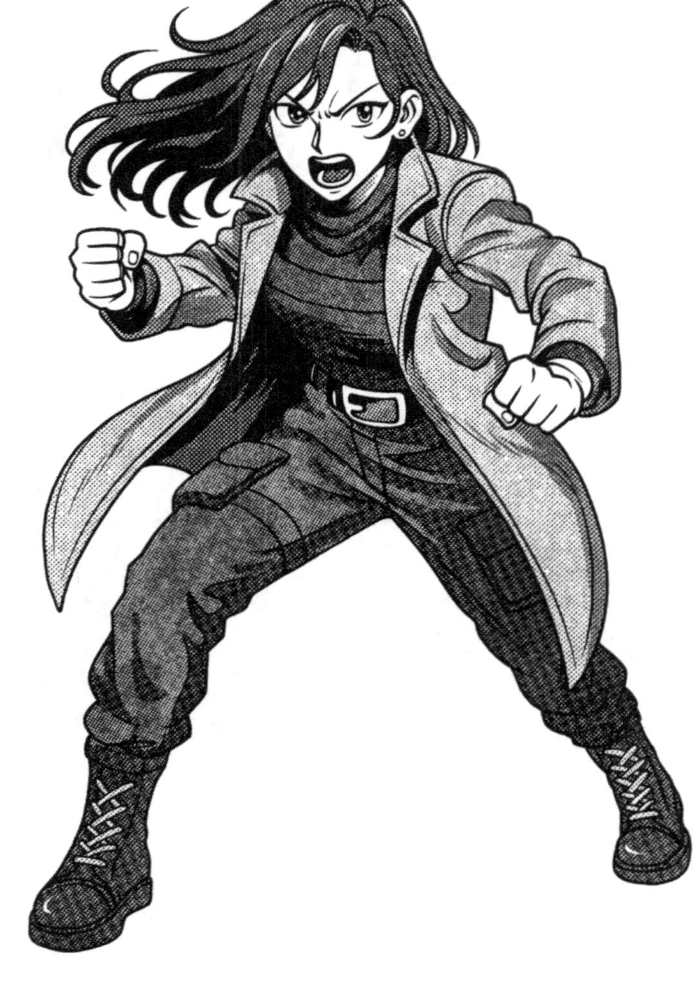

Pro Tip: For a female hero pose, keep the stance wide and low, with the torso leaning forward. Angle the fists toward the viewer to add power and movement.

01

02

03

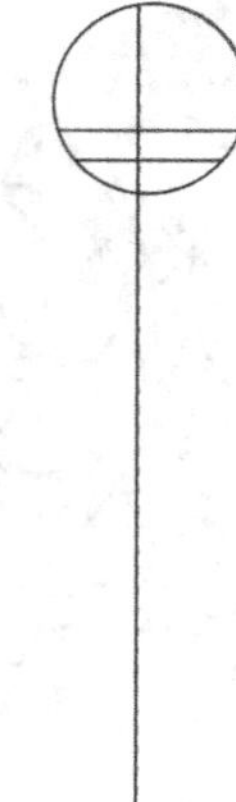

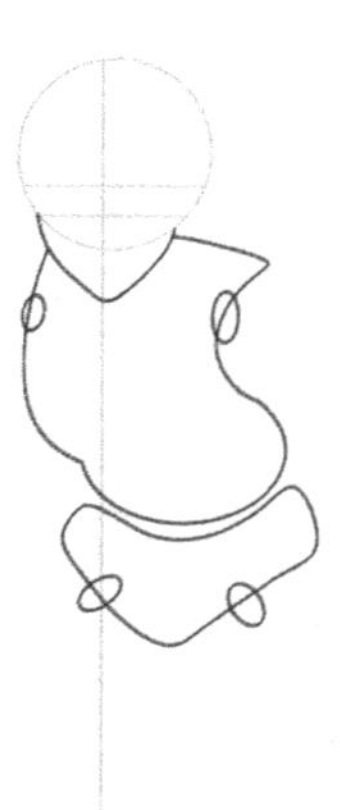

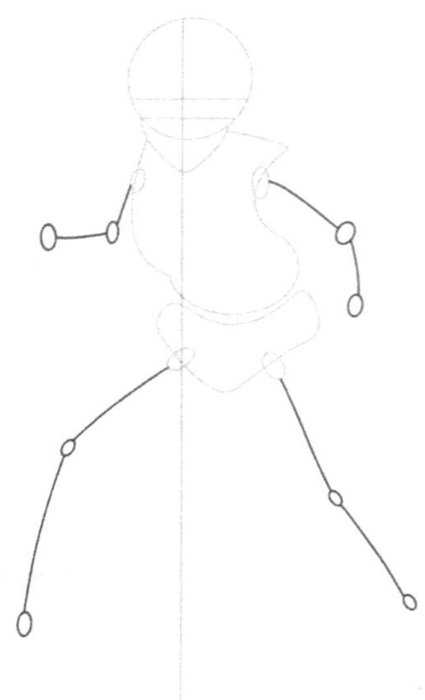

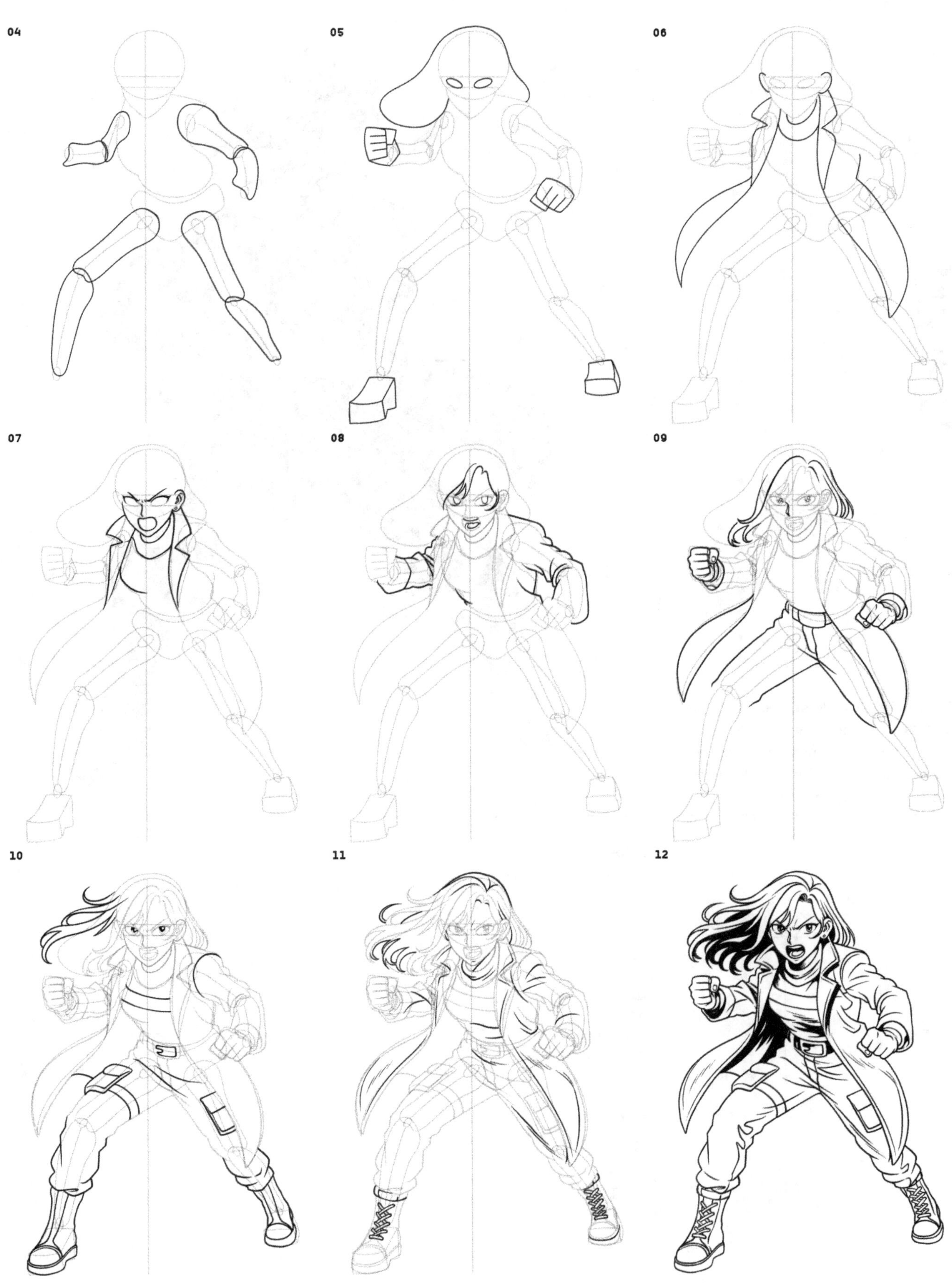

HOW TO DRAW ANIME

SAMURAI

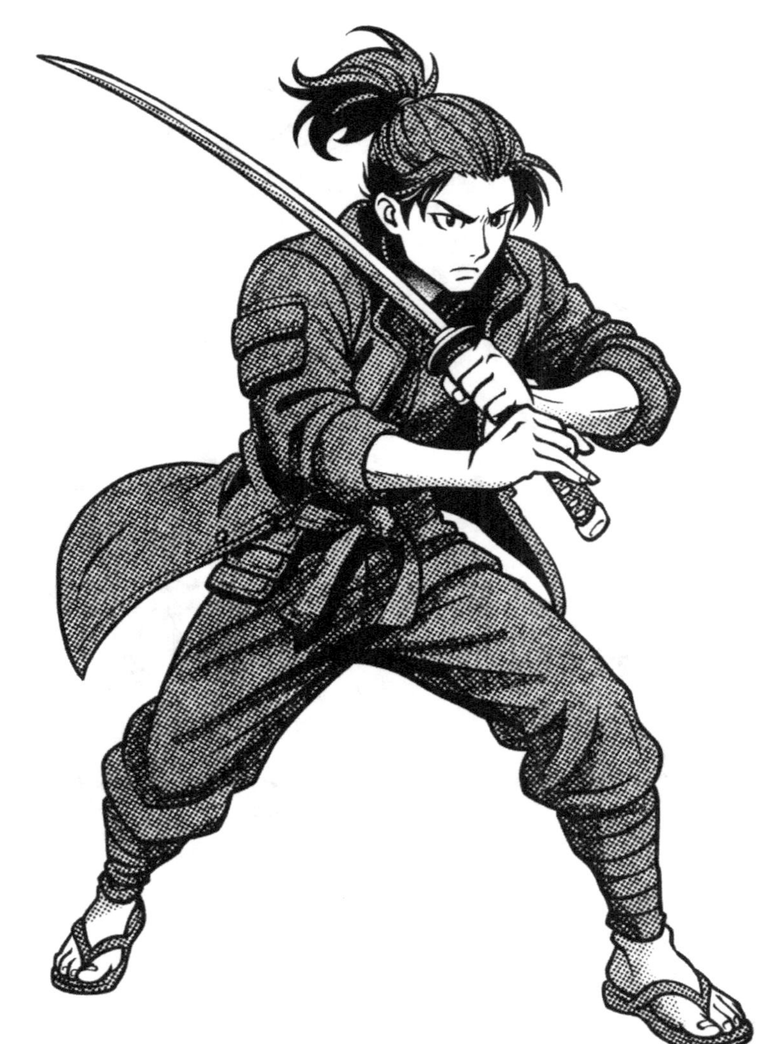

Pro Tip: Keep the knees bent and the feet grounded to show stability. Angle the sword along the centre line of the body to guide the viewer's eye and convey focus and precision.

01

02

03

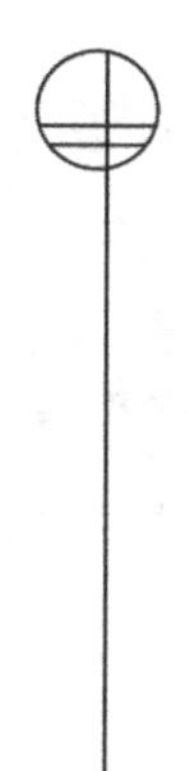

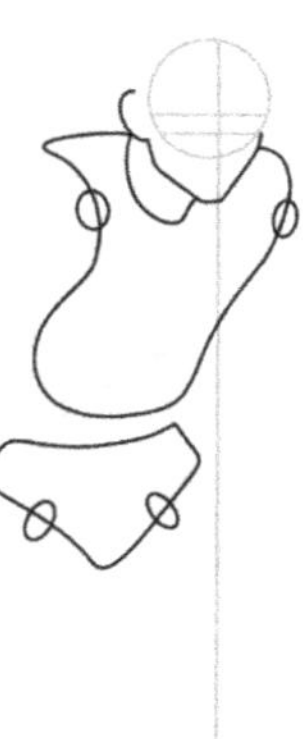

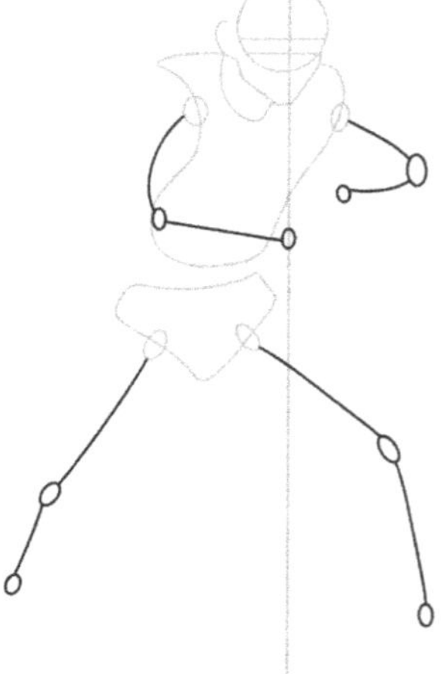

04

05

06

07

08

09

10

11

12

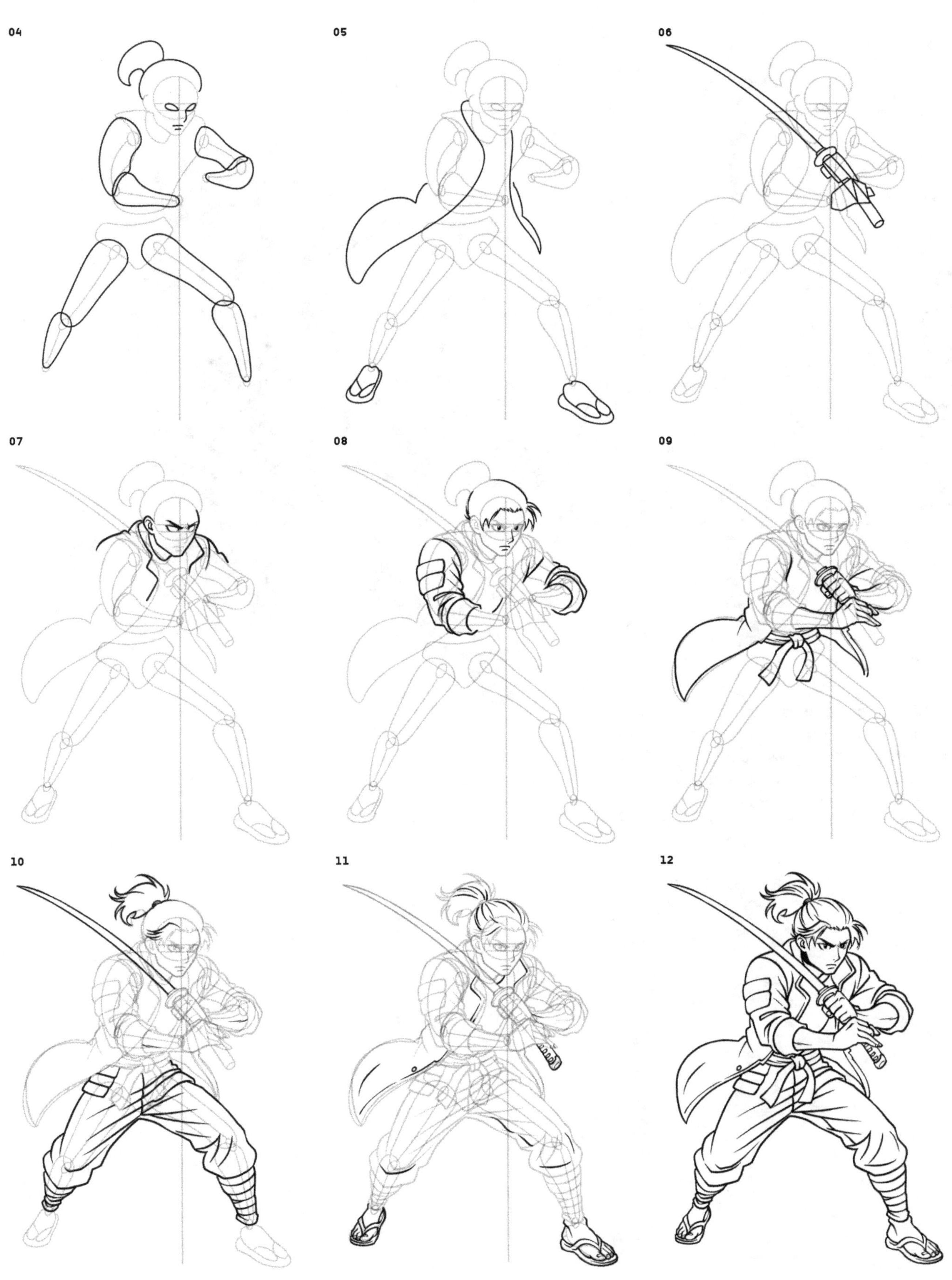

THE ACTION HERO

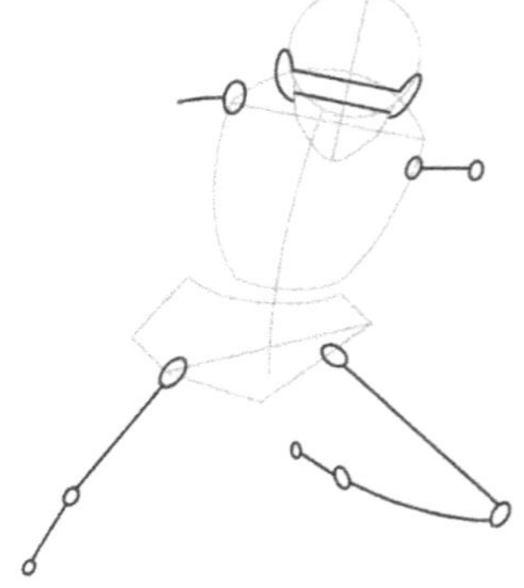

Pro Tip: Use strong foreshortening on the punching arm to push it toward the viewer. Keep the torso twisting with the motion and the back leg bent to show power and forward momentum.

01

02

03

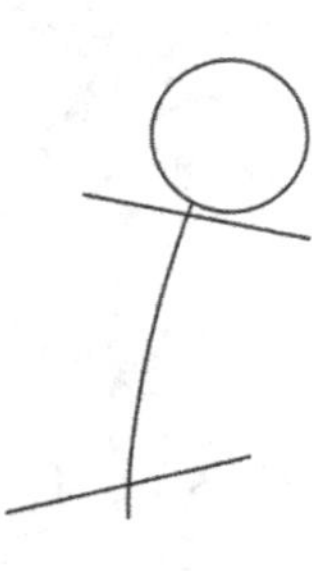

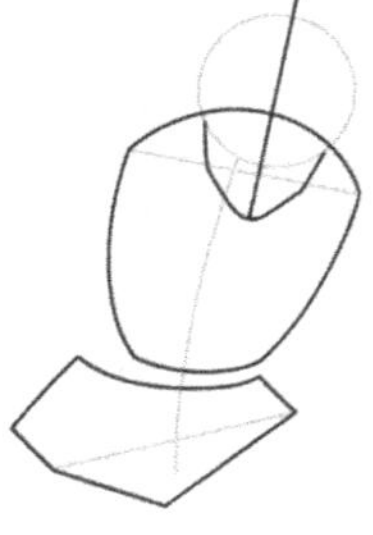

04

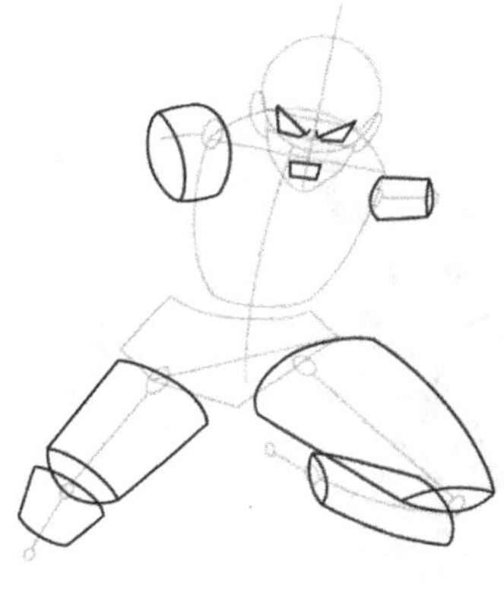

05

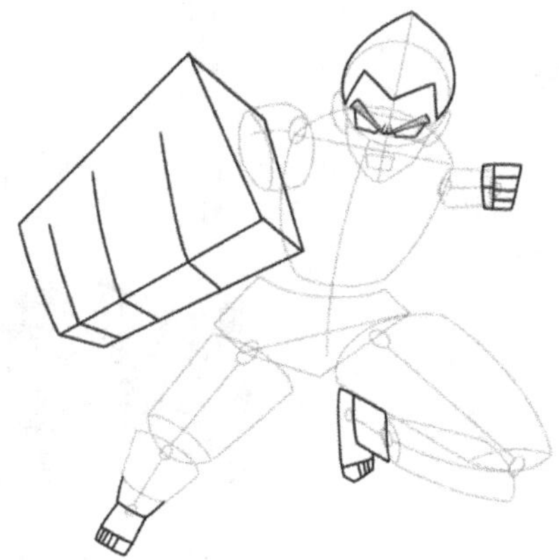

06

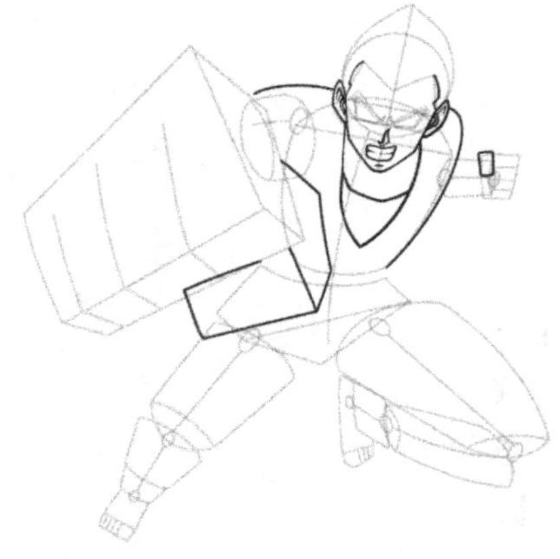

07

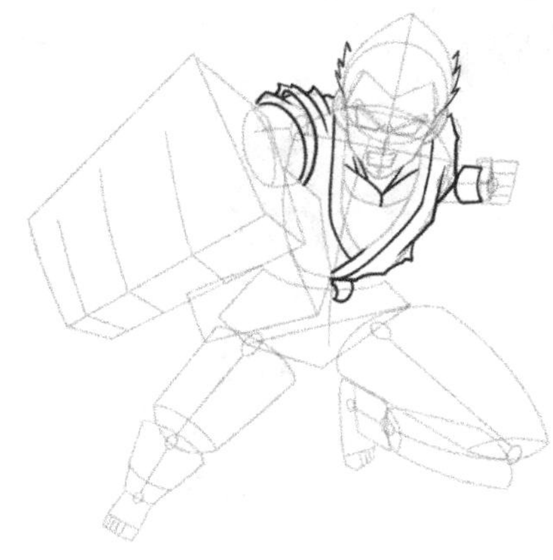

08

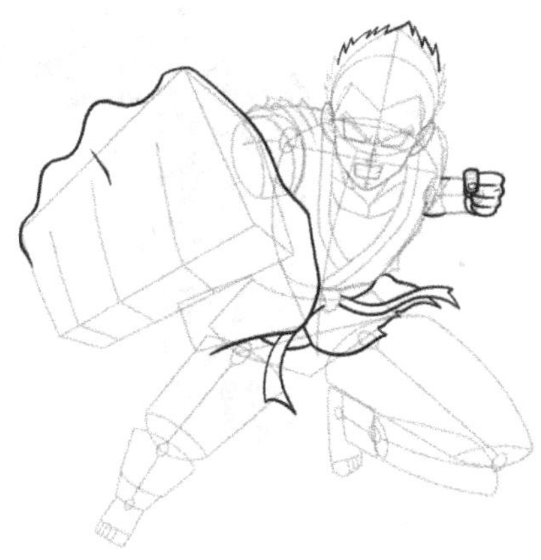

09

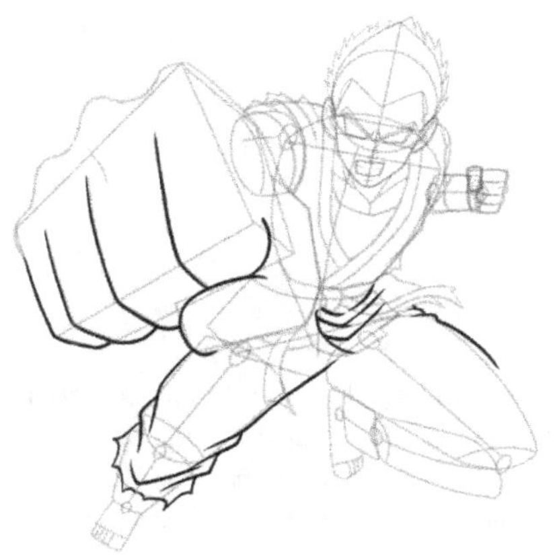

10

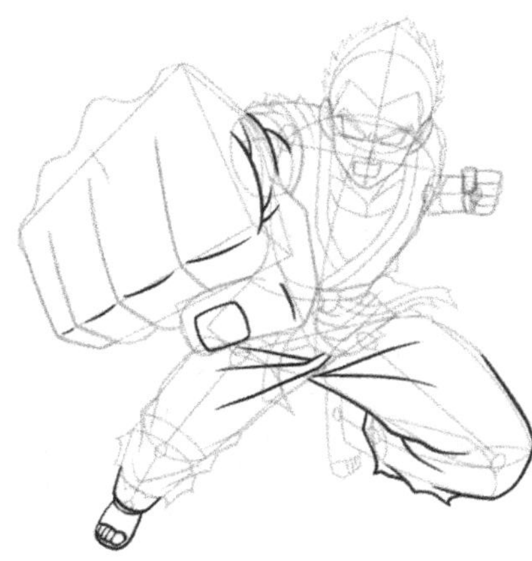

11

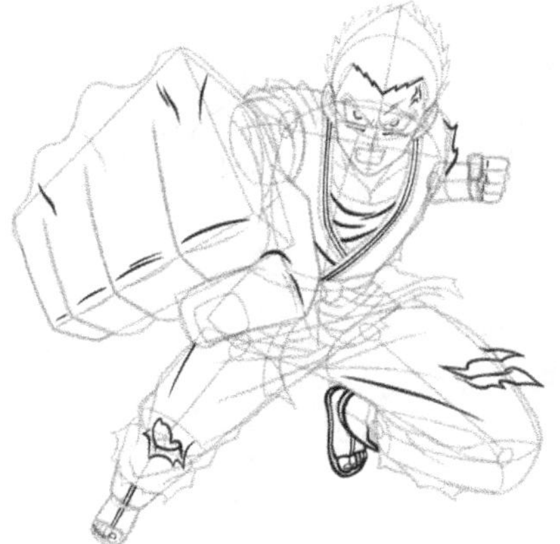

12

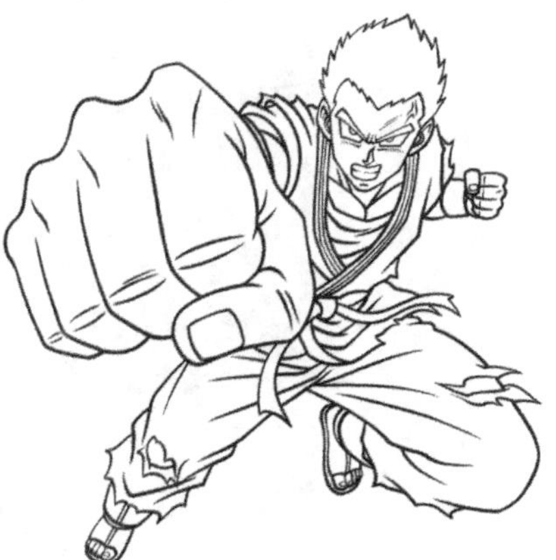

HOW TO DRAW ANIME

THE NINJA

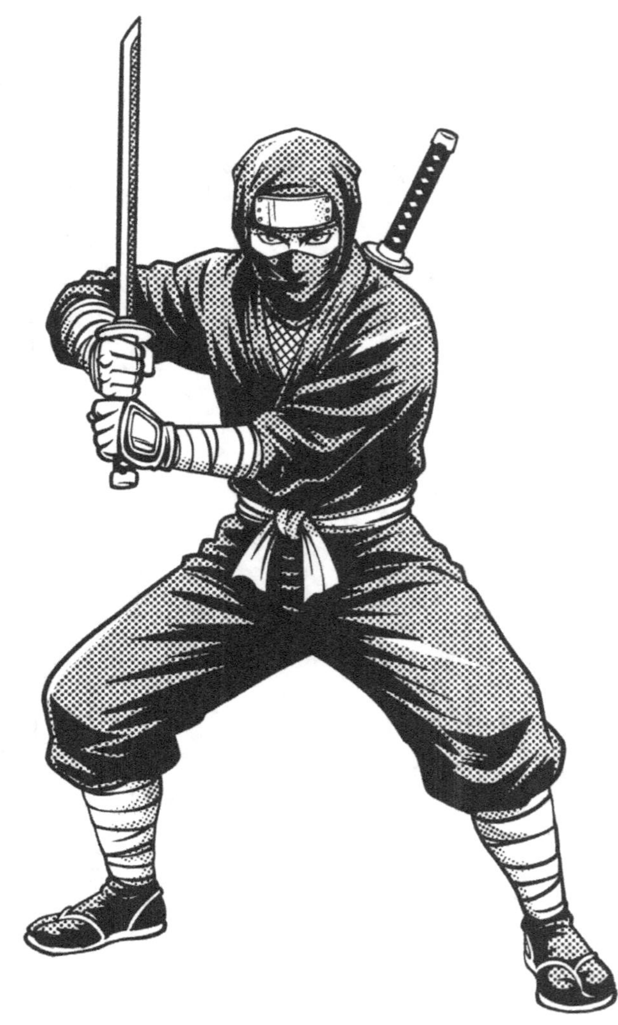

Pro Tip: Keep the stance wide with bent knees to show readiness and control. Angle the sword diagonally across the body to create tension and lead the viewer's eye toward the face.

01

02

03

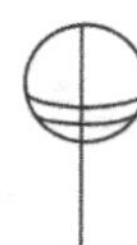

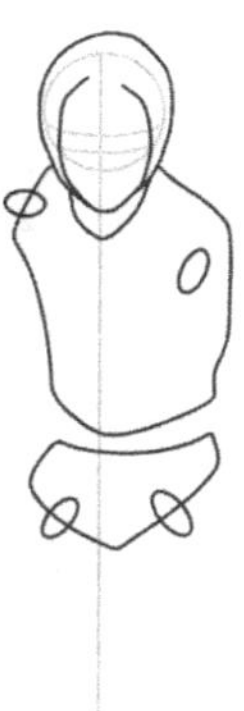

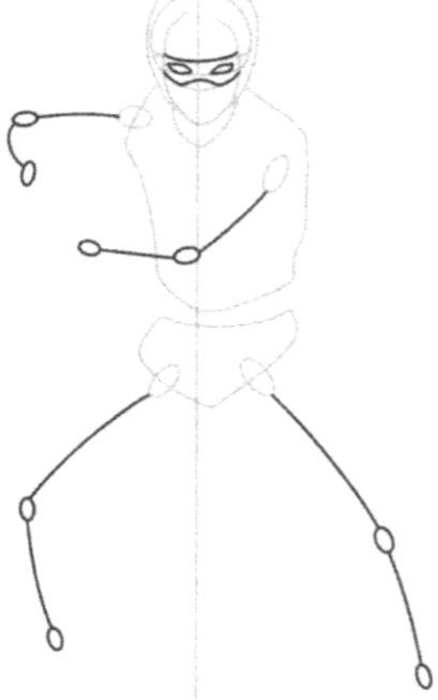

04

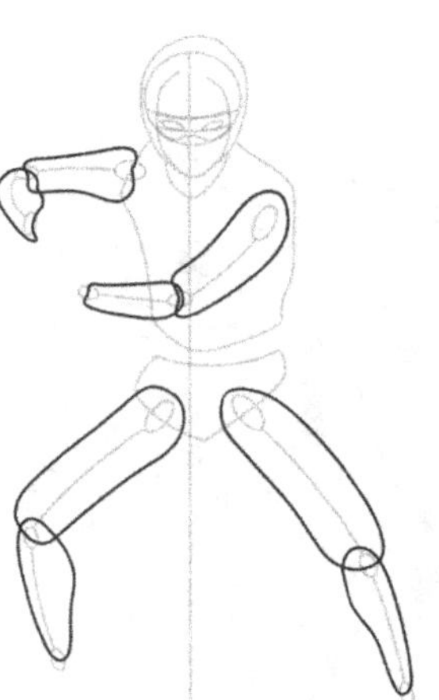

05

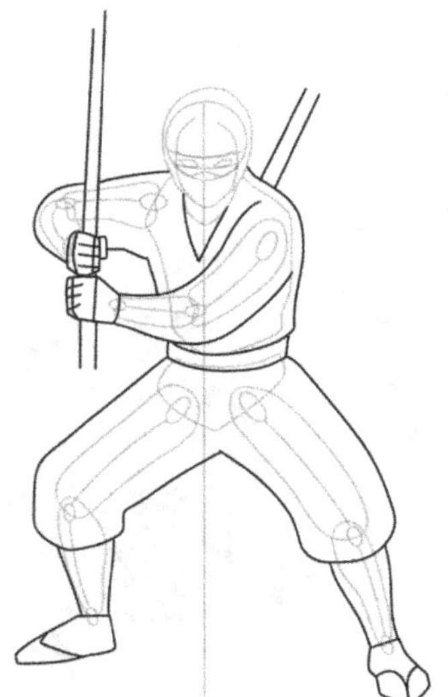

06

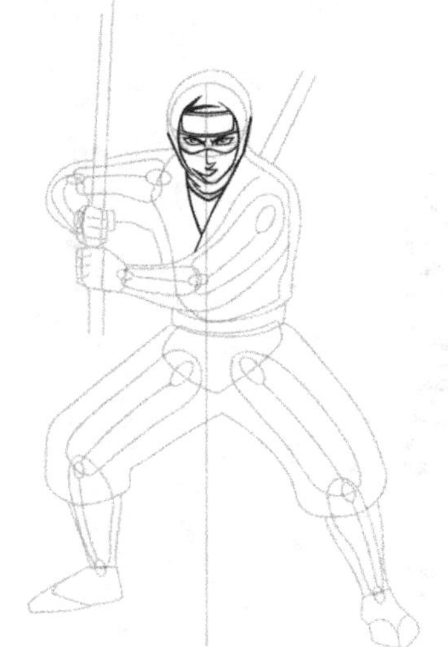

07

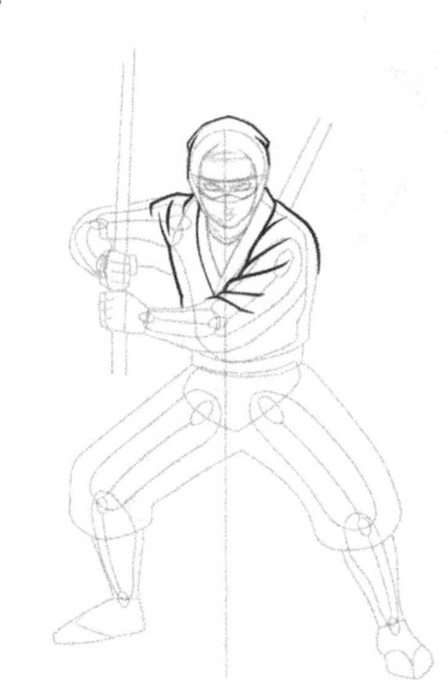

08

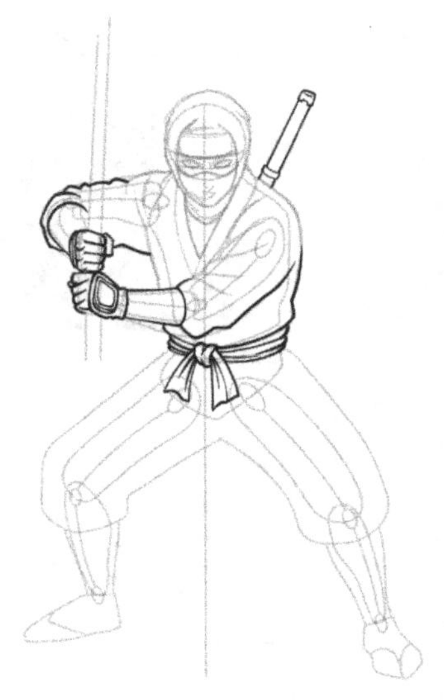

09

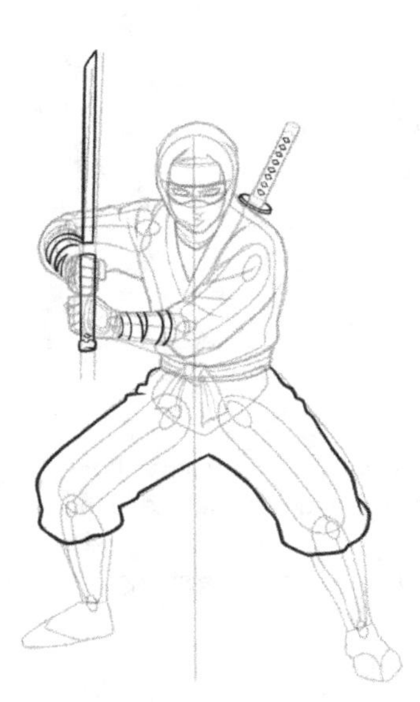

10

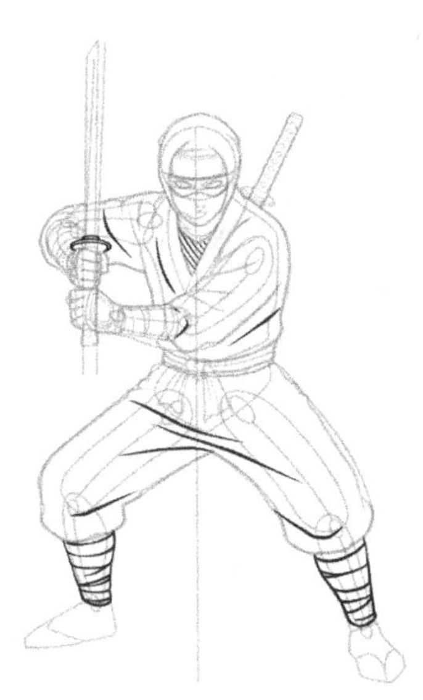

11

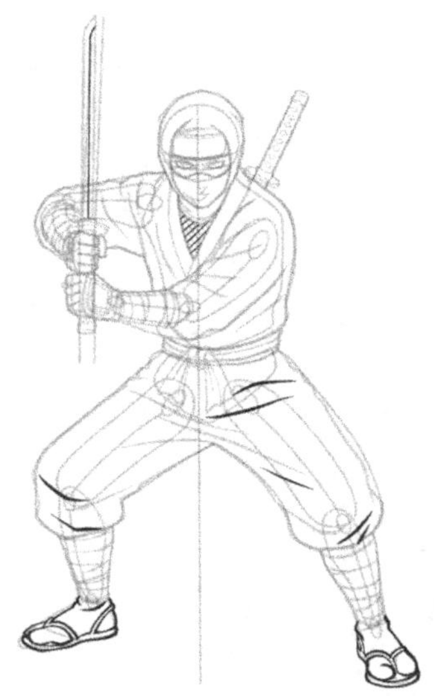

12

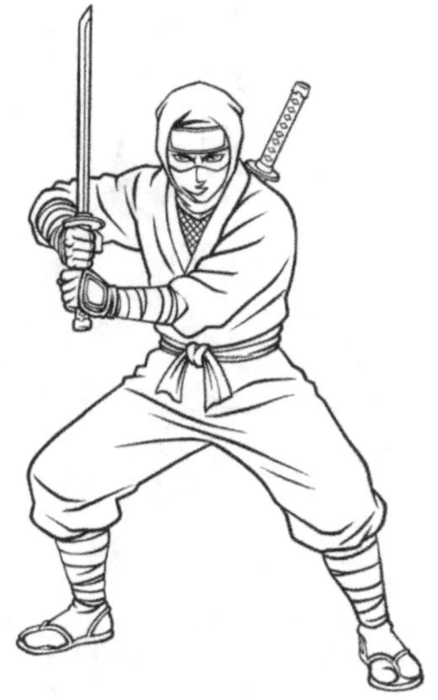

THE ACTION HEROINE

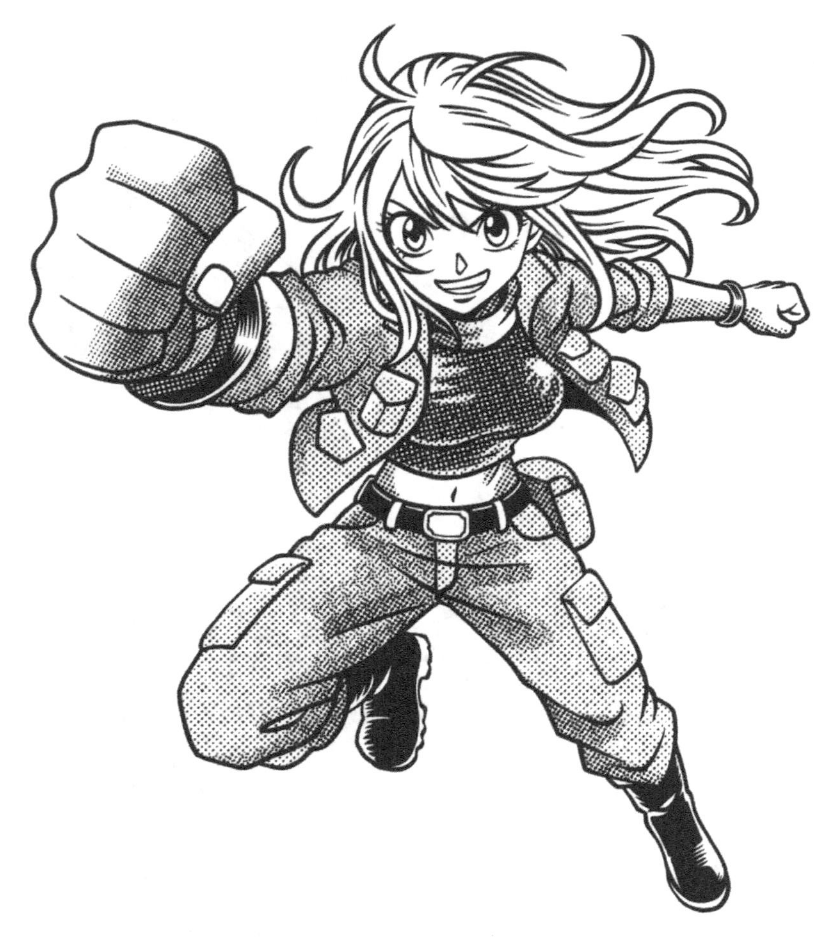

Pro Tip: Twist the torso to show movement and power. Keep the leading arm extended and the back leg grounded to balance strength with agility.

01

02

03

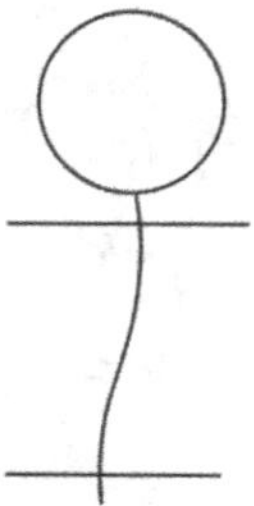

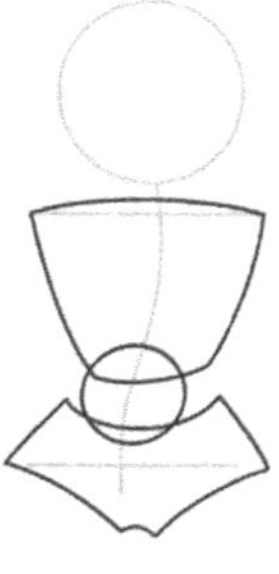

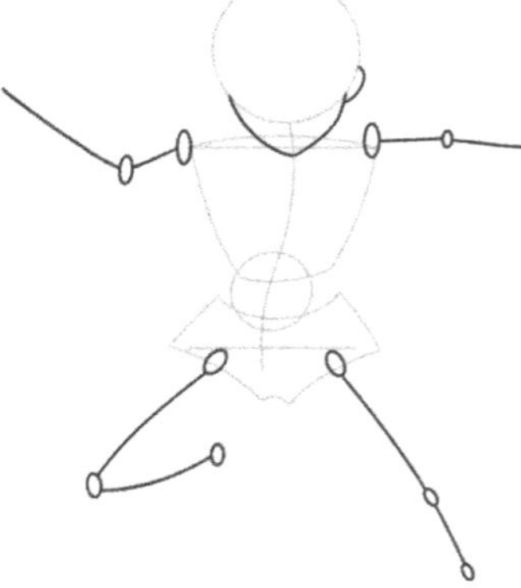

04

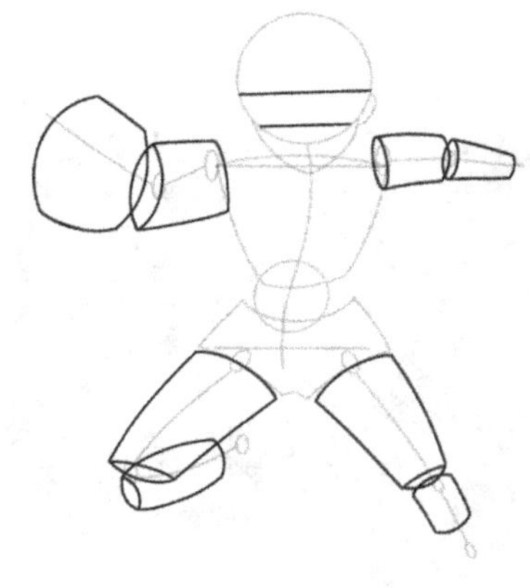

05

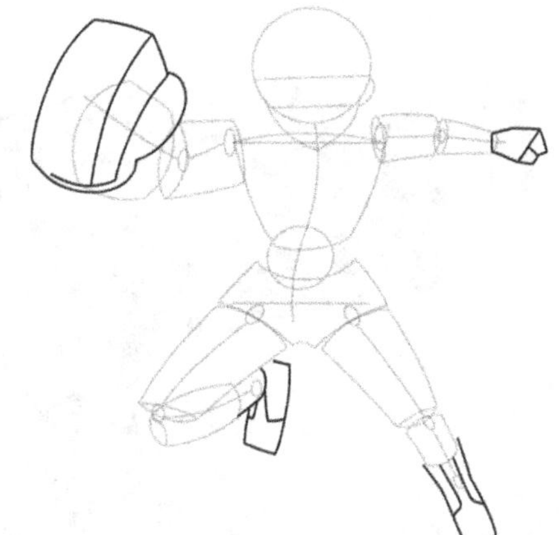

06

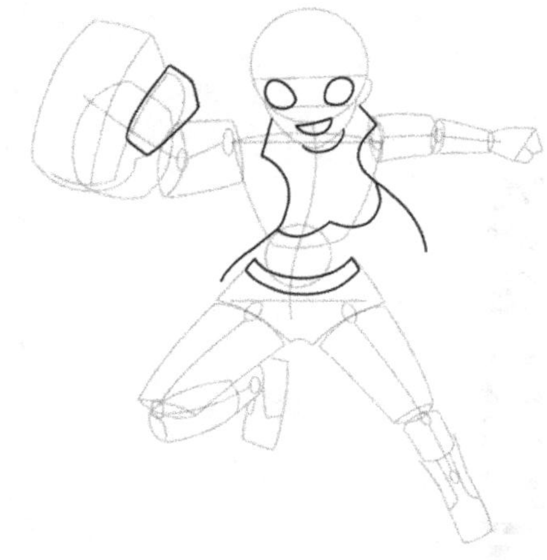

07

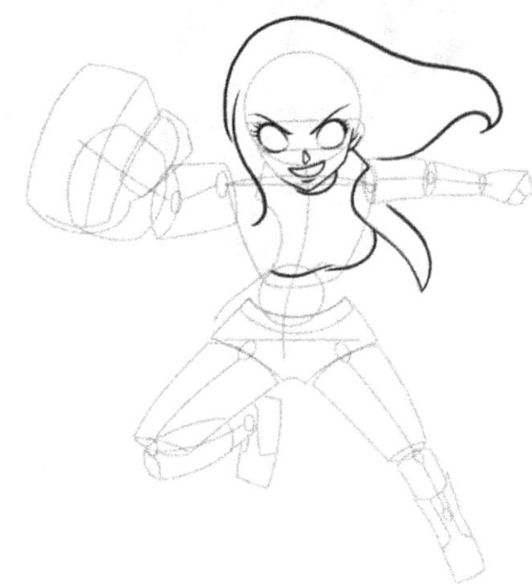

08

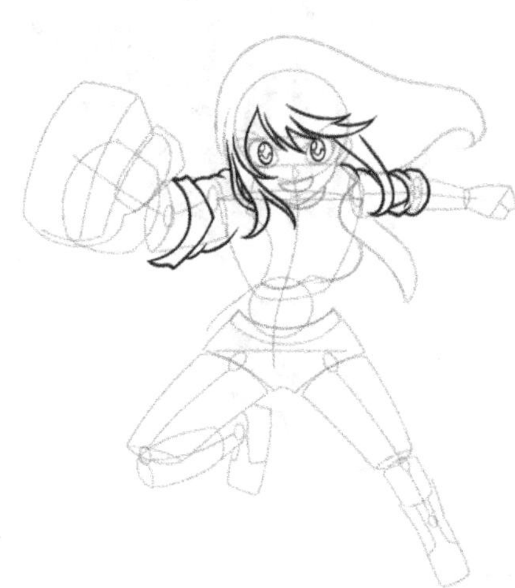

09

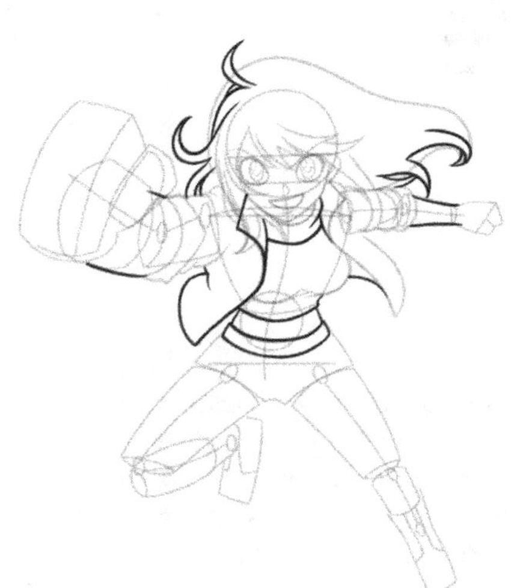

HOW TO DRAW ANIME

10

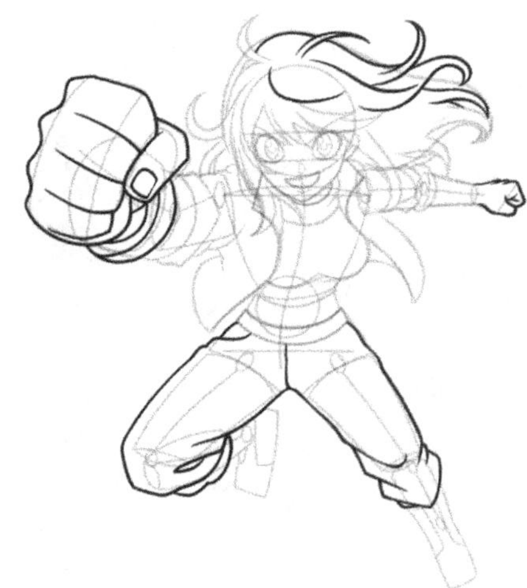

11

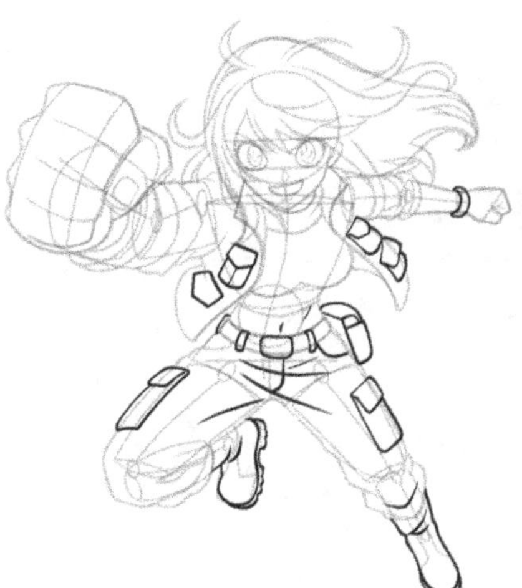

12

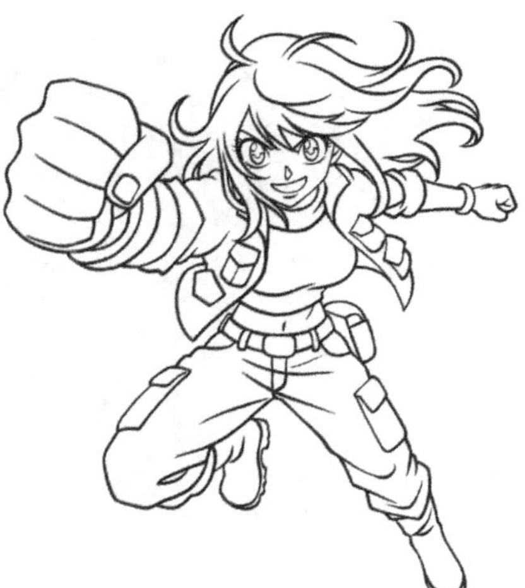

THE MUSCLE MAN

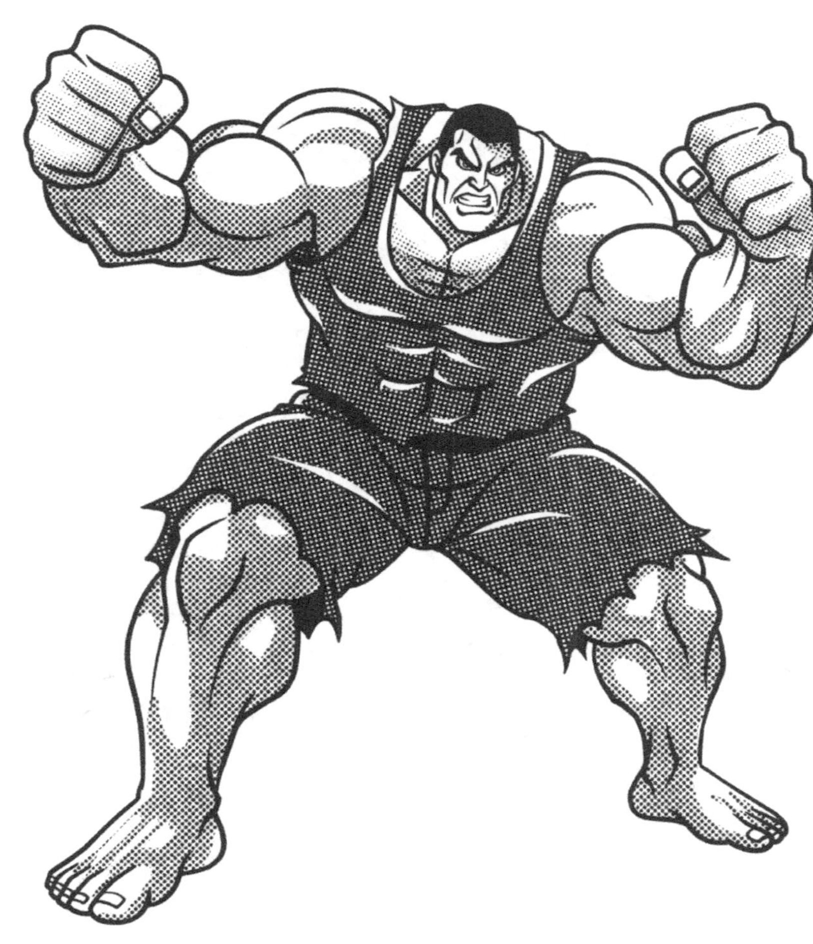

Pro Tip: Make the shoulders about 3.5 heads wide to exaggerate bulk and dominance. Keep the chest broad and the fists pushed forward to amplify the sense of unstoppable power.

01

02

03

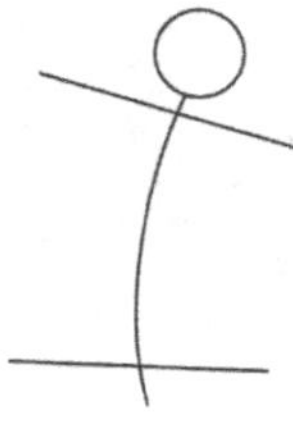

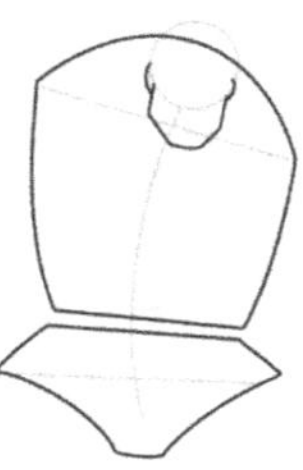

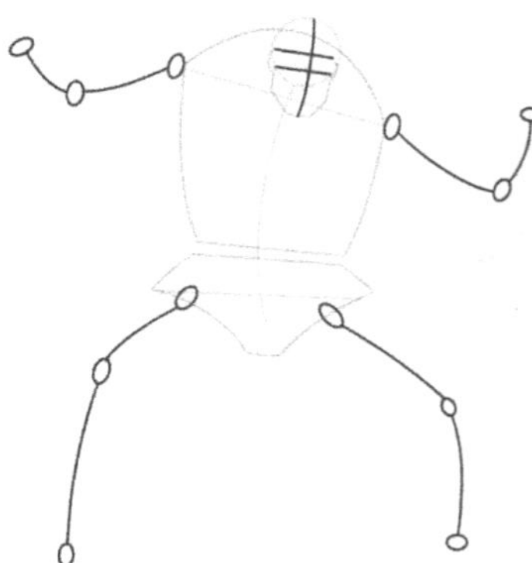

04

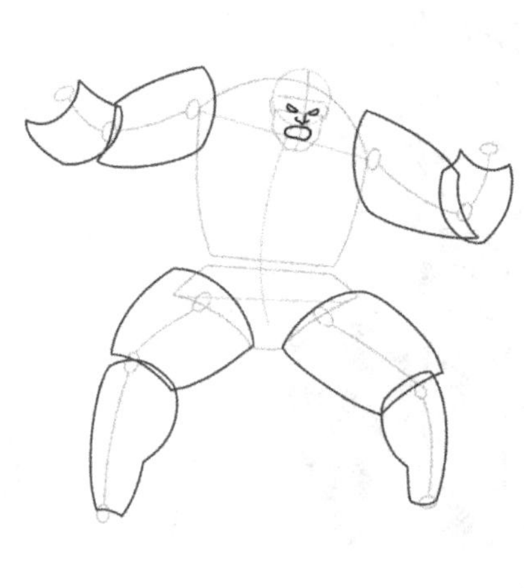

05

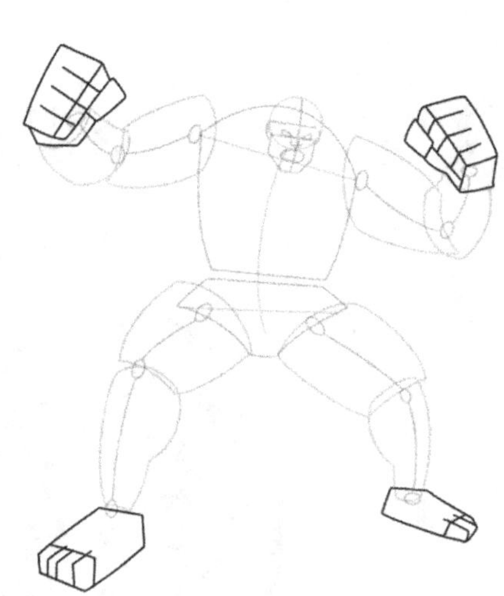

06

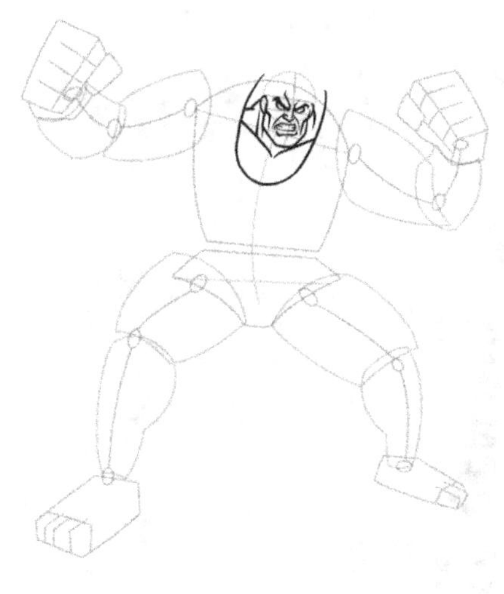

07

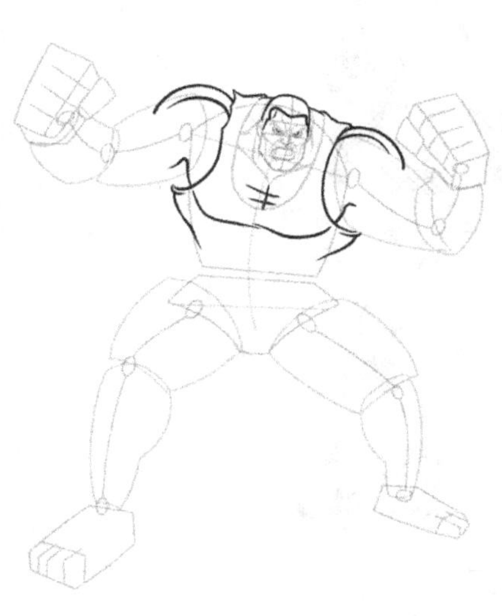

08

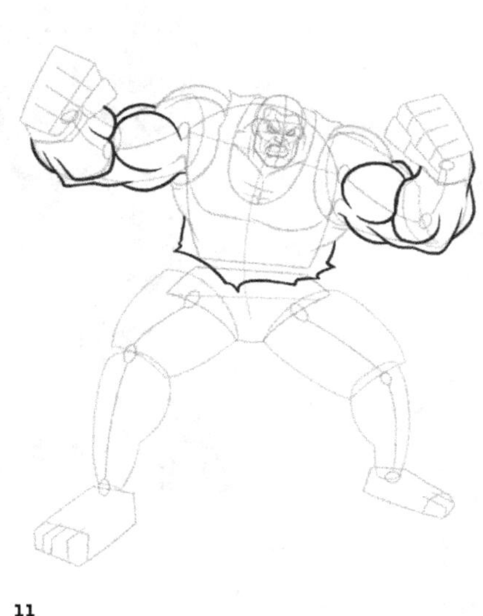

09

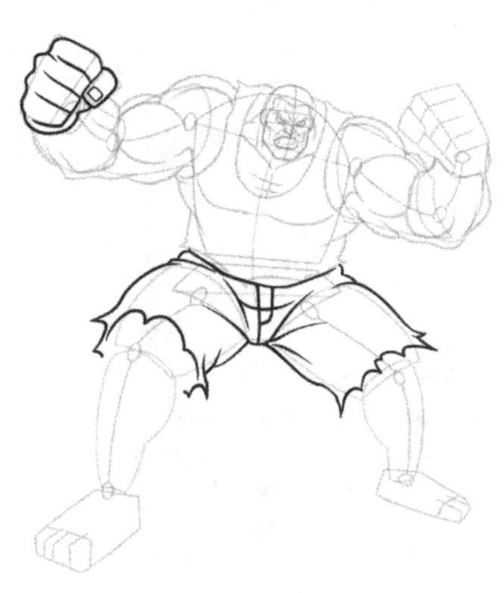

10

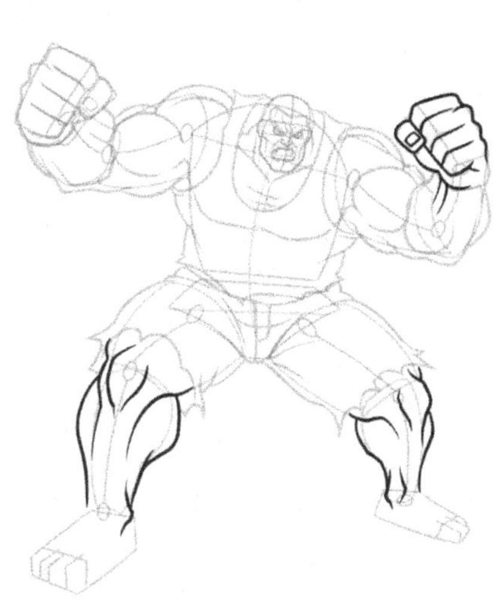

11

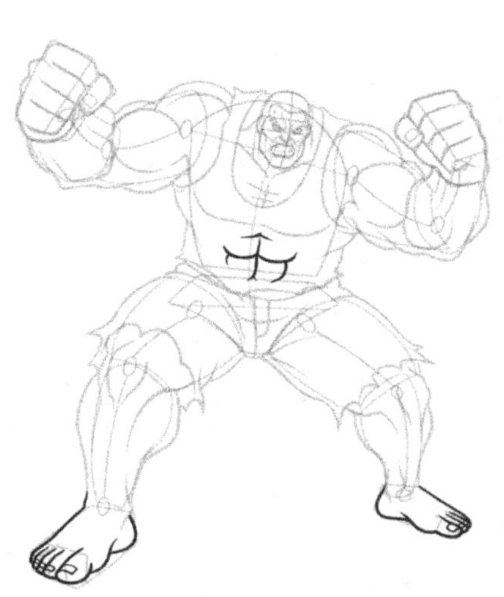

12

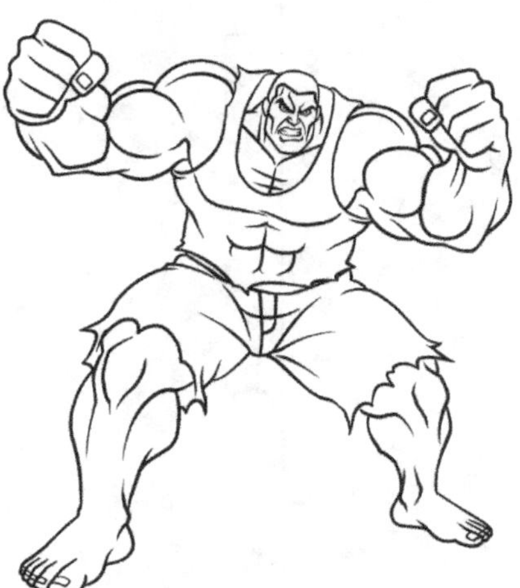

HOW TO DRAW ANIME

THE SENSEI

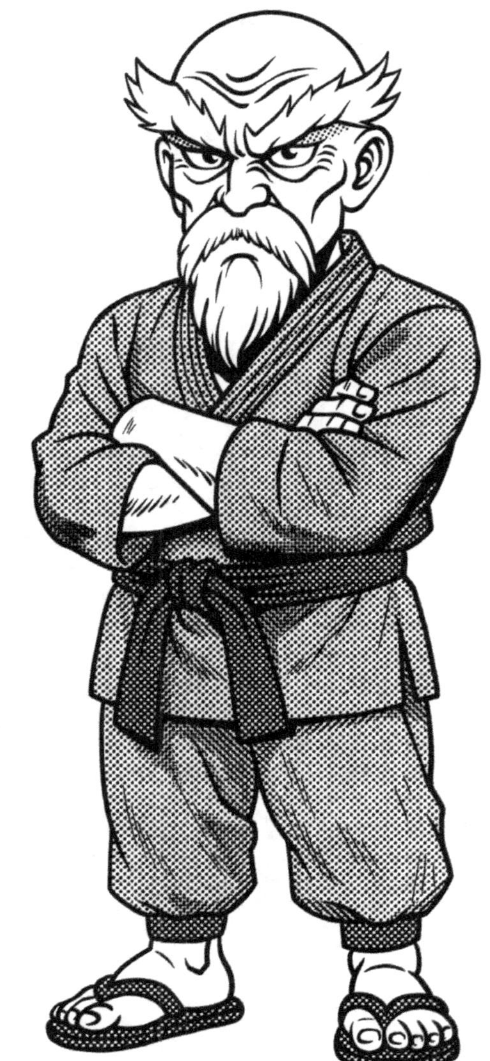

Pro Tip: Keep the figure short and compact with a wide stance to show stability. Cross the arms firmly and angle the eyebrows downward to express wisdom and authority.

01

02

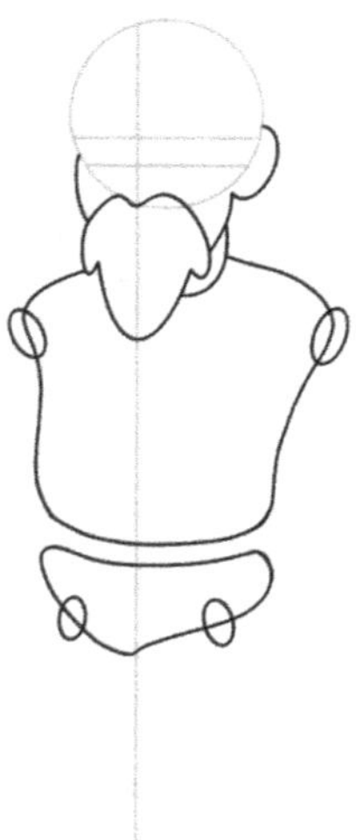

03

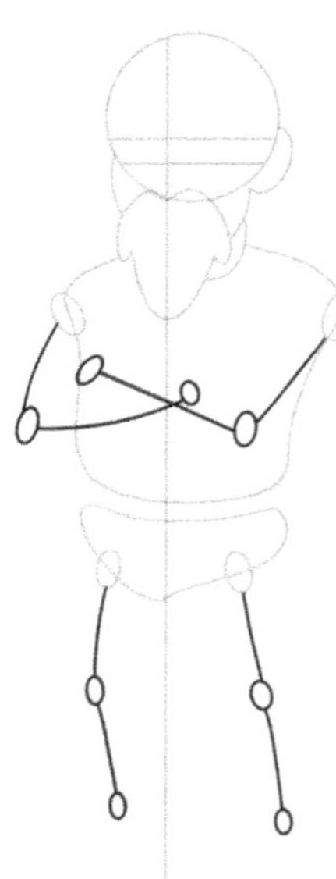

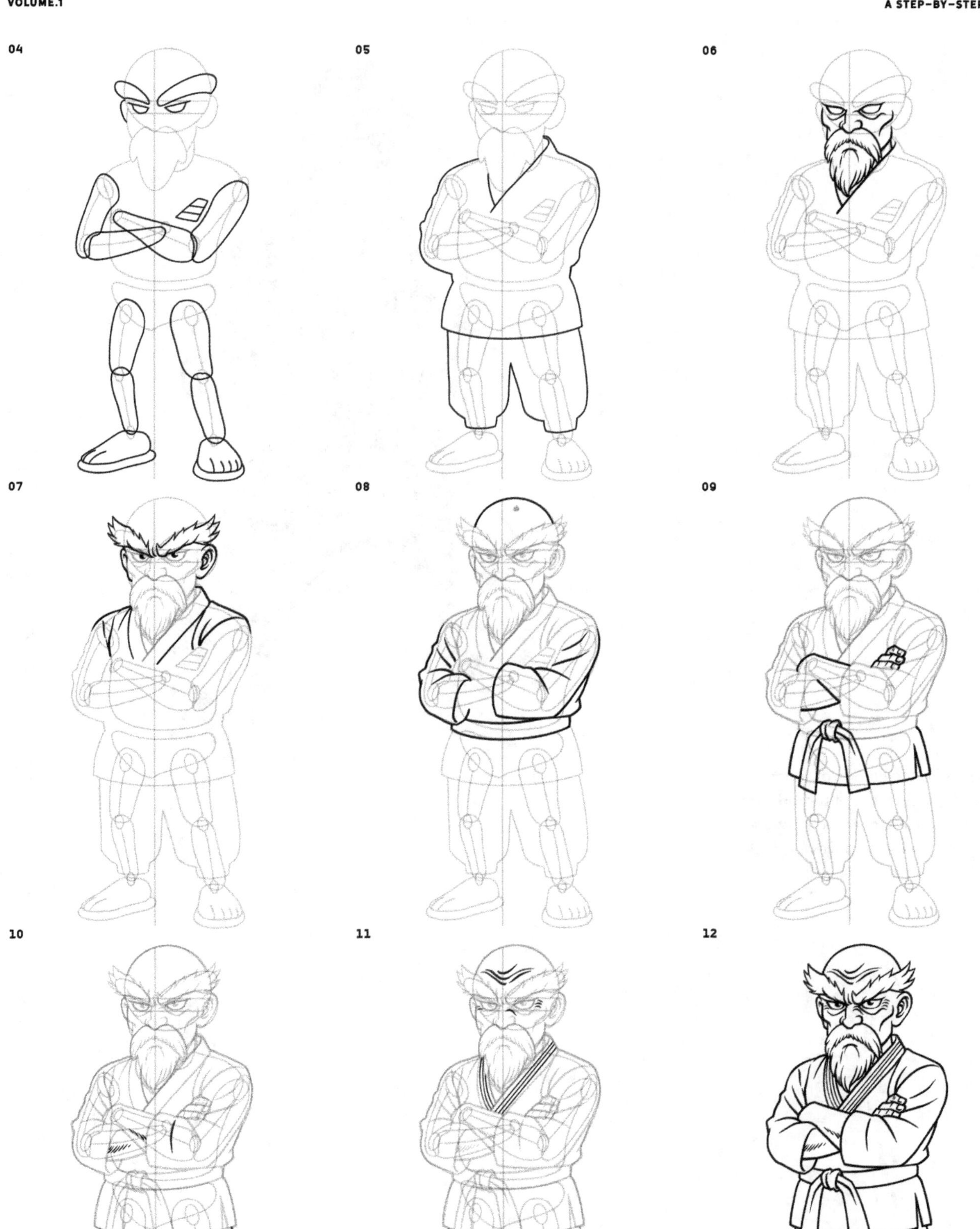

04
05
06
07
08
09
10
11
12
HOW TO DRAW ANIME

THE MARTIAL ARTS EXPERT

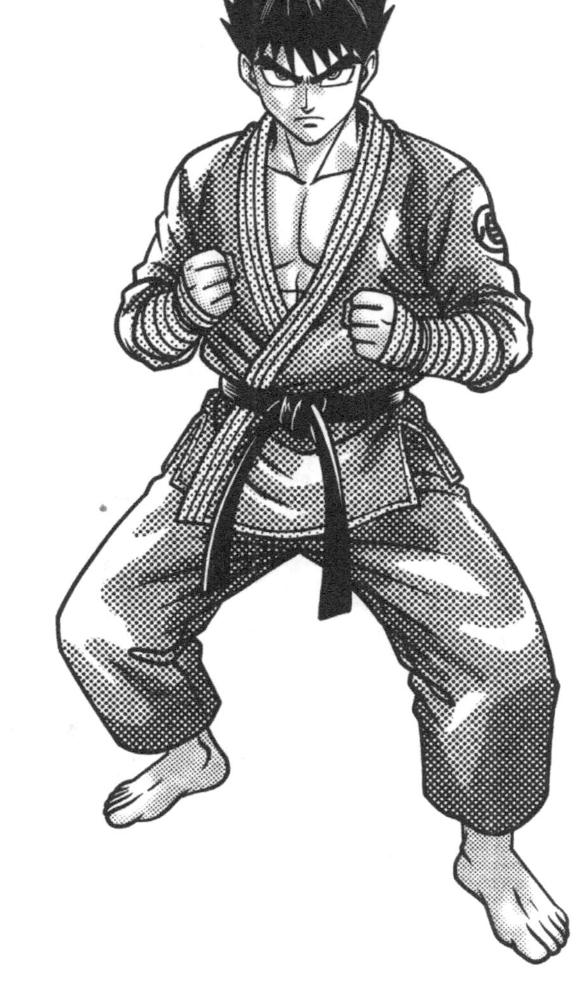

Pro Tip: Keep the stance grounded with bent knees and feet turned slightly outward. Emphasise strong posture and focused eyes to convey discipline, control and power.

01

02

03

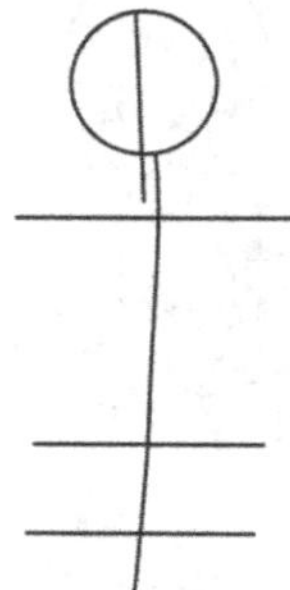

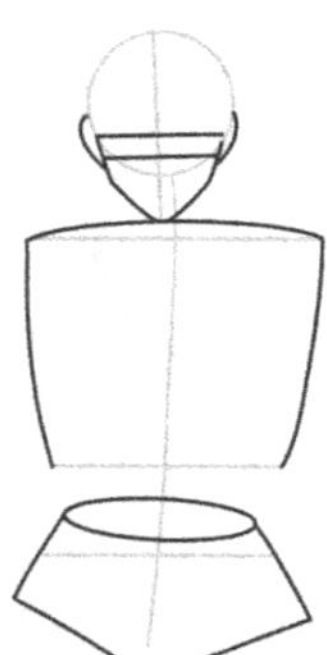

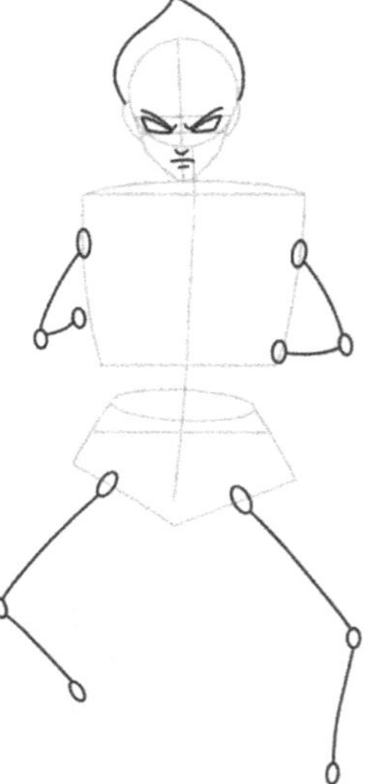

04

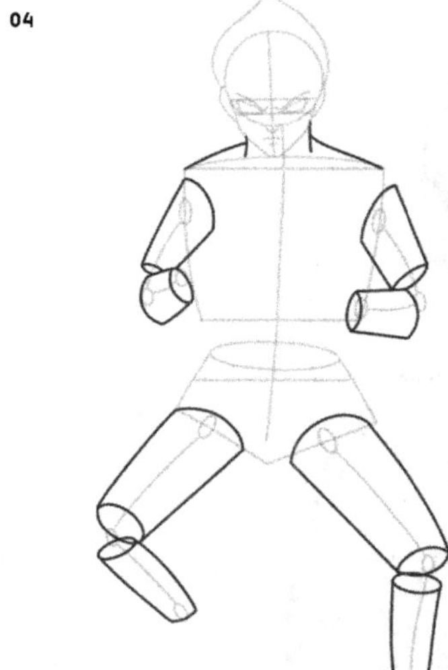

05

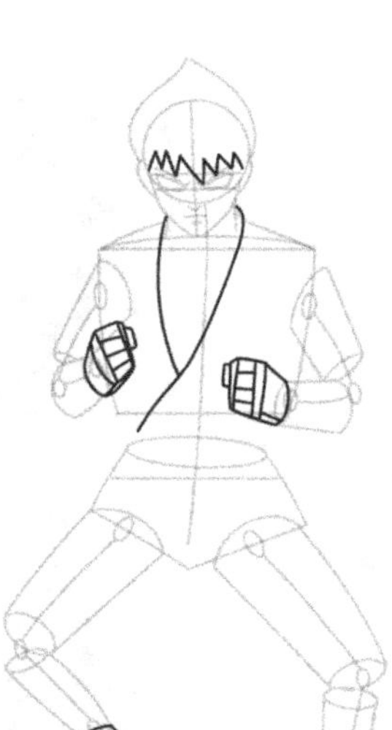

06

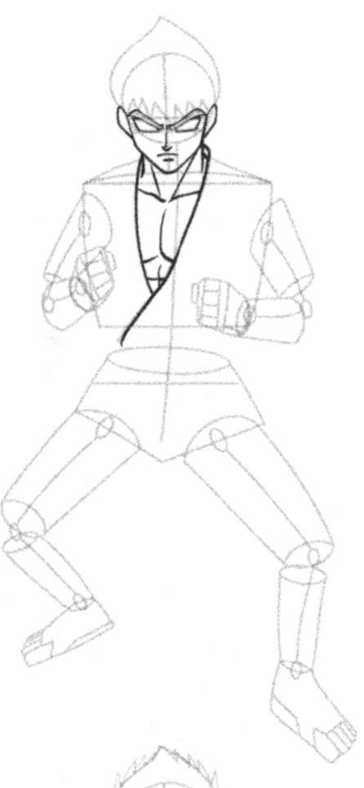

07

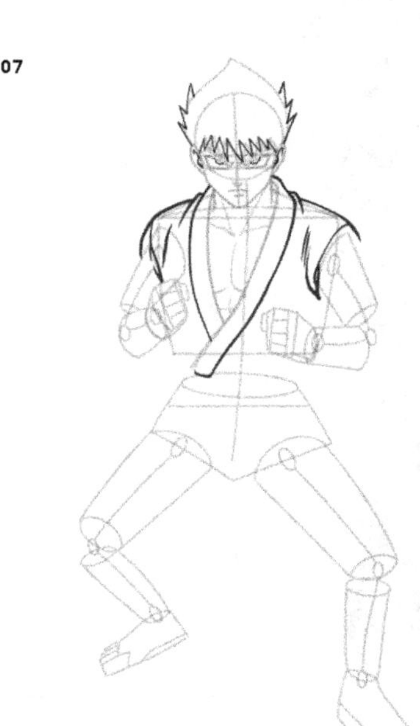

08

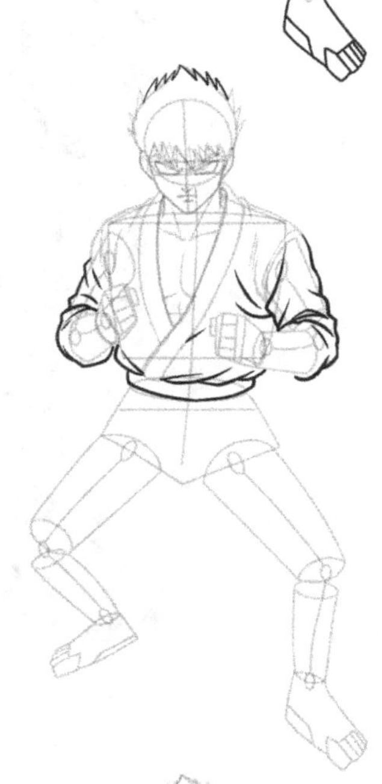

09

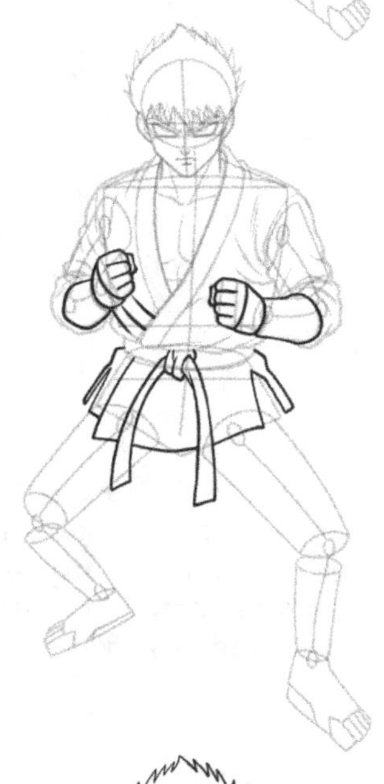

10

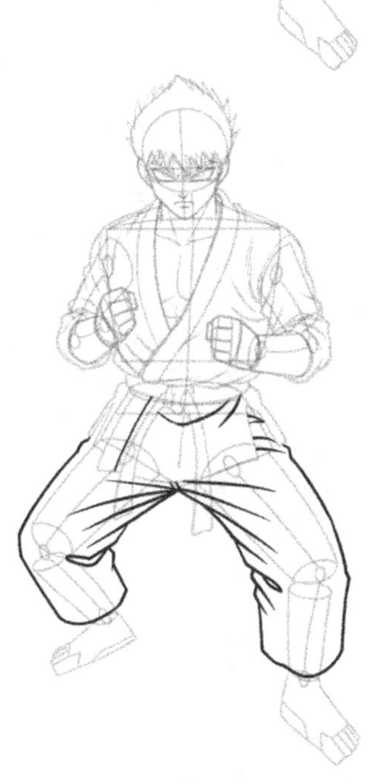

11

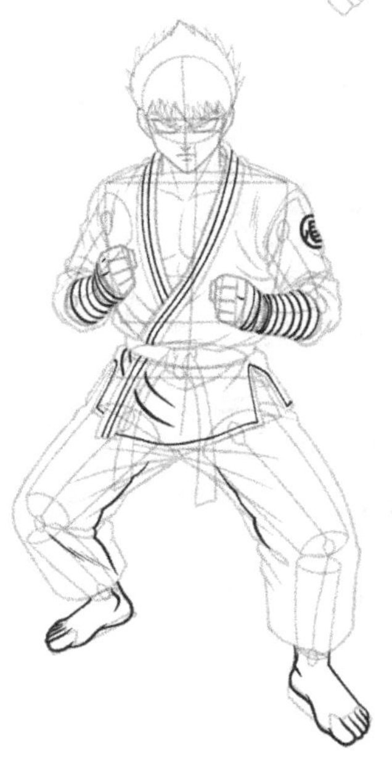

12

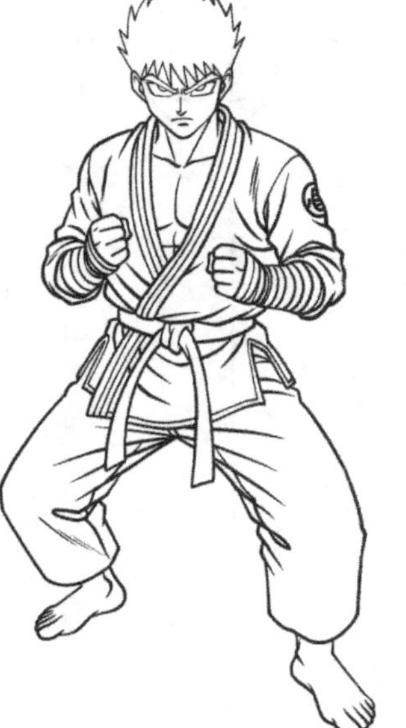

HOW TO DRAW ANIME

THE LONER

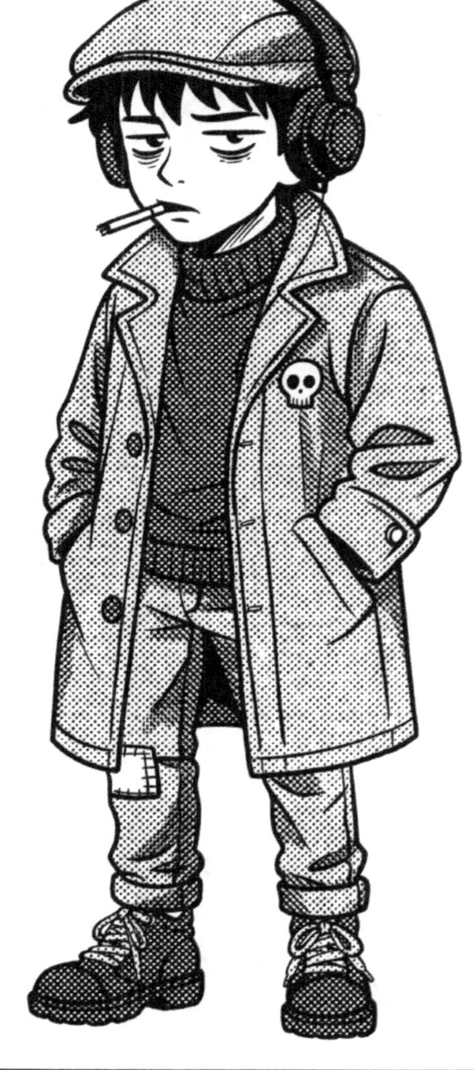

Pro Tip: Shift the weight to one leg and drop the shoulders slightly to show a relaxed, detached attitude. Keep the hands in the pockets and the head tilted down to emphasise the withdrawn mood.

01

02

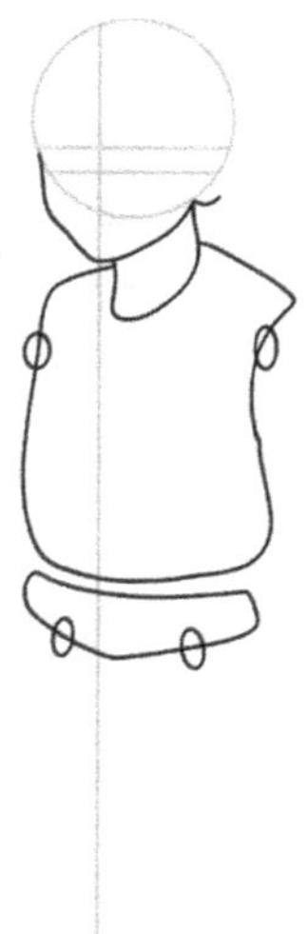

03

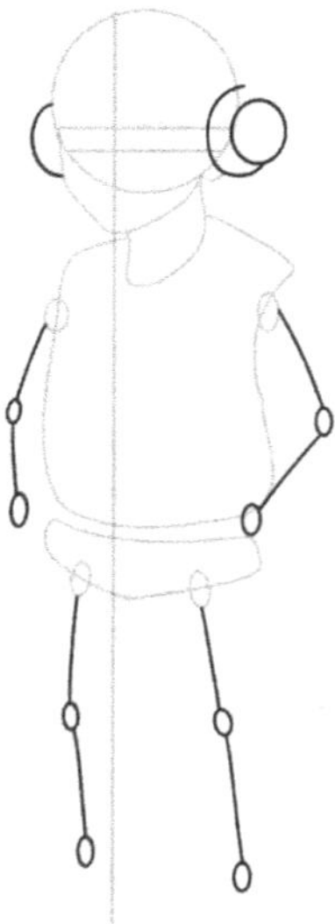

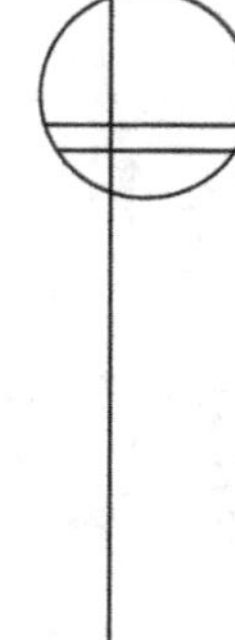

04

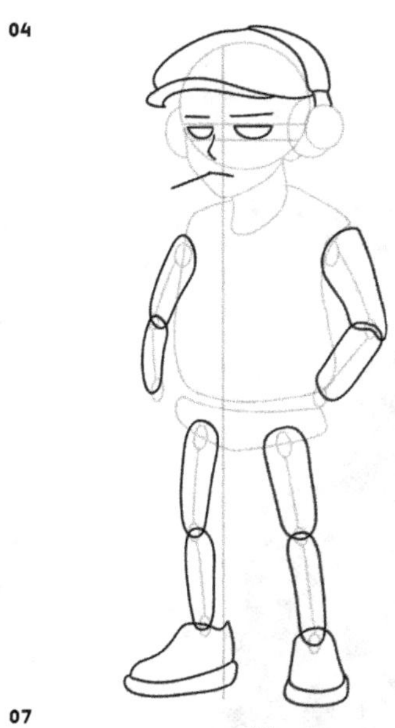

05

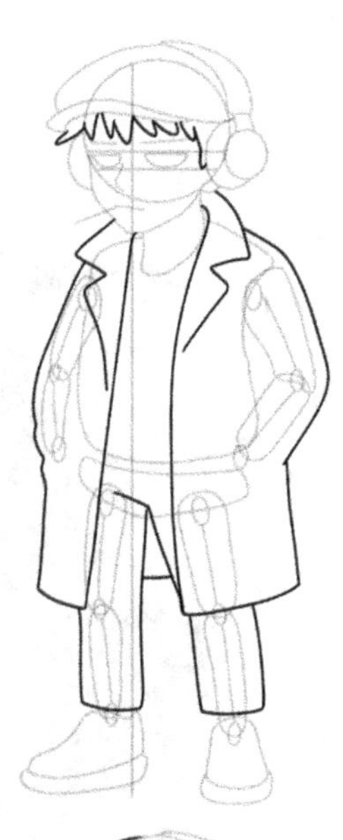

06

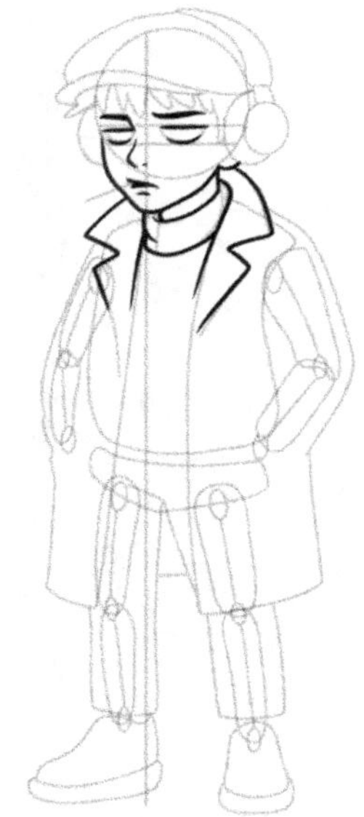

07

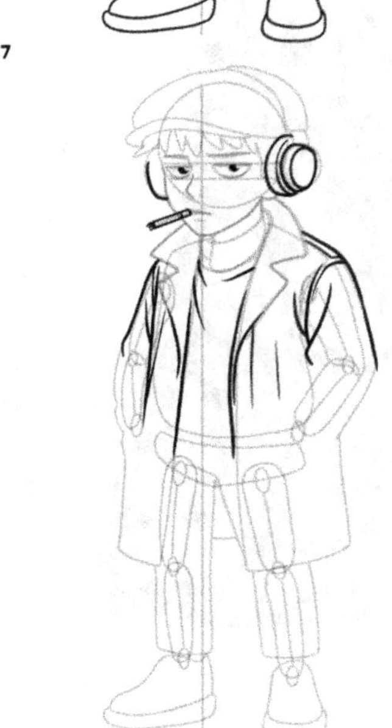

08

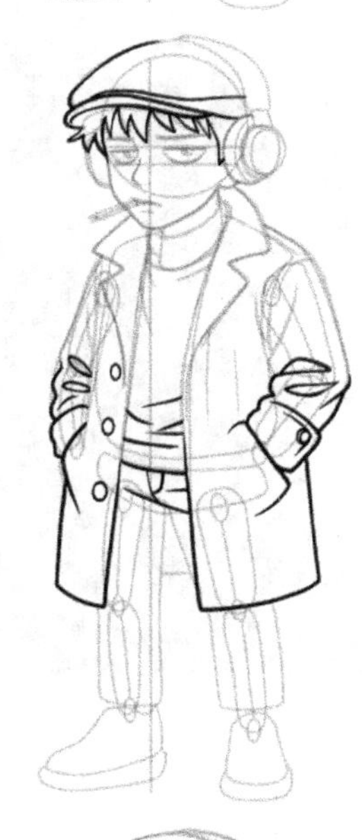

09

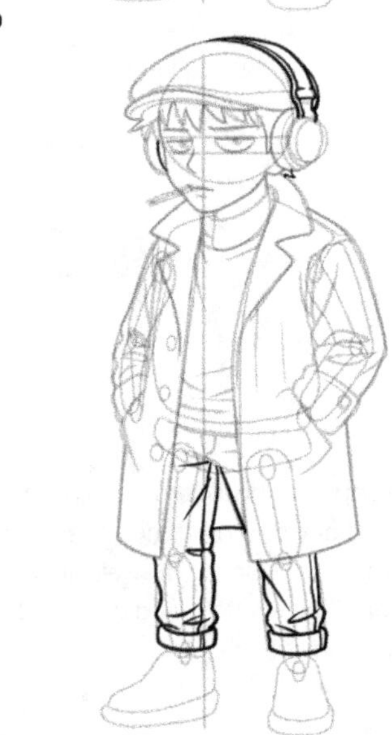

10

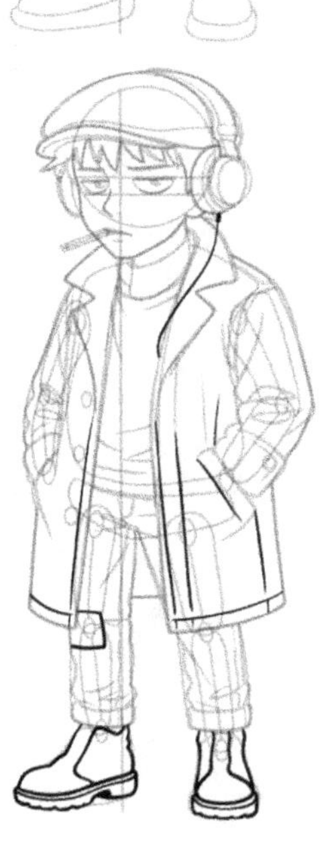

11

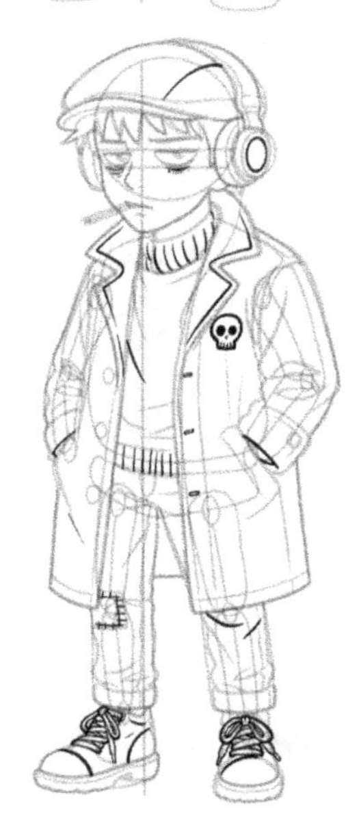

12

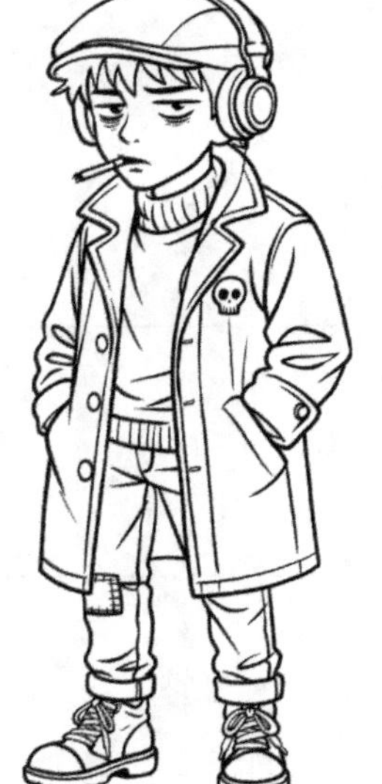

MYSTERIOUS FIGURE

VAULTEDITIONS.COM

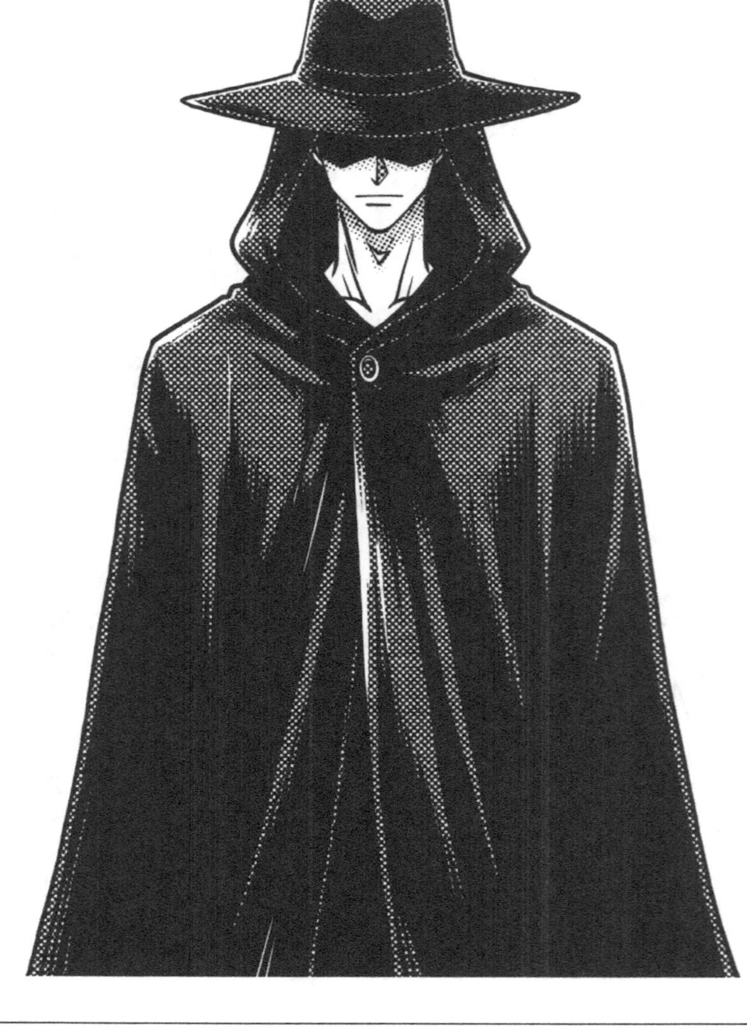

Pro Tip: Keep the shoulders broad and the face partially hidden to heighten the sense of mystery. Use long, straight lines in the cloak to draw the eye downward and emphasise stillness and control.

01

02

03

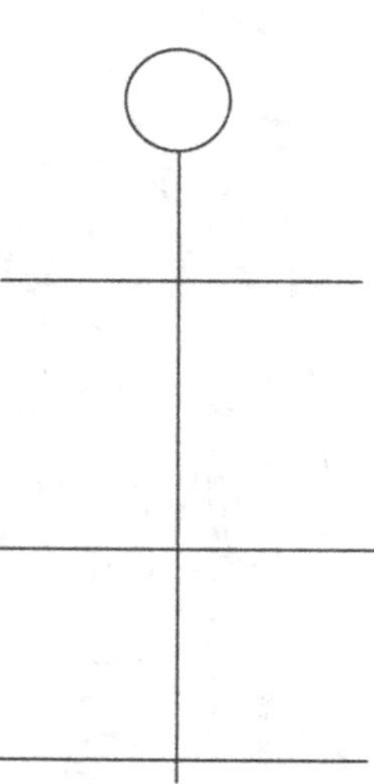

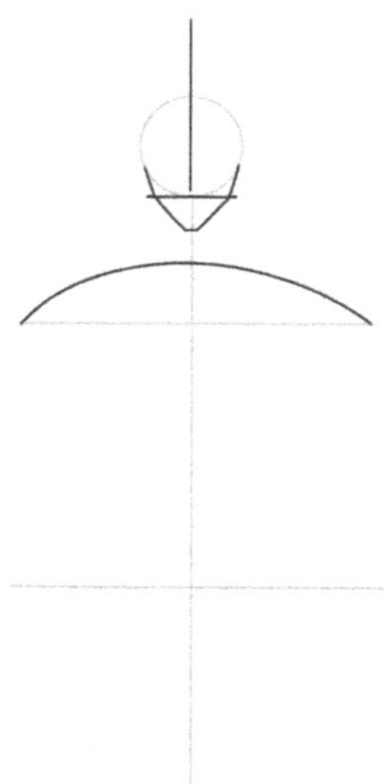

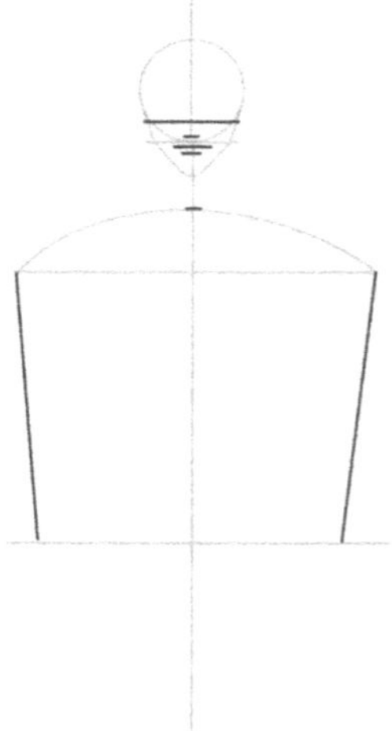

04

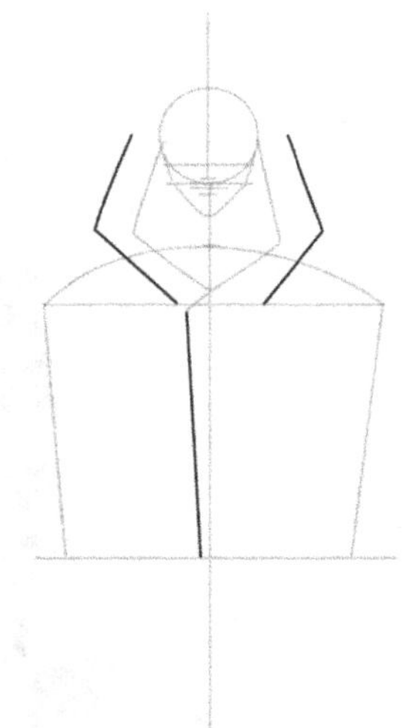

05

06

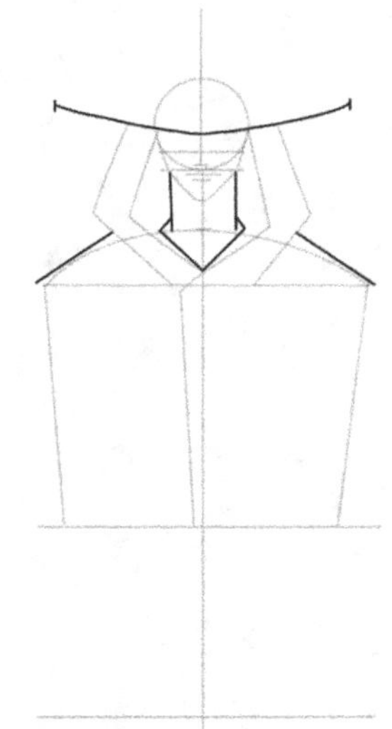

07

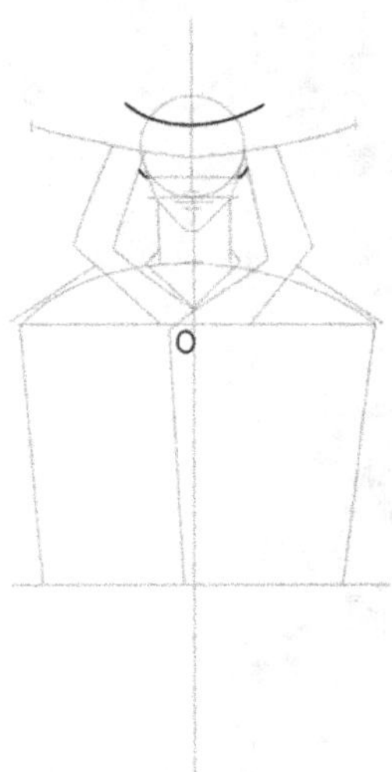

08

09

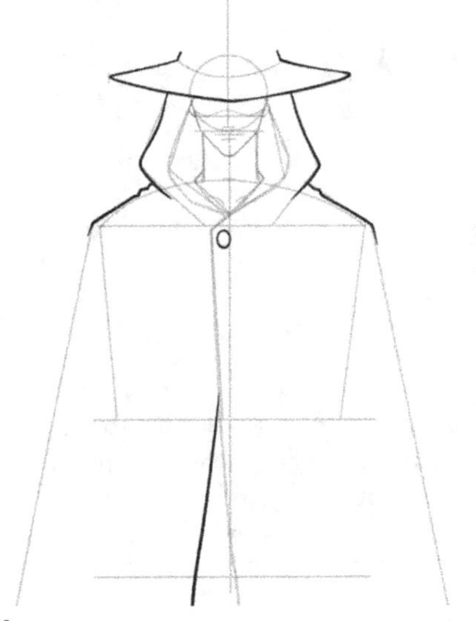

10

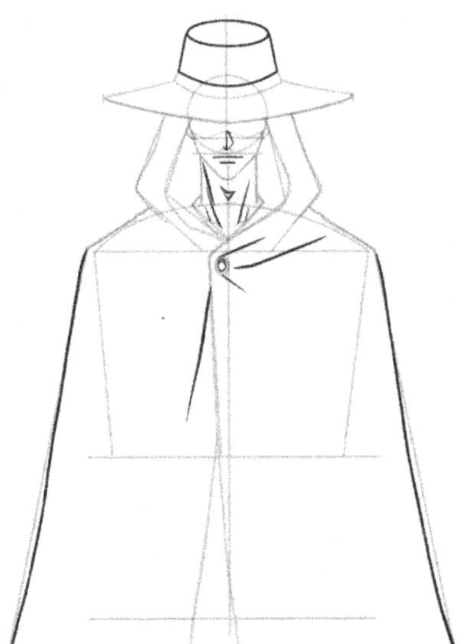

11

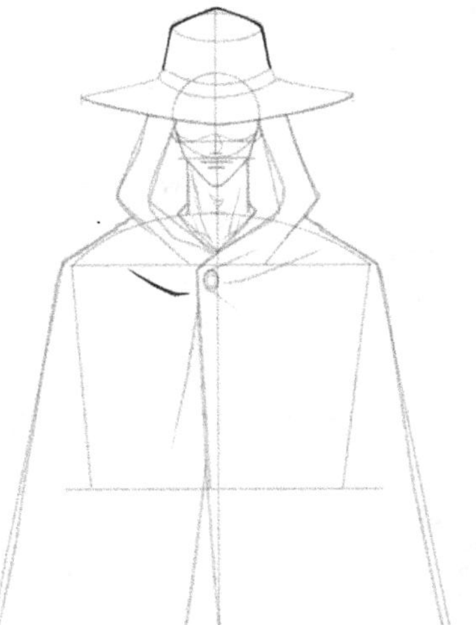

12

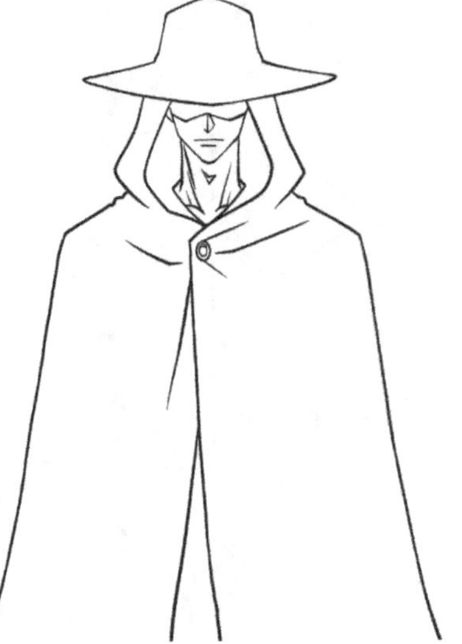

VILLAIN

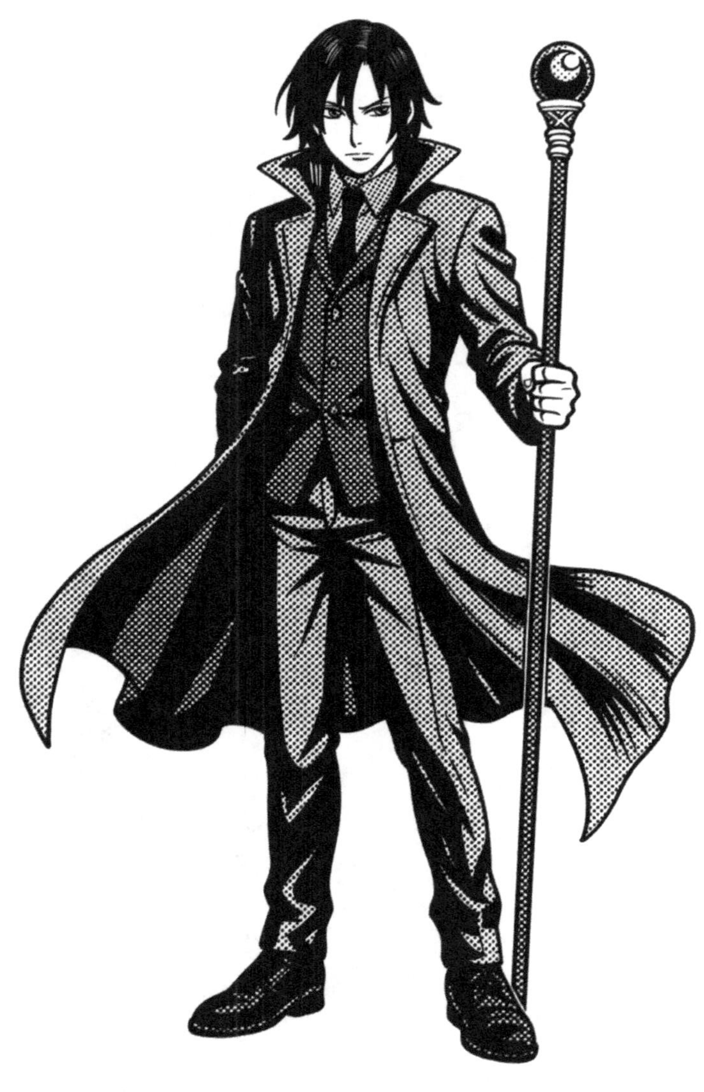

Pro Tip: Keep the shoulders squared and the stance grounded to project confidence. Let the coat flare outward to suggest power, movement and a commanding presence.

01

02

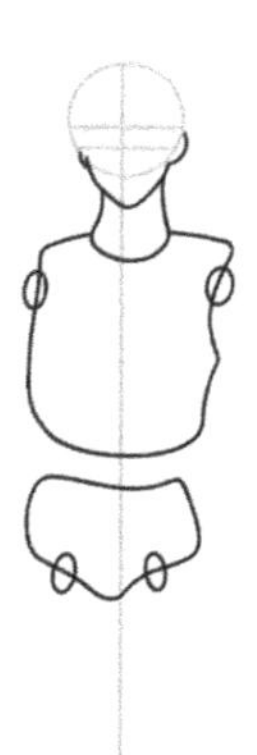

03

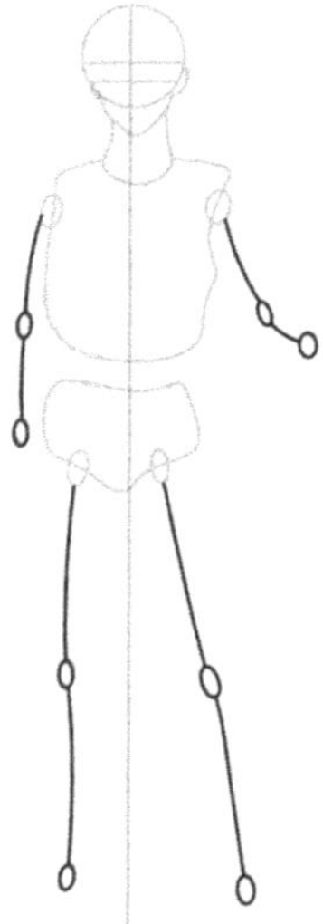

04

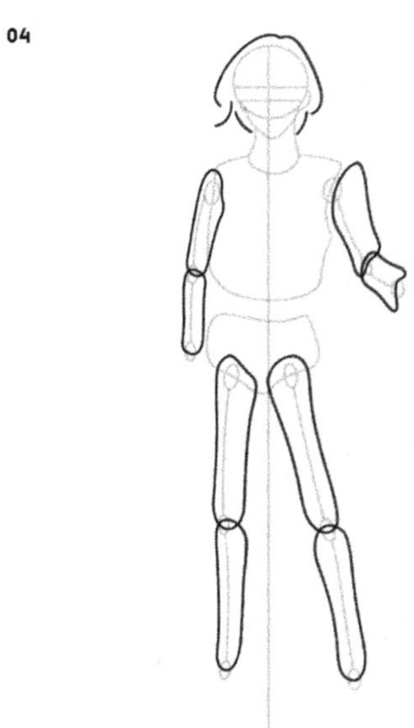

05

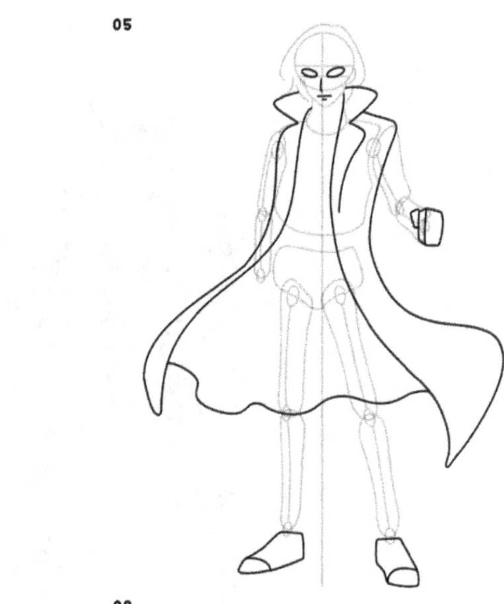

06

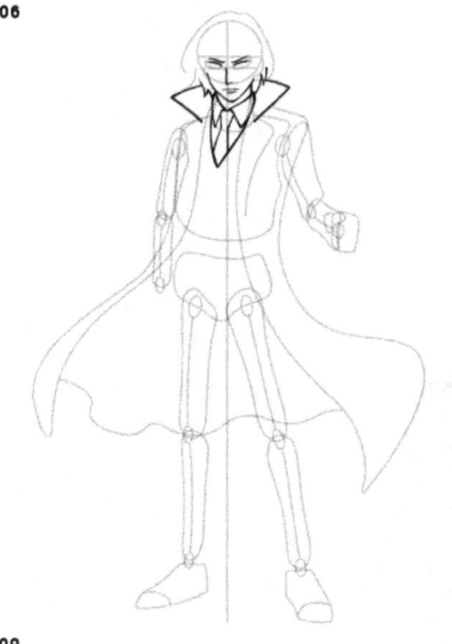

07

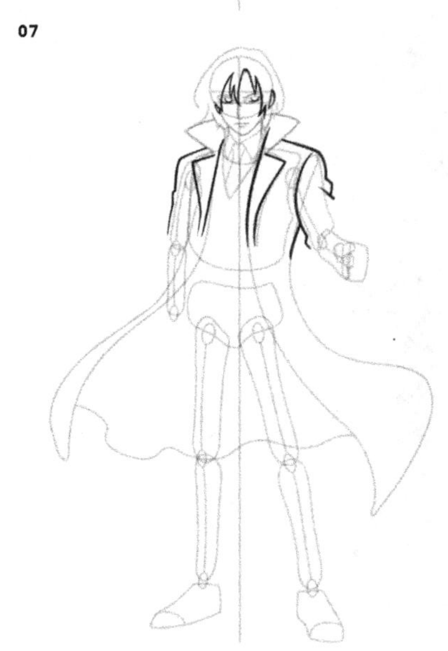

08

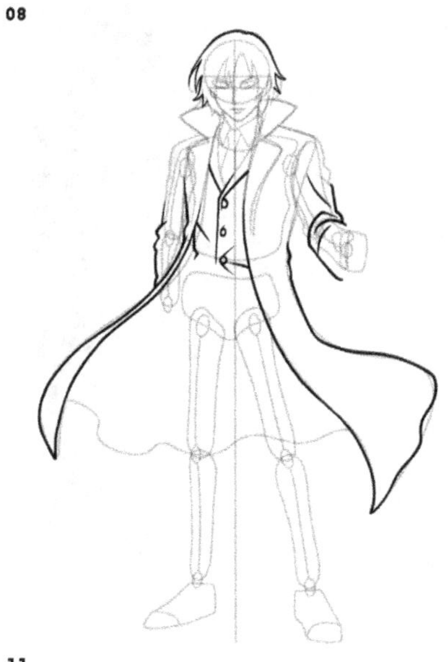

09

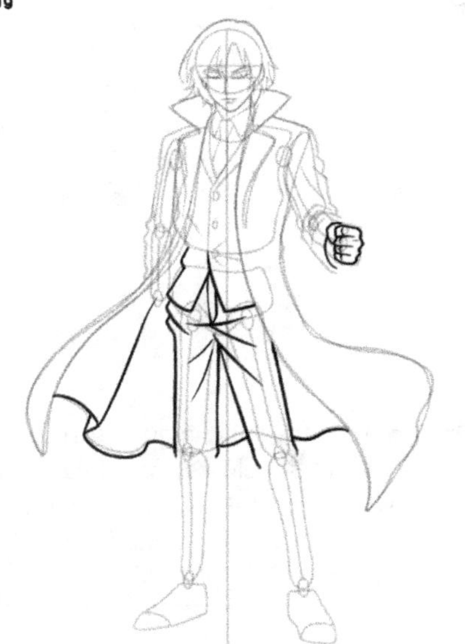

10

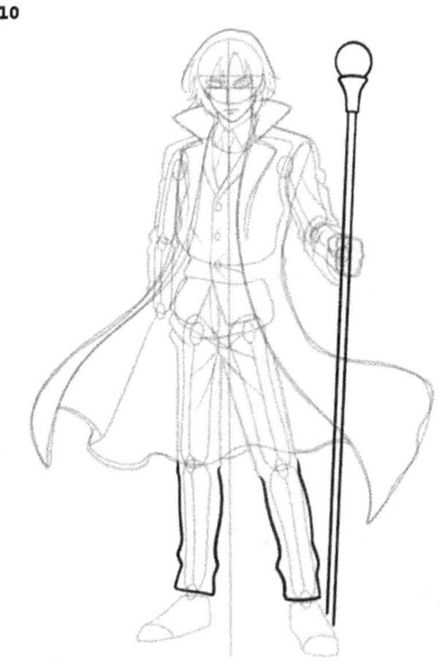

11

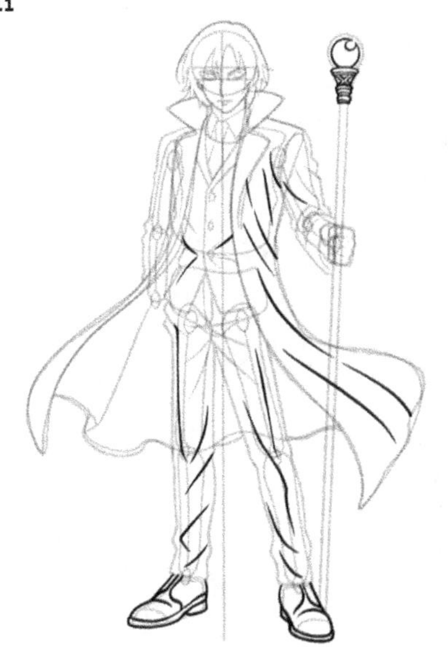

12

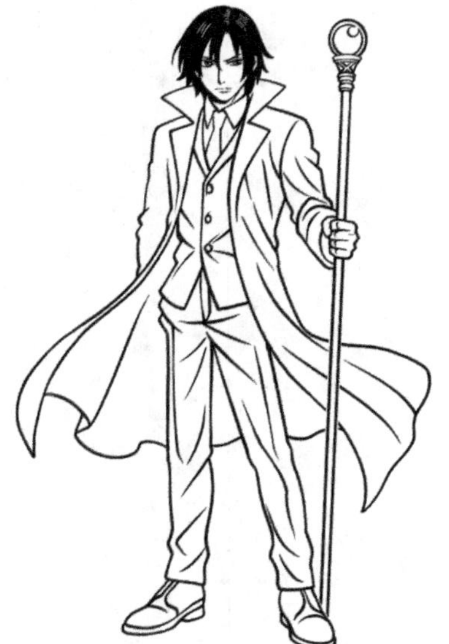

HOW TO DRAW ANIME

THE RIVAL

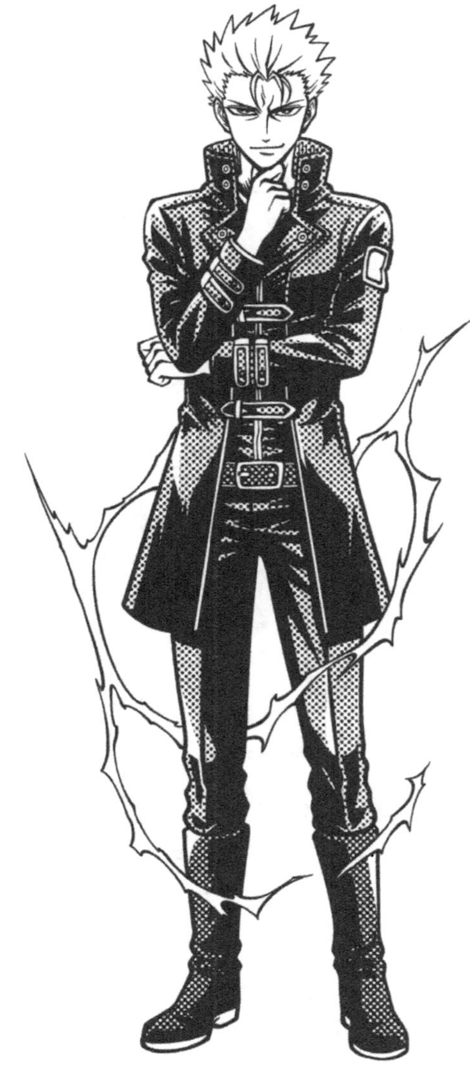

Pro Tip: Keep the figure around seven heads tall with shoulders about two heads wide. Use a relaxed stance and a confident expression to capture the rival's cool, composed attitude.

01

02

03

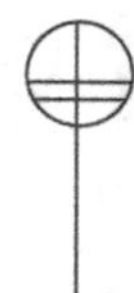

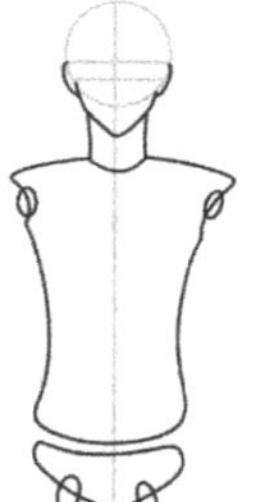

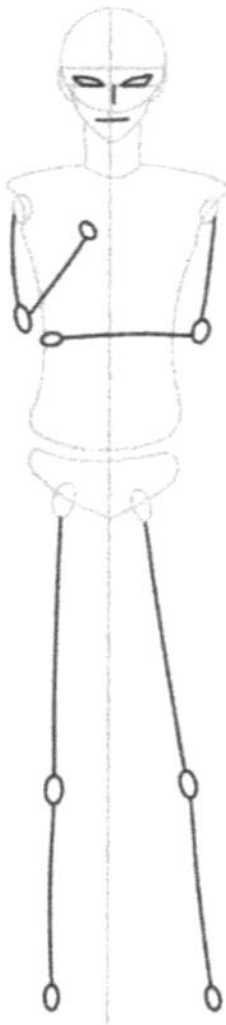

04

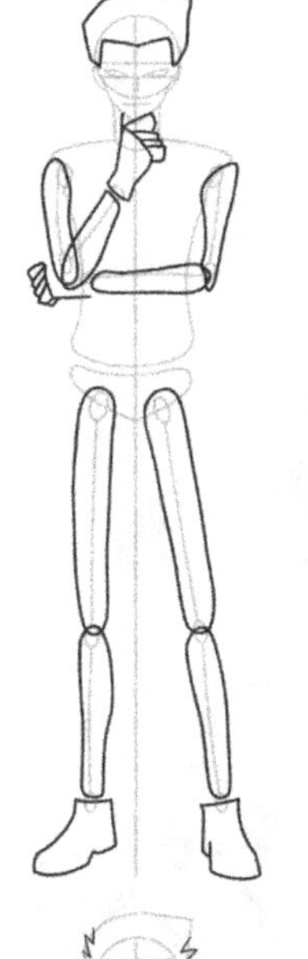

05

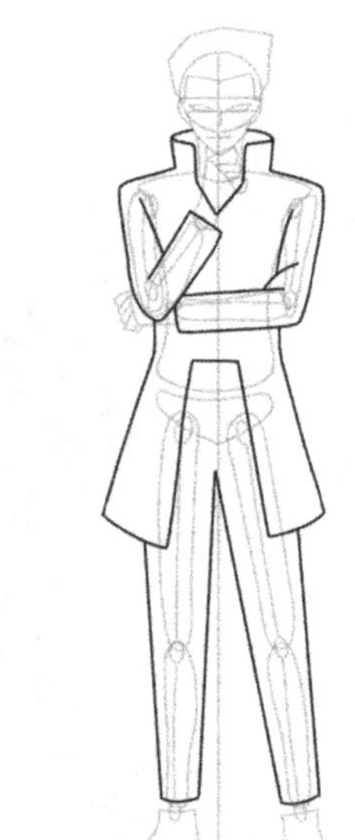

06

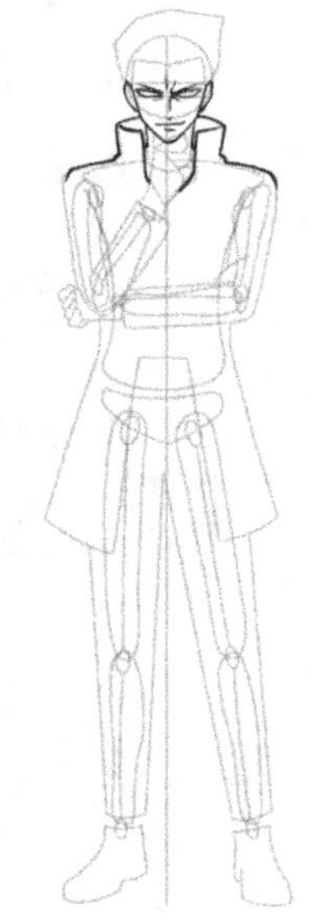

07

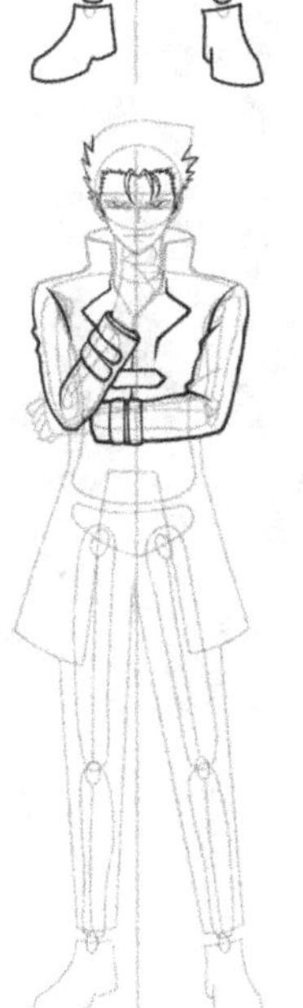

08

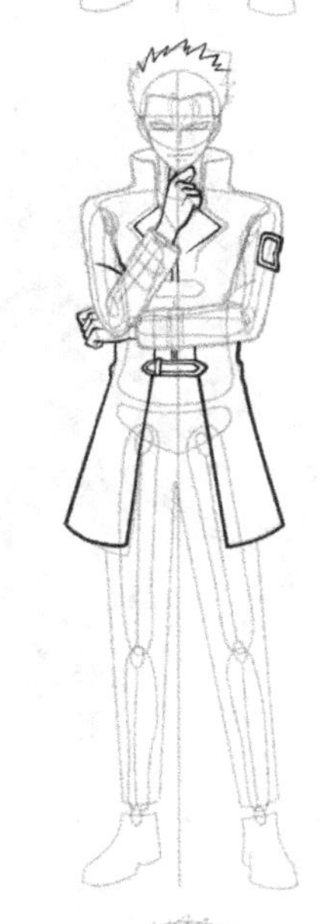

09

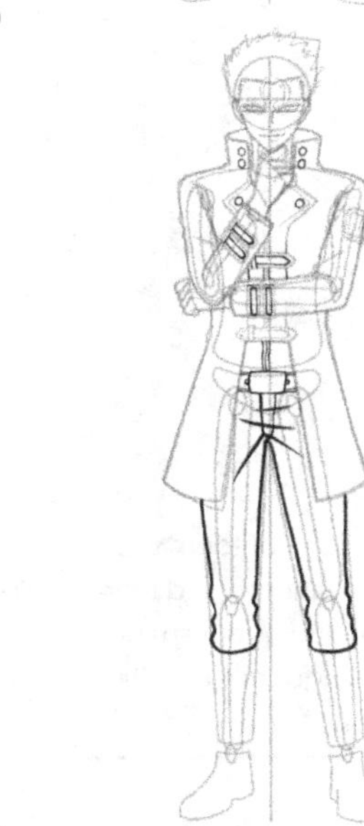

10

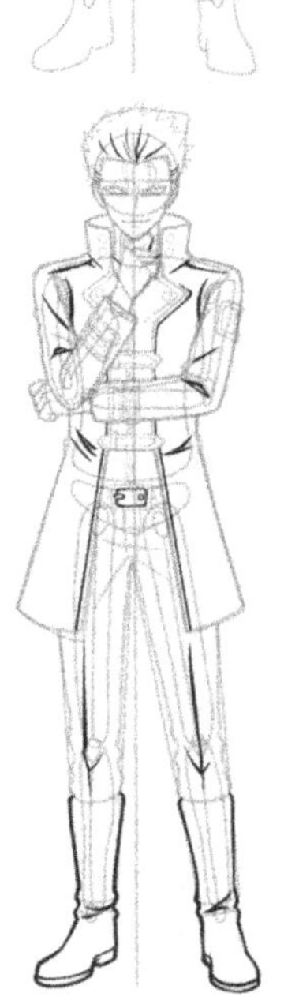

11

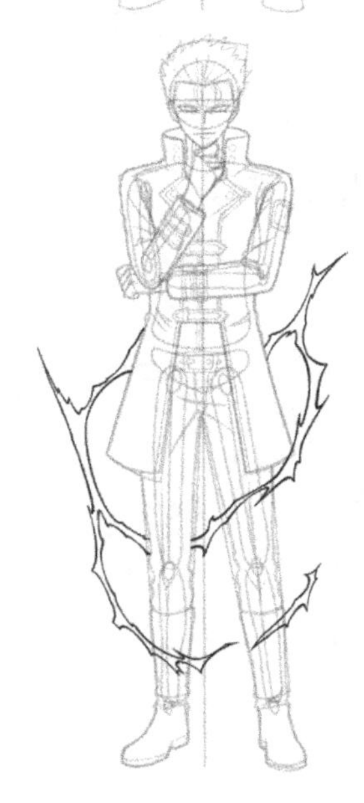

12

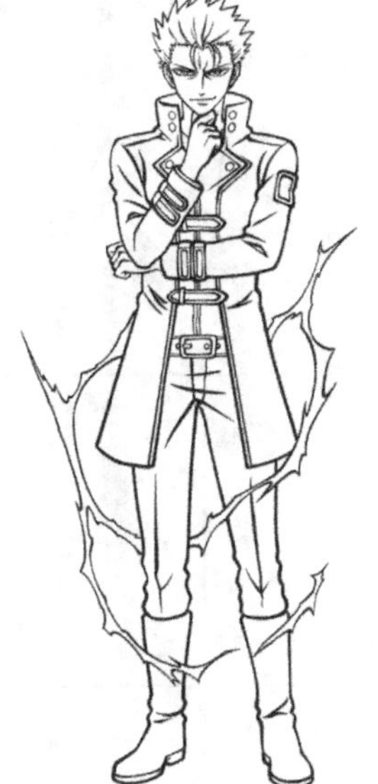

THE DELINQUENT

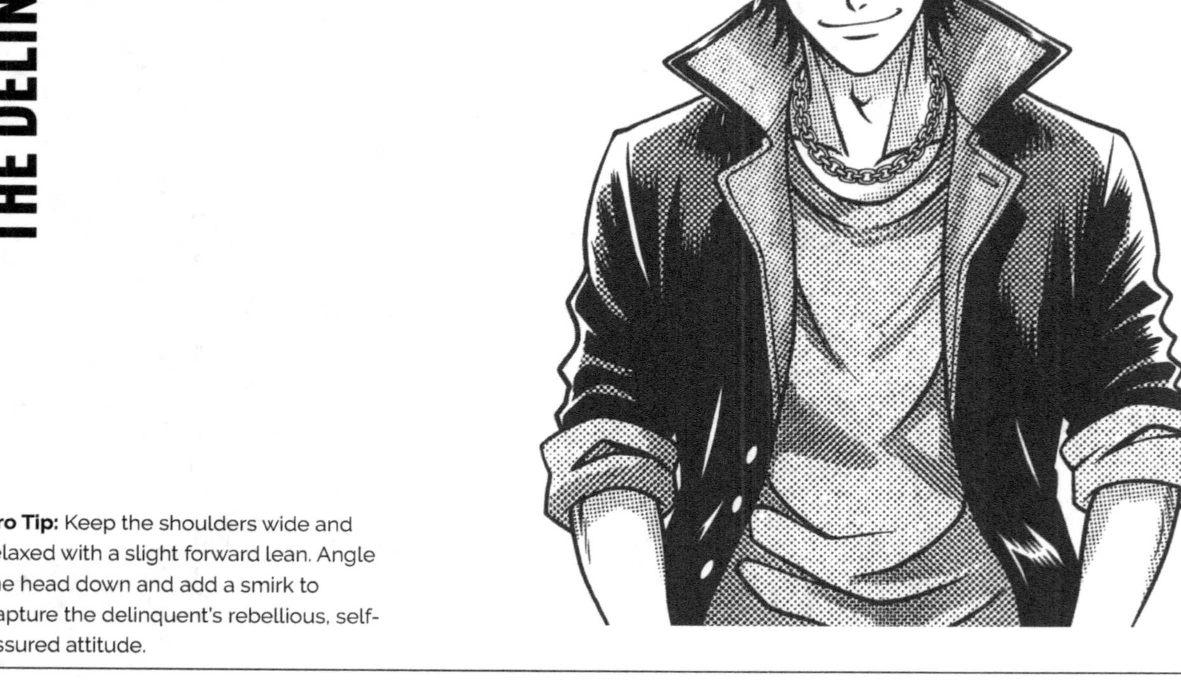

Pro Tip: Keep the shoulders wide and relaxed with a slight forward lean. Angle the head down and add a smirk to capture the delinquent's rebellious, self-assured attitude.

01

02

03

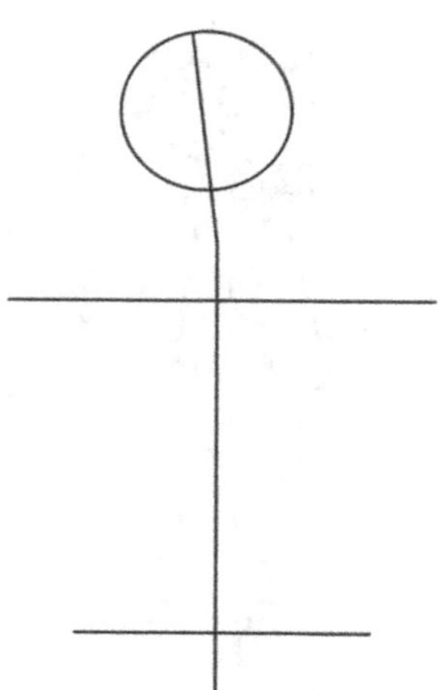

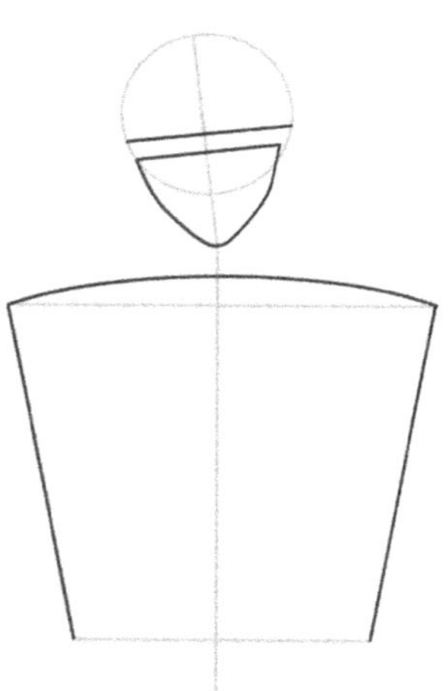

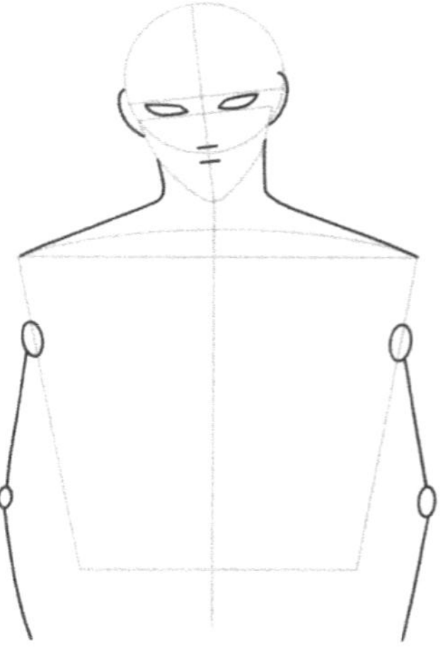

04

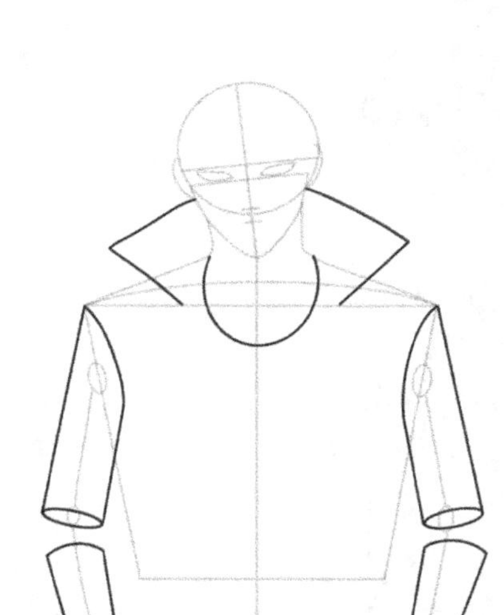

05

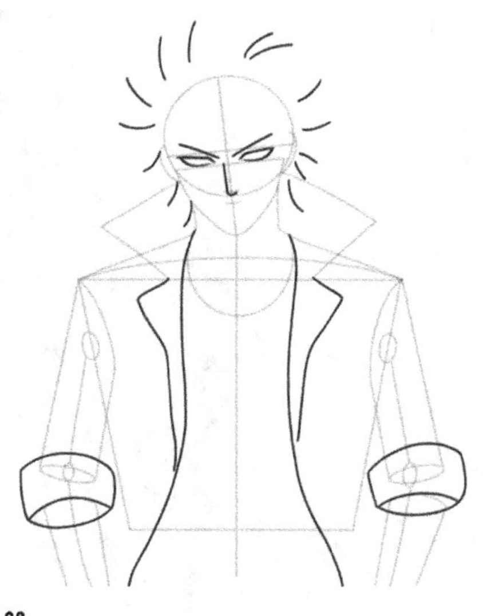

06

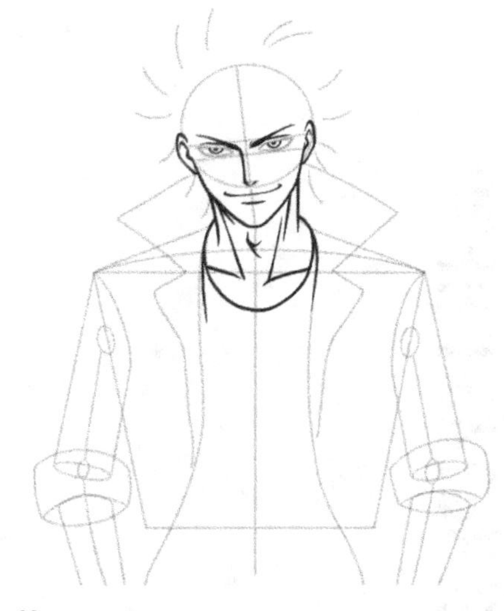

07

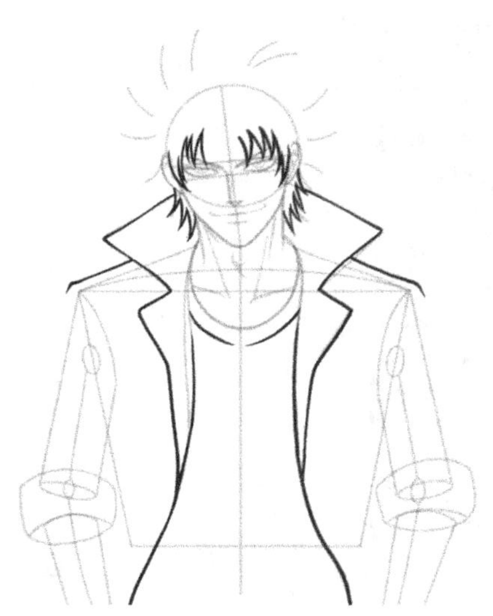

08

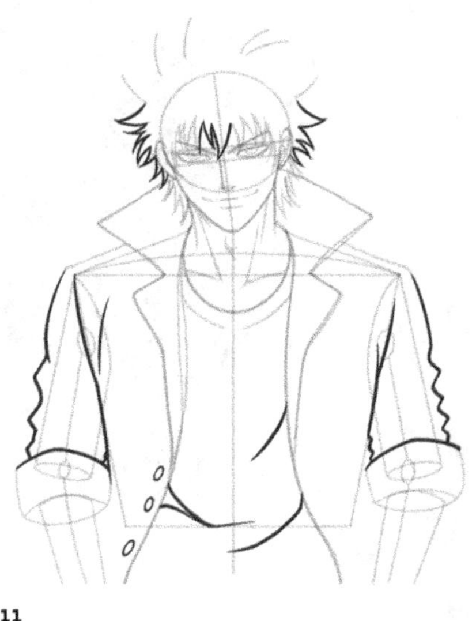

09

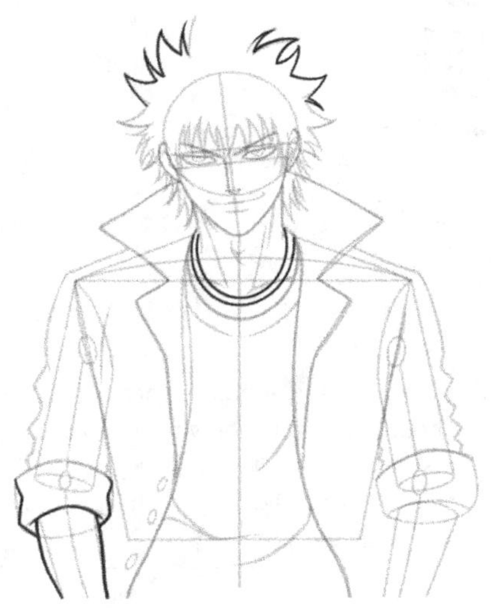

10

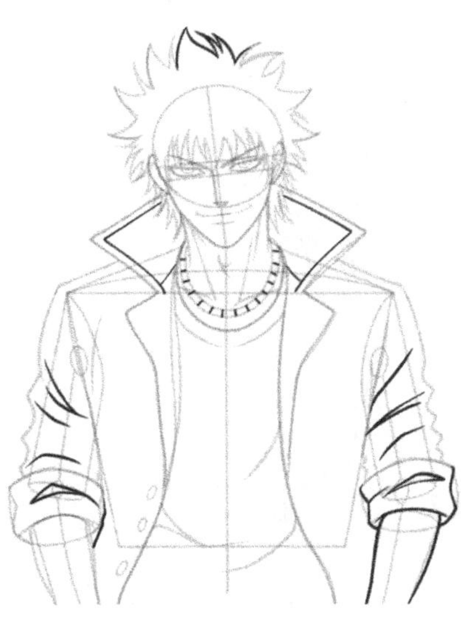

11

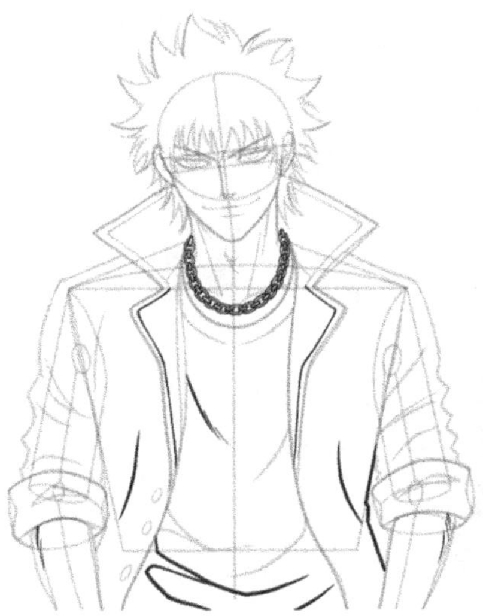

12

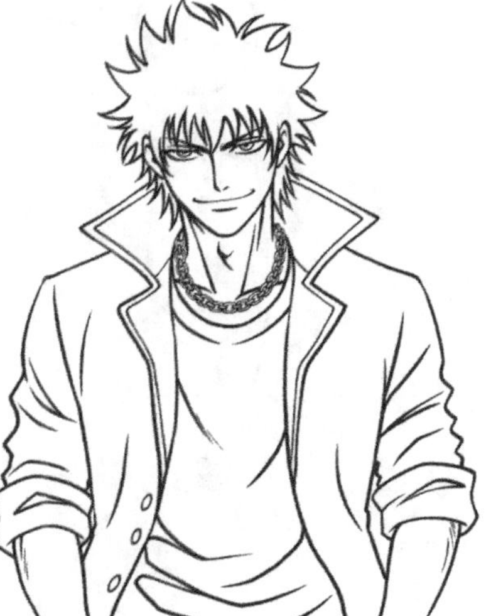

THE RELUCTANT HERO

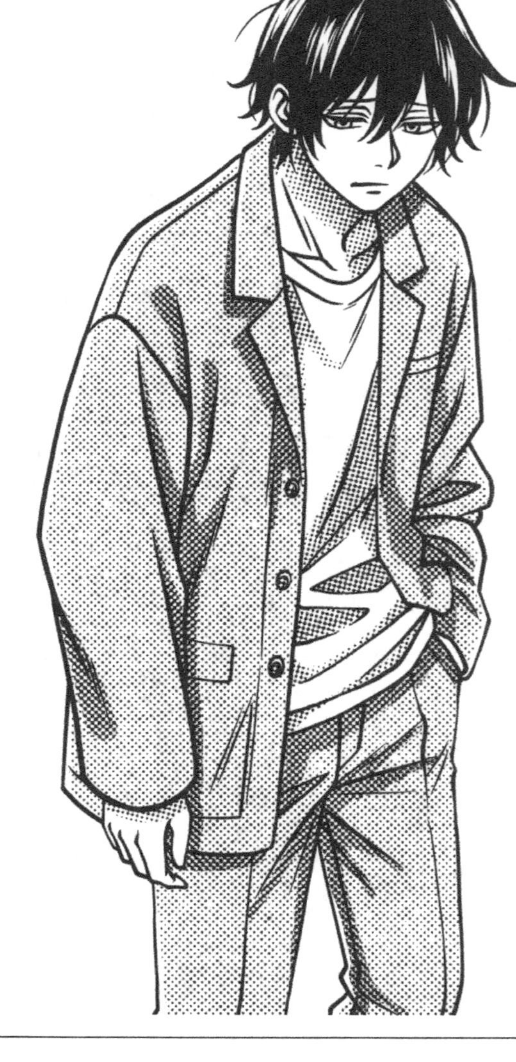

Pro Tip: Drop the shoulders and tilt the head forward to show hesitation. Keep the posture slightly slouched to convey inner conflict while still hinting at underlying strength.

01

02

03

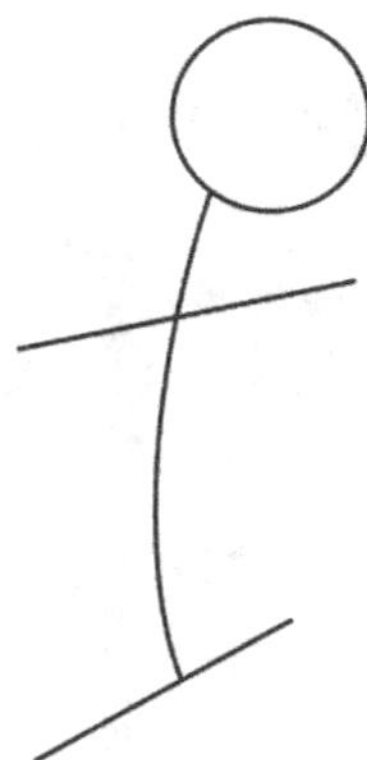

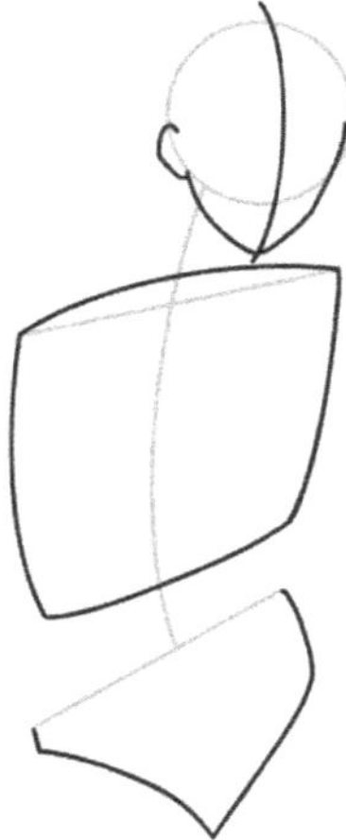

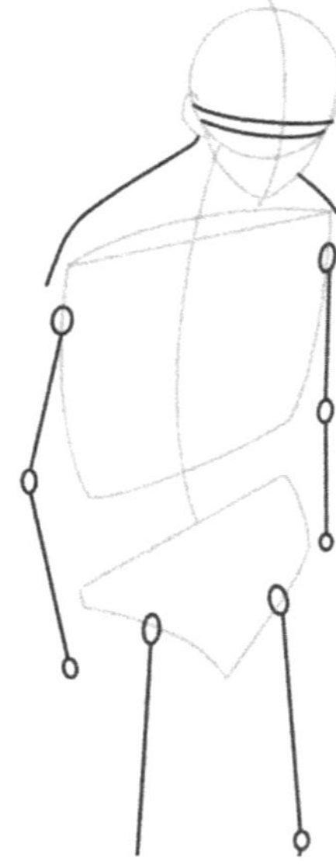

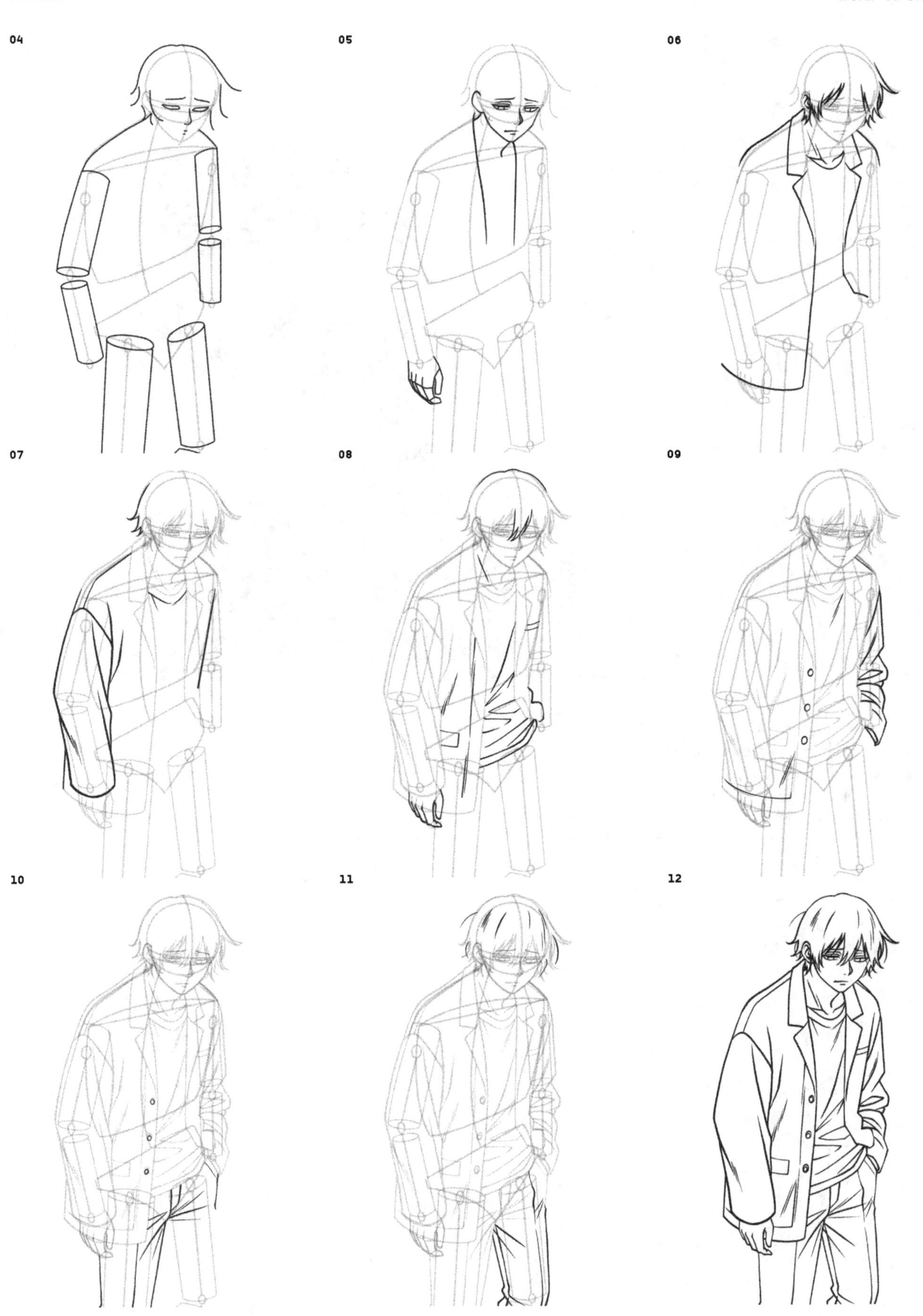

CYBER PUNK

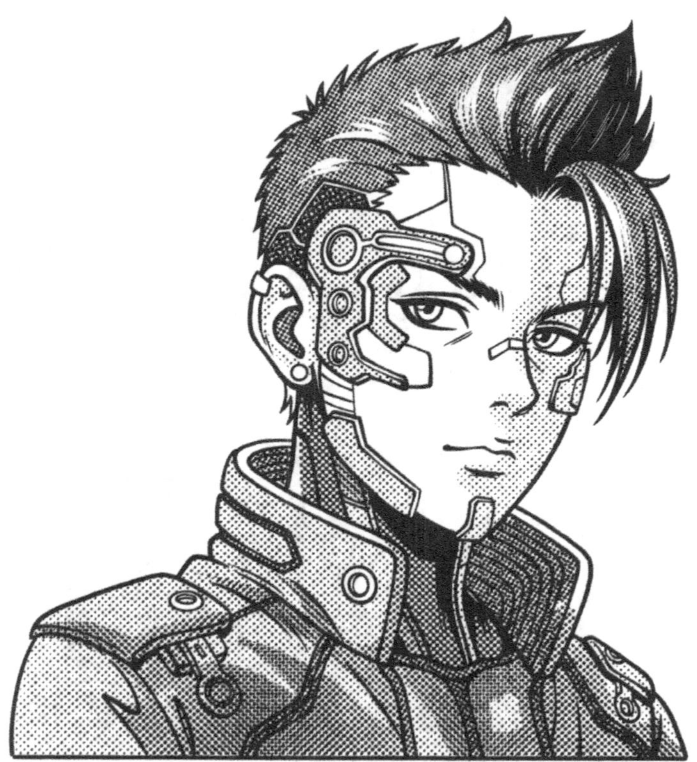

Pro Tip: Angle the head slightly downward and keep the gaze direct to create intensity. Use clean, sharp lines for cybernetic details to contrast with the organic curves of the face.

01

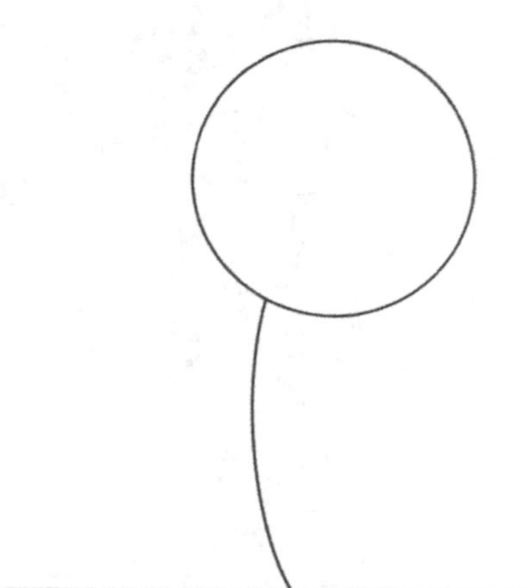

02

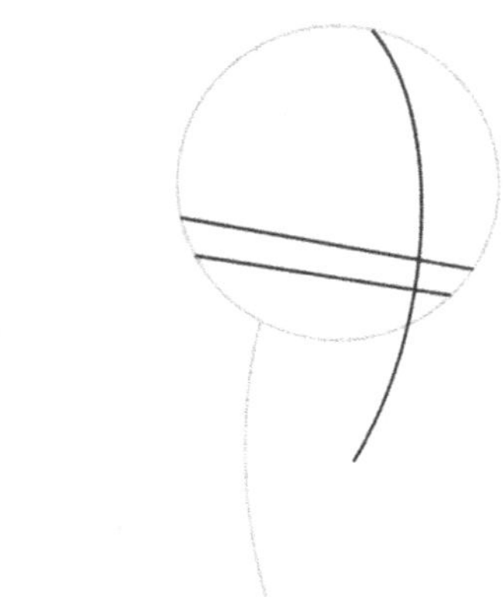

03

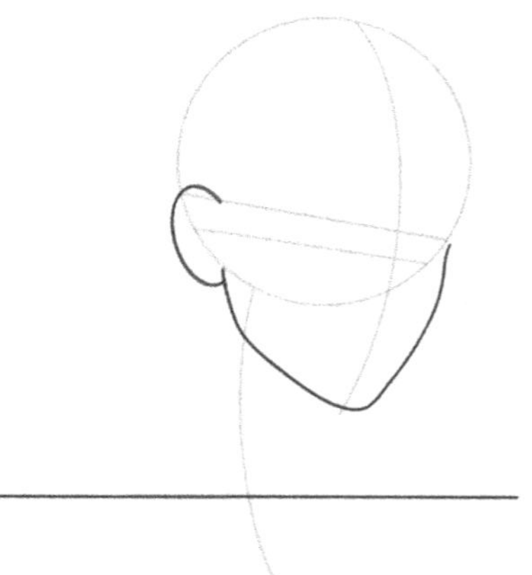

04

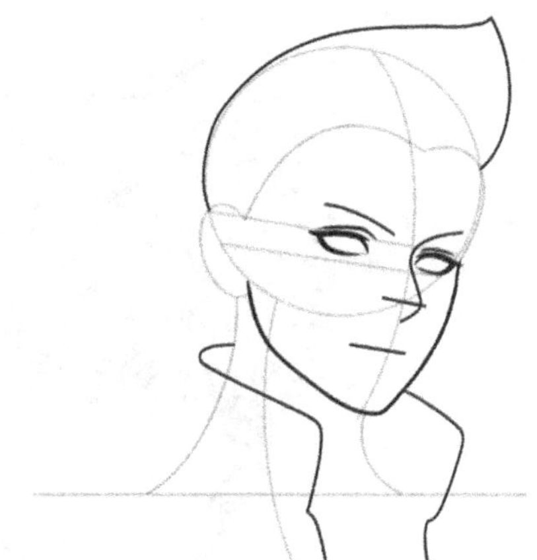

05

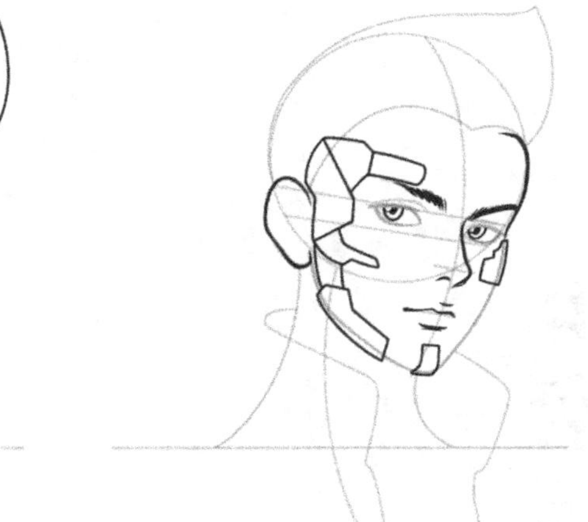

06

07

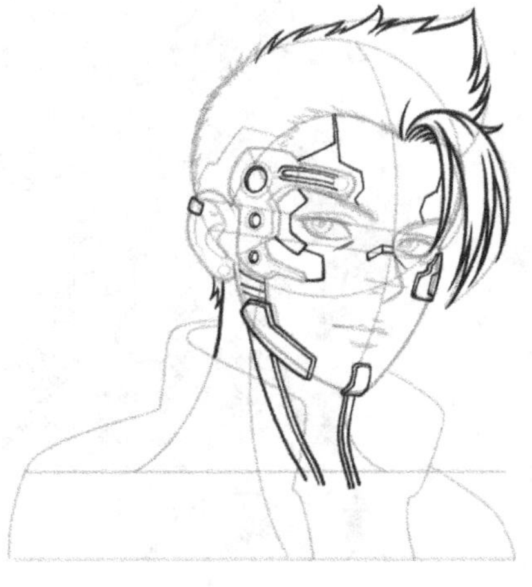

08

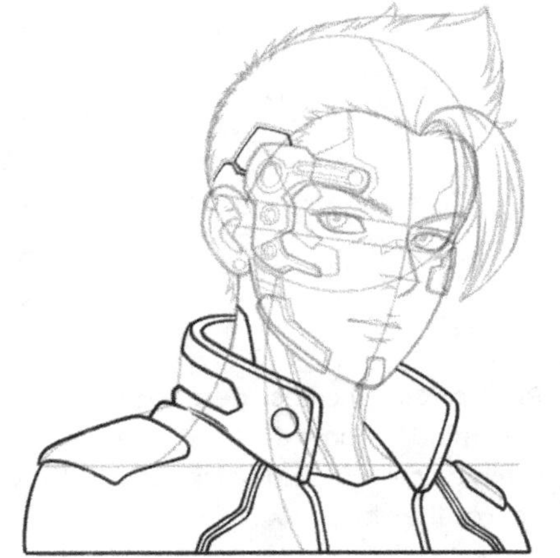

09

10

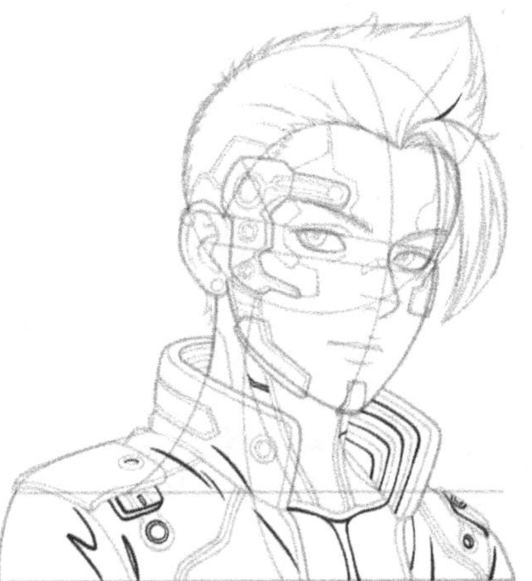

11

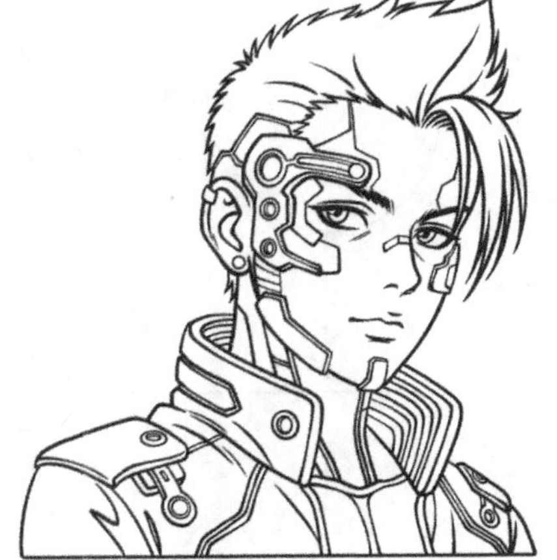

12

MECHA PILOT

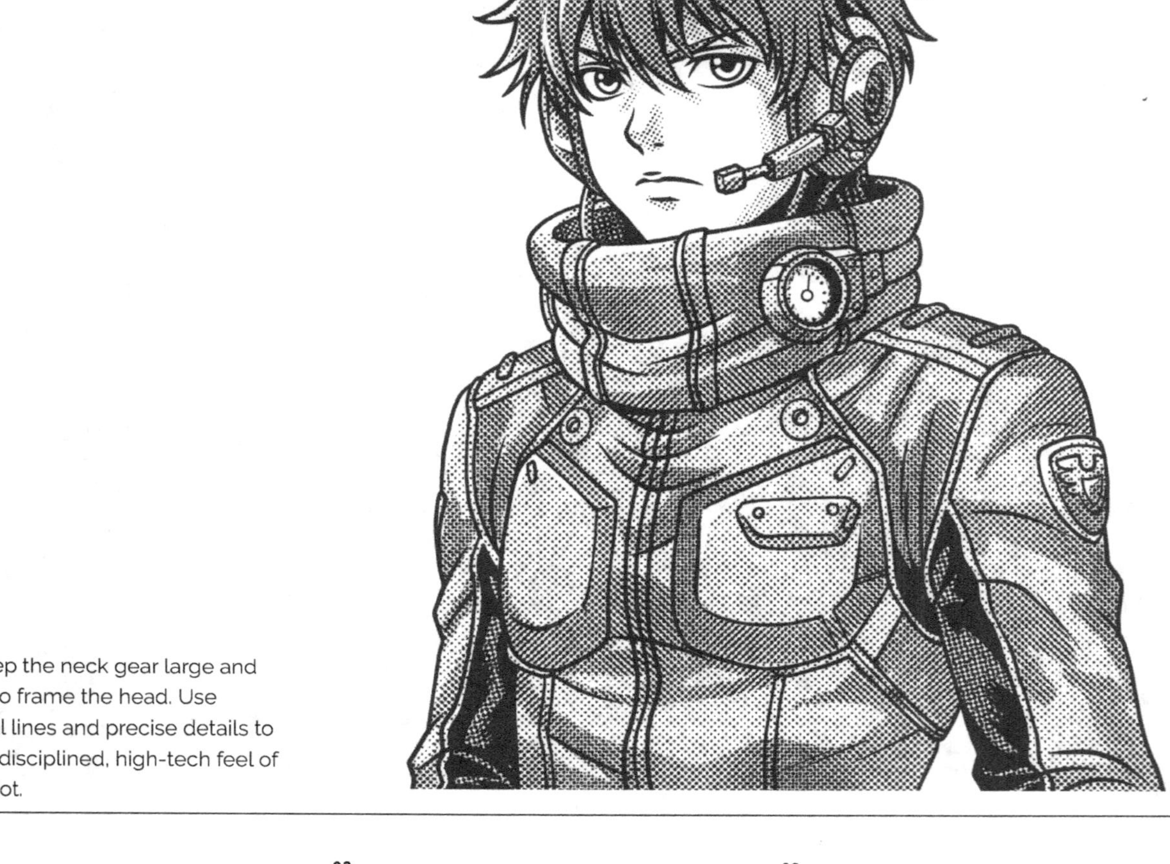

Pro Tip: Keep the neck gear large and structured to frame the head. Use symmetrical lines and precise details to convey the disciplined, high-tech feel of a trained pilot.

01

02

03

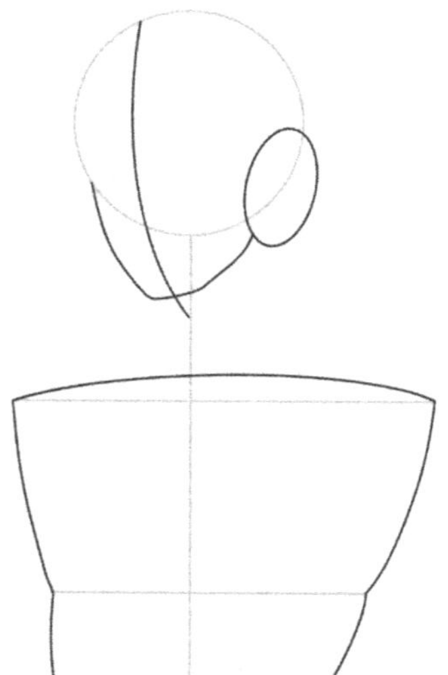

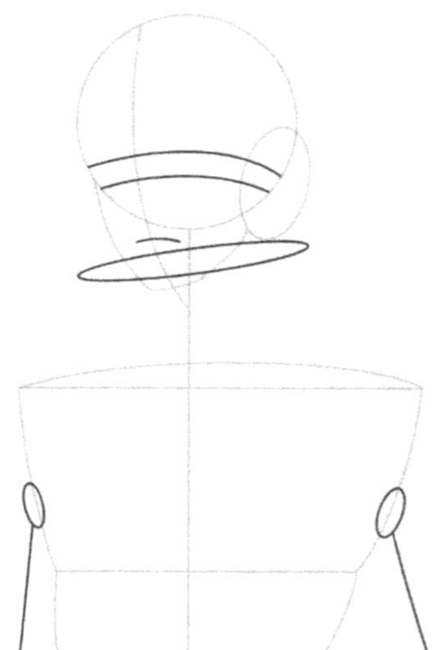

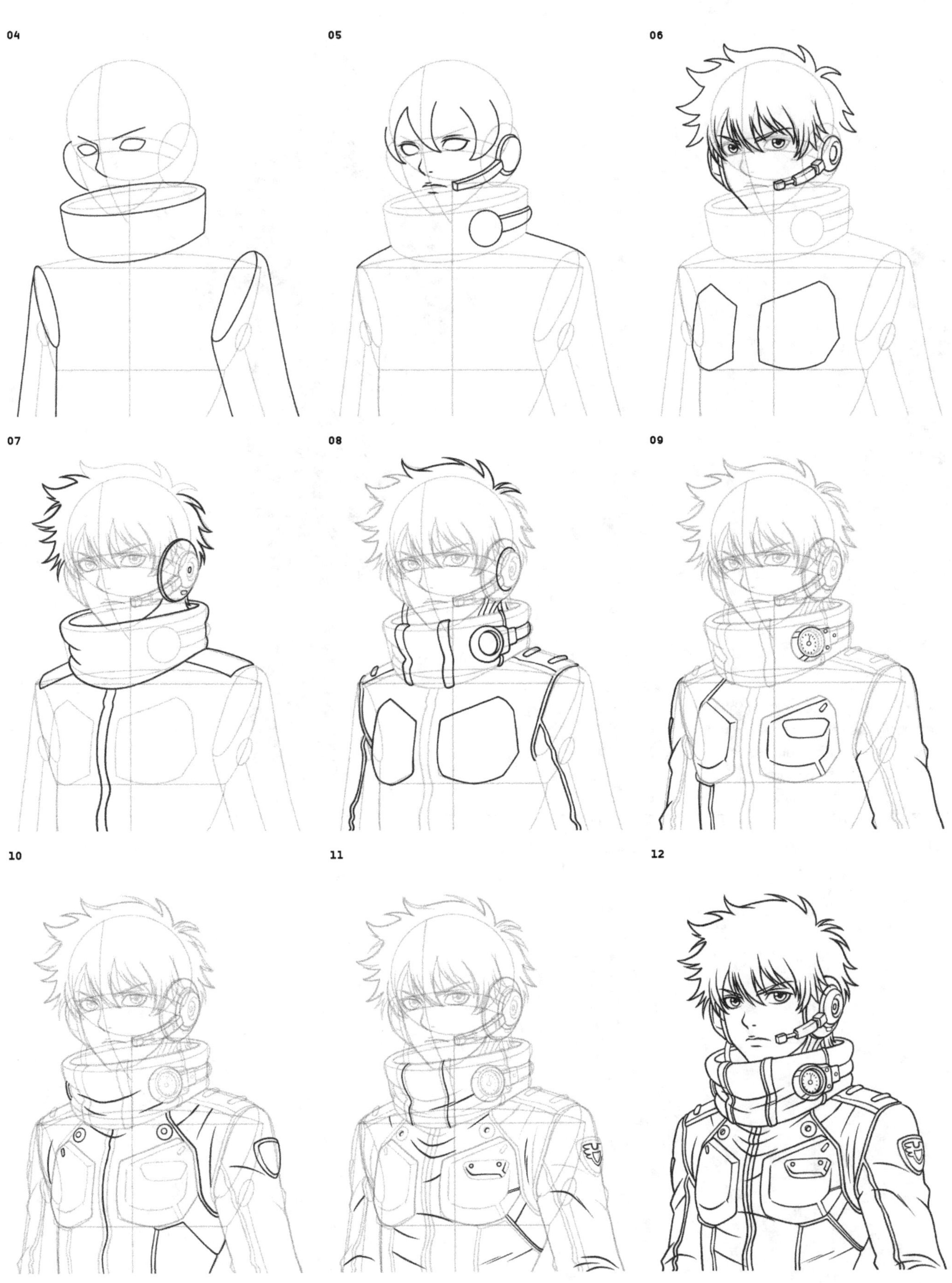
04
05
06
07
08
09
10
11
12
HOW TO DRAW ANIME

THE BUTLER

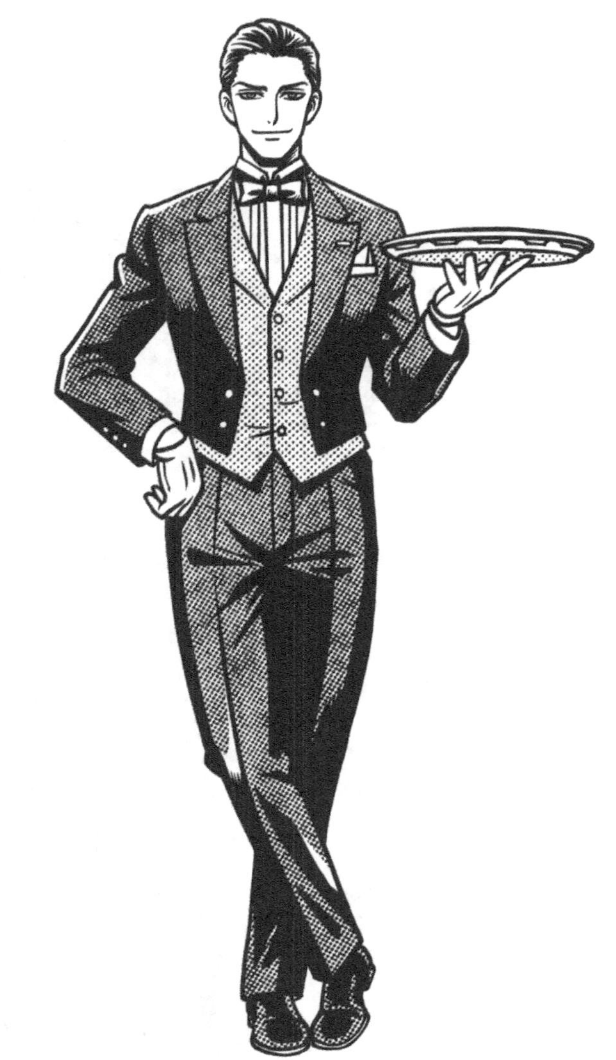

Pro Tip: Keep the spine straight and
the shoulders relaxed to show poise.
Cross the legs neatly and raise one hand
slightly to express calm control and
effortless sophistication.

01

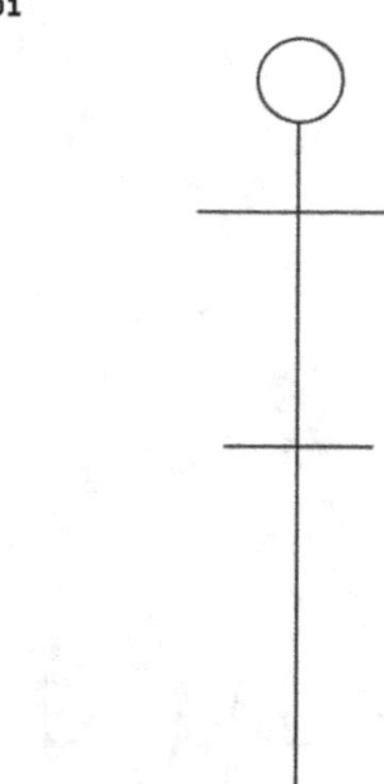

02

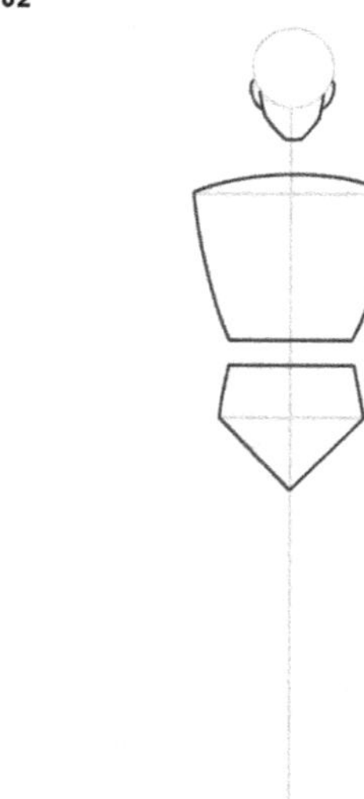

03

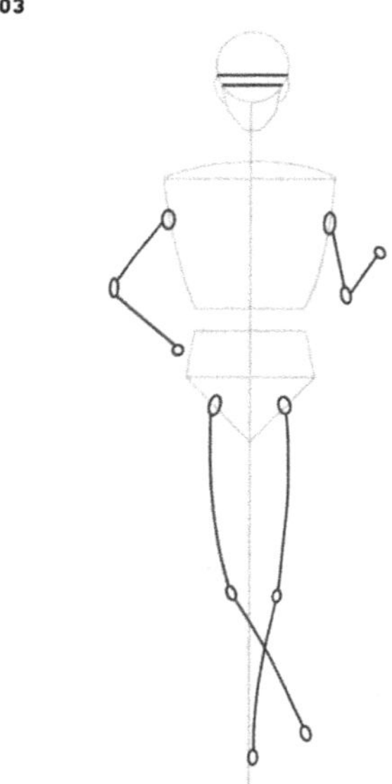

04

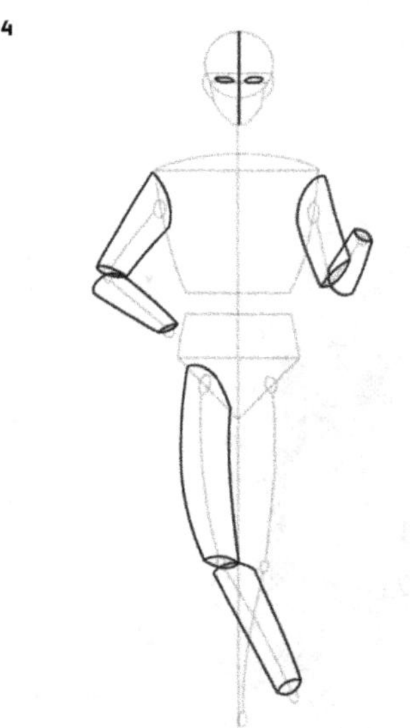

05

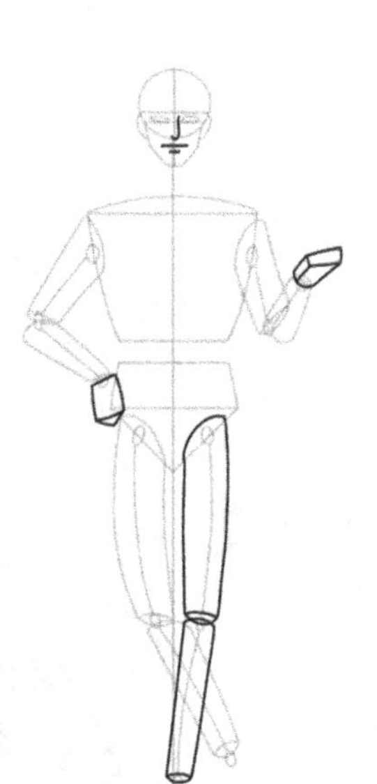

06

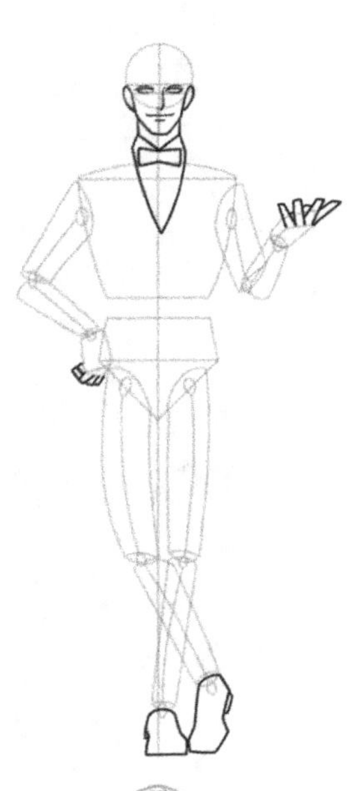

07

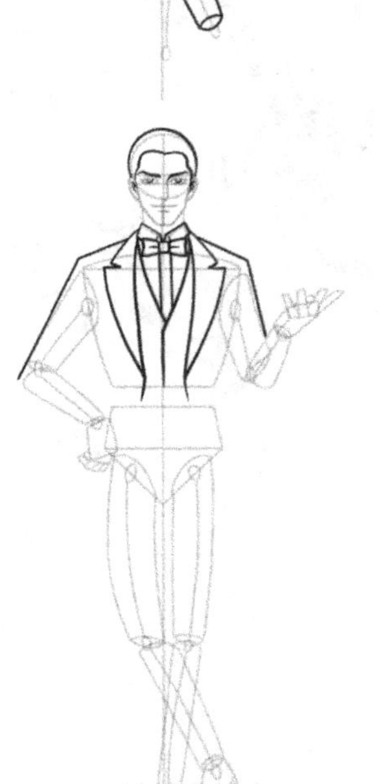

08

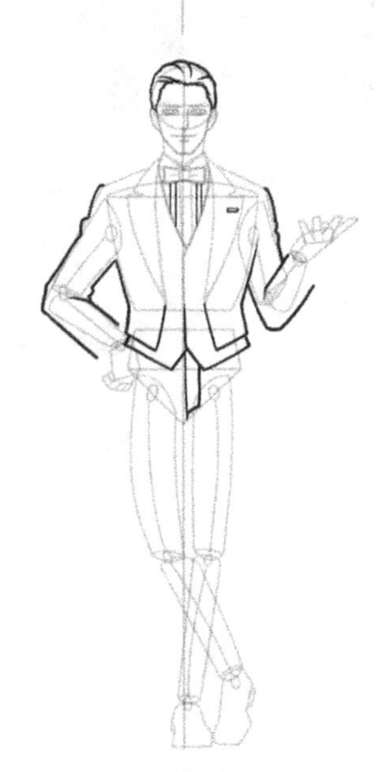

09

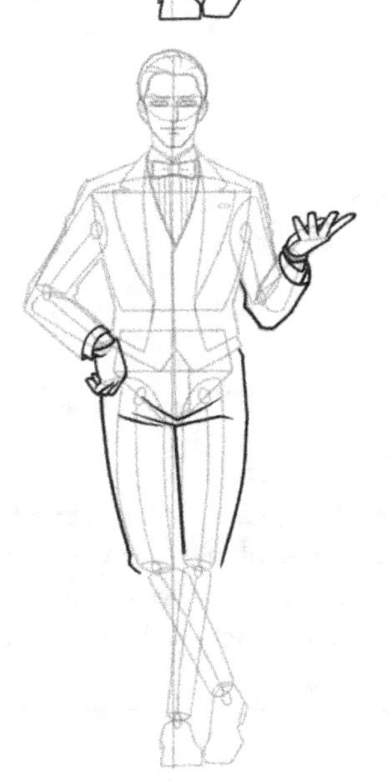

10

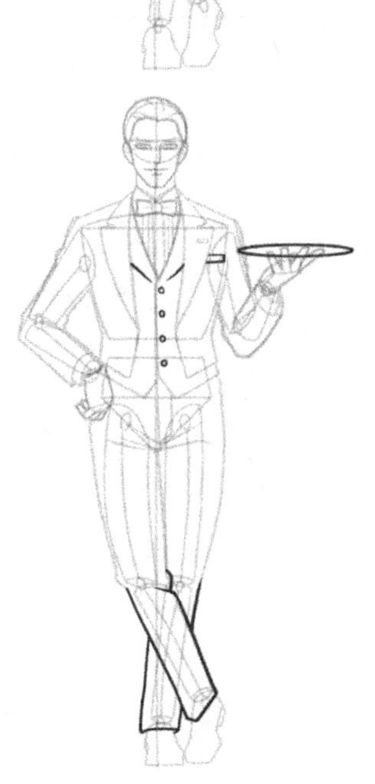

11

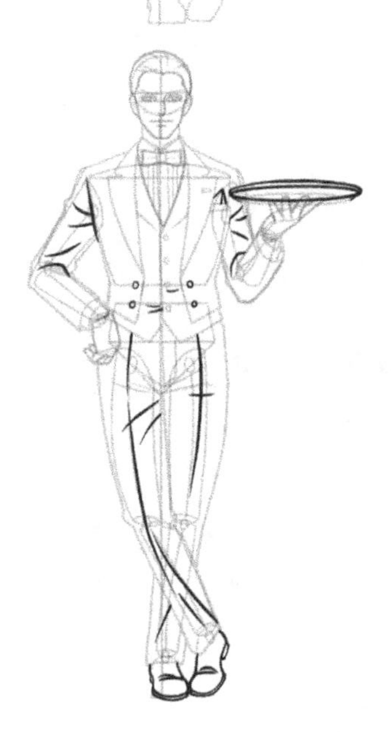

12

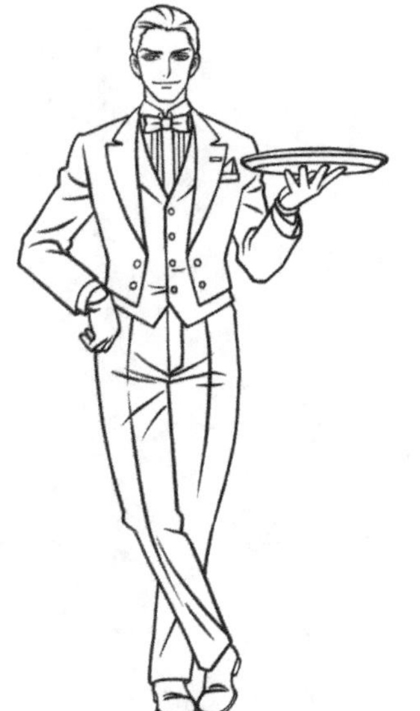

COMIC RELIEF

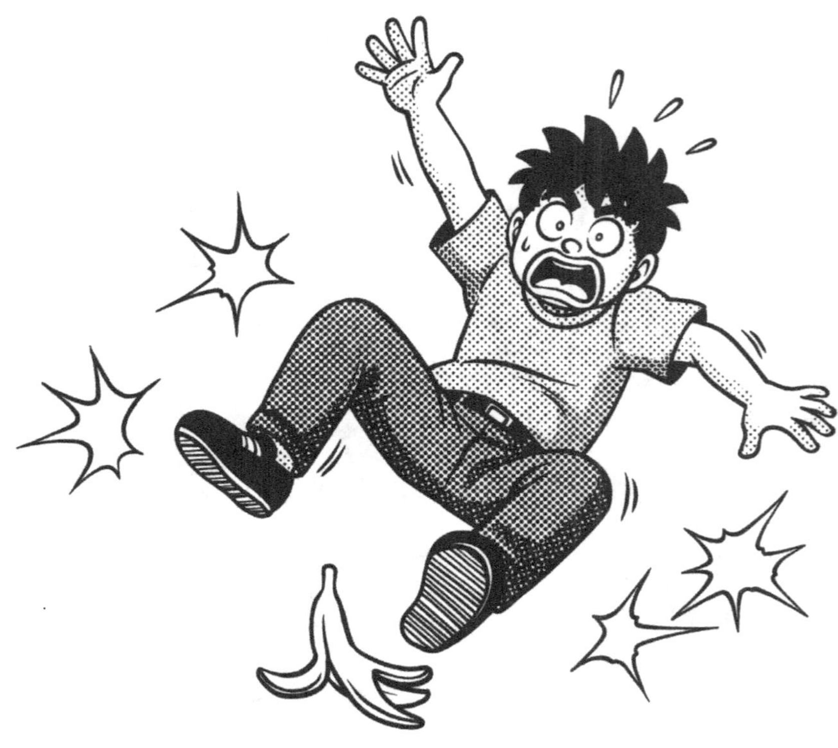

Pro Tip: Exaggerate the limbs and facial features to heighten the sense of panic and motion. Keep the hands open and body off balance to sell the comedic, mid-fall energy.

01   02   03

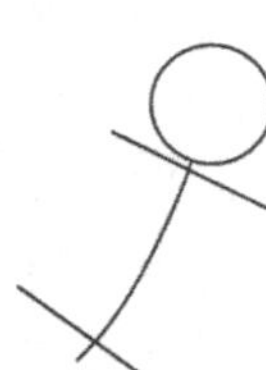

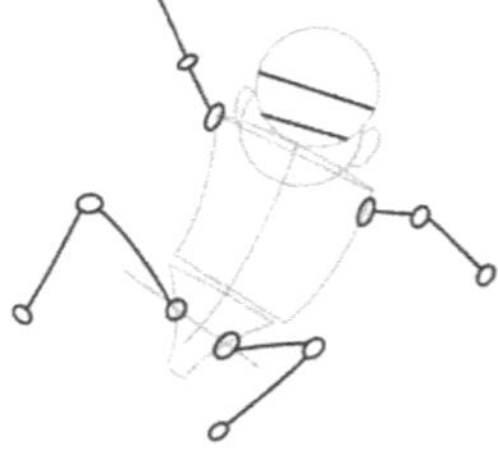

04

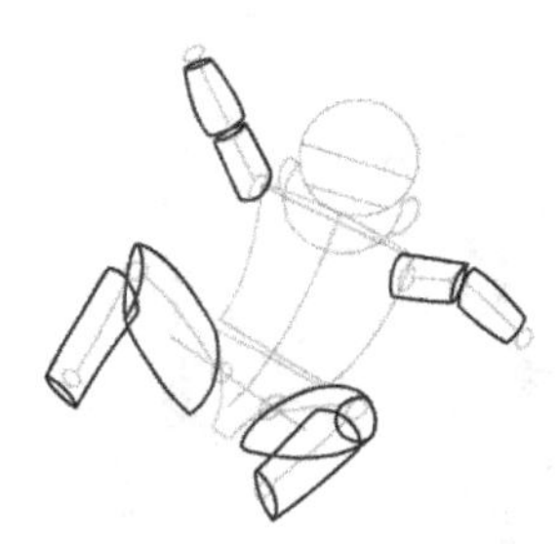

05

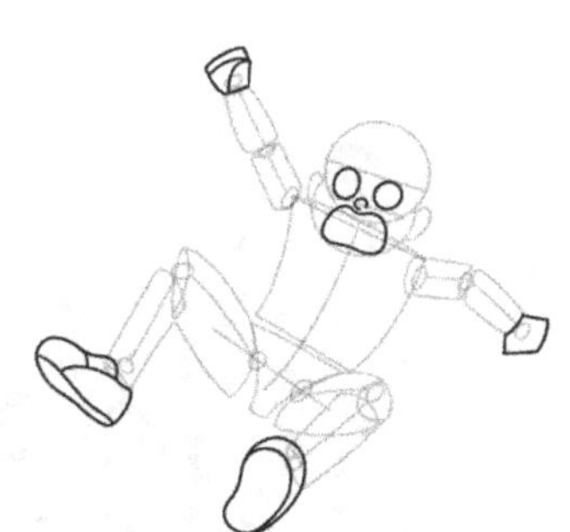

06

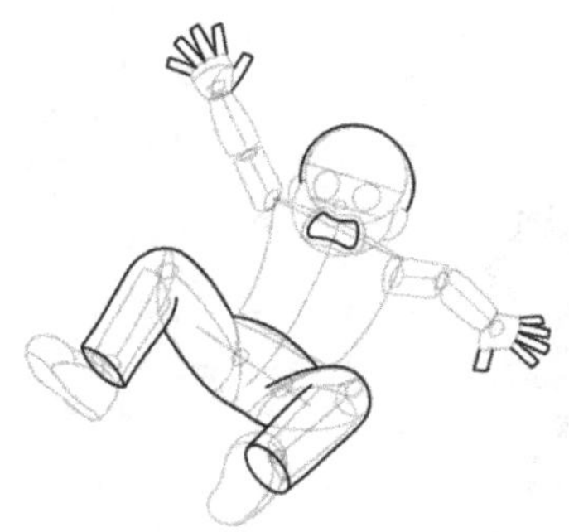

07

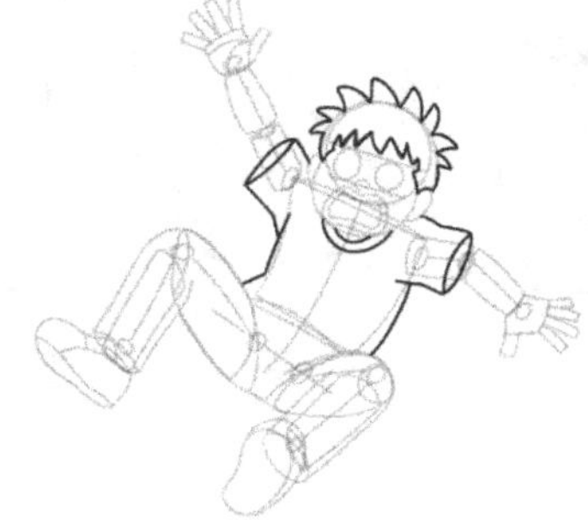

08

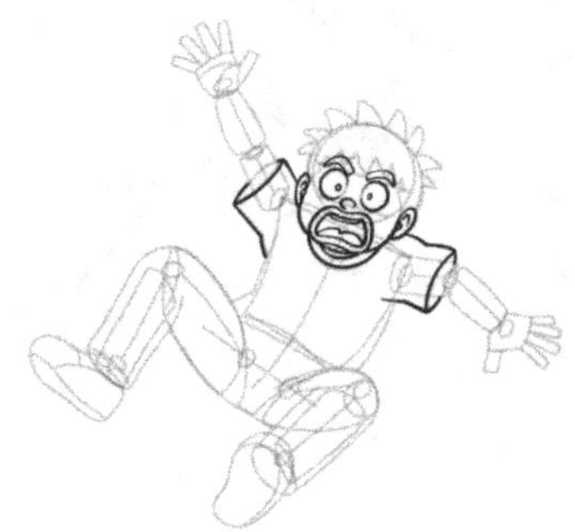

09

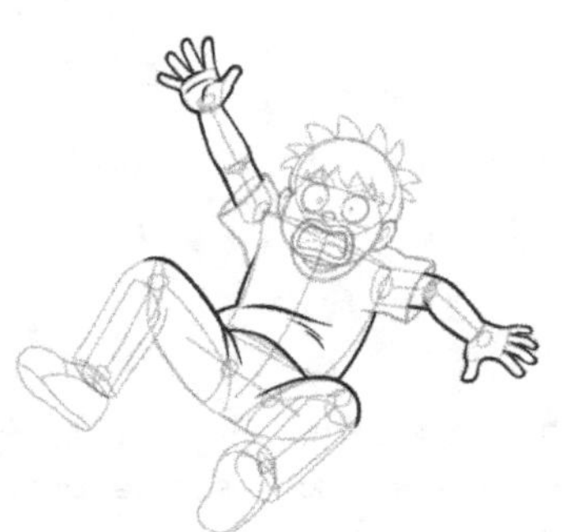

10

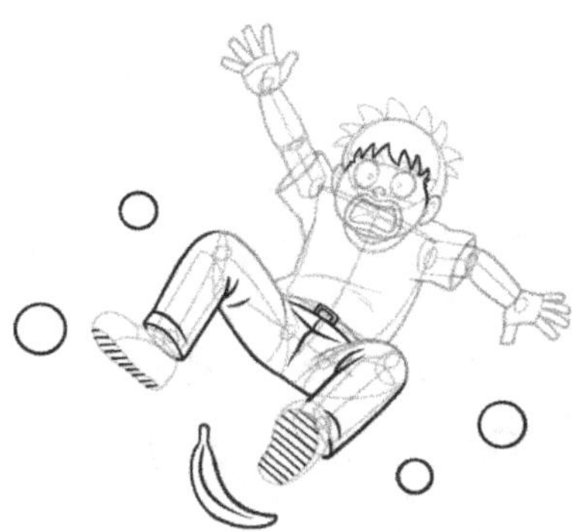

11

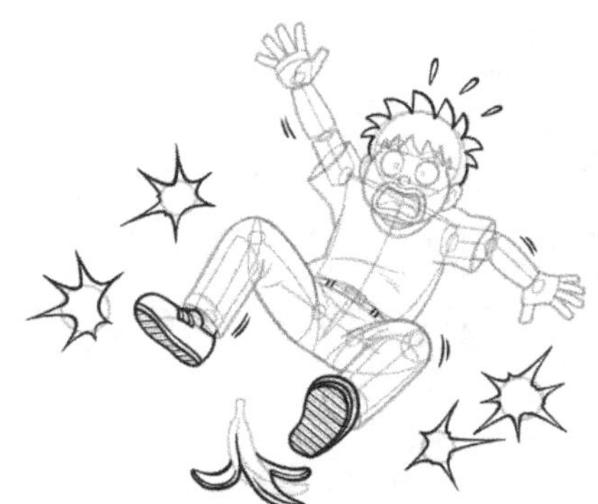

12

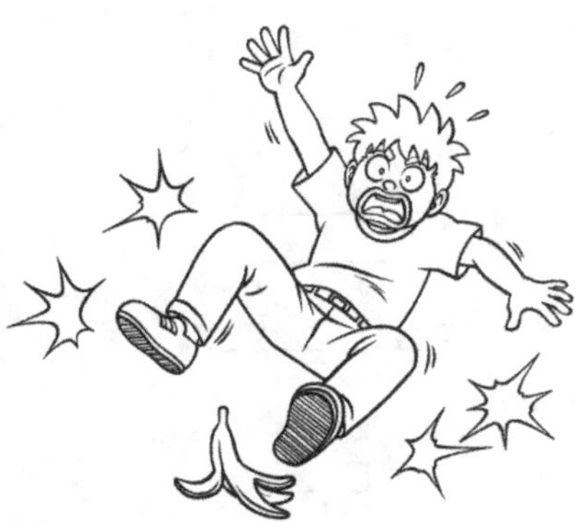

ANIMAL SIDEKICK

Pro Tip: Keep the body compact and rounded to emphasise cuteness and balance. Oversized ears, eyes, and tail help exaggerate personality—perfect for a magical animal companion.

01

02

03

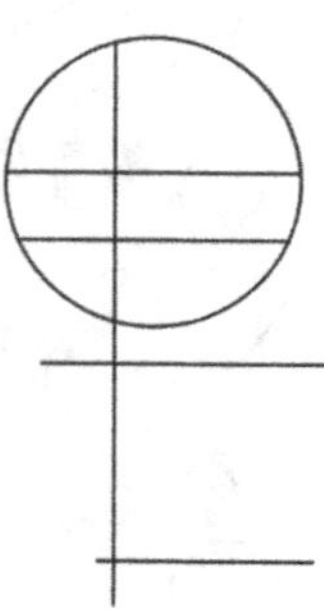

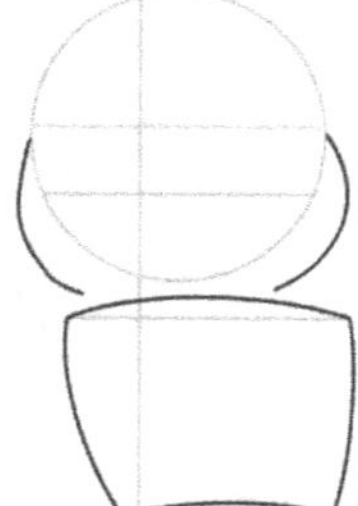

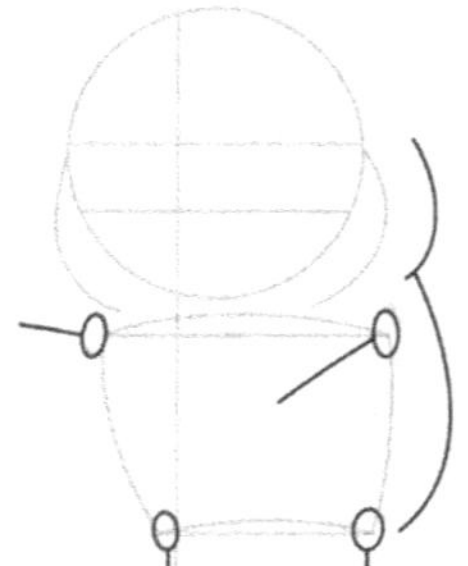

04

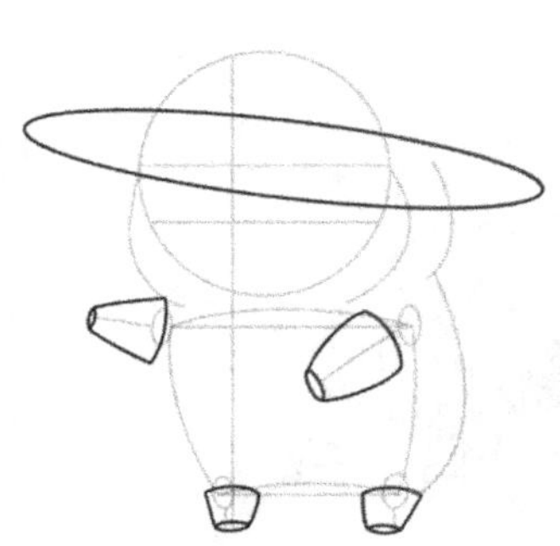

05

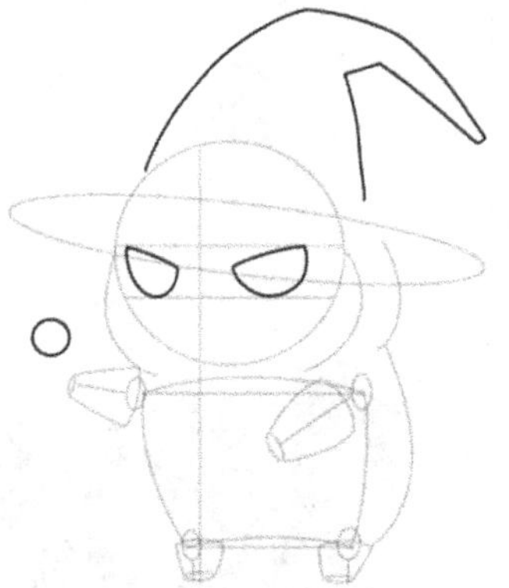

06

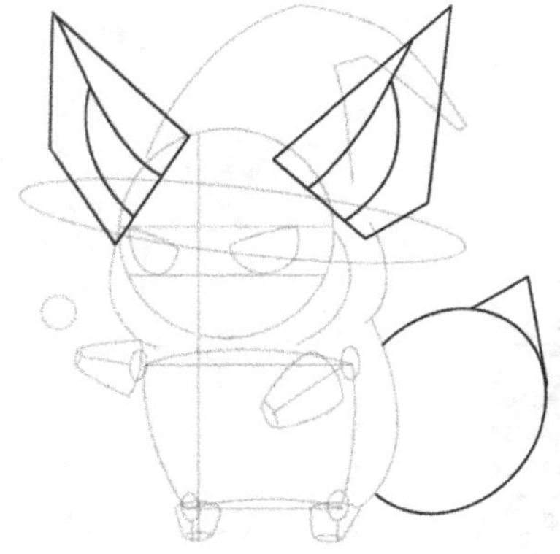

07

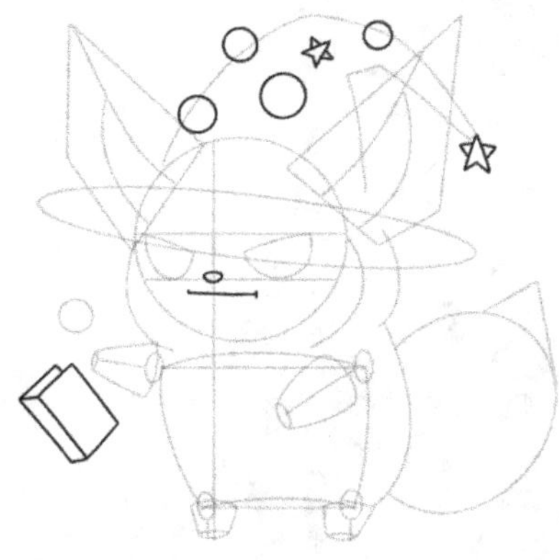

08

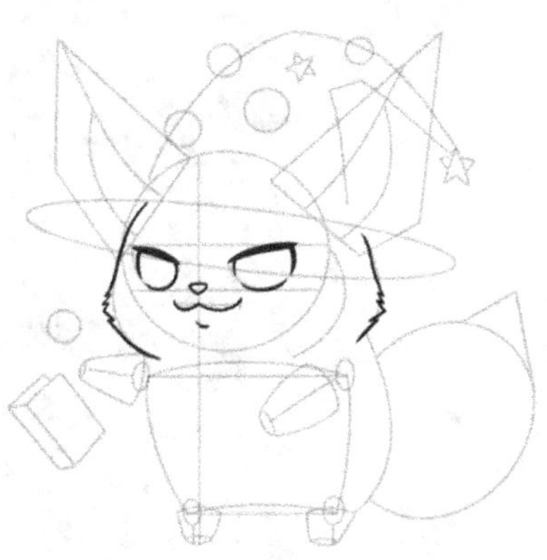

09

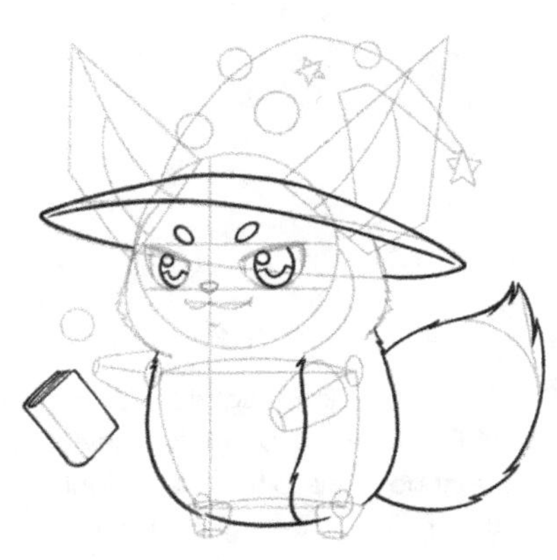

10

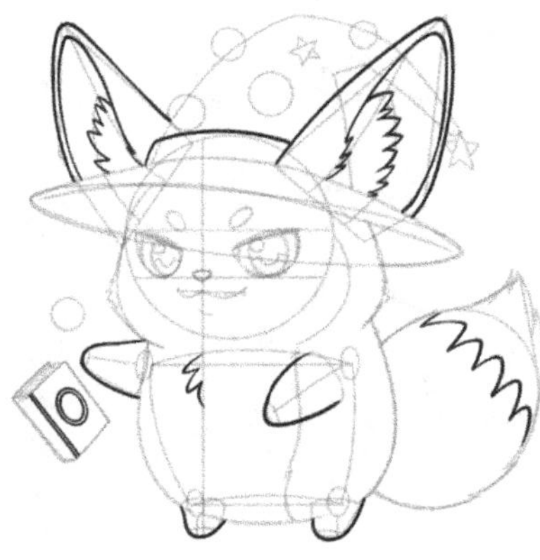

11

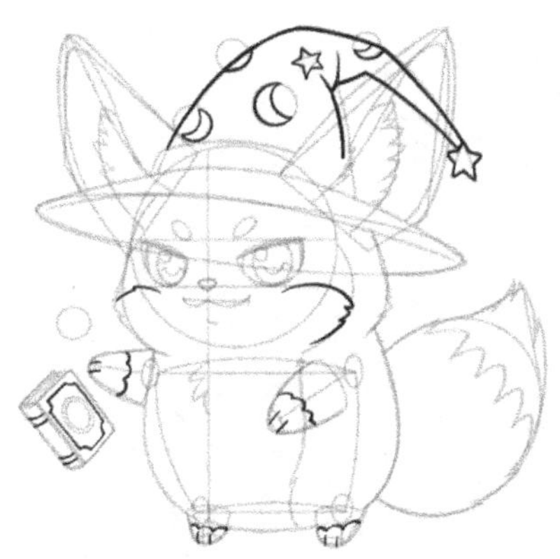

12

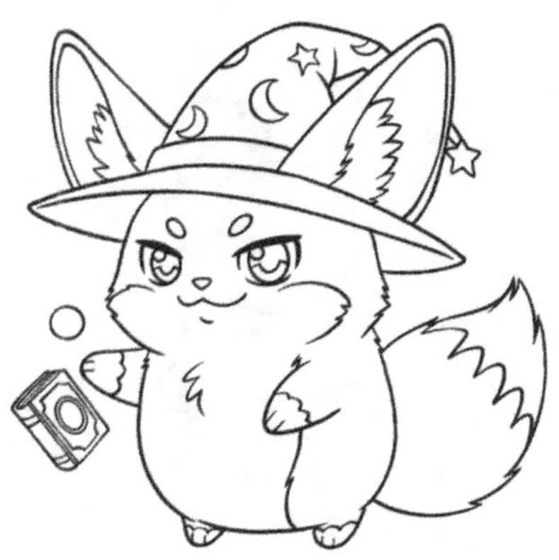

THE WITCH

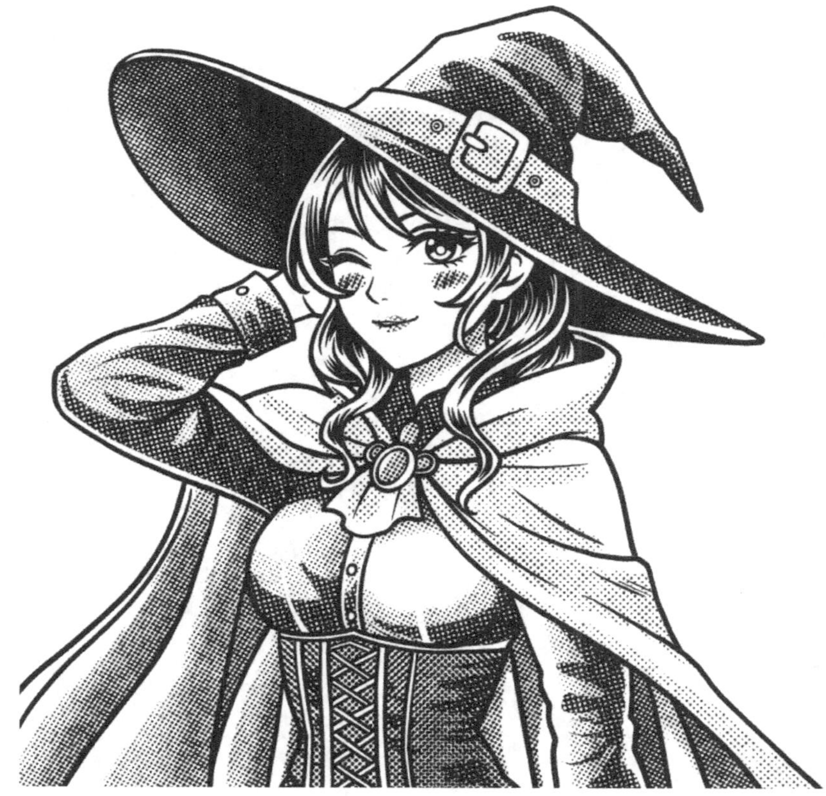

Pro Tip: Tilt the head slightly and lift one arm to touch the hat brim for a playful, confident pose. Keep the eyes bright and the smile subtle to give the witch a charming, mysterious look.

01

02

03

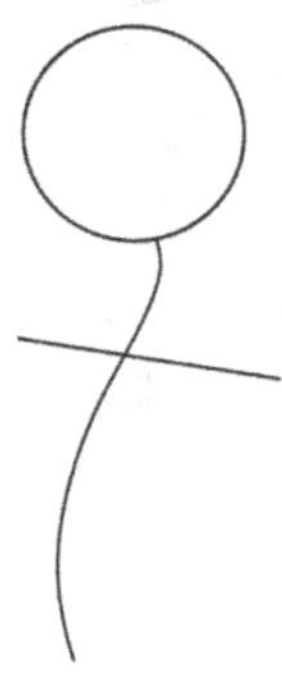

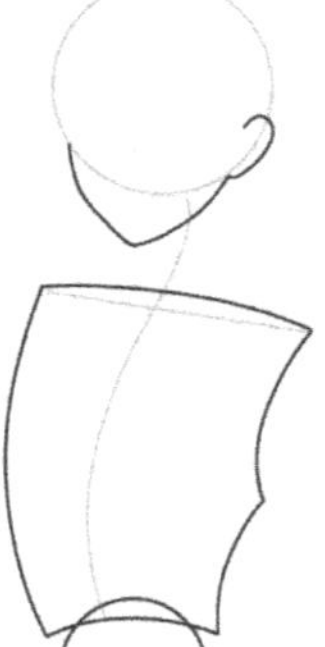

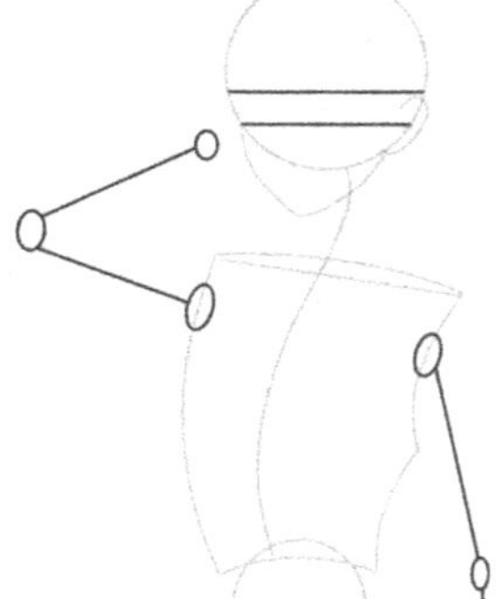

04

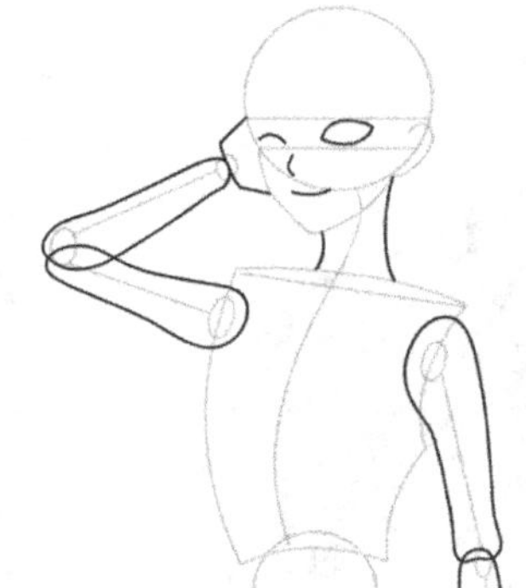
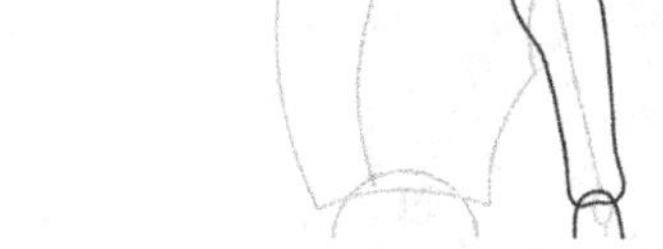

05

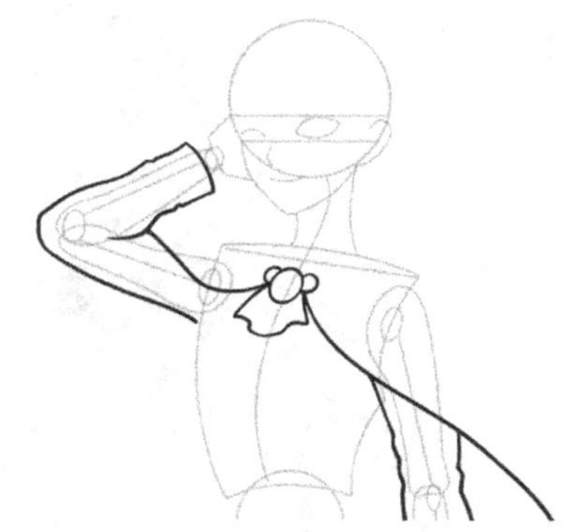

06

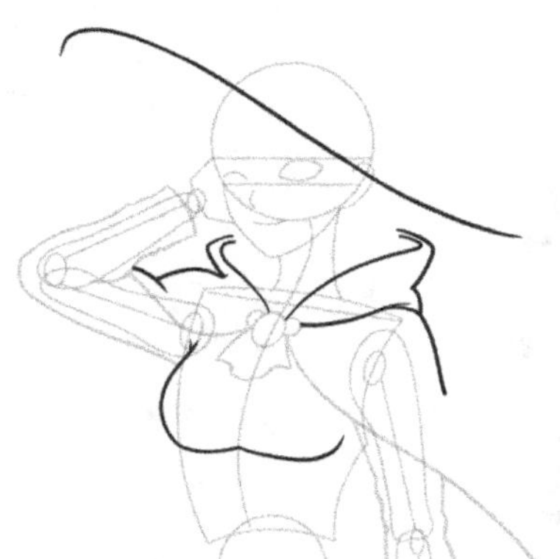

07

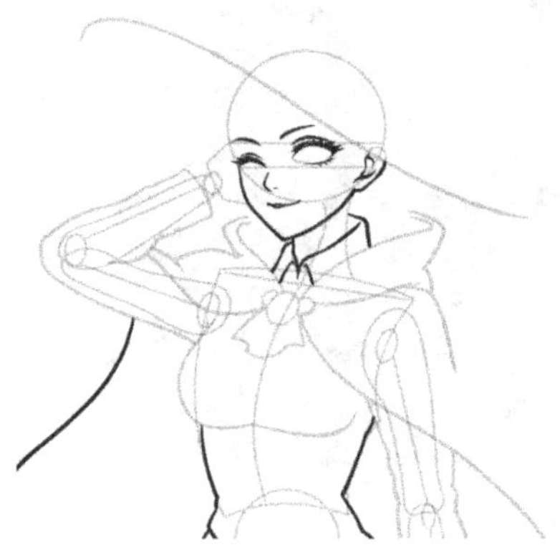

08

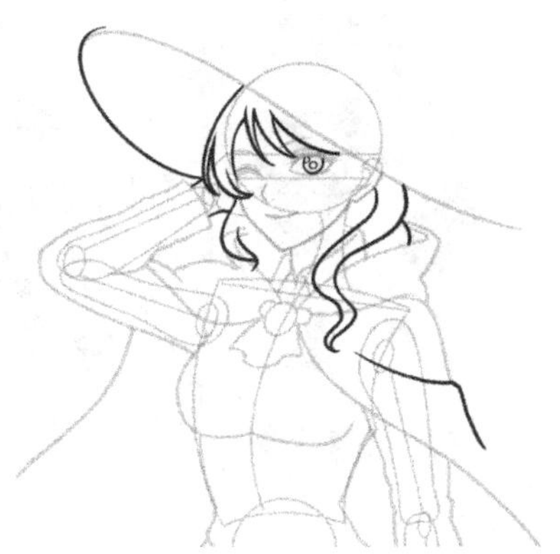

09

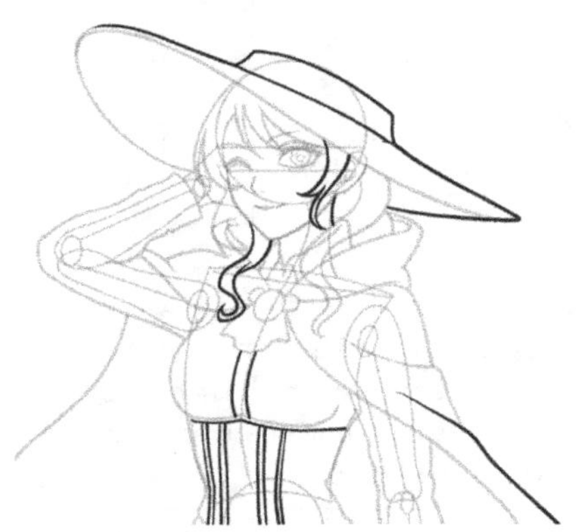

10

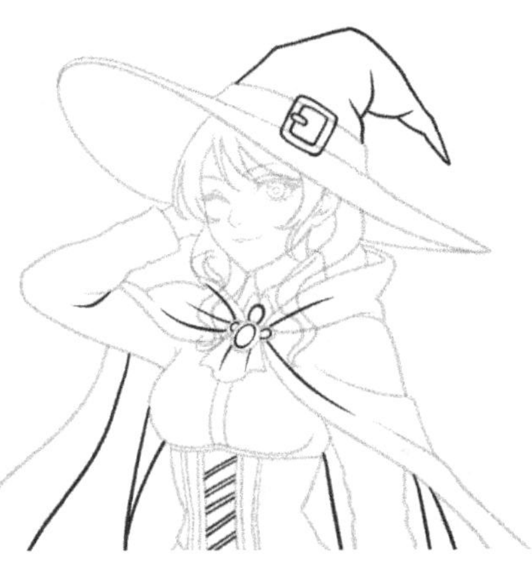

11

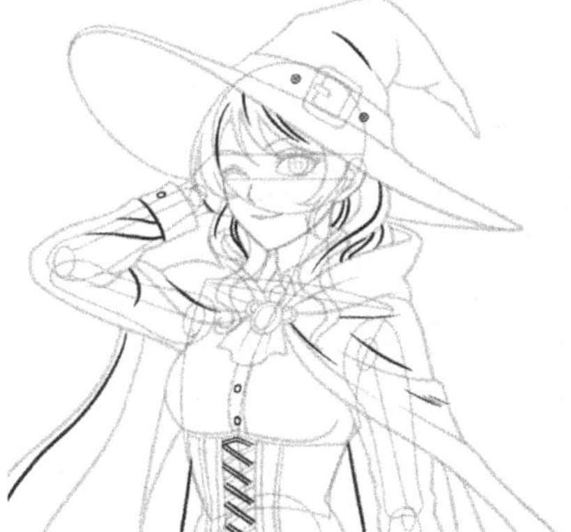

12

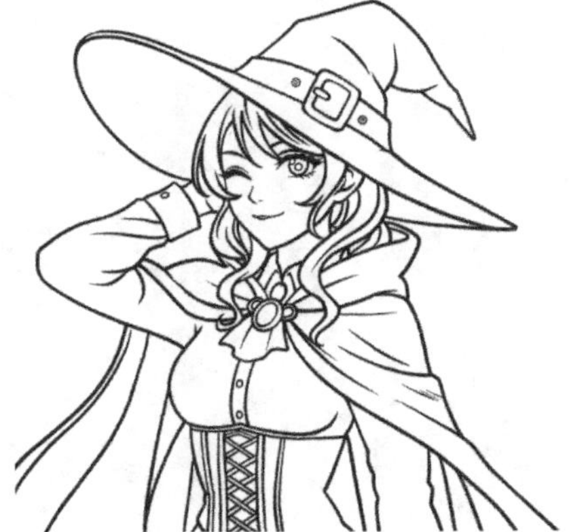

THE GODDESS

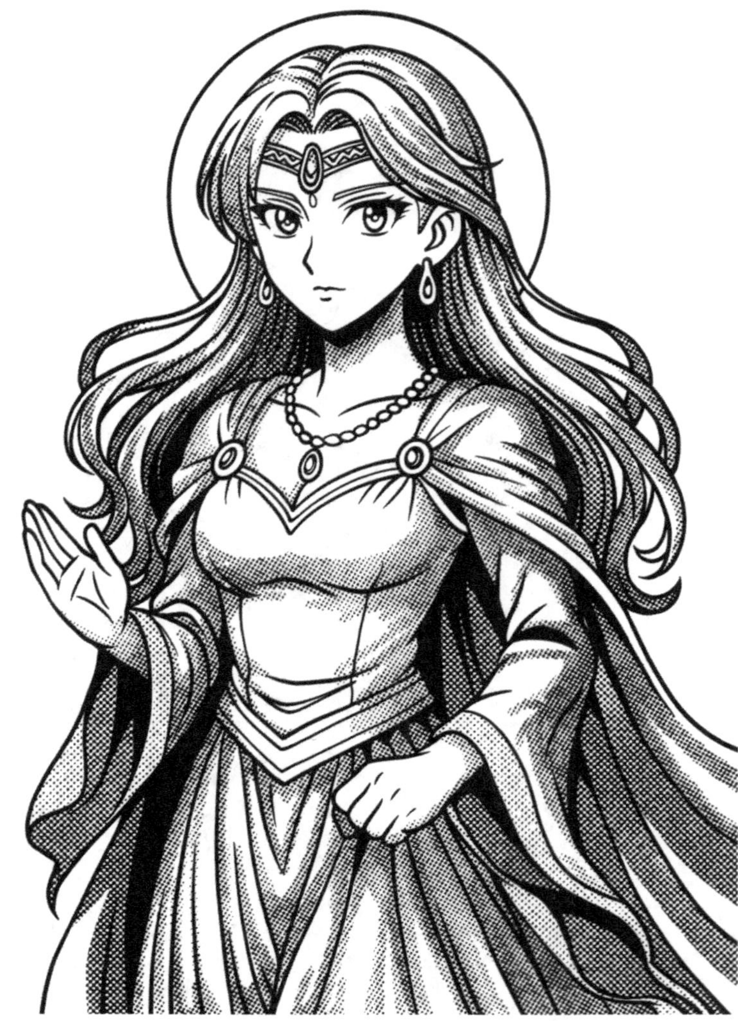

Pro Tip: Keep the posture tall with relaxed shoulders and an open chest to convey grace. Flow the hair and fabric outward to add movement and a sense of divine presence.

01

02

03

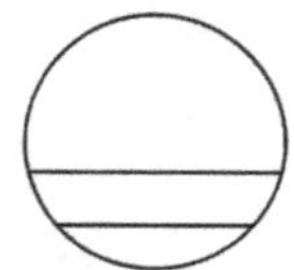

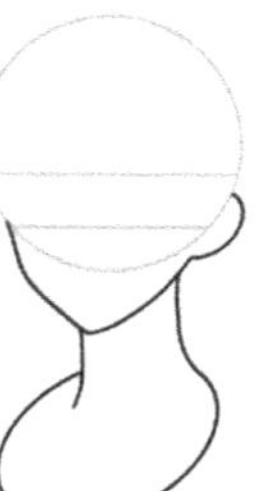

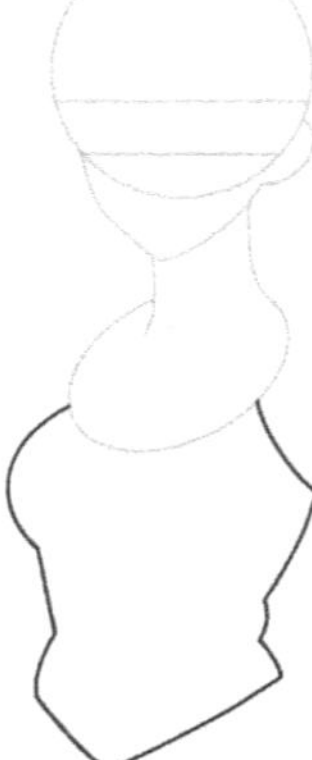

04

05

06

07

08

09

10

11

12

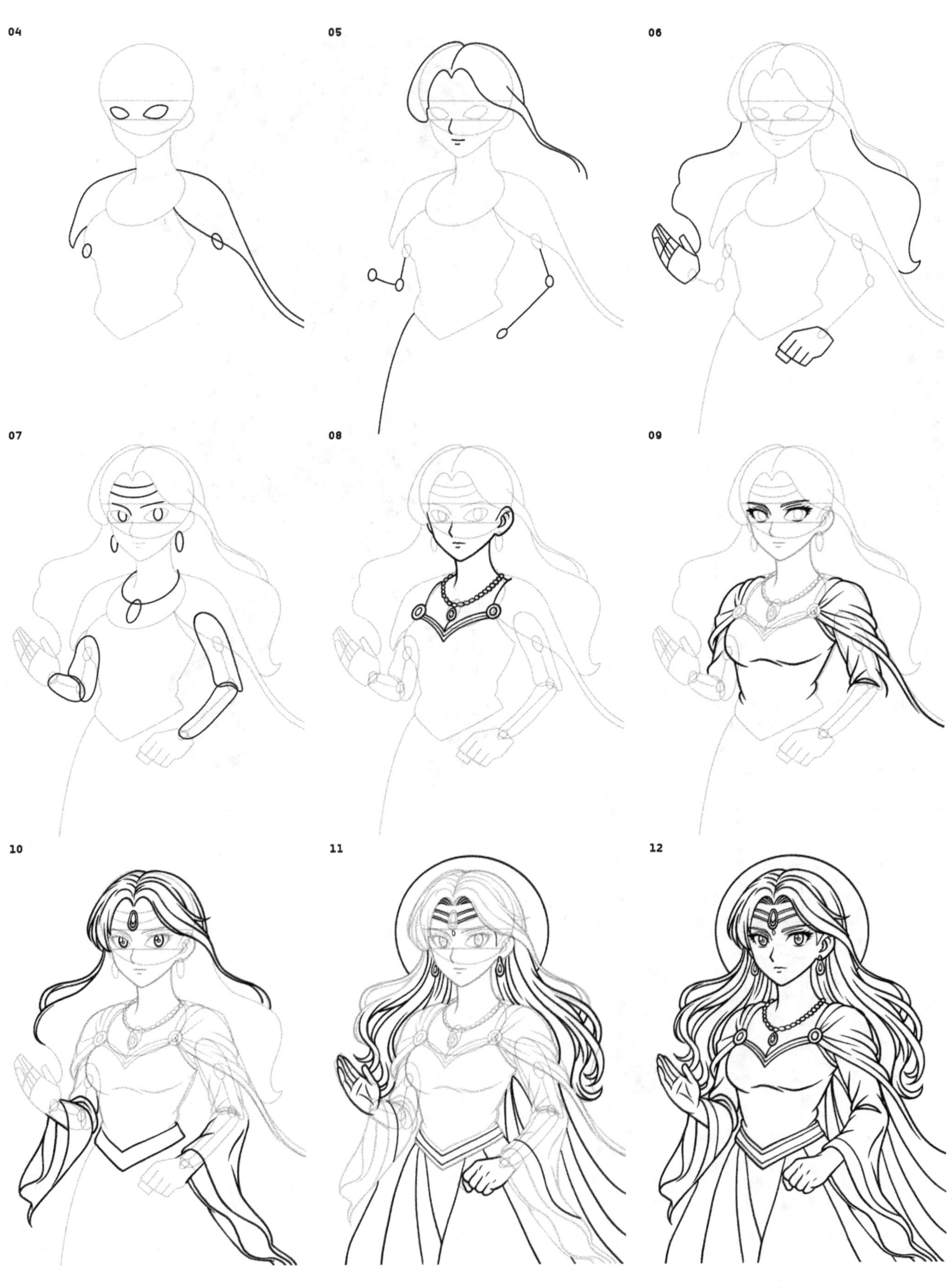

MOE-STYLE CUTE GIRL

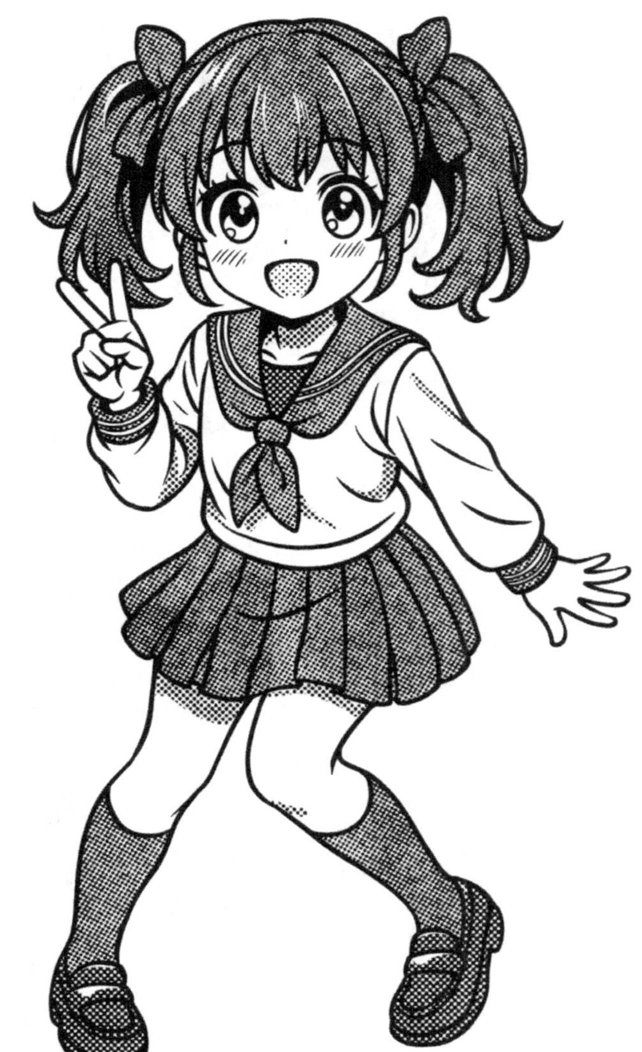

Pro Tip: Keep the head large and the eyes oversized to enhance cuteness. Use a playful pose with bent knees and expressive hands to capture the energetic, cheerful Moe style.

01

02

03

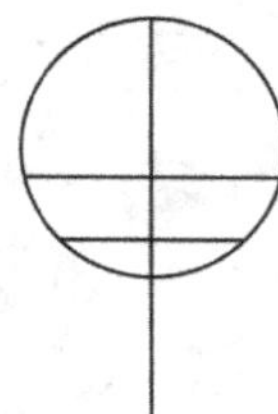

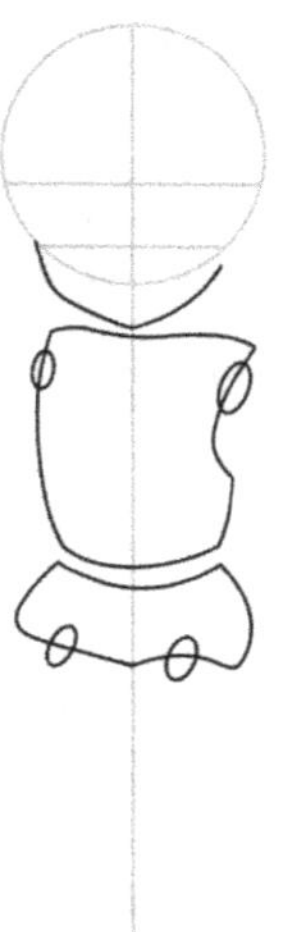

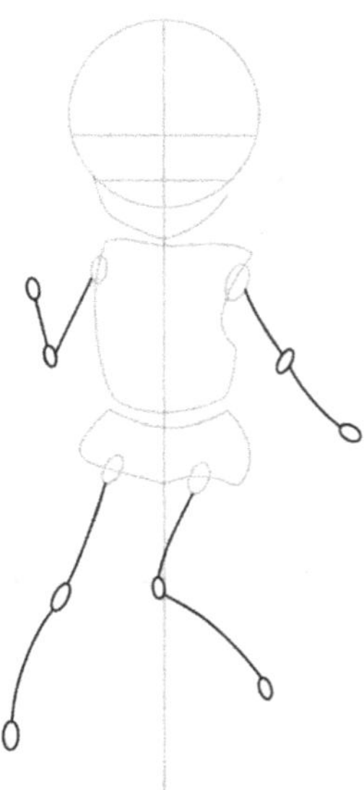

04

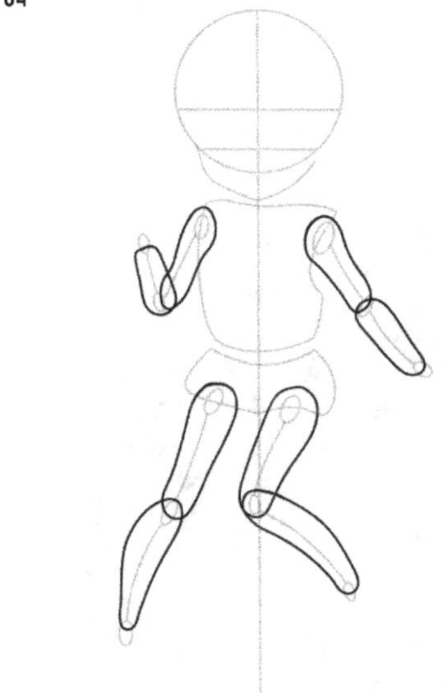

05

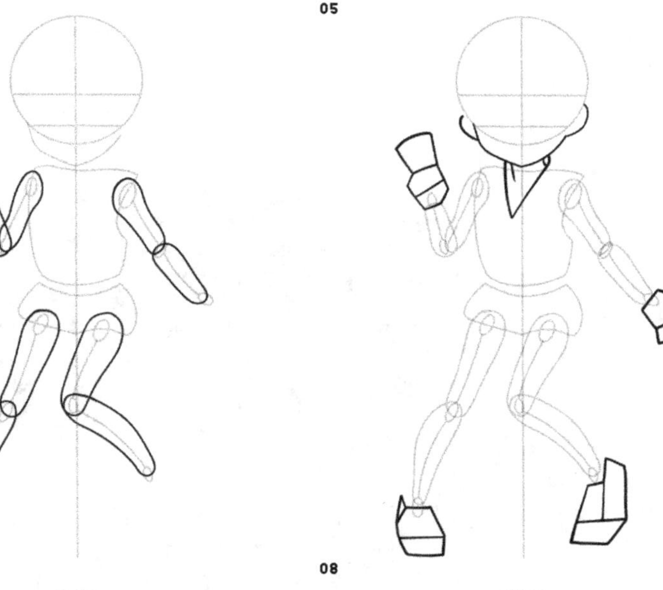

06

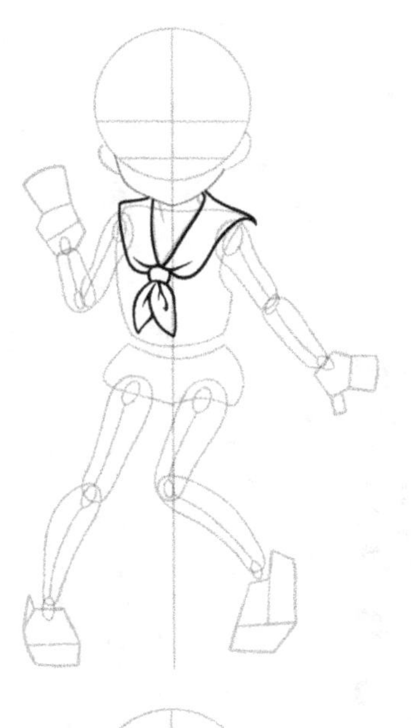

07

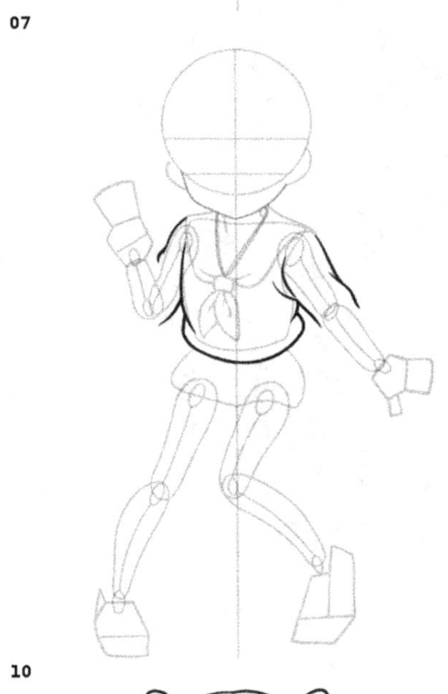

08

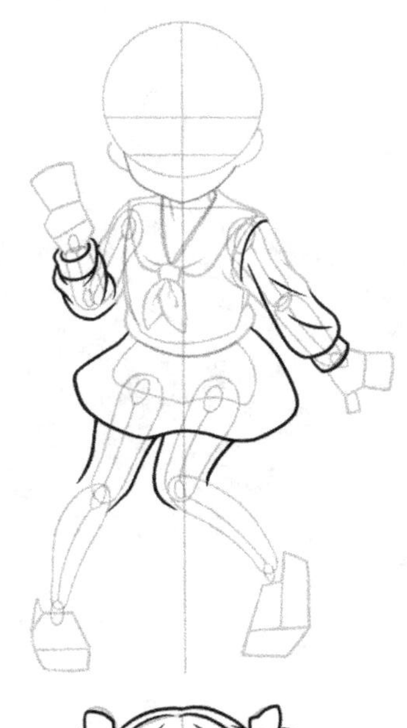

09

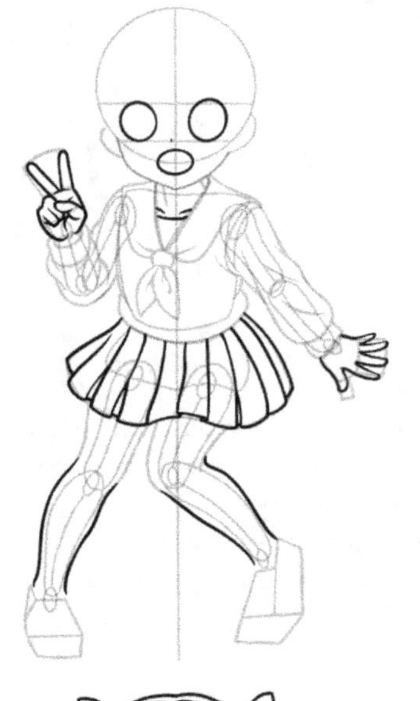

10

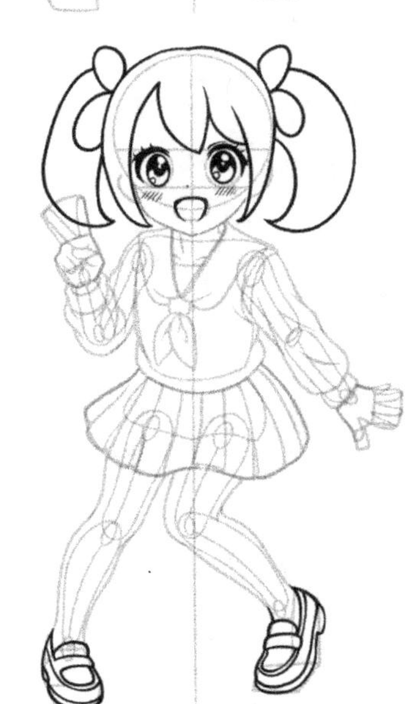

11

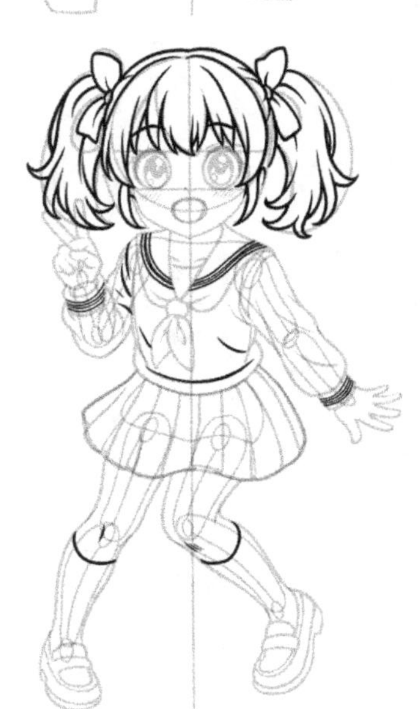

12

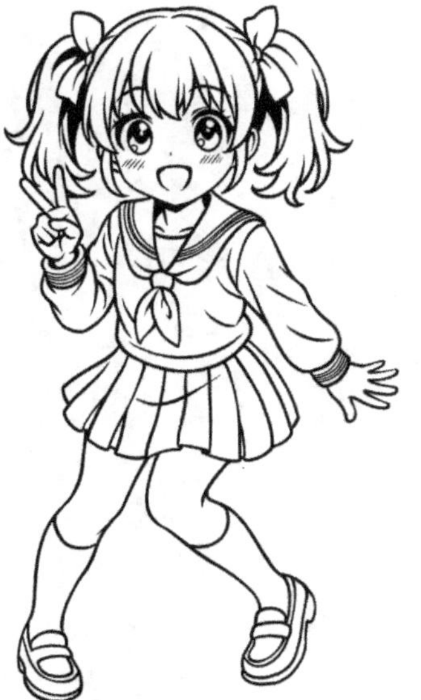

IDOL SINGER

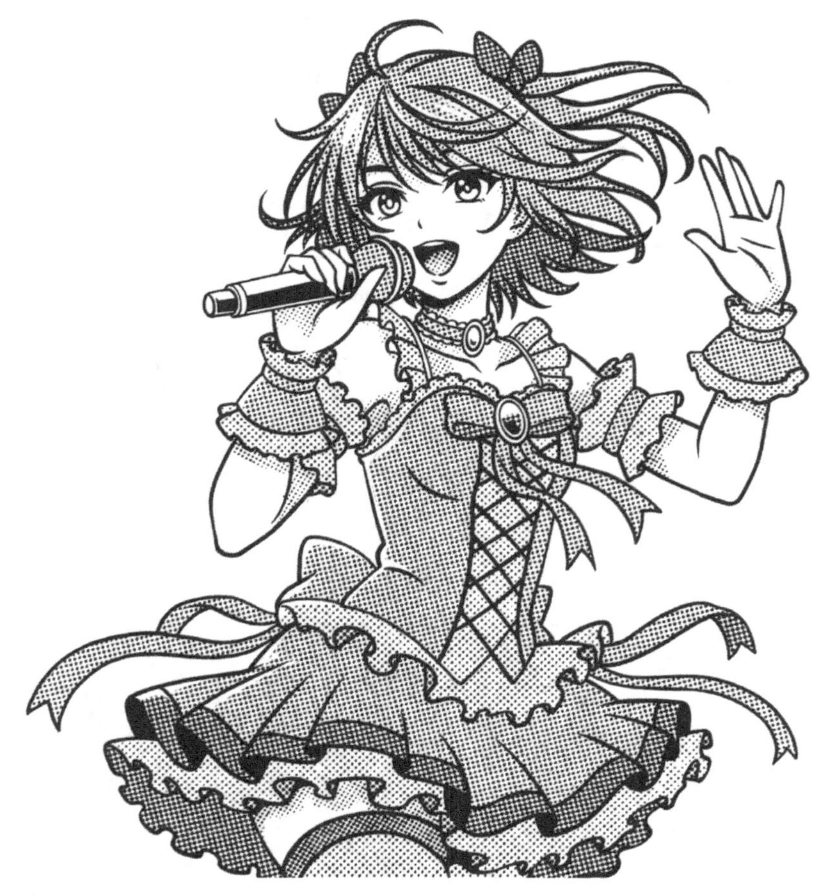

Pro Tip: Keep the pose dynamic with flowing hair and raised arms to show energy and movement. Use big, expressive eyes and an open mouth to capture the idol's joyful stage presence.

01

02

03

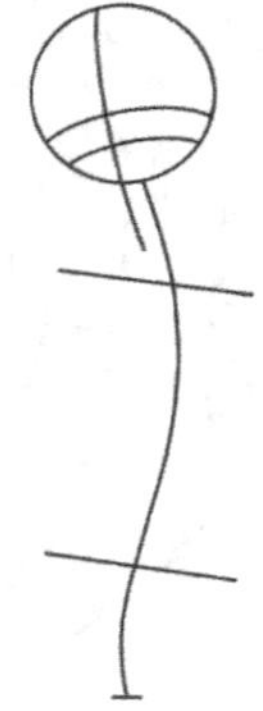

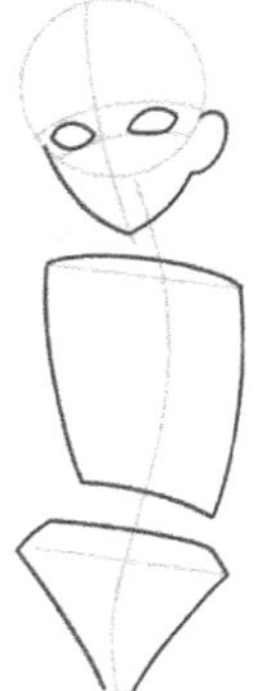

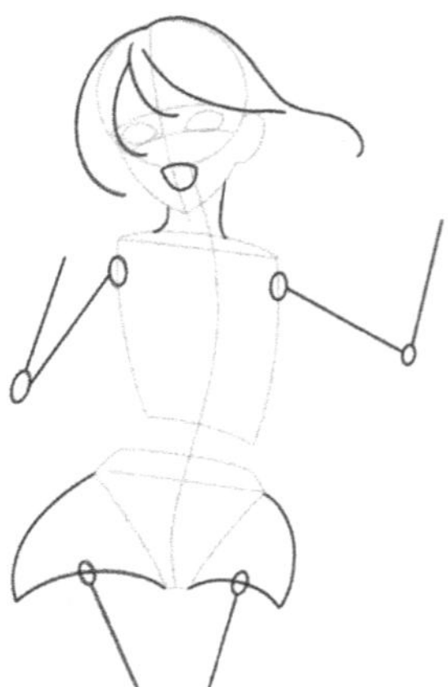

04

05

06

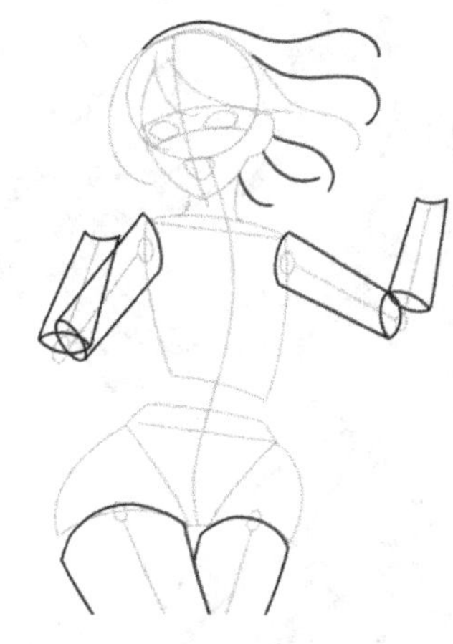

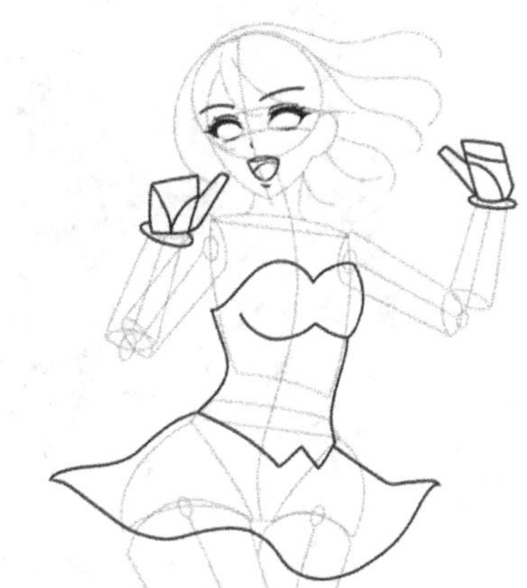

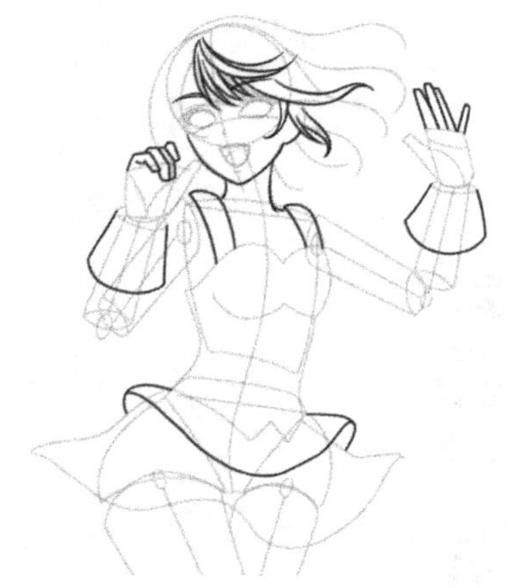

07

08

09

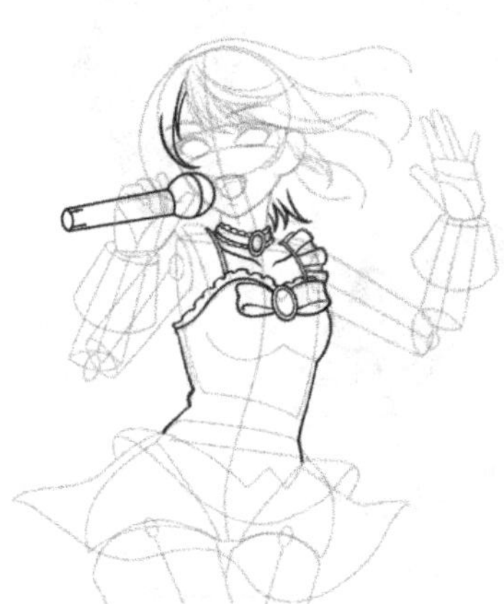

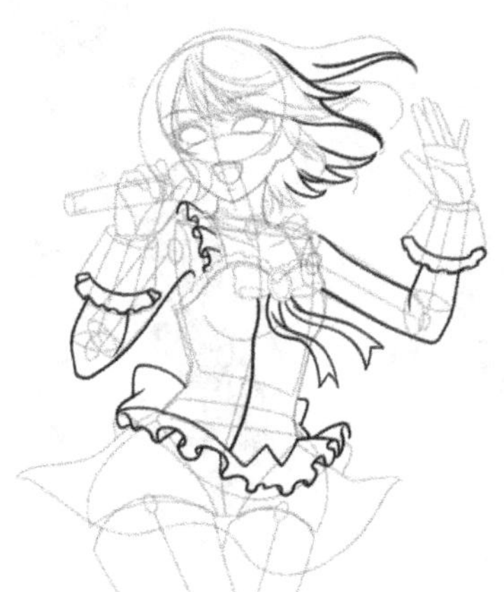

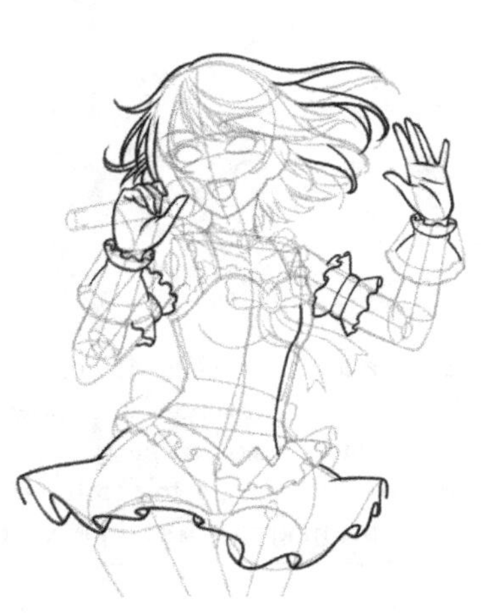

10

11

12

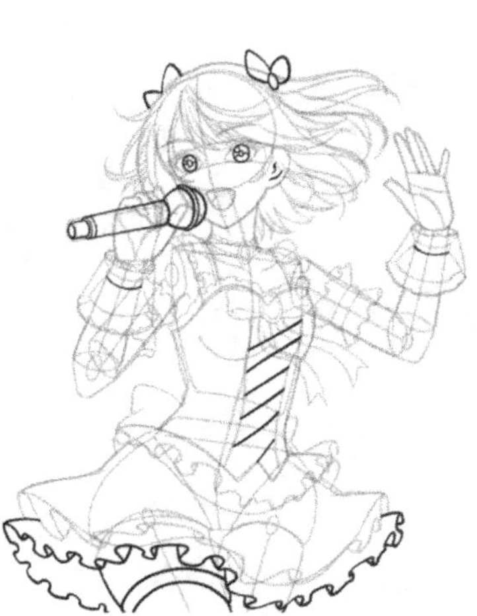

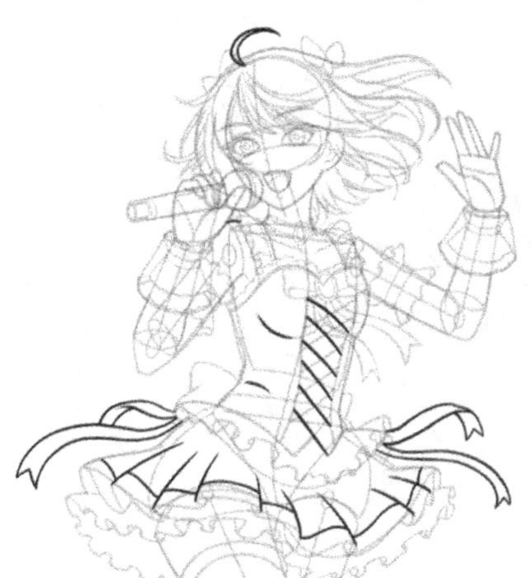

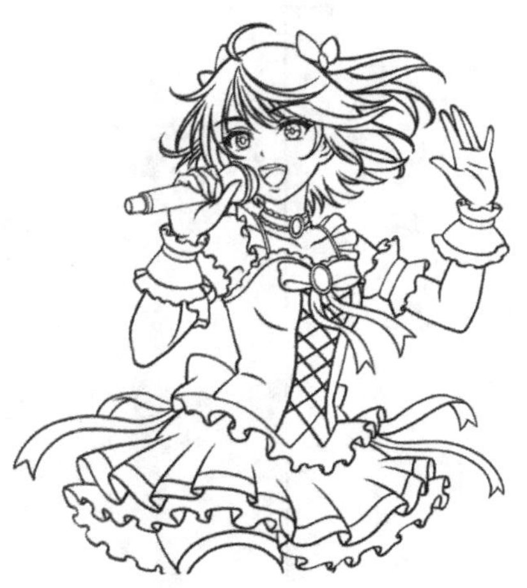

MAGIC GIRL

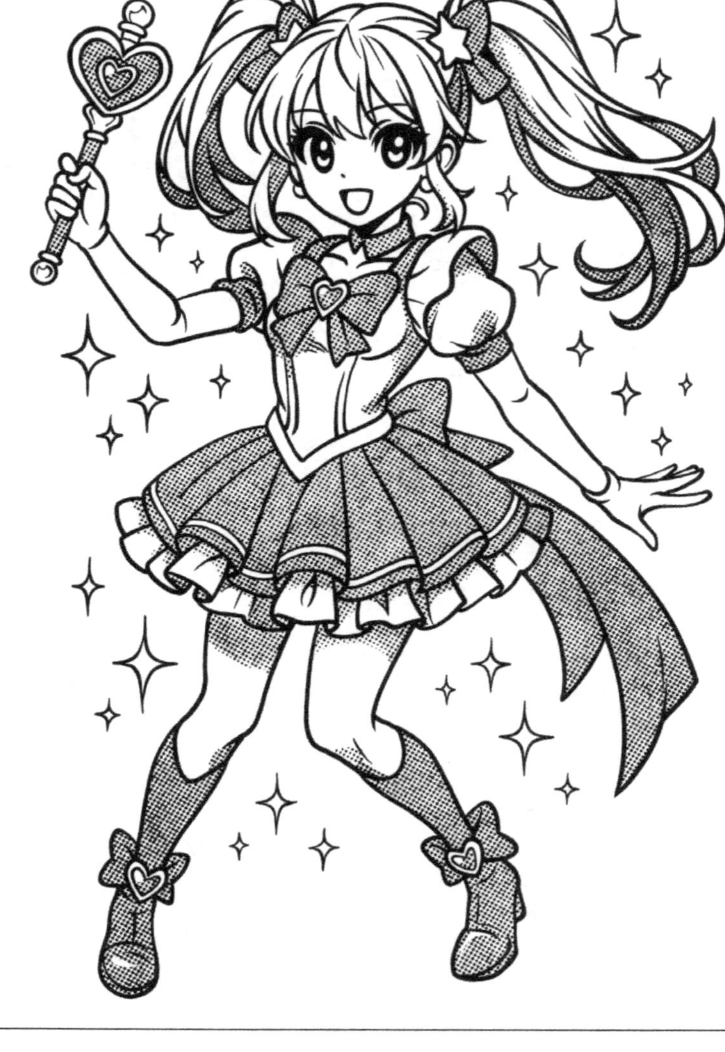

Pro Tip: Keep the pose lively with raised arms and flowing hair to show excitement. Use big, sparkling eyes and dynamic shapes in the costume to capture the magical girl's bright energy.

01

02

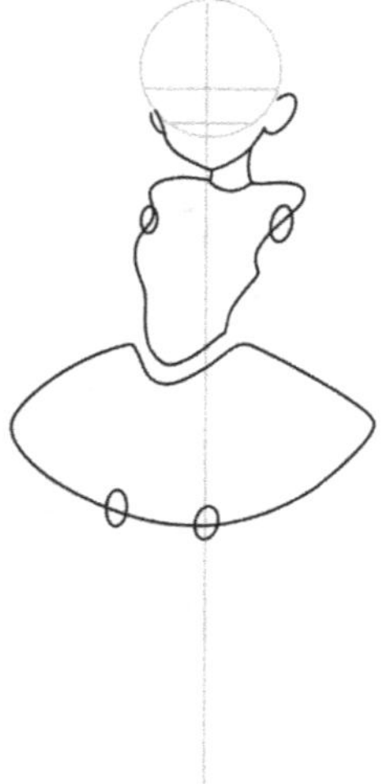

03

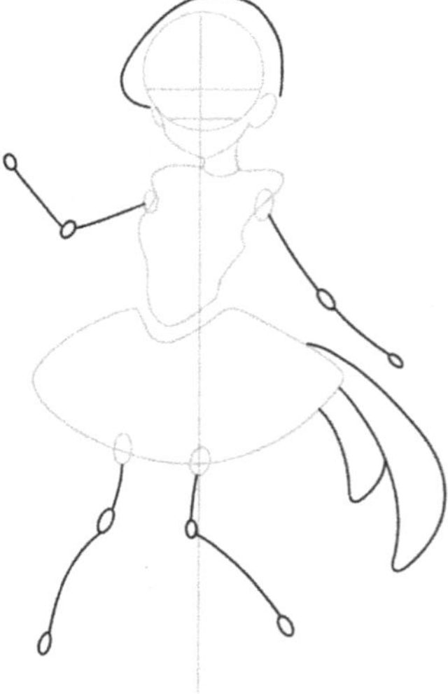

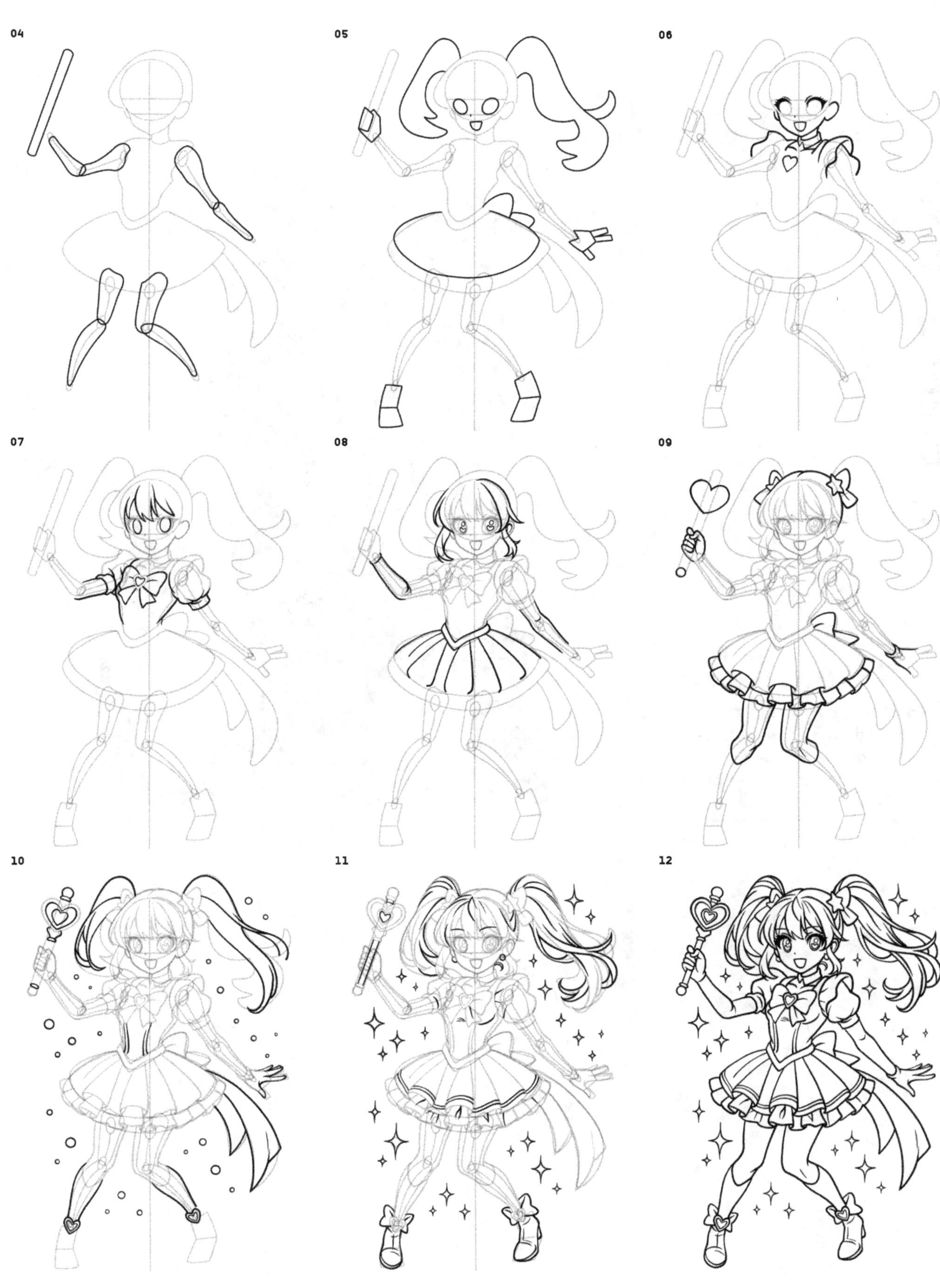

04
05
06
07
08
09
10
11
12
HOW TO DRAW ANIME

KEMONOMIMI GIRL

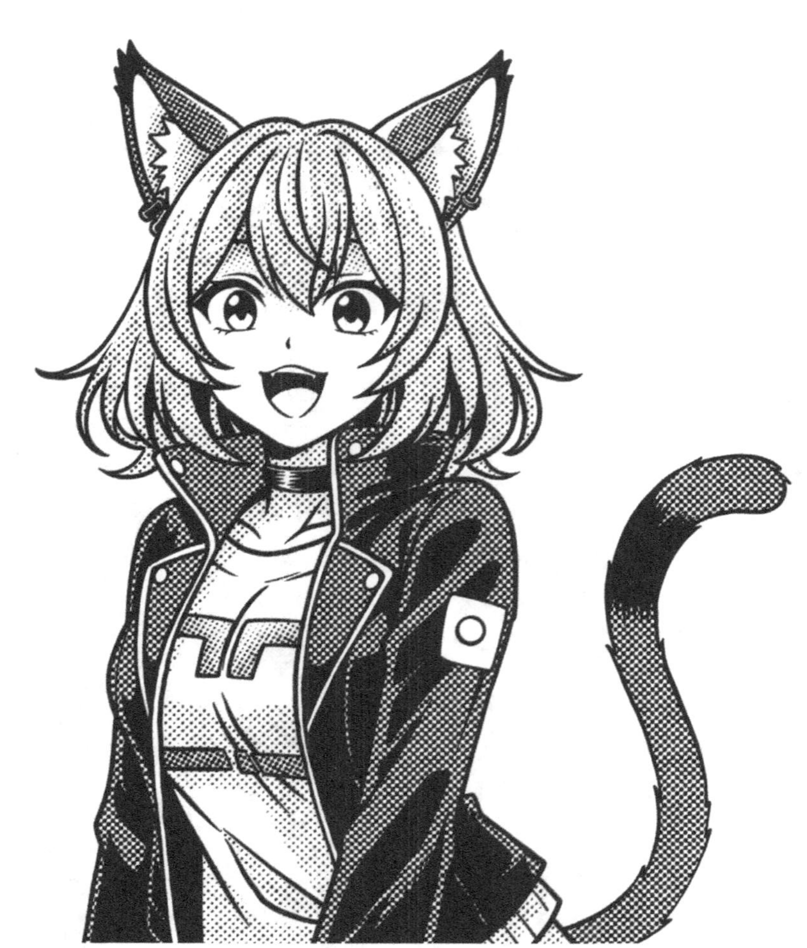

Pro Tip: Align the animal ears with the natural tilt of the head to keep the design believable. Add a flowing tail and wide, sparkling eyes to emphasise the playful, nature of kemonomimi characters.

01

02

03

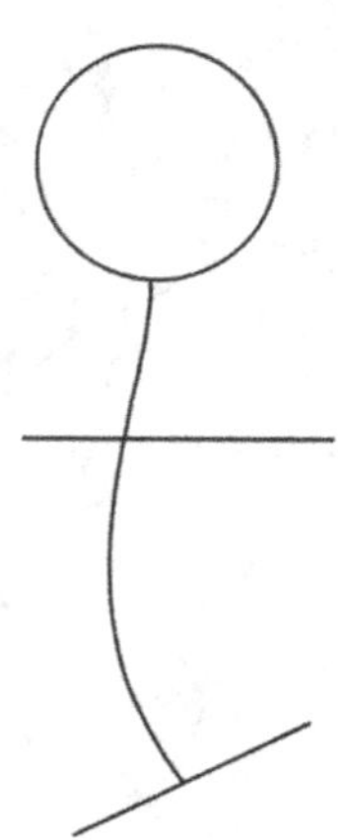

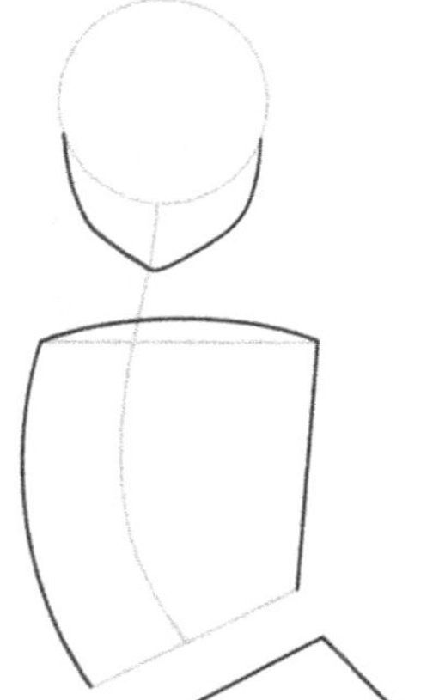

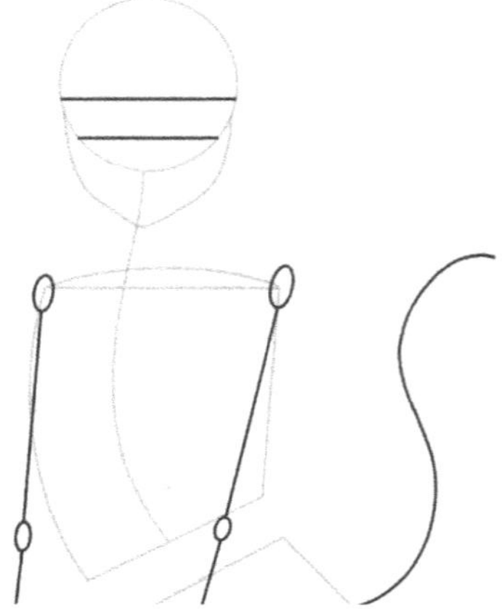

04

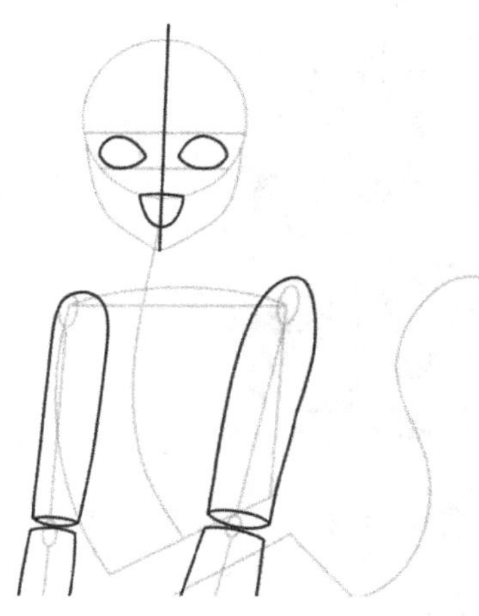

05

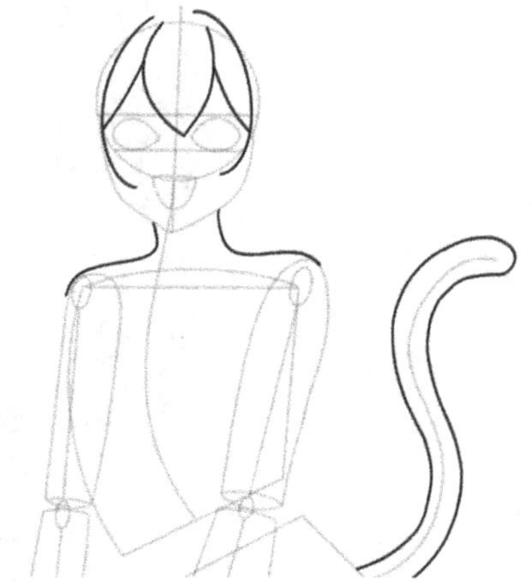

06

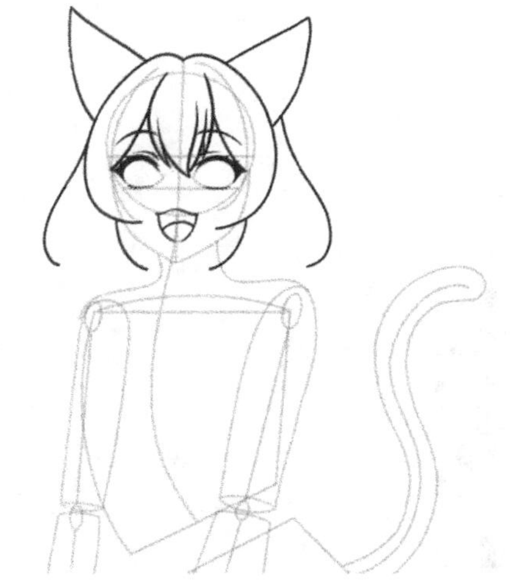

07

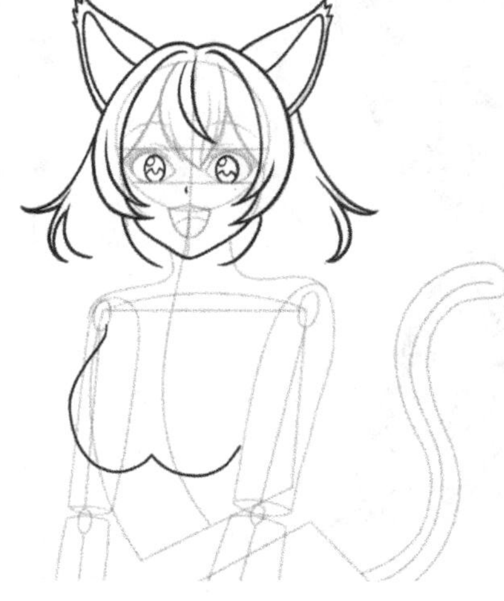

08

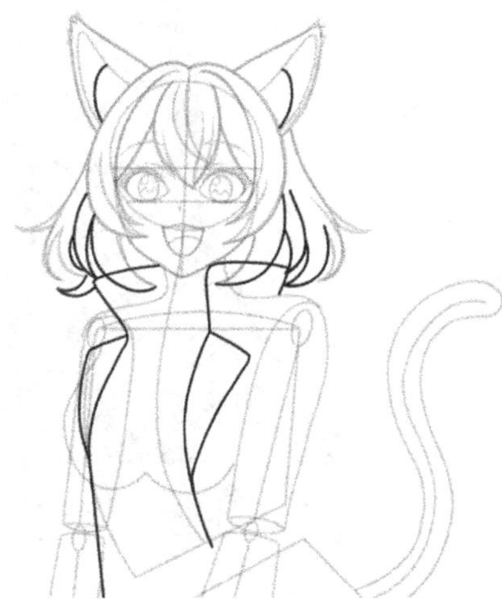

09

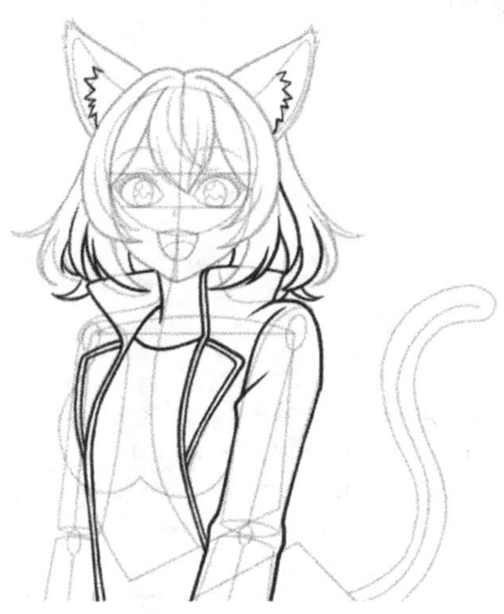

10

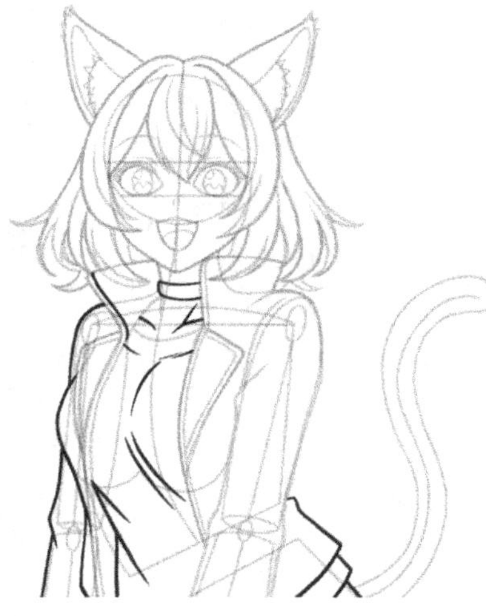

11

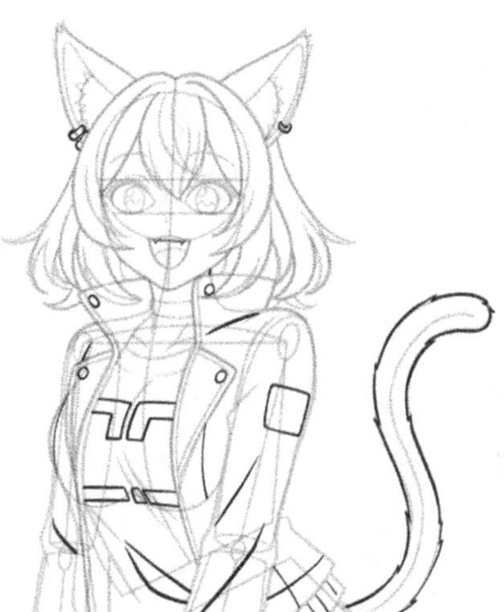

12

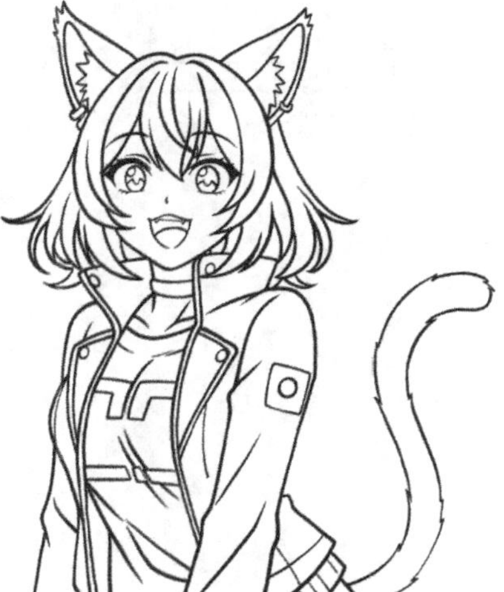

THE DANDERE

Pro Tip: Use a gentle turn of the shoulders and downward gaze to express her quiet emotion. Keep the lines soft and minimal to capture her shy and reserved personality.

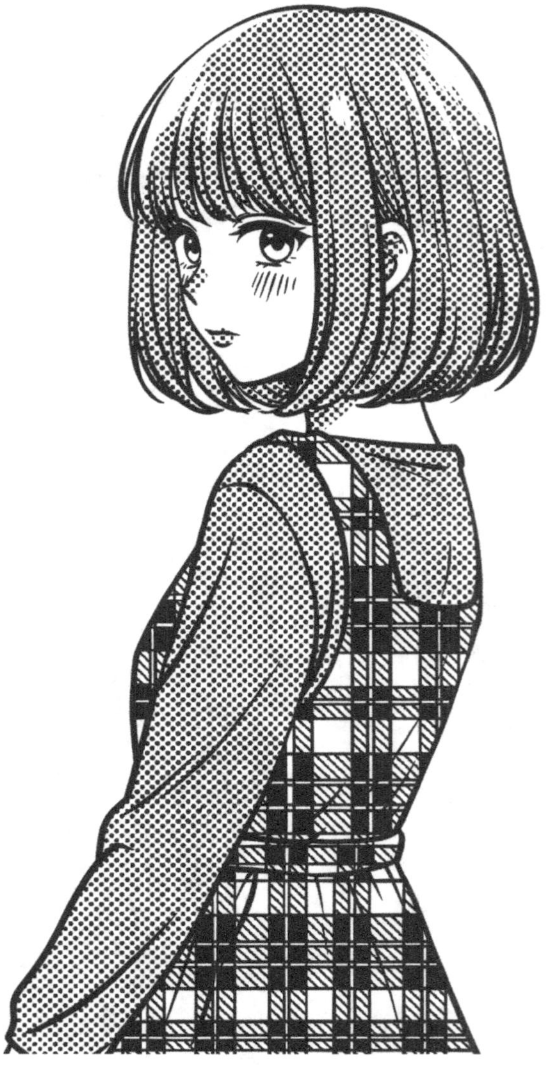

01

02

03

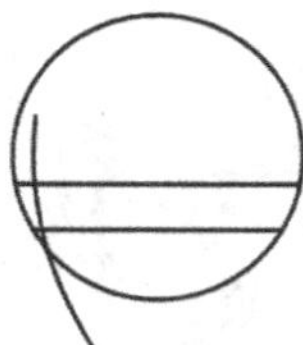

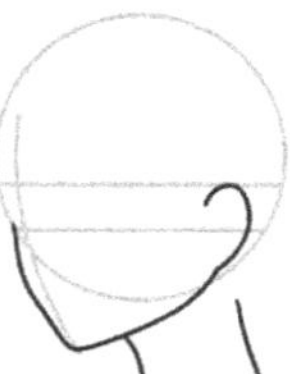

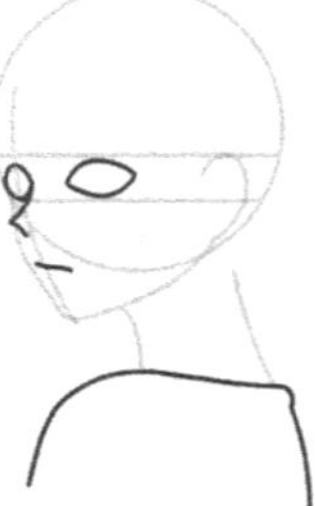

04

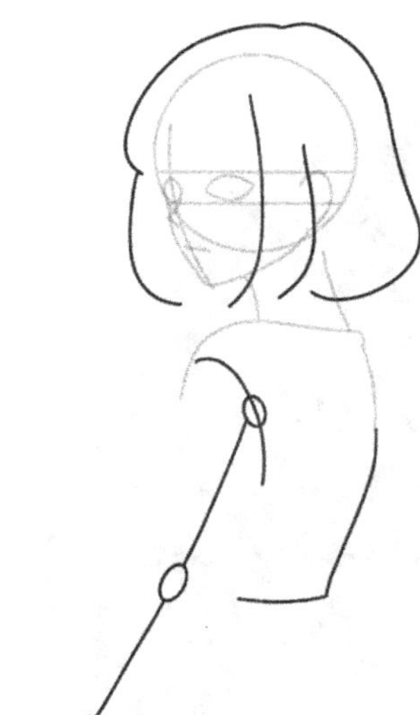

05

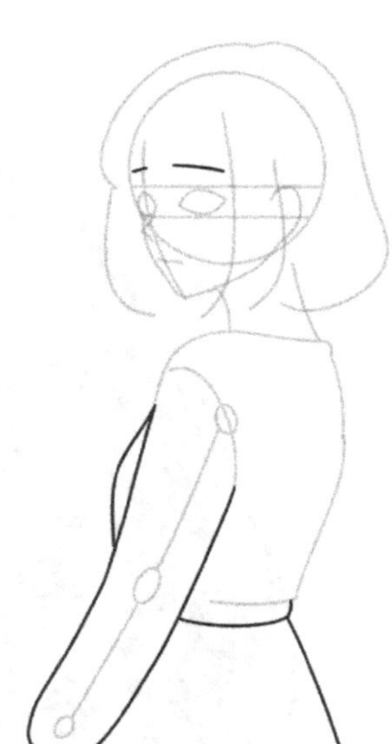

06

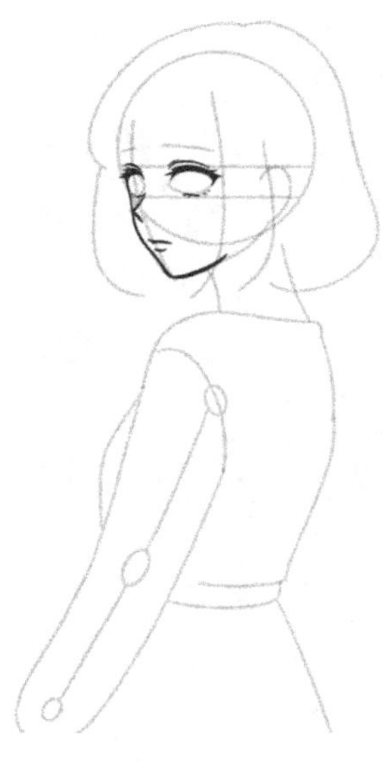

07

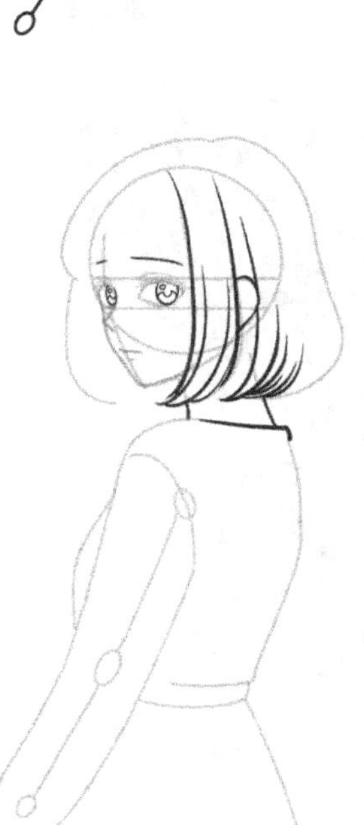

08

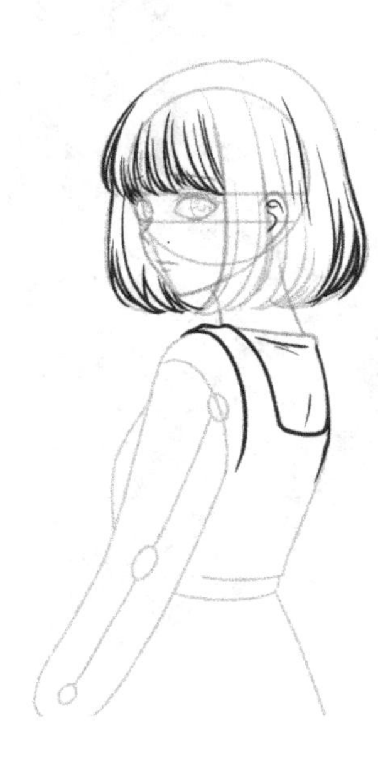

09

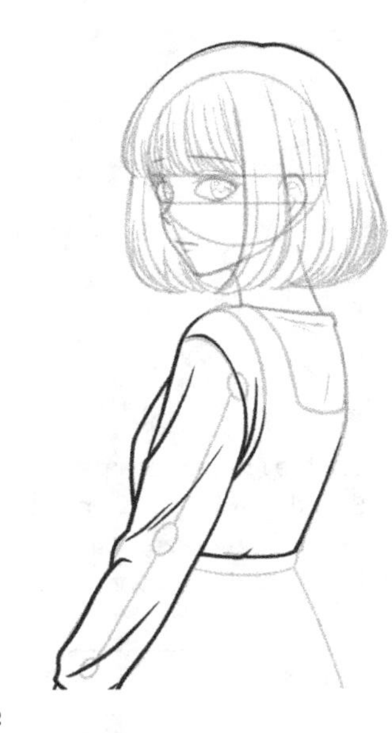

10

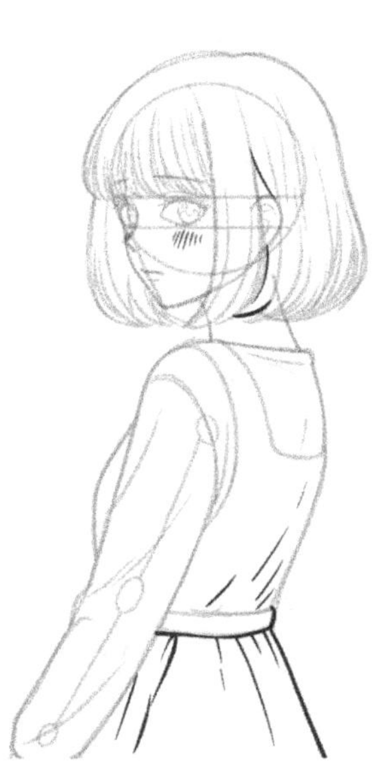

11

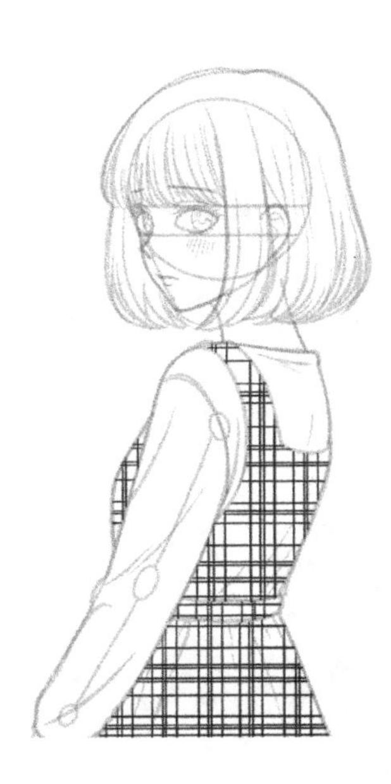

12

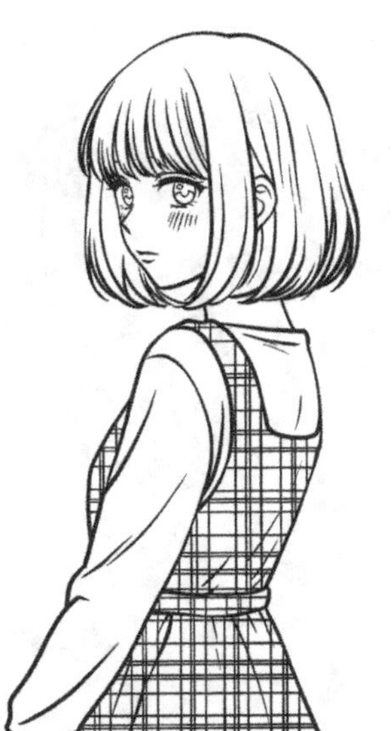

HOW TO DRAW ANIME

THE KUUDERE

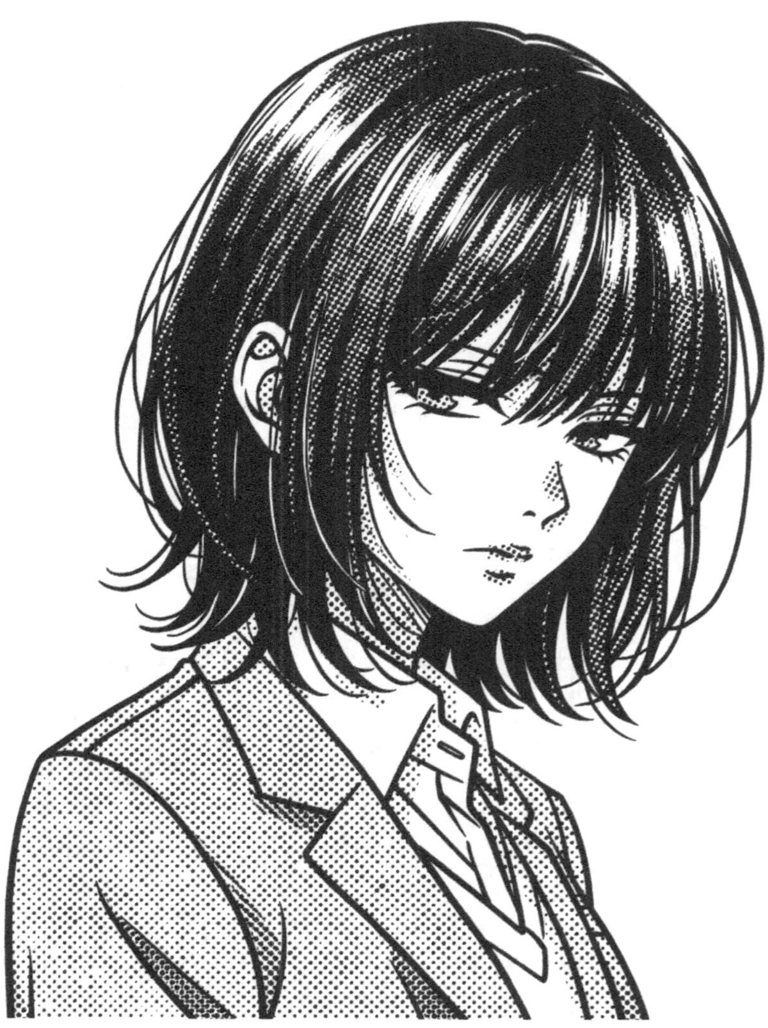

Pro Tip: Keep the features sharp and the pose still. Slightly tilt the head forward and use a cool, steady gaze to suggest quiet confidence and emotional control.

01

02

03

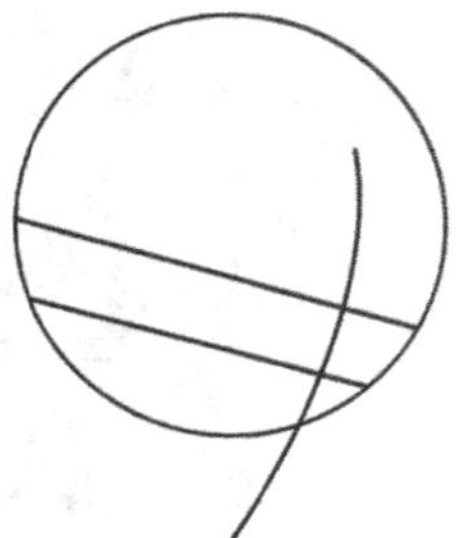

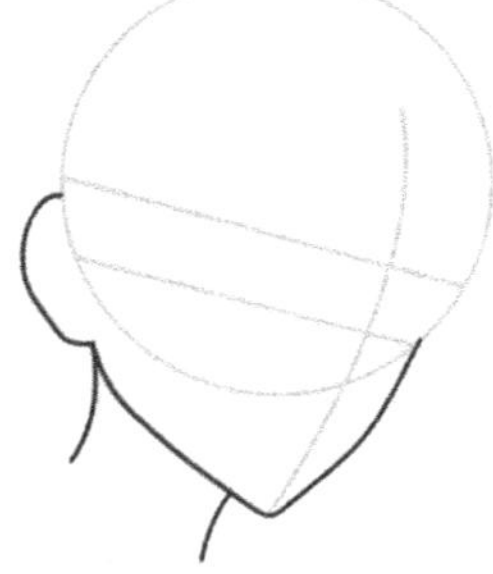

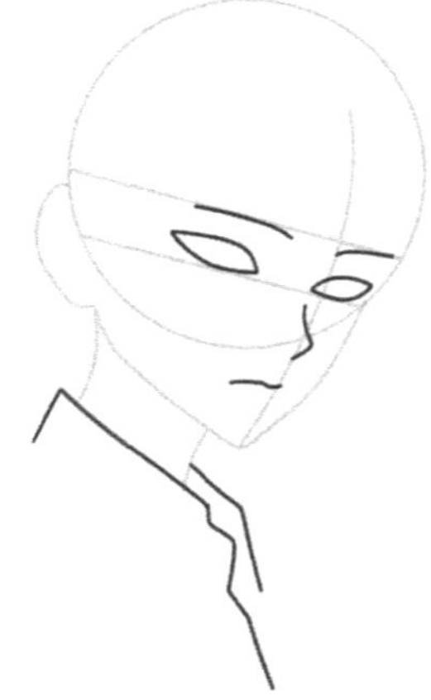

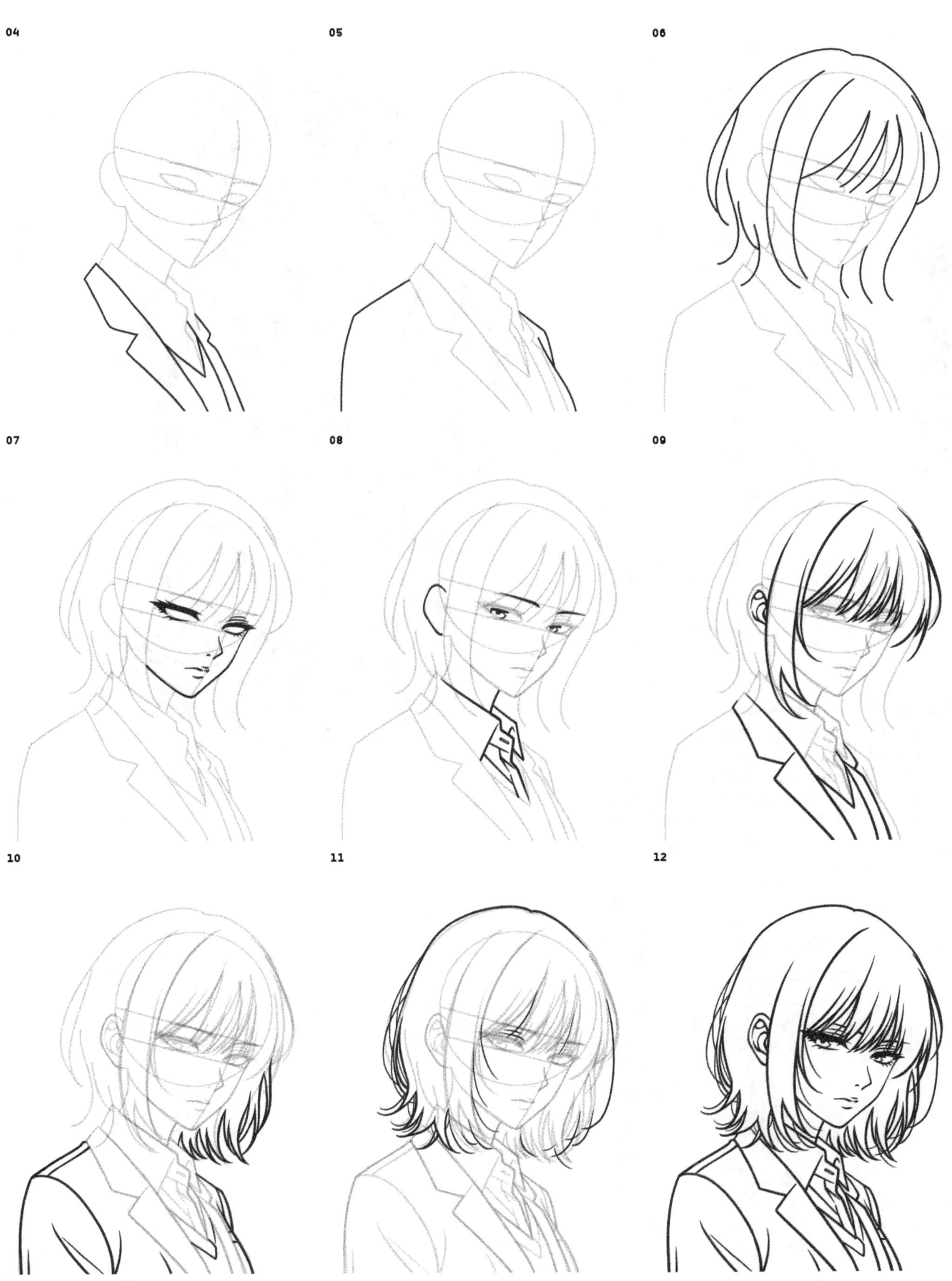

04
05
06
07
08
09
10
11
12
HOW TO DRAW ANIME

THE YANDERE

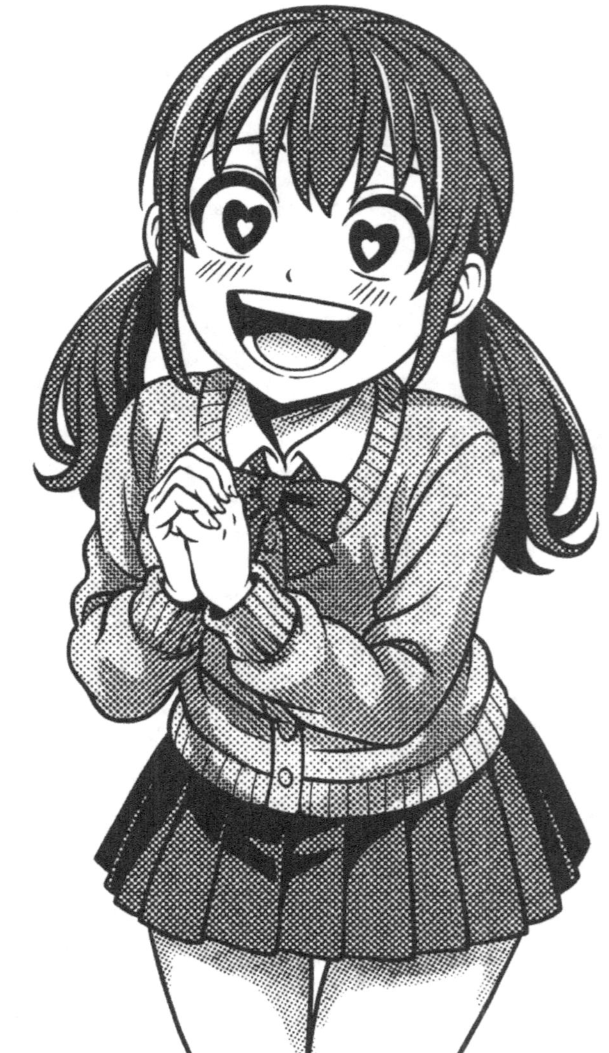

Pro Tip: Exaggerate the eyes and smile to heighten intensity. Keep the hands close to the chest to show obsession, and use symmetry in the pose for a deceptively sweet but unsettling effect.

01

02

03

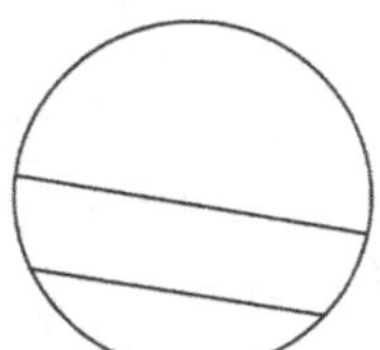

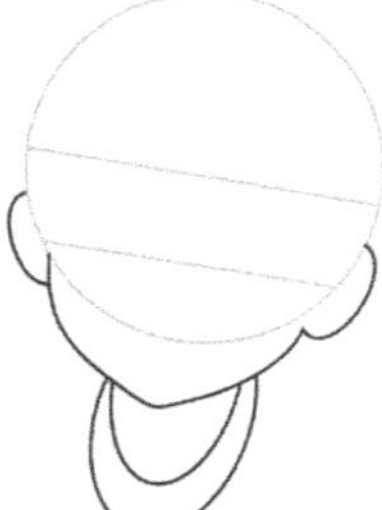

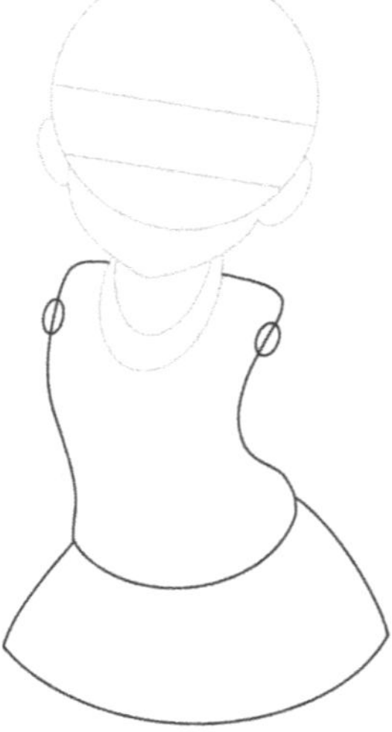

04

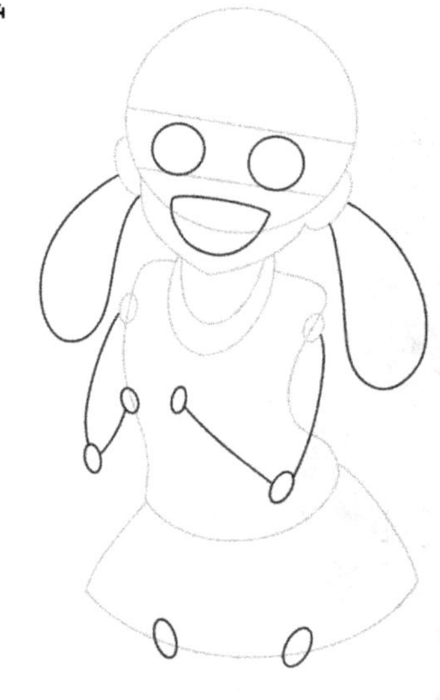

05

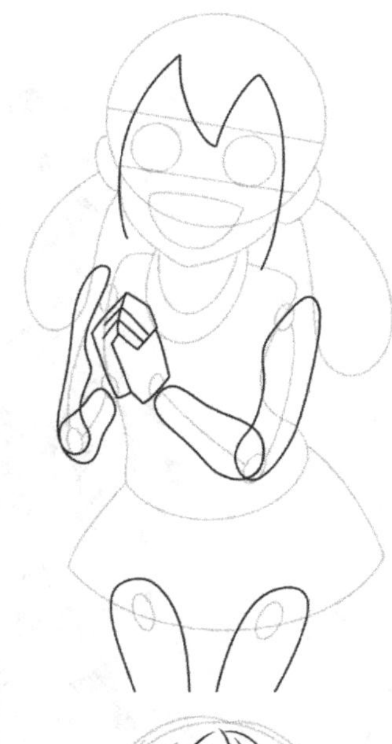

06

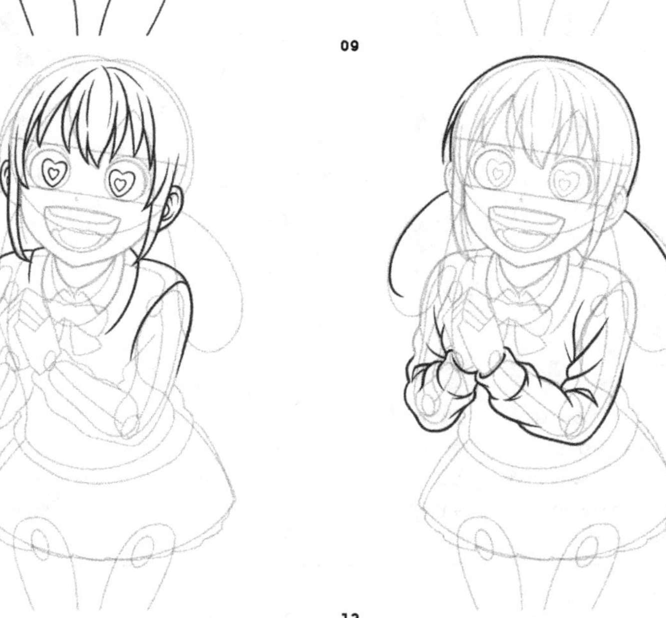

07

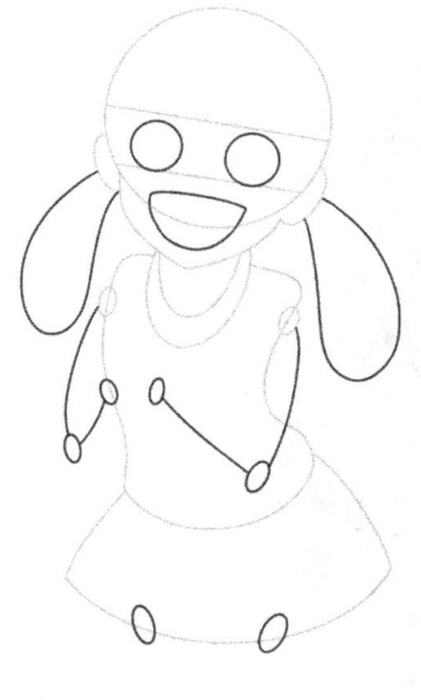

08

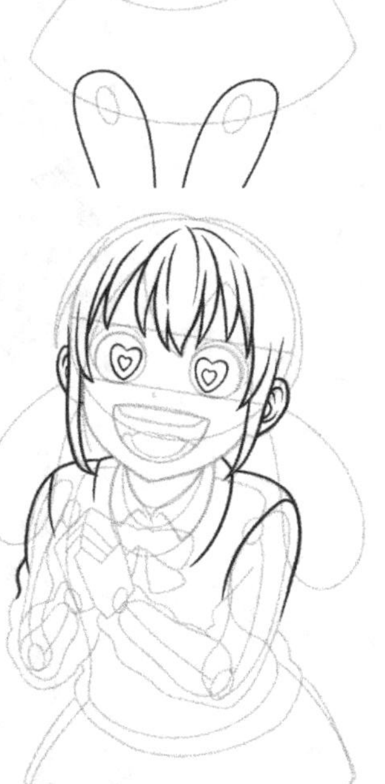

09

10

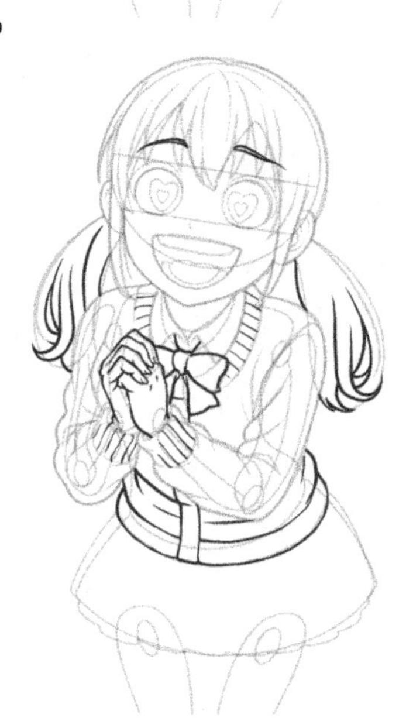

11

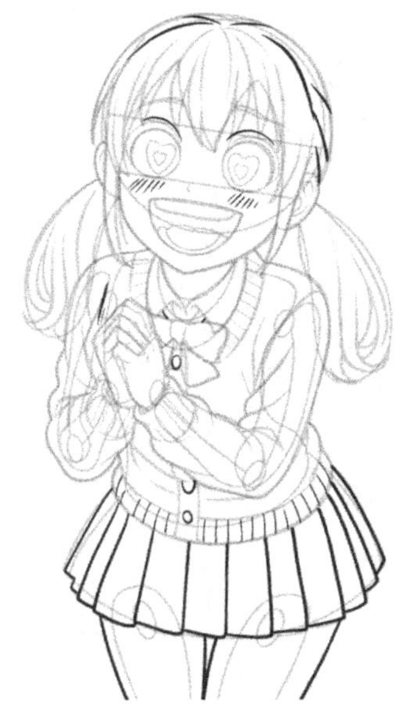

12

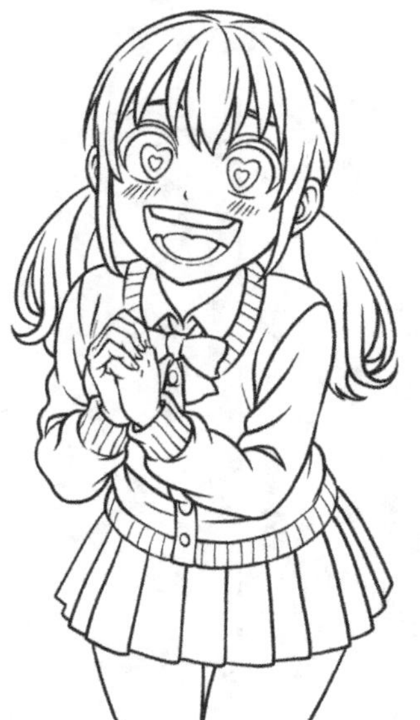

THE TSUNDERE

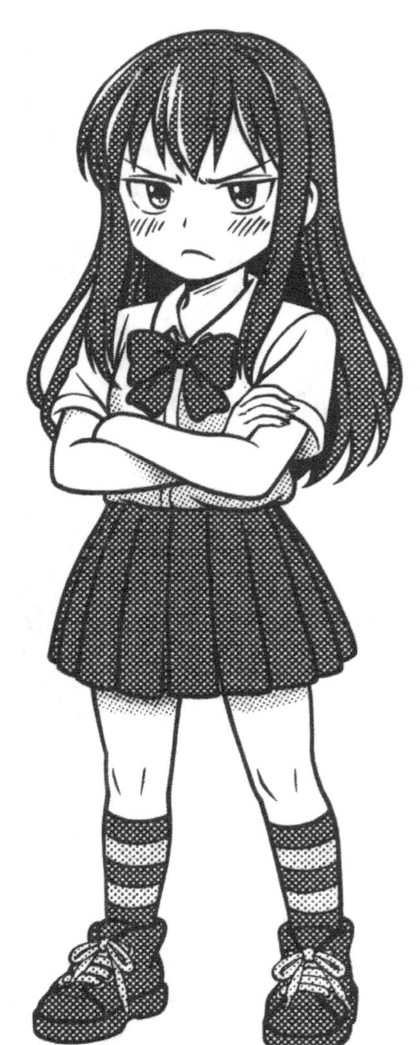

Pro Tip: Crossed arms and a slight forward lean help convey defensiveness. Keep the eyebrows angled and the mouth tight to balance irritation with hidden affection.

01

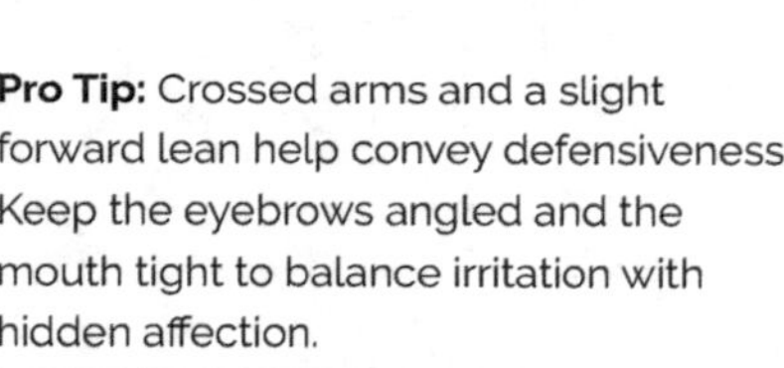

02

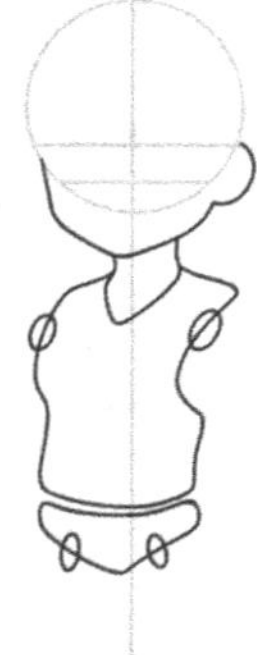

03

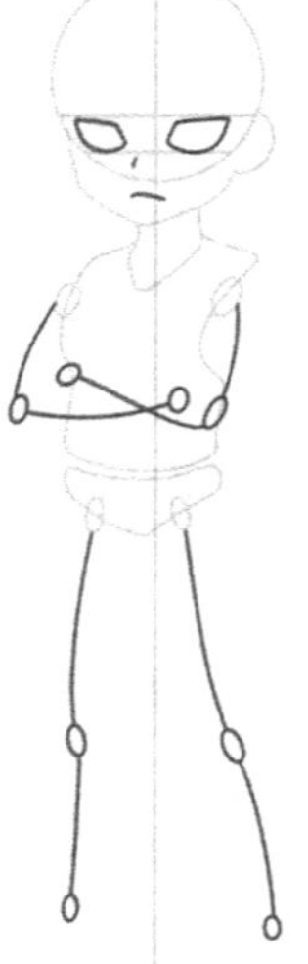

04

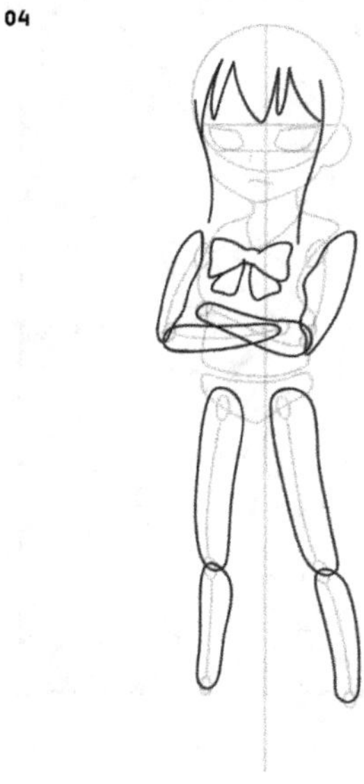

05

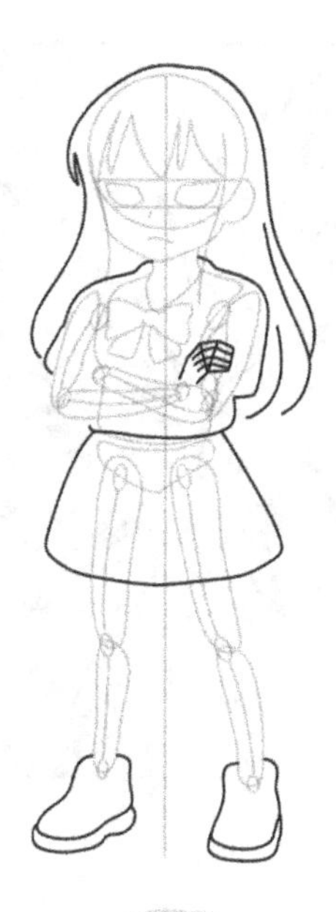

06

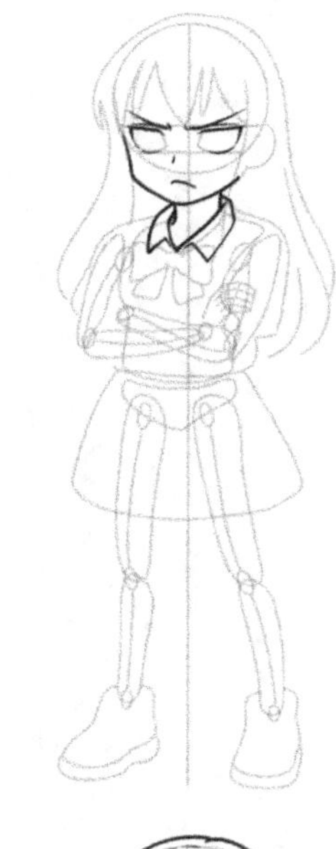

07

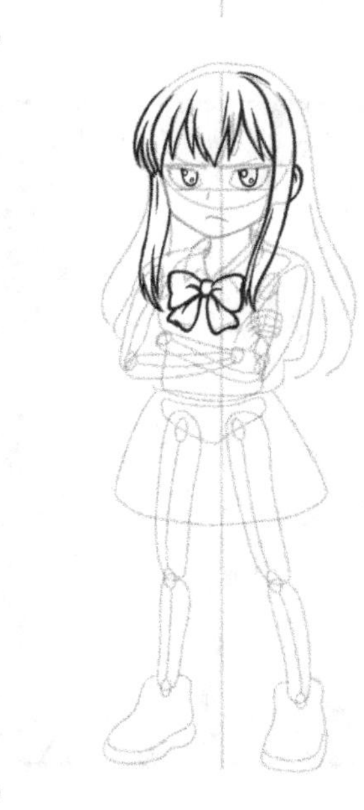

08

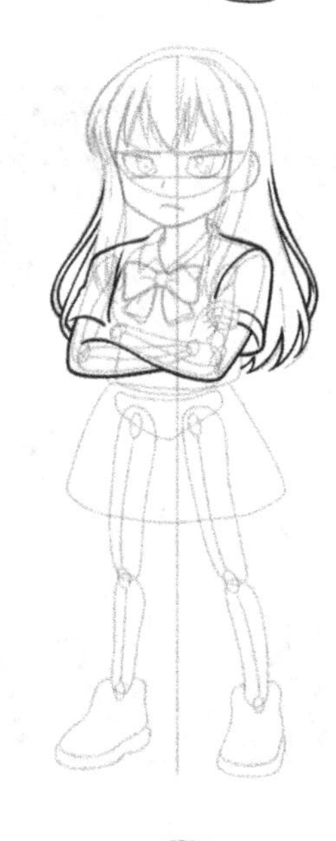

09

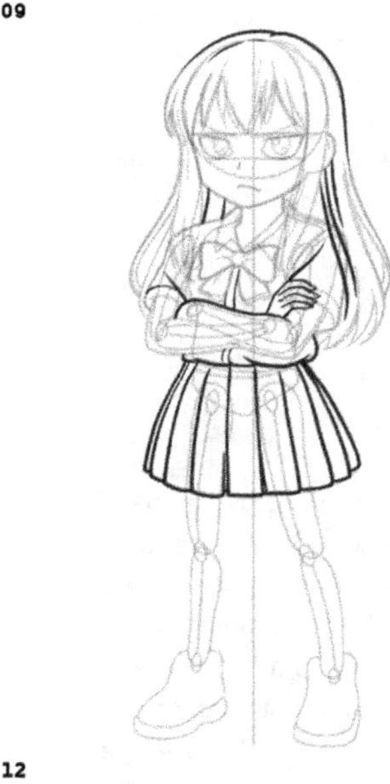

10

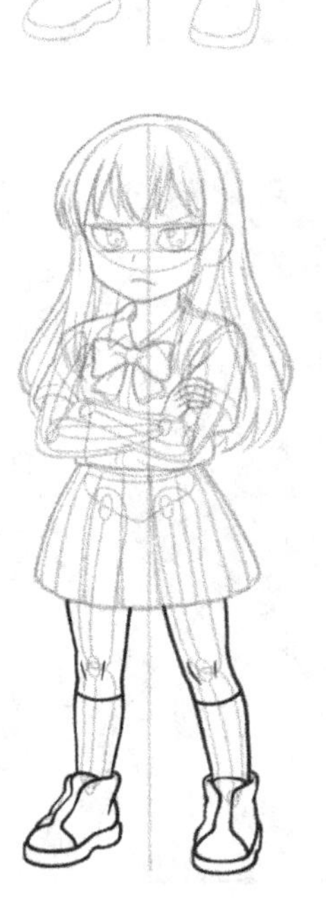

11

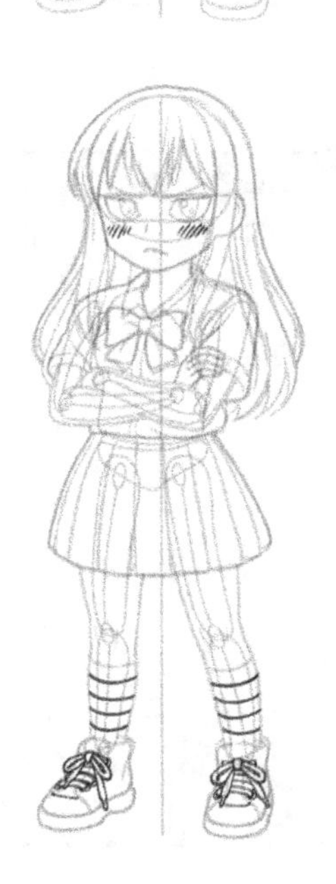

12

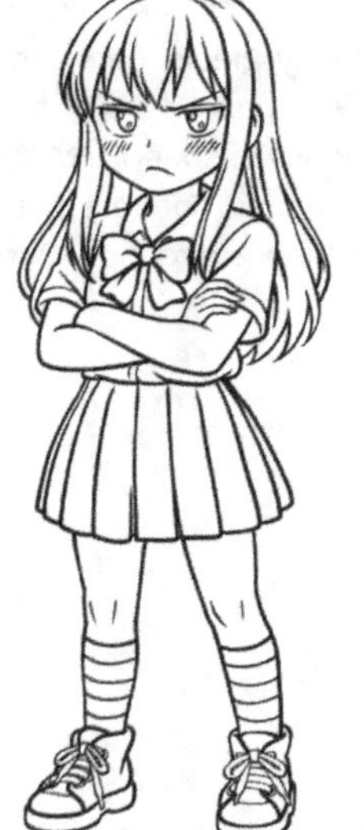

HOW TO DRAW ANIME

IMPACT BURSTS

Impact bursts are explosive line effects used in manga to emphasise force, speed or sudden action. They radiate from a central point, pulling the reader's attention straight to the moment of impact. Different burst styles create different moods, from sharp, jagged energy to softer shockwaves. See how adding a character in the bottom right corner instantly injects more energy into the page. The impact bursts behind her boost the sense of speed and power, creating a dynamic contrast that makes the moment feel energetic, powerful and more dramatic.

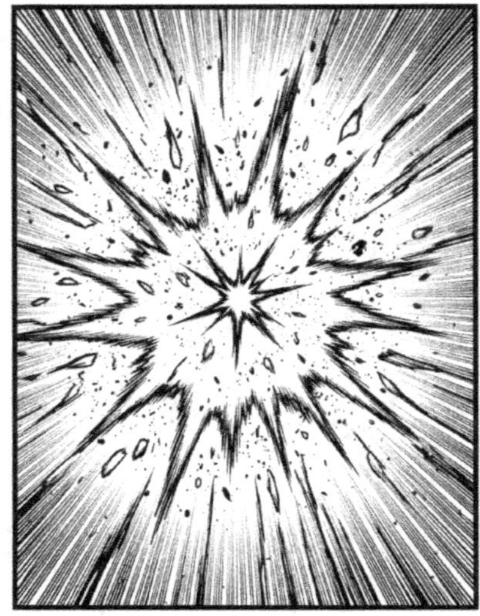
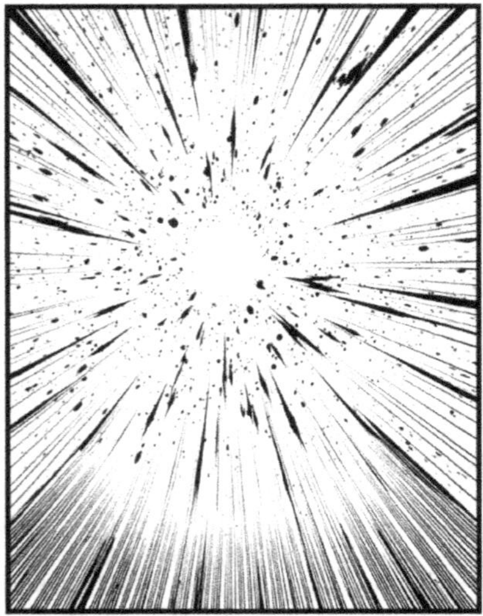
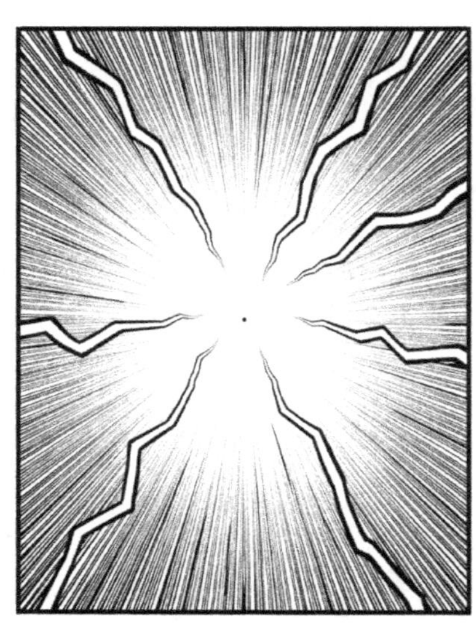
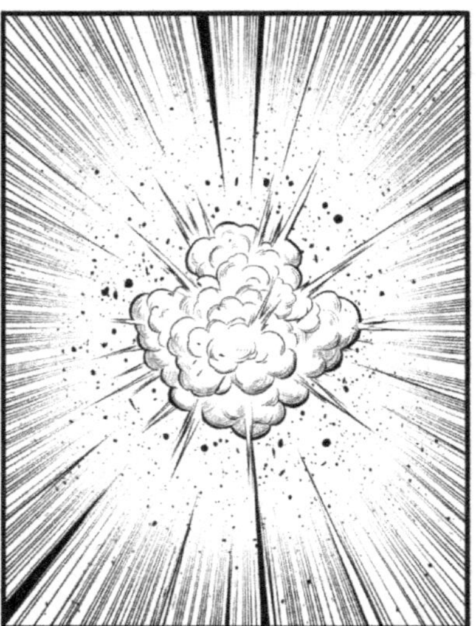
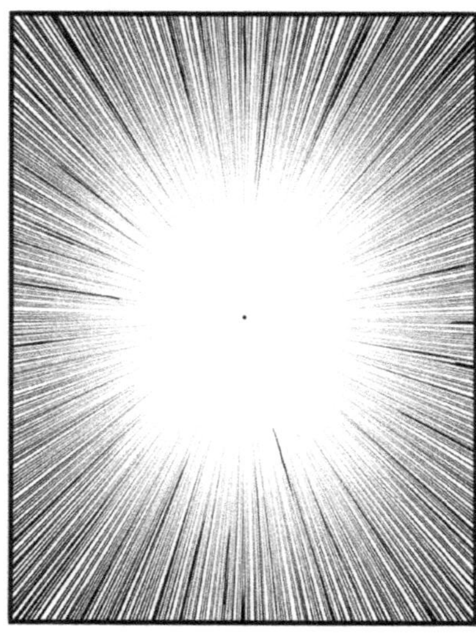
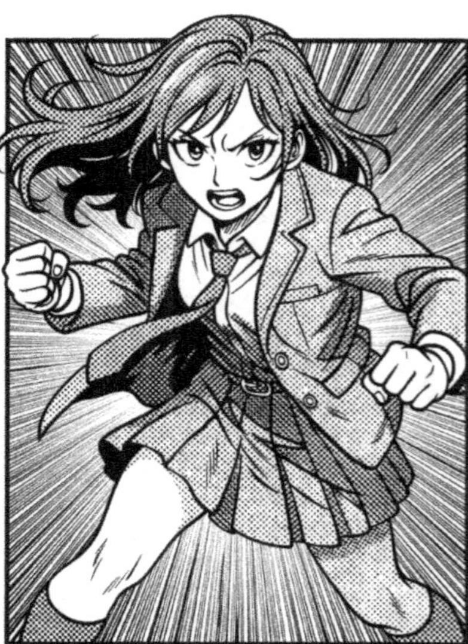

ENVIRONMENTAL ELEMENTS

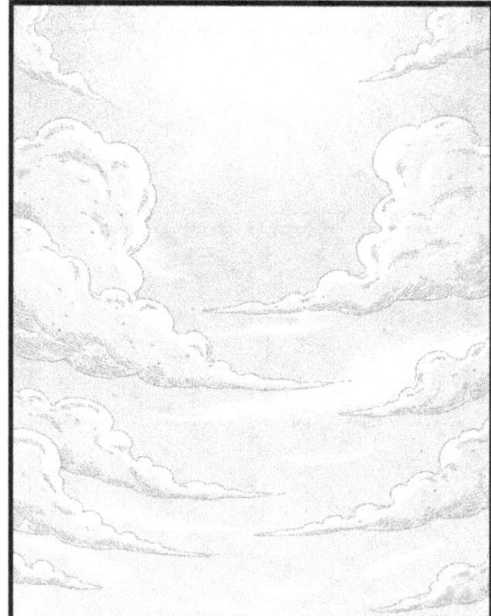

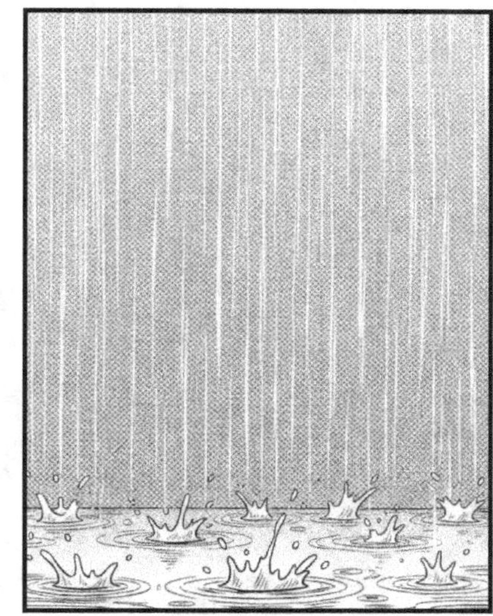

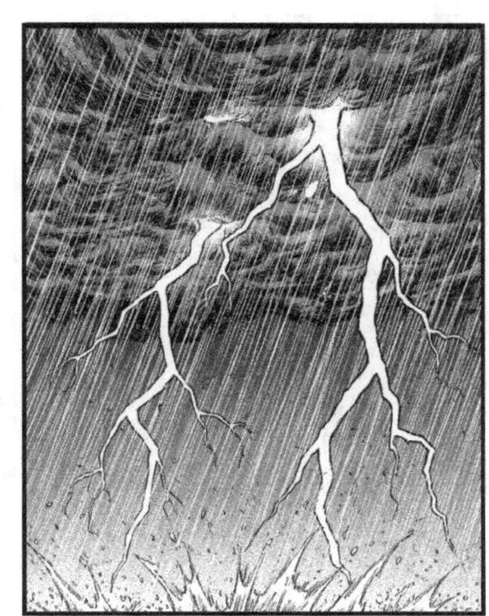

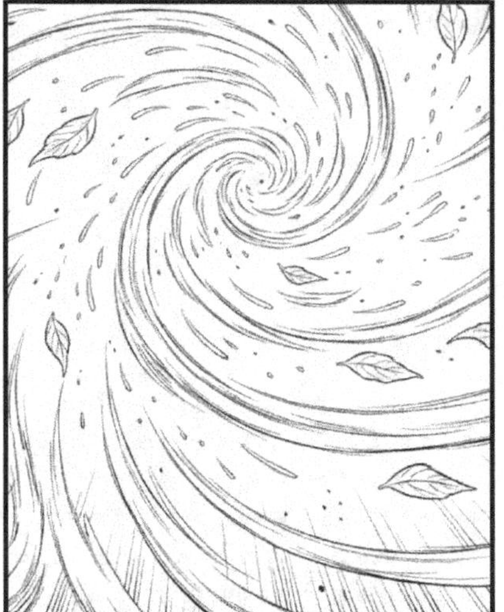

Including environmental elements, such as wind, can instantly enhance the mood in your comic. Swirling leaves or drifting dust add a sense of movement that makes the scene feel alive. These subtle cues help show the direction of action, strengthen the atmosphere and deepen the reader's connection to the moment.

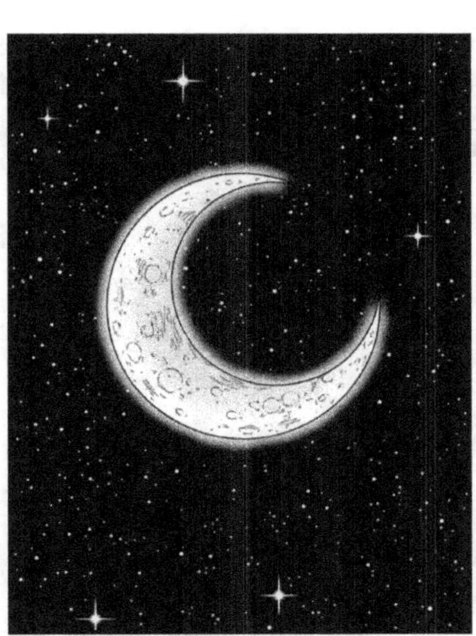

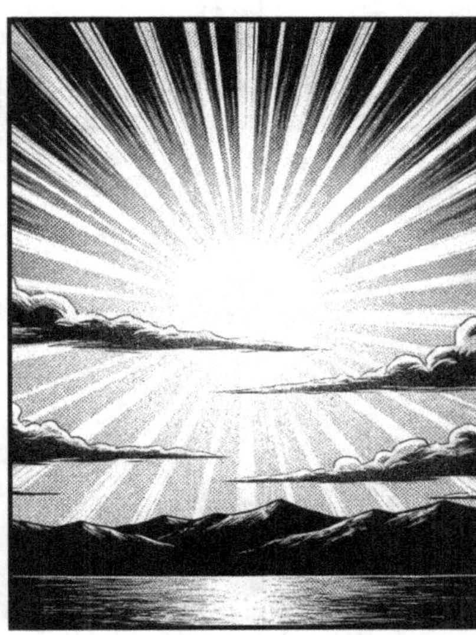

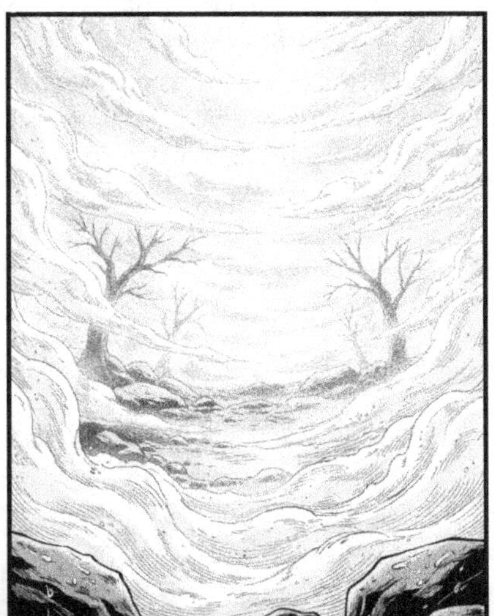

COMIC PANELS

Comic panels are the building blocks of your page and control how your story unfolds. Start with simple rectangles, then vary their size, shape and placement to influence pacing and focus. Larger panels create breathing room for key moments, while smaller or angled panels add energy and urgency. Keep gutters consistent so the page feels intentional, and use changes in panel layout to guide the reader's eye smoothly from one moment to the next. Experiment with compositions, but always design panels in service of clarity and storytelling.

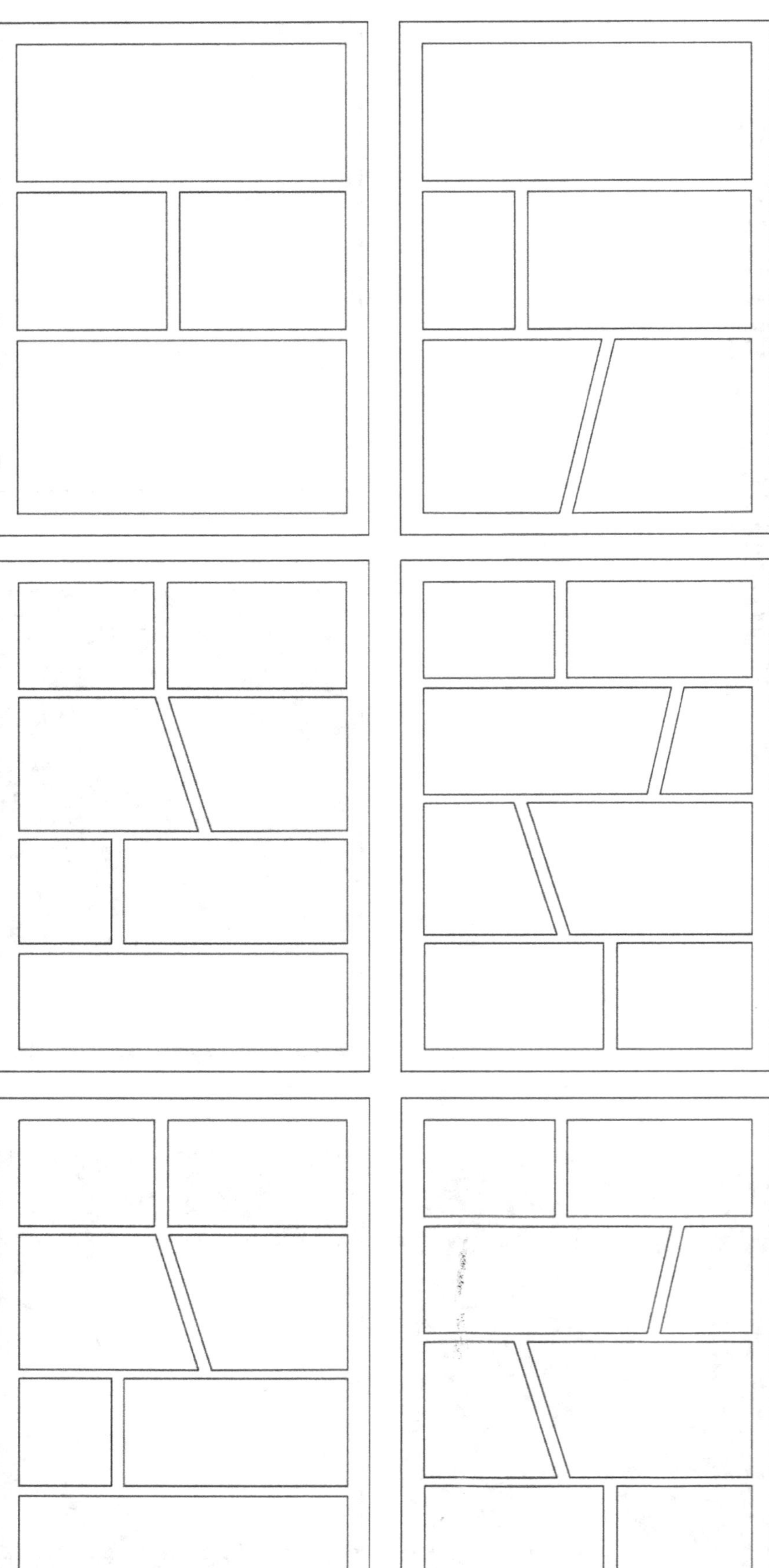

BREAKING THE FRAME

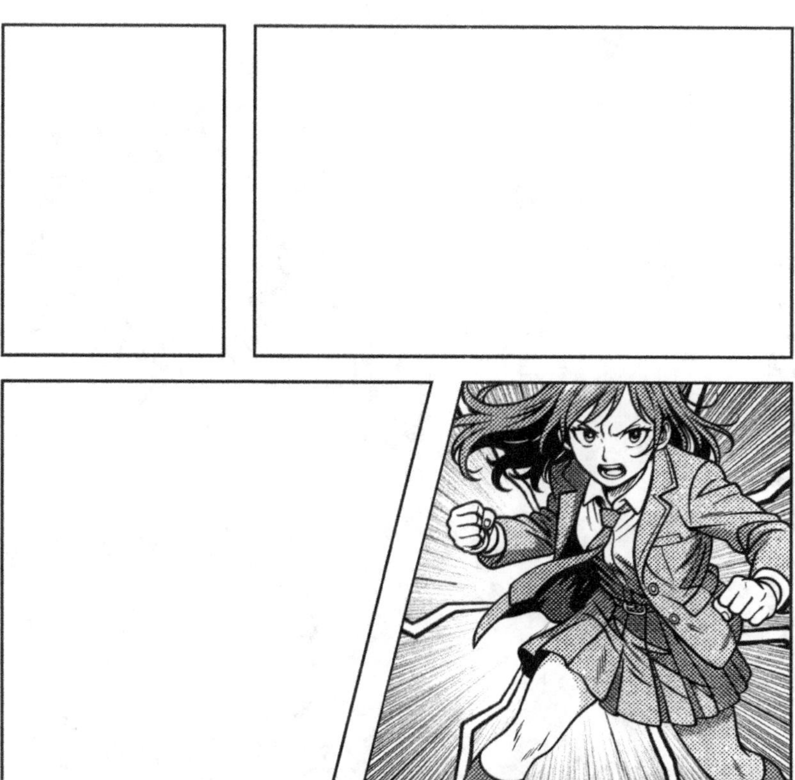

Trompe-l'œil, meaning "to deceive the eye," is an artistic technique that creates the illusion of three-dimensional elements emerging from a flat surface. In comics, you can use this effect by allowing parts of a character or object to break through or overlap the panel borders. A fist punching past the edge, a foot stepping out of the frame, or hair sweeping beyond the border instantly adds depth and motion. These controlled breaks make the scene feel more alive and draw the reader's attention to key actions. Used thoughtfully, trompe-l'œil effects create dynamic moments that feel immediate and cinematic while still keeping the overall page design clear and readable.

In the example at the bottom of the page, the character's head and hand appear to push past the panel edge, creating the illusion that she is bursting forward into the reader's space. By letting her break through the frame, the moment feels more immediate and energetic.

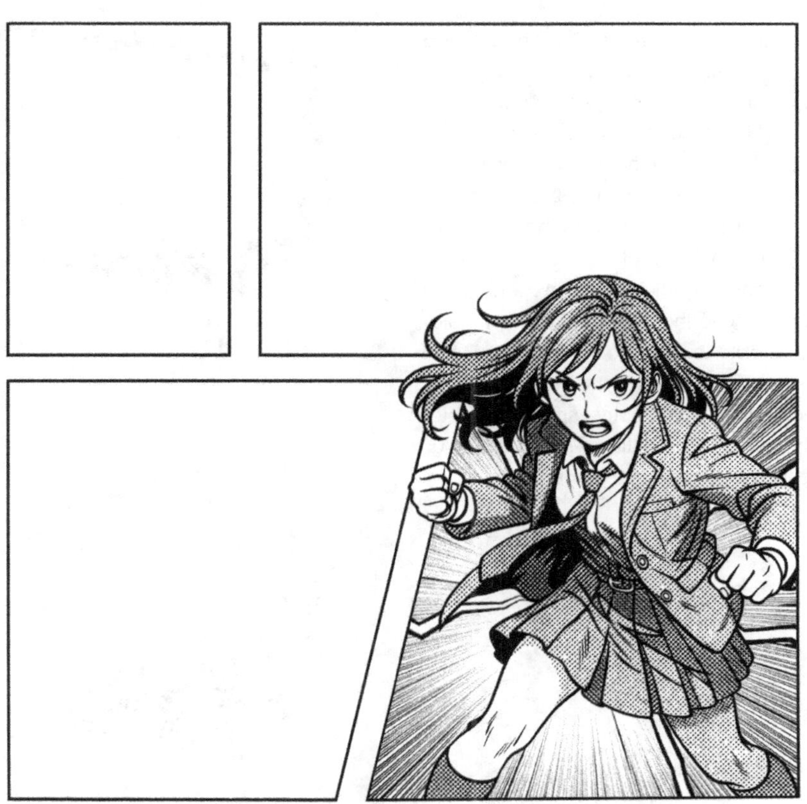

SPEECH BUBBLES

Speech bubbles are essential for guiding dialogue clearly and naturally through your comic. They show who is speaking, control the rhythm of the conversation and help lead the reader's eye through each panel. Keep your bubbles simple, with enough space around the text to stay readable, and place them so they follow the natural flow of the scene without covering important artwork. Tail the bubble toward the speaker's mouth and group bubbles in the order they should be read. Effective speech bubbles support the storytelling without drawing attention away from the action.

HOW TO DRAW VARIOUS PERSPECTIVES

Pro Tip: Learning perspective is essential for creating believable spaces in your manga and gives your storytelling a stronger sense of scale, depth and drama. Mastering one, two and three point perspective allows you to place characters convincingly within rooms, streets, rooftops and entire cityscapes. It helps you control the viewer's eye, build tension and make action scenes feel grounded and dynamic. You'll use perspective constantly in backgrounds, interiors, alleyways, school corridors, urban skylines and dramatic low or high-angle shots. Even simple scenes become richer when the environment is drawn with accurate perspective, giving your world weight and making every moment feel more immersive.

One Point Perspective:

Start by drawing a horizon line across your page, then place a single vanishing point on it. Draw the front face of any object as a simple square or rectangle, and from each of its corners, lightly draw receding lines back to the vanishing point. Decide the depth of the object and add a parallel back edge between those receding lines. Use the same vanishing point for every object in the scene so they all share the same sense of depth, then tidy your construction lines and refine the final drawing.

Two Point Perspective:

Draw a horizon line across your page and place two vanishing points at either end. Start by drawing the vertical edge of your object between them, then connect the top and bottom of this line to both vanishing points to form the receding sides. Decide the width of each side by adding two vertical lines between the receding edges. Every horizontal edge must angle back to one of the vanishing points, while all vertical edges stay straight and upright. Use the same two vanishing points for every object in the scene so everything shares the same sense of depth, then clean up your guidelines and refine the final drawing.

Three Point Perspective:

Draw a horizon line and place two vanishing points along it, then add a third vanishing point either high above or far below your object. Begin with a single vertical edge, but instead of keeping it straight, angle its top and bottom toward the top and bottom vanishing points. Connect the ends of this edge to the two vanishing points on the horizon to build the receding sides. All vertical edges now converge toward the third vanishing point, while all horizontal edges angle back to the left or right vanishing points. Use these same three points for every object so the entire scene shares the same dramatic sense of depth.

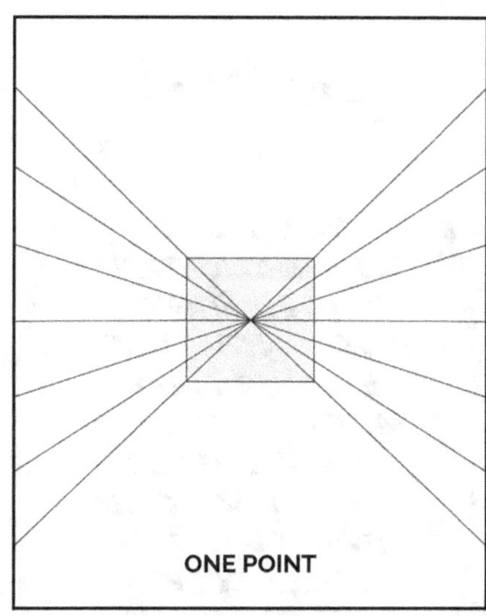

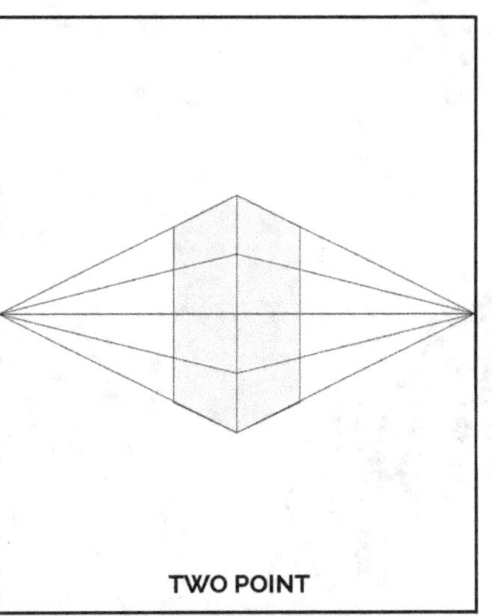

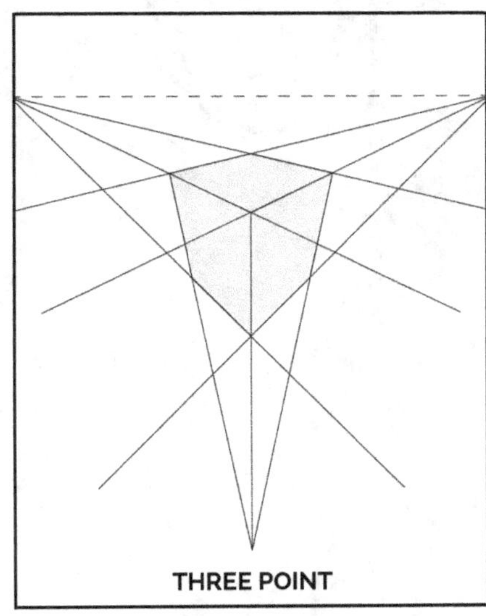

CONCLUSION

Drawing manga is a craft built on consistency, curiosity and deliberate practice. Every exercise in this book has given you a clear method to follow, so you can build strong habits and understand the structure behind the style. You have learnt how to construct characters, pose them with confidence, use perspective, add expression and bring energy to your panels. The skills you now have are the same foundations used by professional manga artists.

As you continue, keep drawing every day, finish your sketches even when they are not perfect and pay attention to the small improvements you make over time. Progress in manga happens line by line. Treat each drawing as a step forward and keep challenging yourself with new characters, new angles and new stories.

Most importantly, enjoy the process. Manga rewards those who stay curious and keep pushing their creativity. You now have the tools. The rest is up to you and the pages you choose to fill next.

LEARN MORE

At Vault Editions, our mission is to provide the highest-quality reference materials for artists and designers, offering meticulously curated resources that inspire and empower creativity. If you've found value in this book, we invite you to explore more of our expertly crafted titles at vaulteditions.com, where you'll discover a world of visual inspiration and practical tools designed to elevate your creative work.

REVIEW THIS BOOK

As a family-owned and operated independent publisher, reviews are essential to the success of our business. Please leave an honest review of this book wherever you purchased it.

JOIN OUR COMMUNITY

Are you the creative and curious type? If so, you will love our community on Instagram. Every day, we share bizarre and beautiful artwork ranging from 17th and 18th-century natural history and scientific illustrations to mythical beasts, ornamental designs, anatomical drawings and more; join our community of 300K+ people today by searching @vault_editions on Instagram.

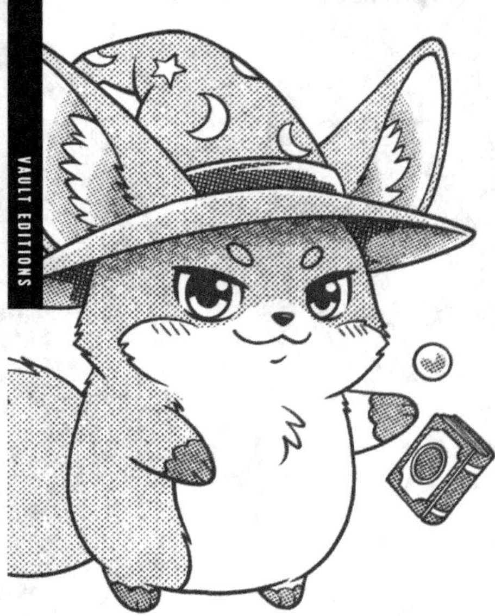

DOWNLOAD YOUR FILES

To enhance your creative journey, *How to Draw Manga for Beginners* comes with a digital PDF version of the book and a specially designed set of Procreate brushes. These resources are tailored to help you refine your skills and streamline your workflow, whether you're working traditionally or digitally.

The digital PDF provides easy access to the book's contents on any device, so you can reference the designs anytime, anywhere. It's perfect for artists on the go, allowing you to study and practice whenever inspiration strikes.

The custom Procreate brushes are designed to replicate the look and feel of traditional manga designs, from bold outlining to shading techniques. These brushes make it easier for digital artists to create authentic-looking designs in a digital medium, offering precision and flexibility as you sketch, refine, and finalise your artwork. Whether you're experimenting with new ideas or perfecting your final designs, these brushes allow you to bring your creations to life.

Download yours now and get creating!

STEP ONE

Enter the following web address on a desktop or laptop computer in your web browser.

vaulteditions.com/pages/hta

STEP TWO

Enter the following password to access the download page:

htm4927sxda

STEP THREE

Follow the prompts to access your high-resolution files.

CONTACT

For technical support, please email: info@vaulteditions.com

Copyright © 2025
Vault Editions Ltd

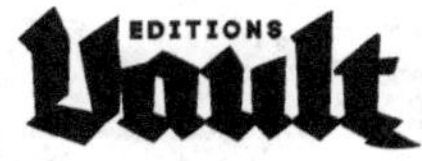

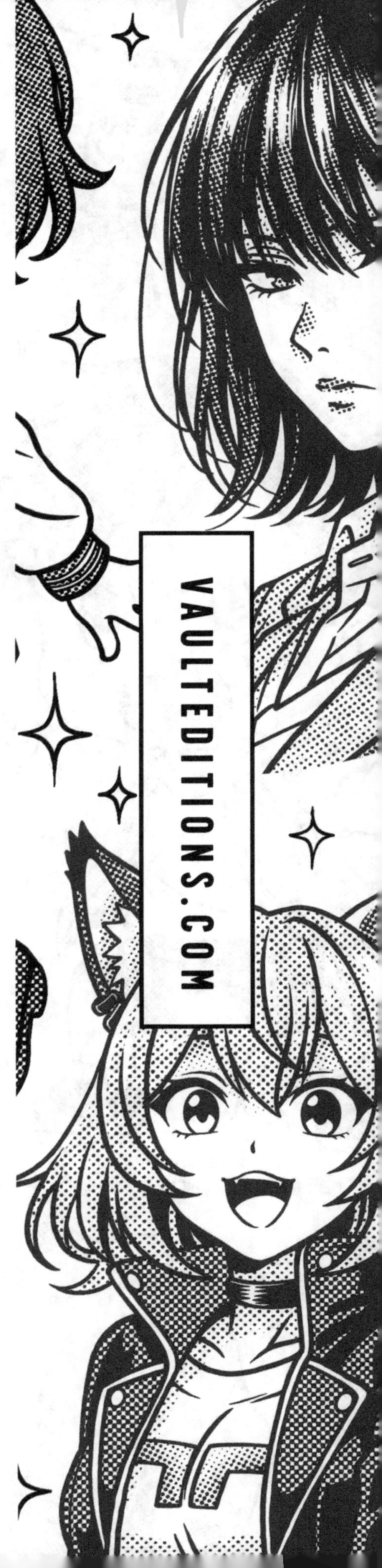

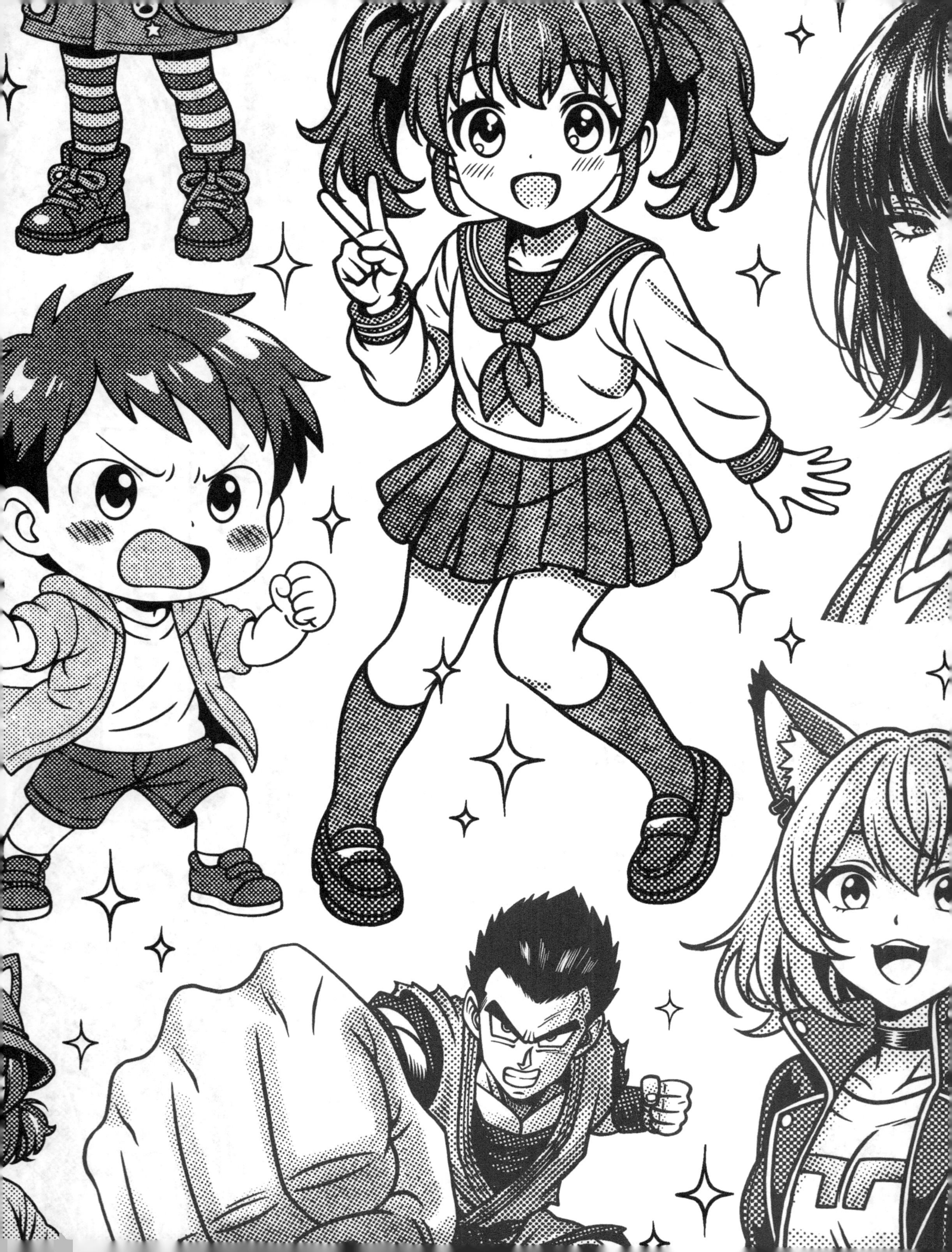